Foundation HTML5 Animation with JavaScript

Billy Lamberta

friendsof ED™

DESIGNER TO DESIGNER™

an Apress® company

Foundation HTML5 Animation with JavaScript

Credits

President and Publisher:
Paul Manning

Lead Editor:
Ben Renow-Clarke

Technical Reviewers:
Robert Hawkes, Brian Danchilla

Editorial Board:
Steve Anglin, Mark Beckner, Ewan Buckingham, Gary Cornell, Morgan Engel, Jonathan Gennick, Jonathan Hassell, Robert Hutchinson, Michelle Lowman, James Markham, Matthew Moodie, Jeff Olson, Jeffrey Pepper, Douglas Pundick, Ben Renow-Clarke, Dominic Shakeshaft, Gwenan Spearing, Matt Wade, Tom Welsh

Coordinating Editor:
Adam Heath

Copy Editor:
Damon Larson

Compositor:
Apress Production (Brigid Duffy)

Indexer:
SPi Global

Artist:
SPi Global

Cover Image Artist:
Corné van Dooren

Cover Designer:
Anna Ishchenko

For Jessica.

—Billy Lamberta

Contents at a Glance

Contents

Part IV: 3D Animation

About the Author

Billy Lamberta is a programmer and multimedia experimenter. After working as a television news photojournalist in his hometown of Richmond, Virginia, he turned his attention to web development and interactive programming using Flash and JavaScript. Billy is interested in the convergence of visual mediums for the purpose of storytelling, and the promise of the open web for distribution. He lives in Buffalo, New York where he watches a lot of hockey.

About the Technical Reviewers

Brian Danchilla is a PHP and Java developer who has written web, numerical analysis, graphics and voip applications. Danchilla has a BA degree as a double major in computer science and mathematics and recently coauthored the book "Pro PHP Programming" (Apress 2011). When not programming, he likes to spend time playing guitar or being outside. He resides in Saskatoon, SK, Canada.

Robert Hawkes thrives on solving problems through code. He's addicted to visual programming, and can't get enough of HTML5 canvas. Most of his waking life is spent working on crazy projects involving all sorts of new and exciting technologies, both on-line and off. Aside from his practical work, Rob has written a book for Apress called "Foundation HTML5 Canvas," which is all about making games with the new Web technology. He works as a Technical Evangelist for Mozilla.

About the Cover Image Artist

 **Corné van Dooren** designed the front cover image for this book. After taking a brief hiatus from friends of ED to create a new design for the Foundation series, he worked at combining technological and organic forms, the results of which now appear on this and other book covers.

Corné spent his childhood drawing on everything at hand and then began exploring the infinite world of multimedia—and his journey of discovery hasn't stopped since. His mantra has always been, "The only limit to multimedia is the imagination"—a saying that keeps him constantly moving forward.

Corné works for many international clients, writes features for multimedia magazines, reviews and tests software, authors multimedia studies, and works on many other friends of ED books. You can see more of his work at and contact him through his website at `www.cornevandooren.com`.

Acknowledgments

This book owes a debt of gratitude to the people in the JavaScript and Flash communities who have contributed countless programs and tutorials for everyone to learn from. My programming knowledge is a direct result of the free-software movement, and the willingness of other programmers to share their code. Thank you for my education.

Thank you Keith Peters, who this book is just not possible without.
I've learned much from your work, and am honored to contribute, if just a little, to it.

Thanks to all the great people at Apress who worked very hard, and through my shortcomings, to put this book together. A special thank you to Ben Renow-Clarke and Adam Heath for their guidance, and to Brian Danchilla and Rob Hawkes for the fantastic feedback that made this book better.

Finally, thanks to my family: my parents who had the foresight to get a crazy and impractical home computer for us kids, even if I had to teach them how to turn it on; and to my sisters, who have always supported me. And, of course, thank you Jessica for being very patient with me during this entire process. I love you all.

Introduction

This book is about how to create interactive animations for the web using computer code and math. But don't worry if you can't remember anything from your high school algebra class, you'll just need a minimal understanding to get started. The purpose of this book is to give you the tools to create and express your ideas, it's not about memorizing equations or theory—although I do explain the underlying ideas—but the practical application of techniques to incorporate in your work. These are concepts and formulas that you will see working, in real-time, right in front of you. Think of this book as the elements of motion, a catalog of ideas to mix, match, and reference.

There are plenty of examples to play with, and it's very satisfying to watch something you've created move around on screen—as if almost alive. But it can be even more satisfying to share this experience with your friends by simply giving them a link to follow in their web browsers—this is the great benefit to distribution using the Internet.

This book is a rewrite of the brilliant work by Keith Peters, Foundation ActionScript Animation. However, instead of targeting Flash, this book uses modern web technologies like the HTML5 and JavaScript. The malleability of this book is a result of the portability of its underlying concepts—the math is the same. When you understand these basic building blocks, you are no longer reliant on the tools provided by someone else, but you can implement these ideas wherever your programming life takes you.

Since the examples in this book are implemented using HTML5 and JavaScript, I'll step you through the particular programming techniques you'll need to understand them. JavaScript is a fun, powerful, and relatively small language, but it can be quirky and idiosyncratic largely because of its flexibility. While other, more structured, languages impose a particular way to program, JavaScript allows you to write code in many different styles. This freedom is powerful, but it can be confusing for a beginner to work out the main ideas of the language. If this is your first time using JavaScript, it would be wise to skim through a proper introduction before working through the examples in this book. The biggest confusion when learning JavaScript is the assumptions you bring from other languages. Keep the reference documentation handy and, if in doubt, test your code snippets in your browsers development console. If you are Flash developer, resist the temptation to think of JavaScript as a variation of ActionScript. It has it's own unique program structure and style, and you will avoid problems later on by leaving behind any preconceived ideas about the language now.

This was a fun book to write, and I hope you have fun working through it. Write your programs, experiment with them, share, and learn from others. Creativity is an active process, and not something you sit around and wait for, so let's get coding!

Part I

JavaScript Animation Basics

Chapter 1

Basic Animation Concepts

What we'll cover in this chapter:

- What is animation?
- Frames and motion
- Dynamic versus static animation

Oh, how far the web browser has come! What started as a program for accessing text files over the network, soon revolutionized how we communicate and share, and has now evolved into a fully graphical, interactive programming environment. The most recent markup standard for these documents, HTML5, adds graphics capabilities that were previously available only with native applications. After a period of stagnation, modern web browsers benefit from a new wave of competition and innovation with HTML5 and JavaScript. The new canvas element provides a way to create standards-compliant games, applications, and animations that work across modern web browsers and mobile devices, including popular phones and tablets such as iPhones, iPads, and Android devices.

This book covers programming, math, and physics techniques used to make animations with the HTML5 canvas element and JavaScript. As you'll see, this provides developers with levels of power, control, and interactivity that, for the first time, are available in a standards-compliant web browser.

Before we dive into specific techniques and formulas for moving things around with JavaScript, let's take a quick look at exactly what animation is, some of the basic techniques behind it, and some concepts that you can use for your animations to make them more dynamic and interesting.

Whether this is your first time drawing with computers or you have previous experience using tools such as Adobe Flash, this book is a great guide to programmed animation. This book has undergone many changes since being ported from Flash to JavaScript, but it also demonstrates that the underlying techniques and mathematical concepts are language-agnostic. We target the web browser here, but given modest graphics support wherever your coding environment, these formulas and examples are applicable anywhere.

Sure, you can skip this chapter if you can't wait to write some code. But it's strongly suggested you come back to it at some point. If nothing else, you'll find some insights into how animation works.

What is animation?

Animation is motion. Motion is a change in the position of an object over time—one minute it is here, the next minute it is over there—and space between those two points. By applying mathematical formulas to an object's location, you can determine its next position and affect the behavior of the movement—breathe life into it.

But animation is not just movement, it's change in any visual attribute: shape, size, orientation, color, etc. A ball squishes, plants grow, faces contort—something changes. Some of the earliest computer animations cycled colors to simulate movement; for instance, you can make a waterfall composed of pixels in various shades of blue that appears to alternate hues with such frequency to look like falling water, though nothing on the screen has actually changed position.

Time is a fundamental component of animation. It is the mechanism used to express change in an object from one position to the next. And without time, there is no motion—it is a still image and not an animation. Consequently, without motion, we have no sense of time, even if it is present. Take for example, a video of an empty parking garage from a security camera. Without movement, it is impossible to decide if you are watching a live stream, a frame from 5 seconds ago, or an unchanging still image. Only when a plastic bag blows across the screen are you assured that time is present and further change can occur. Without time, nothing else happens in the picture.

This brings up another point, animation keeps us interested. If something changes, our brains naturally become curious. What changed? Why did it change? Did I cause it to change? Does this change fit within the mental model I've constructed for this object or do I need to adjust my assumptions? Temporal media types such as music and film are compelling because, as in life, we are not sure what will happen next. We may have a general idea, and discerning these patterns is pleasurable, but we find joy in tickling the boundaries of the unexpected. Nontemporal media—images, paintings, text—do not change; we may explore the details of the work and our understanding and interpretation might change over time, but the work will not. This is what makes animation so gripping. Change is inherent to the medium; it captures a part of our experience that we are naturally attuned to. Thus, we are able to get lost in a movie for hours or enthralled by a video game for days. If something is going to happen, generally we want to know what that is.

Frames and motion

Animation is a process that creates the *illusion* of motion. Nearly every form of projected motion media uses *frames* to accomplish this.

Frames are a series of discrete images shown in rapid succession to simulate motion or change in an object. Frames are the basis for anything you see on a computer, television, or movie screen. This idea goes back to the earliest cartoons. Animators drew individual pictures on sheets of cellophane (known as *cells*), and the earliest motion pictures used a similar technique with multiple photographs.

The concept is simple: You show a bunch of images that vary slightly from one to the next, and the mind blurs them together as a single, moving image. But why do we insist on calling it an *illusion of motion*? If you see a man walk across the room on a movie screen, is that not motion? Of course it's only an image of a man, not a real person, but that's not the reason we don't consider it motion.

Remember, moving objects travel from a point here to a point there by passing through the intervening space. That is real motion; objects move through space smoothly, not in several jumps. But frame-based motion does just that. It doesn't move from spot to spot, it disappears and reappears in another location in the next frame. The faster it's moving, the bigger jump it takes.

If you were shown a picture of a man on the left side of a room and then a few seconds later another picture of the same man on the right side of the room, you'd infer that there are two pictures, not an animation. If you were shown a half dozen pictures of the man in the process of crossing the room, you'd still interpret these as a series of individual photographs. (See Figure 1-1 for an example of this.) If the images were presented fast enough, it wouldn't change the fact they remain a bunch of still photos, but, you would no longer see it that way. Your mind will process it all as a man moving across the room. It is no more real motion than the original two photos were, but at some point, the mind gives up and buys into the illusion.

Figure 1-1. A series of still photographs by Eadweard Muybridge

This point has been extensively examined by the film industry. Researchers have found that at a rate of 24 frames per second, people will accept these frames as a single moving image. Go much slower than that, and the jumpiness gets annoying and starts to break the illusion. And it seems that the human eye can't distinguish frame rates higher than that—showing 100 frames per second won't make your animation seem any more realistic (although higher frame rates in a programmed animation can result in more responsive interaction and will seem smoother).

Frames as records

The whole concept of frames makes three things possible: storage, transmission, and display. You can't store, transmit, and display an actual man walking across a room, but you can store many pictures of that man walking across the room. You can also transmit the images and display them. Thus, you can show an animation almost anywhere and at any time, as long as you can interpret the stored images and have a means to display them.

Now, we need a more general definition of what a frame is. So far, we've referred to a frame as a still image or a drawing. Let's call it a record of a system at a specific point in time. That system can be the midway point of a man walking across a room; then the record is that image. On the other hand, that system can be a collection of virtual objects, and the record is their shapes, colors, and positions at a particular moment in time. Thus, your animation becomes not a series of still images, but rather, it is a series of image descriptions. Instead of displaying only the image, the computer takes that description, creates the image from it, and then displays it. You can even take this idea a step further by using programmed frames.

Programmed frames

Because you have at your disposal a computer that can perform calculations as needed, you don't need a long list of frame descriptions. You can cut it down to a description of the first frame, and then you follow some rules for building the subsequent frames. Now the computer is not merely creating an image from a description; it's creating the description first, creating the image based on this description, and then finally displaying the image.

Consider how much file space you can save using this approach. Images take up hard disk space and bandwidth, and 24 images per second will add up fast. If you can decrease that to one description and a set of rules, you can possibly reduce the file size to a fraction of what it was. Even a complex set of rules for how the objects should move and react takes up less space than a single medium-sized image. Indeed, one of the first things people notice about programmed animation is just how small the files are.

Naturally, there is a trade-off. As your system gets larger and your rules get more complex, the computer must work furiously to calculate the next description, and then it must work additionally to display it. If you're trying to maintain a particular frame rate, that gives the computer a limited amount of time (milliseconds) to process it. If the computer can't calculate the scene in time, your frame rate suffers. On the other hand, image-based animation doesn't care about what's in the scene or how complex it is; it just shows the next picture, and generally it is right on time.

Dynamic versus static animation

The great advantage of programming an animation is that it becomes dynamic. The images are not defined until runtime. Instead of watching a predetermined sequence of frames—such as a movie's ending that will never change no matter how many times you watch it—you can generate new images, effectively creating a unique visual experience for each viewing. If you calculate an object's position using user-provided values, such as a mouse cursor, the media can responsively update the display to interact with the user, creating a level of immersion not capable with other media types.

But a coded animation isn't necessarily interactive. You can take an object and, using code, move it from a particular position across the screen. Each time the animation is played, the same code runs, causing the same movement. This is an example of what we'll call a *static* animation. Each frame, from start to finish, is predefined. Similar to a movie, you're watching a predetermined sequence of images that do not change on another viewing.

But what if you create an object, and again, using code, determine a random point to place it and a random direction and speed to move it? Now, each time you play the animation, something different happens. Or, what happens if, when the animation starts, you determine the time of day and month of the year, and use that data to create a scene—a winter morning, a summer afternoon, visually distinct images depending on the date the program is run?

Or, maybe you have some factors in your animation that change using input from the keyboard and mouse while it runs. This enables the user to interact with the objects on the screen, and about as far from static as you can get.

Perhaps the most interesting aspect of dynamic animation, and the focus of this book, is the application of real-world mathematics and physics principles to objects in the animation. You're not limited to moving an object in some random direction; you can also give it some gravity, so that as it moves, it falls down. When it hits the "ground," it bounces, but not as high as it started out. Then it eventually settles down and just sits there. You can also add some user interaction, enabling the user to "pick up" the object with the mouse or move it around with the keyboard. As the user throws the object around, she gets the feeling of handling a physical object.

With this kind of animation, the user is no longer a passive recipient of a sequence of frames that plays out, but has entered an environment you created. You can construct a world that models the physical constraints of your own, providing a more realistic experience, or, you can completely disregard such worldly confines. As the programmer, you are free to express your vision as you see fit. These are the joys of creative coding; by offloading tasks to the computer and having a constantly updating visual display, you can create rich scenes that involve the viewer in a way no medium in human history has been able to do before. How long will viewers stay there? They will remain as long as the environment keeps them interested. The more they interact with it, the more likely they'll come back for more.

Summary

In this opening chapter, the basics of animation theory have been summarized. We build on the concepts of frames and dynamism to create motion and interactivity in our animations.

In the following chapters, we examine the mathematical elements of movement and build a collection of tools that you'll incorporate into your programmed animations to create motion, and include lessons on how to use them. What you create with these tools is entirely your decision. The most obvious applications of the techniques in this book are for game creation. Games are essentially interactive animations with some goals for players to achieve. But this is not simply a game-programming book. These techniques are applicable to a wide range of animated projects—from navigational systems, to advertisements, to educational applications, and to interactive art.

A new era of web programming creativity has begun thanks to the innovation driving modern browsers. With the HTML5 canvas element, you have a standards-compliant, cross-platform component for creating advanced web graphics. This book is an exploration into the principles of programmatically generated movement for creating these next-generation graphic interactions.

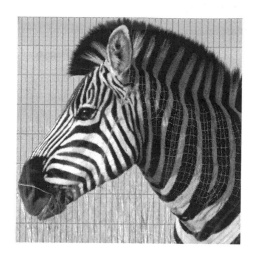

Chapter 2

Basics of JavaScript for Animation

What we'll cover in this chapter:

- Basic animation
- An introduction to HTML5
- Animating with code
- JavaScript objects
- User interaction

If the first chapter is a somewhat philosophical overview of animation, this one is a technical overview of what it takes to create an HTML5 document and how to animate using a canvas element and JavaScript. This chapter covers the essentials of document structure, animation loops, JavaScript objects, and user interaction. The techniques you learn here are used throughout the rest of the book.

Basic animation

To start off, let's review what Chapter 1 covers:

- Animation is made with frames, and each frame is slightly different in presenting the illusion of motion.
- Frame-by-frame animation contains an image or a description of an image for each frame.
- Dynamic animation contains an initial description of an image and rules that are applied to alter the description on each frame.

This book focuses on the rules for dynamic animation, providing different techniques to change the image description, which results in realistic motion. In this chapter, you see how to structure the initial description, how to apply those rules on each frame, and how to tie the program together. You will create plenty of working examples as you progress.

An introduction to HTML5

In this book, we create HTML5 documents that are viewed in a web browser. HTML5 is the latest iteration of HTML, Hypertext Markup Language, a language for structuring and presenting content for the World Wide Web. HTML elements are the building blocks of web pages. At the time of writing, the HTML5 specification is still in development, but a number of features are considered stable and ready to use, such as the canvas element. HTML5 improves on HTML4, which was standardized in 1997, by adding new elements and support for multimedia content, such as audio and video. Because these new, semantically meaningful elements expose properties and controls that are accessible in the document, you can manipulate them programmatically using JavaScript, giving you a powerful way to control and create media.

HTML5 is a *collection* of individual features. When assessing a particular browser's HTML5 support, this is not an all-or-nothing classification; rather, you test if a browser supports a specific feature of the defined specification. Different browsers have different support for different features. This can make it difficult to target individual HTML5 elements without knowing how a user will view the document. As browsers continue to improve, cross-platform feature detection becomes less of a concern, but for now, you should always test the user's web browser for the HTML5 features you target and provide a backup solution if it fails—even if it's just a politely worded message instructing your user to upgrade his browser.

Canvas support

The good news, at least for this book, is that all the major browser vendors have implemented support for the canvas element. This means that you can be relatively confident that your user can see the animation you create, provided she has upgraded to a recent version of her browser. Games and animations provide an excellent way to push users into upgrading their browsers, because, after decades of video games, most people understand that cutting-edge graphics require the latest hardware and software. At least it's easier to convince someone to upgrade her browser rather than buy a brand new gaming console.

In case the canvas element is not supported in a web browser, in your HTML document, you can provide backup content by including it within the canvas tags:

```
<canvas width="400" height="400">
  <p>This browser does not support the<code>canvas</code> element.</p>
</canvas>
```

The warning message appears only if the browser does not recognize the canvas tag. If the browser does support it, then it renders the canvas element and ignores the nested `<p>` element.

To programmatically test whether the browser supports the canvas element, you can add the following JavaScript to your document:

```
if (document.createElement('canvas').getContext) {
  console.log("Success! The canvas element is supported.");
}
```

This code creates a new canvas element and tests for the existence of its getContext property, which the object has if it's a valid HTML5 canvas element. If the browser does have support, it prints a message to the debugging console letting you know.

Table 2-1 lists the most popular web browsers and the minimum version required for basic support of the canvas element.

Table 2-1. Canvas Element Support for the Major Browsers

IE	Firefox	Safari	Chrome	Opera	iOS Safari	Android Browser
9	3.5	3.2	9	10.6	3.2	2.1

Performance

Programming graphics has always been—and for the foreseeable future, will be—a very computationally demanding operation. The reason is simple: The more you can do, the more you want to do and the more demands you place on the performance of the system. The past 25 years of video game history has been an amazing journey of technical advances, evolving from the blocky characters featured in dedicated arcade machines, to fully immersive 3D worlds run on today's consoles. But still, we want more. Sometimes we judge computer animation against features of the natural world: character realism, lighting effects, and physics. It's quite a marvel that these simulations can hold up to the scrutiny of human perception, and yet, they often do. We're still at the dawn of computer animation, and as long as computers keep getting faster—with the help of Moore's Law—and developers keep refining their techniques, our abilities for visual creation in the future seem almost unlimited.

But animation on the web using the canvas element is at the incubation stage, only now considered a viable alternative to using plug-ins like Adobe Flash. In recent years, developers have pushed the boundaries of speed and performance in web browsers and JavaScript engines, and because this is still a highly competitive area, we can look forward to more optimizations and improvements to come.

The examples in this book are written so they run at a smooth, reasonable performance on a relatively modern computer and web browser. The capability of your computer will differ from mine, so as you examine the source code in this book, feel free to adjust the values so the examples run smoothly on your machine. Plus, there is no better way to learn how the formulas work than by experimenting with their parameters and observing the output.

However, before you share any animations with the world, test them on as many different devices as you can. As more people use mobile phones and tablets—instead of more traditional desktop computers—to access the web, developers need to account for a wide range of device performance differences. Testing and measuring on all these platforms is the only way to ensure your code remains performant.

A basic HTML5 document

One of the best parts of web development is how easy it is to create and view a document—all you need is a text editor and a web browser. This simple snippet provides the setup for all of the examples contained in this book. After you walk through the structure of these elements, we'll add a couple of minor additions for clarity, but this is the basic HTML5 file you will use:

```
<!doctype html>
<html>
 <head>
  <meta charset="utf-8">
  <title></title>
  <link rel="stylesheet" href="style.css">
 </head>
 <body>
  <canvas id="canvas" width="400" height="400"></canvas>
  <script>
  window.onload = function () {
    //Our code here...
  };
  </script>
 </body>
</html>
```

Save this file as 01-skeleton.html and load it in your web browser. You won't actually see anything because it's a blank document, but the page did load and is a completely valid HTML5 document. (You can always view the source in your browser to confirm that something is there.)

Now let's go through the elements step by step. The first line simply declares that this is an HTML5 document type. If you have any familiarity with all the various HTML4 document types, you'll see that this declaration is quite simple:

```
<!doctype html>
```

Next, we declare the root html element and the header:

```
<html>
 <head>
  <meta charset="utf-8">
  <title></title>
  <link rel="stylesheet" href="style.css">
 </head>
```

At the top of the head element, set the document character encoding to utf-8. UTF-8 is an encoding for Unicode, which is a universal character set that defines the characters used in most of the world's languages. The browser uses this encoding to read the characters from a file and display them as properly formatted text. These documents are stored in a sequence of bytes contained in a file on a server somewhere, transmitted across the network, then reassembled on the client's computer and displayed in a web browser. The character encoding tells the browser how to convert this sequence of bytes into a sequence of characters, which is then processed and displayed as a web page. If you don't include the encoding declaration, the browser might attempt to guess the character encoding of the file (wrongly), or use a default setting (wrongly), causing the page to display incorrectly. It's best to explicitly set the character encoding here and avoid the potential confusion.

All valid HTML5 documents contain a `title` element, which is also placed in the header. Because we use a CSS stylesheet, create a `link` element that points to an external file. This contains the style definitions for our document; we'll look at the `style.css` file in a moment.

With the header set, let's look at the rest of the document:

```
<body>
  <canvas id="canvas" width="400" height="400"></canvas>
  <script>
  window.onload = function () {
    //Our code here...
  };
  </script>
</body>
</html>
```

In the **body** element, we place a `canvas` element. This is what we draw to and reference from our scripts. Give the canvas an `id` name and a `height` and `width` value so you can see it, and use its `id` to access the element with the DOM interface.

After the canvas element, add a `script` tag that includes the JavaScript code for each example. We've placed the `script` after the other elements, right before the closing **body** tag, so that the browser loads the rest of the document before executing the script. Also, if the script is loaded from a file—possibly from a different server—it won't hold up the rest of the document while waiting to download. This makes loading faster and the document more responsive.

The skeleton script is simple and effectively does nothing. The `window` object is the top of the Document Object Model and how we access the DOM. When the document has finished loading, the window object executes the function assigned to its `onload` property:

```
<script>
window.onload = function () {
  //Our code here...
};
</script>
```

The example code in this book is placed within the `window.onload` callback function. Because this method is executed after all the document elements have been loaded, we can be assured that the canvas element is ready to go by the time the code is called. Consequently, if your document contains a lot of data embedded in it, such as large images, you can wait a long time for `window.onload` to execute. In this situation, it might be better to load the assets using JavaScript, which I show you how to do in Chapter 4.

Finally, we close out our `script`, **body**, and `html` tags. We're finished creating a basic but perfectly valid HTML5 document.

CSS stylesheet

In the document header, we created a `link` to a CSS stylesheet. Now, let's look at that file. The style definitions for this book are intentionally minimal; only the background color of the document **body** and **canvas** element has been declared. By default, the canvas background color is transparent, which might be the color you want, but has been changed to white so you can see exactly where the element is positioned in the document. Here's the stylesheet for the `style.css` file:

```css
body {
  background-color: #bbb;
}

#canvas {
  background-color: #fff;
}
```

This assumes the document contains an element with an `id` of `'canvas'`. As a document gets more complicated, so does its stylesheet. The HTML file defines the structure of the document, whereas the CSS stylesheet defines the style or look of the elements. In general, it's best to organize your content, style, and scripts in separate files.

Additional scripts

As the examples get more complicated and you need to reuse portions of code, it becomes convenient, if not necessary, to move these pieces into separate files for clarity. This is done when declaring new classes that are used across multiple exercises and for functions whose verbosity would distract from the point at hand.

Throughout this book, we'll maintain a file of these utility functions; it's named `utils.js`. This script contains functions that set up boilerplate code for the examples, so that you can concentrate on the underlying animation principles. Each function is explained as they are introduced, so you don't have to think of this file as a black box.

In this file, many of the utility functions will be added as properties to a global JavaScript object named `utils`. This way, you can avoid cluttering up the global namespace with a bunch of functions. Be sure that at the top of the `utils.js` file you've declared an empty object like the following:

```js
var utils = {};
```

To import this file and other scripts into your document, create a `script` element and set its `src` attribute to the location of the file. Include these immediately before the example code to be certain that everything has loaded properly before attempting to use it:

```html
<script src="utils.js"></script>
<script>
window.onload = function () {
  //Our code here...
};
</script>
```

Importing boilerplate js(?)

writing new js inline

14

Debugging

One of the most important aspects of writing code is debugging it. Back in the old days of web development, this usually meant throwing pop-up alert windows. Thankfully, web browsers now offer increasingly sophisticated debugging tools for code introspection and performance analysis. These tools enable you to step through a running application and interact with it, so you know exactly what's going on in your code at a given time.

It's a safe bet that every modern, HTML5-capable browser has some built-in developer tools and a console to input JavaScript statements and print out the results. You might have to dig around the menus of the application, but they're in there somewhere.

For example, in the Chromium web browser, click the wrench icon near the upper right corner, scroll down to *Tools*, and then click *JavaScript Console*. This is where the logging messages print out. Figure 2-1 shows an open debugging session in Chromium. The Firefox web browser has something similar: In the File menu, click *Tools*, and then click *Web Console*. Likewise, Internet Explorer 9 and Opera each has its own developer environments. It's important you get comfortable with these tools in all the major browsers because to maintain cross-browser compatibility, you debug in all of them. If you're having trouble finding a particular browser's web development tools, be sure to check its help section.

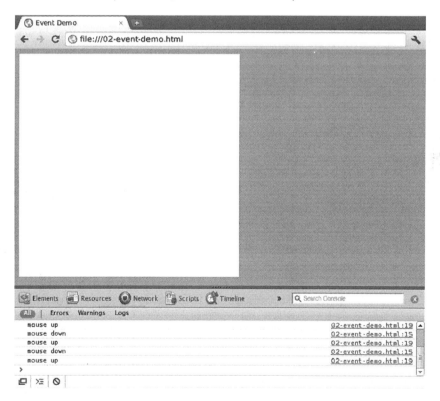

Figure 2-1. The Chromium browser debugging console

How t writing to the console

After you have opened a web developer console, you can type JavaScript expressions directly into the browser and have them evaluated. Try it by entering these statements:

```
console.log("Hello, World!");
2 + 2
```

From the console, you can access DOM elements and script variables to inspect their values (provided they are in the proper scope), which makes it easy to reason about how your program runs. This is a great way to test and debug small sections of code before committing them to a larger program. Find those bugs as early as possible!

Animating with code

With the document structure in place, you should now understand enough of the basics to start coding. You need a text editor to input the examples and an HTML5-capable web browser to run them. For debugging, you should be familiar with your browser's built-in developer console. After you have these tools—which may already be on your computer—you're ready to go. Let's dive in to some animation!

Animation loops

Almost all programmed animation is expressed as some kind of loop. If you think about a frame-by-frame animation, you might create a flowchart resembling a series of images, where each frame just needs to be drawn, as shown in Figure 2-2.

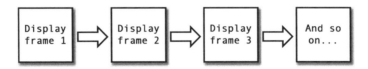

Figure 2-2. Frame-by-frame animation

When you start drawing shapes, though, things are a bit different. JavaScript code won't create and store a new image for each frame, even in a frame-by-frame animation. For each frame, we store the position, size, color, and other attributes of every object drawn to the canvas. So, if you had a ball moving across the screen, each frame would store the position of the ball on that frame. Maybe frame 1 would indicate the ball is 10 pixels from the left side, frame 2 would indicate it's 15 pixels, and so on. The code reads this data, draws the object according to the description given, and displays that frame. From that process, you can derive a flowchart, as shown in Figure 2-3.

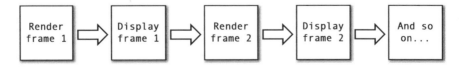

Figure 2-3. Rendering and then displaying frames

But when you consider how we described a dynamic, coded animation, the flowchart looks more like Figure 2-4.

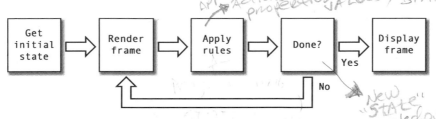

[handwritten annotations: PROGRAMMING; Apply Actions properties VALUES / STATEMENTS; New "STATE" created after "rules" applied]

Figure 2-4. Scripted animation

As you see in Figure 2-4, there is no concept of frame 1, frame 2, and so on. Programmed animation generally can, and usually does, all occur in just one frame. Here, you can start to see what we mean by a loop.

First, you set up an initial state, such as by drawing a circle to the screen using the built-in canvas drawing API. You then render and display the frame. Next, you apply your rules. The rules can be as simple as, "The ball will move 5 pixels to the right," or they can be made up of dozens of lines of complex trigonometry. The examples in the book cover that entire spectrum. Applying the rules results in a new state—a new description that is then rendered and displayed. Then you apply the same rules all over again.

The same set of rules is applied over and over; you don't have one set of rules for the first frame, and then another set for the next. So, your challenge is to come up with a set of rules that can handle every possible situation that can arise in your scene. What happens when the ball moves so far to the right that it's off the canvas? Your set of rules needs to account for this. Do you want the user to interact with the ball using a mouse? Your rules need to take that into account as well.

[handwritten margin note: ONLY ONE set of Rules that Repeat Resulting IN A Loop. Rules include HANDLERS FOR All possible situations]

It sounds daunting, but it's not that complex. You start off with some simple behavior by creating a rule or two, and when that works, you add another rule. The "rules" we've been referring to are actually programming statements. Each rule can be a single statement or composed of several statements. In the example of moving the ball 5 pixels to the right, the rule is expressed in JavaScript like this:

```
ball.x = ball.x + 5;
```

[handwritten: whatever x's current position is... Add (5) to it]

This says to take whatever the ball's x position (horizontal axis) is, add 5 to it, and make that its new x position. You can even simplify the expression like this:

```
ball.x += 5;
```

The += operator adds the value on the right to the variable on the left and assigns the result back to that variable.

Here's a more advanced set of rules that you'll see later in the book:

```
var dx = mouse.x - ball.x,
    dy = mouse.y - ball.y,
    ax = dx * spring,
    ay = dy * spring;
```

[handwritten: Add this value (on the right); BALL.X += 5; To This VARIABLE (on the left)]

17

```
vx += ax;
vy += ay;
vy += gravity;
vx *= friction;
vy *= friction;

ball.x += vx;
ball.y += vy;
ball.draw(context);
```

Don't worry about what it all means, just know that we need to run this code over and over to generate each new frame.

So, how do these loops run? Here's a misguided attempt, which reflects an error that many beginning programmers make. It's based on the **while** loop structure that exists in almost every programming language. You set up a loop to run indefinitely, updating the ball from within:

```
while (true) {
  ball.x += 1;
}
```

It seems simple: The **while** evaluation always passes because we're testing a value of **true**, so the loop keeps executing. We increment the ball's x position by 1 each time through the loop, from 0 to 1 to 2, 3, 4, etc. Each time it moves across the canvas from left to right.

If you've made the same mistake, you know that the ball doesn't move across the canvas, and in fact you won't see it at all—it's already moved past the right side of the screen. Why doesn't it move to all the points in between? Actually, it did! But you didn't see it because the canvas element was never updated. Figure 2-5 is another flowchart that shows essentially what happens.

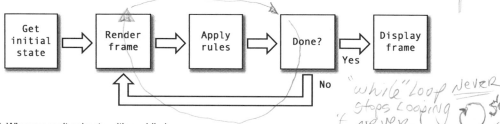

Figure 2-5. Why you can't animate with a while loop

You applied the rules and moved the ball into position, creating a new scene, but it never got displayed because you didn't draw the object to the canvas at the end of a frame. This is an important point.

Here is the sequence of actions you must take on each frame to animate:

1. Execute all the code that needs to be called for that frame.

2. Draw all objects to the canvas element.

3. Restart the process to render the next frame.

Keeping these steps in mind, we'll create a function that we can call repeatedly to update the object's position and draw it to the canvas element. We then create a JavaScript timer to set up the loop:

```
function drawFrame () {
  ball.x += 1;
  ball.draw(context);
}

window.setInterval(drawFrame, 1000/60);
```

Here, we've set up the **drawFrame** function to update the ball and render it to the canvas using its **draw** method (which we haven't created yet). We pass **drawFrame** as an argument to **window.setInterval**, which repeatedly executes the function at an interval specified in milliseconds by the second argument. In this example, that's **1000/60**, which is 60 frames a second, or about 17 ms.

For a long time, this was the way developers had to set up an animation loop using JavaScript. If you really wanted to, you could still use this method in the example code throughout this book. The problem is that JavaScript timers were never intended to be used for animation. They are not accurate to the millisecond—timer resolutions vary across browsers—so you cannot count on them for high quality animations. Furthermore, the delay specified by the second argument is only a request to be executed at a given time. If there are other jobs in the browser's execution queue that need to be run, then the animation code has to wait.

Because animation was never a feature of the previous HTML specification, browser vendors had not placed much priority on these kinds of optimizations. However, with HTML5's canvas element and a new emphasis on multimedia content, browsers are once again competing against each other on performance and speed. Recognition that animation has become an increasingly important component of web applications has led browser vendors to invent new solutions to handle the demands placed on them.

An animation loop using requestAnimationFrame

Because of the increased interest in HTML5-based animation, web browsers have implemented an API that lets developers indicate they're using JavaScript specifically for animation, which allows for browser-based optimizations. The function **window.requestAnimationFrame** accepts a callback function as an argument and executes it prior to redrawing the screen. In some browsers, a second, optional parameter is implemented that specifies an HTML element that provides the visual bounds of the animation. Changes to the program that are made in this function argument happen before the next browser repaint. To create an animation loop, chain together multiple calls to requestAnimationFrame:

```
(function drawFrame () {
  window.requestAnimationFrame(drawFrame, canvas);

  //animation code...
}());
```

This might be a small snippet of code, but it's important you understand exactly how it works because it provides the core animation loop used in the book examples. We've defined a function, **drawFrame**, that contains the animation code to run on every frame. On the first line in this function, we make a call to **window.requestAnimationFrame** and pass a reference to the same **drawFrame** function that we're defining. The second optional argument is the canvas element that we'll draw to. You might find it surprising that we can pass a function as an argument to another function before we have finished defining it. Just keep in mind, by the time it is needed here as an argument, it has already been defined.

When we execute the `drawFrame` function, `window.requestAnimationFrame` queues the `drawFrame` function to be run again at the next animation interval, which repeats this process. Because we keep requesting that the function run again, we've chained together a loop. Therefore, any code we place in this function is called again and again, allowing us to animate the canvas at discreet intervals.

To start the loop, after `drawFrame` has been defined, wrap the function in parentheses and immediately invoke it. This is a more space-efficient—and arguably clearer—alternative to defining the function first, then immediately invoking it on the following line.

Because `requestAnimationFrame` is a relatively new feature, browsers are still working on their own implementations of it. Because you want your code to be cross-platform, here is a little code snippet that you can use to normalize the function across multiple browsers:

```
if (!window.requestAnimationFrame) {
  window.requestAnimationFrame = (window.webkitRequestAnimationFrame ||
                    window.mozRequestAnimationFrame ||
                    window.oRequestAnimationFrame ||
                    window.msRequestAnimationFrame ||
                    function (callback) {
                      return window.setTimeout(callback, 1000/60);
                    });
}
```

This code tests whether the function `window.requestAnimationFrame` is defined, and if it's not, runs through the known browser implementations and assigns that as the function. If it cannot find a browser-specific version of the function, then it falls back to a JavaScript timer-based animation using `setTimeout` at an interval of 60 frames a second.

Because this environment check is used in all of the examples, include it in the `utils.js` file to import into our documents. This way, you can be sure the animation loop works across multiple browsers, keeping the scripts uncluttered so we can concentrate on understanding the core ideas of each exercise.

JavaScript objects

In this book, the focus is on the various principles and formulas needed to create animations with JavaScript instead of teaching specific coding methodologies. As such, we won't create large framework libraries or complex data structures; instead, we'll keep things as simple as possible.

The animation concepts you learn here can be incorporated into more advanced JavaScript projects; however, the goal is not to hand you a collection of pre-built code for you to copy and paste, but to convey an understanding of the principles that make each one work.

Because this book is written using JavaScript, you need to know some of the main ideas of the language to appreciate what's going on in the examples. Since the most important things in JavaScript are objects and functions (which is just a special kind of object), we'll look at those first.

[Handwritten at top: An "object's" A data structure containing "properties": VARIABLES, FUNCTION — AKA "it's Method", other objects]

Basic objects

JavaScript has been designed as a simple object-based system. An *object* is a data structure that contains *properties*. These properties can be variables, functions, or other objects. When a function is assigned to a property, it is known as an object's *method*. Objects are predefined in the browser, or you can create your own. For example, to create an empty object and store it in a variable to reference later, you write:

```
var objA = {};
```

[Handwritten: ← creates an empty object]

This creates an object with no properties and stores it in the variable objA. Because JavaScript objects can be modified by default at any time, we can add a new property to it like this:

```
objA.name = "My Object A";
```

[Handwritten: ← name is objA's name property Assigned A string value]

This creates a new property called name on the objA object and assigns it a string value "My Object A". You can always access the object's property value using the notation objA.name. You can also create properties when declaring a new object, as follows:

```
var objB = {
  name: "My Object B",
  hello: function (person) {
    console.log("Hello, " + person);
  }
};
```

[Handwritten: "Name" property's Assigned A string]
[Handwritten: "hello" property w/ a function stored inside it, the hello Function when called Accepts the VALUE (the name of the person you're addressing)]
[Handwritten: This defines the Function: display this concatinated string]

Here, we've created a new object, objB, that contains two properties: the property name, which contains a string, and the property hello, within which we've stored a function. Because a function is also an object in JavaScript, you can pass it around and assign it to variables like any other value. This example method takes a string as an argument and prints a message to the browser's debugging console:

```
objB.hello("Gentle Reader"); //prints: "Hello, Gentle Reader"
```

Creating new kinds of objects

[Handwritten: this calls the "hello" function & passes in the VALUE (name of the person you're Addressing)]

We've declared objects with properties as we've needed them, but what if you want to create multiple objects with the same property definitions? You can create them one by one, but it's more efficient to use a *constructor* function. A constructor is a special kind of function that creates a new object based on the properties assigned to that constructor. After it's set up, you can create a new object instance by invoking the constructor with the new command. To distinguish a constructor function from a regular function, use the convention of starting the name with a capital letter:

```
function MyObject (person) {
  this.name = person;
  this.say = function () {
    console.log("It's " + this.name);
  };
}

var objA = new MyObject("Gentle Reader");

objA.say(); //prints: "It's Gentle Reader"
```

[Handwritten: MyObject is a "constructor" function, CONSTRUCTOR is like a "CLASS" (class "constructor")]
[Handwritten: The "say()" function's defined internally inside the constructor function — it includes the console.log]
[Handwritten: this is the "name" property, passed in when the new MyObject function's called]
[Handwritten: the new VAR objA 's assigned ". SAY()" property (call)]
[Handwritten: Constructors = class]

In the constructor, notice the special object `this`, which we can add properties to. This is the object that is returned from the constructor. Any variables declared in the constructor function that are not attached to the `this` object cannot be directly accessed from outside the constructor.

Prototypes

Using constructors to create object instances is exactly what we'd do in a more class-based language. In fact, when you see references to classes in JavaScript documentation, this is typically what it's referring to, the constructor function. Sometimes this terminology overlooks that JavaScript is, in fact, a prototype-based language.

When you create a new object instance in JavaScript, you actually create a new object that inherits properties from its constructor object—this is its prototype. You can directly access this object from the constructor's `prototype` property. Any properties you assign to the prototype are shared by all objects derived from its type. Building off the previous example constructor, here is the code:

```
MyObject.prototype.hello = function () {
  console.log("Hello, " + this.name);
};

objA.hello(); //prints: "Hello, Gentle Reader"

var objB = new MyObject("Inspired Coder");

objB.hello(); //prints: "Hello, Inspired Coder"
```

Here we've added the `hello` function to the constructor prototype, and in doing so, we added this method to both object instances: the one previously declared and a newly created object.

Throughout this book, we create classes (a constructor function and prototype properties) that are shared across many examples. Typically, we keep these in a separate file that can be imported into documents.

Functional style

One strength of the JavaScript language is that functions are first-class objects. This means you can assign functions to variables, pass them around, and use them as arguments to other functions. This is a powerful concept and a feature that is not available in many programming languages. Although the implications of this idea can be fairly complex, the concept is simple, and something we take advantage of throughout the book. If you can understand it, you're on your way to becoming a successful JavaScript programmer.

You've already used functional arguments earlier in the chapter when you created an animation loop: `setInterval` and `requestAnimationFrame` each take function callbacks as parameters. But, we can also use functions to structure code clearly. For example, here is a typical `for` loop used to iterate over values in an array. We create a counter variable, `i`, that increments each loop cycle, using it to access the array values. We've declared an array of three elements and printed each one in turn to the console:

*[handwritten: 1st class objects = pass funct. to other functions —
• use funct. as other functions' arguments
• Assign funct. to variables
(FUNCTIONS)
AS ARGUMENTS • funct...
CALLBACKS = AS PARAMETERS —]*

```
var arr = [1, 2, 3];
for (var i = 0, len = arr.length; i < len; i++) {
  console.log(arr[i]);
}
```

[handwritten: ARRAY method]

You can also express iteration functionally. Every JavaScript array object has a method named `forEach`, which takes a function as an argument. `forEach` iterates over all the array elements, passing each one as the first argument to the user-defined function, and the second, optional, argument is the element's index position. Here's how the previous example looks using this method:

[handwritten: TAKES A FUNCTION AS AN ARGUMENT]

[handwritten: 1st Argument = FUNCTION ---- of "FOR Each" method]

```
var arr = [1, 2, 3];
arr.forEach(function (element, i) {
  console.log(element);
});
```

*[handwritten: what's "element" ?/?
Element is each element in the array]*

This code snippet does the same thing as the previous one—printing out each array element value to the console—but it is structurally different. There are a couple of benefits to this approach. For one, we didn't declare any temporary variables used only for iteration that linger around after this code has executed. But perhaps more important, this style allows you to reason about the code at a functional level. This means you can understand how the code works by examining the function that is passed as an argument and the parameters it accepts. You do not have to worry about the state of the loop or if any dependent variables are setup correctly. This can have advantages when debugging, because when something goes wrong, you can dig down through the function calls in the stack trace to determine where exactly the error occurred.

*[handwritten: Reason ABOUT the code AT A FUNCTIONAL LEVEL"?
EXAMINE the FUNCTION Being PASSED AS AN Argument & it's PARAMeters.]*

[handwritten: SLOWER than FOR LOOPs —]

The drawback to functional iteration is that it's typically slower than a for-loop, due to the increased computation needed to execute the function. As is often the case when writing programs, the developer needs to consider both readability of the code and the speed of its execution, and that can be determined only by testing. Generally, you should write programs that are clear and easy to understand, and let the browser makers worry about getting the code to run fast.

We use both kinds of iteration throughout this book, depending on speed requirements and the need for clarity. More often, and central to working with JavaScript and the DOM, is the need to pass function arguments as event handlers. We look at how these work in the next section on user interaction.

User interaction

User interaction is probably one of the main reasons you're reading this book. After all, if it weren't for interaction or some sort of dynamic input going into the animation, you might as well watch a movie. User interaction is based on user events, and these are generally mouse events, touch events, and keyboard events. Let's quickly go through the various user event types and how to handle them.

Events and event handlers

[handwritten: TRIGGER (OBJECT) ACTION (function)]

To understand events, you must understand a couple of additional concepts: listeners and handlers. A *listener* determines whether an element should act on a particular event, and a *handler* is a function that is called when the event occurs.

The shapes that we draw to the canvas element have no built-in means for detecting events. But, the HTML elements do, which means that we can capture user input using the DOM interface, calculate where the event occurred relative to the drawn objects, and make decisions based on this information. In this section, we look at how to capture DOM events, and in later chapters, we'll see how to use them to add interaction to an animation.

Listeners and handlers

As just stated, a listener is an object that listens for events. You can specify a DOM element as a listener for a particular event by calling its method addEventListener. You pass it a string as the first argument, which is the type of the event to listen for, and a handler function that is called when the element receives this event. Here's what the syntax looks like:

```
element.addEventListener(type, handler [, useCapture]);
```

The third argument is usually optional, however, in some browser implementations it is not. For that reason, in this book, we always pass a value of false for useCapture, which is the default. This affects how an event bubbles up the DOM tree, but is not applicable to the examples in this book. For details about DOM event model flow, see the specification at http://www.w3.org/TR/DOM-Level-3-Events/#event-flow.

A typical example is listening for a mouse press on a canvas element (mouse events are discussed shortly):

```
canvas.addEventListener('mousedown', function (event) {
  console.log("Mouse pressed on element!");
}, false);
```

The first argument, the event type 'mousedown', is a string. Make sure you double-check the spelling of the event type you're listening for, because a typo here can mean you're waiting for an event that doesn't exist. addEventListener happily listens for any event type you specify, so this can be a difficult bug to track down (and you won't be happy when you do).

Now, I've said a listener listens for events, but perhaps a more accurate description is that a listener is *notified* of events. Internally, the object that generates events keeps a list of every object that has added itself as a listener. If an object is capable of generating different types of events, such as mousedown, mouseup, and mousemove, it keeps a list of listeners for each event type it can generate. Whenever one of these events occurs, the object runs through the corresponding list and lets each object in that list know what event has occurred.

Another way of describing events is that the object that becomes a listener is *subscribing* to a particular event. The object that generates the event is *broadcasting* the event to all its subscribers.

Additionally, if you no longer want an object to listen for a particular event, you can tell it to stop listening, or unsubscribe, by calling its removeEventListener method. Notice it has the exact same parameters as the addEventListener method:

```
element.removeEventListener(type, handler [, useCapture]);
```

USE this Code

This tells the object to remove the listener from its list of listeners for that particular event, so it will not receive further notifications.

Let's go ahead and see this in action. Start out with the skeleton document presented earlier, and add the code to that:

```html
<!doctype html>
<html>
 <head>
  <meta charset="utf-8">
  <title>Event Demo</title>
  <link rel="stylesheet" href="style.css">
 </head>
 <body>
  <canvas id="canvas" width="400" height="400"></canvas>
  <script>
  window.onload = function () {
    var canvas = document.getElementById('canvas');

    canvas.addEventListener('mousedown', function (event) {
      console.log("mouse down");
    }, false);

    canvas.addEventListener('mouseup', function (event) {
      console.log("mouse up");
    }, false);
  };
  </script>
 </body>
</html>
```

The window loads -(window.on Load); CAlls Anonymous Function: VAR "CANVAS" declared And A DOM property (getElement byId) Assigned to the VAR using the string VALUE "CANVAS".

Now MY CANVAS ELement can Listen FOR A "mouse down" EVENT, using the "addEventListener" FUNCTION & it's 1st "ARGUMENT" is the specific mouse event to Listen for; it's 2nd ARGUMENT is AN ANONYMOUS function (tells VAR "CANVAS" whAt Action to do) in this cASE "write this string to console";

HANDLERS

INLINE FUNCTIONS HANDLER

STRING

In this example, first we accessed the canvas element (that has an id of `'canvas'`) through the DOM interface using `document.getElementById` and stored it at the variable `canvas`. We then added listeners for two events, mouseup and mousedown. As handlers, we passed in callback functions that are defined in-line (remember, functions are objects that can be passed around), which print a message to the debugging console. The handlers get passed an event object as an argument that contains some information about the event; minimally, it contains the name of the event and information about what object triggered it. In the case of mouse events, it contains information about the mouse location at the time of the event, which mouse button was pressed (if any), and so on. For keyboard events, it would have information about what keys were pressed at the time of the event.

At time of EVENT: iNFO

the 3rd Argument is: "FALSE" BecAuse you don't wAnt to "use CAPTURE"

Save this example as `02-event-demo.html`. When you load the file in your web browser, you'll see that it prints a message to the debugging console each time the mouse is pressed or released on the canvas element. Make sure you get this exercise working, and the path to your CSS file is correct. It's a simple exercise, but it's a good test to ensure your development environment is set up correctly.

If you are new to JavaScript and can get this example working and understand it, congratulations—you've just moved from beginner up to intermediate status!

Now that you know a little bit more about handlers, you can get a better understanding of listeners. An object generates an event, broadcasts that event, or notifies its listeners of the event. How does it do that

Listeners create a list of frequency of occurance of their specific event

exactly? Well, all it does is call the function on that object that has the correct handler name. In the previous example, document `02-event-demo.html` added the canvas element as a listener for a couple of mouse events. Internally, the element keeps a list for each event. So it has a list for the **mousedown** event and another list for the **mouseup** event.

When the user presses the mouse button on the canvas element, the element responds, "Hey! Mouse down! Must notify listeners!" It then goes through its **mousedown** list and sees what is in there. The element finds a reference to the function that was specified as a handler and then calls that function on the listener. If other objects had registered as listeners to the **mousedown** event, they would also be on the list, and whatever handlers they had defined would be called.

The same thing happens when the mouse is released, except it looks at its **mouseup** list.

Those are the basics of events and handlers. Next, we introduce you to some of the event types used for interaction.

Mouse events   *— Types of Mouse Events*

To capture a mouse event, you must add a listener to a DOM element to handle the event. Mouse event types are defined by strings, and different browsers have varying levels of support for particular events. Here is a list of the most common ones:

- mousedown
- mouseup
- click
- dblclick
- mousewheel
- mousemove
- mouseover
- mouseout

ALL lower case

These mouse event types are self-explanatory. To get a feel for them, create and run the following document, which prints to the console each mouse event as it occurs on the canvas element. You can find this file with the rest of the example code, `03-mouse-events.html`:

```
<!doctype html>
<html>
 <head>
  <meta charset="utf-8">
  <title>Mouse Events</title>
  <link rel="stylesheet" href="style.css">
 </head>
 <body>
  <canvas id="canvas" width="400" height="400"></canvas>
  <script>
  window.onload = function () {
```

```
var canvas = document.getElementById('canvas');

function onMouseEvent (event) {
  console.log(event.type);
}

canvas.addEventListener('mousedown', onMouseEvent, false);
canvas.addEventListener('mouseup', onMouseEvent, false);
canvas.addEventListener('click', onMouseEvent, false);
canvas.addEventListener('dblclick', onMouseEvent, false);
canvas.addEventListener('mousewheel', onMouseEvent, false);
canvas.addEventListener('mousemove', onMouseEvent, false);
canvas.addEventListener('mouseover', onMouseEvent, false);
canvas.addEventListener('mouseout', onMouseEvent, false);
};
</script>
</body>
</html>
```

Notice that we're using the same handler function for every mouse event type, and it prints the type of event that has been dispatched.

Because we can reference only the canvas element, and not what has been drawn to it, we can't add an event listener to specific lines or shapes. If you've drawn a rectangle to use as a button, the canvas has no way of determining where the button boundaries are. To detect a button click, it's up to you to capture the canvas element's mouse event, determine the position relative to the button, and perform the calculation yourself. As we work through the book examples, you'll see some ways to do this.

Mouse position

Every mouse event contains two properties to determine the current location of the mouse cursor: pageX and pageY. By combining these values and the offset of the canvas element, you can determine where on the canvas element the mouse is. Unfortunately, these mouse event properties are not supported across all browsers, so in these cases, you can use clientX and clientY.

Having to calculate the offset every time you need the mouse position is a bit unwieldy. Because we want to keep the examples uncluttered, add this cross-platform mouse position code into an utility function utils.captureMouse to include in the file utils.js. We import this into our documents:

```
utils.captureMouse = function (element) {
  var mouse = {x: 0, y: 0};

  element.addEventListener('mousemove', function (event) {
    var x, y;
    if (event.pageX || event.pageY) {
      x = event.pageX;
      y = event.pageY;
    } else {
      x = event.clientX + document.body.scrollLeft +
          document.documentElement.scrollLeft;
      y = event.clientY + document.body.scrollTop +
          document.documentElement.scrollTop;
```

```
    }
    x -= element.offsetLeft;
    y -= element.offsetTop;

    mouse.x = x;
    mouse.y = y;
  }, false);

  return mouse;
};
```

[handwritten annotations: wtf "element"? Is it the canvas of the mouse event?]

This function takes a DOM element as an argument, attaches a mousemove event handler to it, and returns an object with x and y properties. When the mouse moves over the element, the event handler calculates the mouse position using the event's location (as supported by the browser) and the document offset position of the element. It then assigns these values to the object we returned, which we can access from our main script. The mouse x and y positions are relative to the top-left corner of the element, which is the coordinate (0, 0).

For example, you invoke this function at the start of the script, passing the canvas element as an argument:

```
var canvas = document.getElementById('canvas'),
    mouse = utils.captureMouse(canvas);
```

[handwritten annotation: initializes "mouse" object]

After the mouse object has been initialized, you can query its x and y properties whenever you need to determine the current location of the mouse cursor. Here's a complete example that demonstrates how this function is used throughout the rest of the book:

```
<!doctype html>
<html>
 <head>
  <meta charset="utf-8">
  <title>Mouse Position</title>
  <link rel="stylesheet" href="style.css">
 </head>
 <body>
  <canvas id="canvas" width="400" height="400"></canvas>
  <script src="utils.js"></script>
  <script>
  window.onload = function () {
    var canvas = document.getElementById('canvas'),
        mouse = utils.captureMouse(canvas);

    canvas.addEventListener('mousedown', function () {
      console.log("x: " + mouse.x + ", y: " + mouse.y);
    }, false);
  };
  </script>
 </body>
</html>
```

[handwritten annotation: refs external js - "captureMouse"]

Run this file (04-mouse-position.html) in your browser with the debugging console open. Make sure you've included the utils.captureMouse function in utils.js and imported that file into the document.

When you click on the canvas element, you'll see a message displaying the current mouse position using the `mouse.x` and `mouse.y` properties.

Touch Events

Because touch screen devices are gaining in popularity, it's a good idea to see how to use them with JavaScript. Touch events are similar to mouse events, but have a few key differences. A touch point can be thought of like a mouse cursor; however, a mouse cursor will always stay on the screen, whereas a finger will press, move, and release from the device, so there will be times when no cursor is available. When querying the touch position, you must take this into consideration. Secondly, there is no touch event equivalent to `mouseover`—there is either a touch or there isn't, there is no finger hovering. Finally, multiple touches can occur at the same time. Each touch is stored in an array on the touch event, but for these examples we just use the first one.

Here's the touch events we use to interact with our animations:

- touchstart

- touchend

- touchmovc

These are demonstrated in example `05-touch-events.html`, so if you want to see this in action then make sure you are on a device or emulator that can support touch events:

```
<!doctype html>
<html>
 <head>
  <meta charset="utf-8">
  <title>Touch Events</title>
  <link rel="stylesheet" href="style.css">
 </head>
 <body>
  <canvas id="canvas" width="400" height="400"></canvas>
  <script>
  window.onload = function () {
    var canvas = document.getElementById('canvas');

    function onTouchEvent (event) {
      console.log(event.type);
    }

    canvas.addEventListener('touchstart', onTouchEvent, false);
    canvas.addEventListener('touchend', onTouchEvent, false);
    canvas.addEventListener('touchmove', onTouchEvent, false);
  };
  </script>
 </body>
</html>
```

This code does the same thing as the mouse events example (`03-mouse-events.html`): When a touch event is detected on the canvas element, it prints out the type to the debugging console.

29

Touch position

Like the `utils.captureMouse` function, you can use the `utils.captureTouch` utility to determine the location of the first finger touch on an element. The two functions are similar, but because there might not be a finger touching the screen, the property `isPressed` has been added to the returned object. This property contains a Boolean value indicating whether a touch is detected. Also, when there is no active touch present, the properties `x` and `y` are set to `null`. Add the following function to the `utils.js` file:

```
utils.captureTouch = function (element) {
  var touch = {x: null, y: null, isPressed: false};

  element.addEventListener('touchstart', function (event) {
    touch.isPressed = true;
  }, false);

  element.addEventListener('touchend', function (event) {
    touch.isPressed = false;
    touch.x = null;
    touch.y = null;
  }, false);

  element.addEventListener('touchmove', function (event) {
    var x, y,
        touch_event = event.touches[0]; //first touch

    if (touch_event.pageX || touch_event.pageY) {
      x = touch_event.pageX;
      y = touch_event.pageY;
    } else {
      x = touch_event.clientX + document.body.scrollLeft +
          document.documentElement.scrollLeft;
      y = touch_event.clientY + document.body.scrollTop +
          document.documentElement.scrollTop;
    }
    x -= offsetLeft;
    y -= offsetTop;

    touch.x = x;
    touch.y = y;
  }, false);

  return touch;
};
```

The function definition is similar to the mouse position version, but with a few extra event listeners. It takes an element argument and returns an object with properties `x`, `y`, and `isPressed`. The `touchmove` event handler keeps track of the position of the first touch relative to the element, using some cross-browser code to calculate the offset. There are also also event handlers added for `touchstart`, which sets `isPressed` to `true`, and `touchend`, which sets `isPressed` to `false`. It also sets the `x` and `y` properties to `null`, because there is no longer an active position.

You can initialize the `touch` object like before:

```
var canvas = document.getElementById('canvas'),
    touch = utils.captureTouch(canvas);
```

You must be certain that there is a touch present before accessing the x and y properties; otherwise, their values will be **null** and potentially mess up the animation calculations. Therefore, for any touch location queries, be sure to check whether there is an active touch press:

```
if (touch.isPressed) {
  console.log("x: " + touch.x + ", y: " + touch.y);
}
```

Touch events won't be used much in this book because we're concentrating on the underlying math that makes the examples work. But, this should give you an idea about how to use them if you wanted to experiment with a touch device.

Keyboard events

Keyboard event types, like all event types, are defined as strings. There are only two:

- keydown

- keyup

You can listen for keyboard events on elements that support character input—such as a text area element—the same way you listened for mouse events on the canvas element. But, you first need to set the focus to that element to capture these keyboard events. Assuming you have an HTML **textarea** element stored at the variable **textarea**, you can set its focus and capture a **keydown** event, like so:

```
textarea.focus();
textarea.addEventListener('keydown', function (event) {
  console.log(event.type);
}, false);
```

In many cases, though, it makes more sense to listen for keyboard events on the web page, regardless of what has focus. To do that, attach a keyboard event listener on the global **window** object. The following example detects when you press and release a key, regardless of what element has focus (example 06-keyboard-events.html):

```
<!doctype html>
<html>
 <head>
  <meta charset="utf-8">
  <title>Keyboard Events</title>
  <link rel="stylesheet" href="style.css">
 </head>
 <body>
  <script>
  window.onload = function () {

    function onKeyboardEvent (event) {
      console.log(event.type);
    }
```

```
    window.addEventListener('keydown', onKeyboardEvent, false);
    window.addEventListener('keyup', onKeyboardEvent, false);
  };
  </script>
 </body>
</html>
```

Key codes

More often than not, within the event handler function, you'll want to know which key has been pressed. Earlier, when introducing events, you saw that an event handler gets passed an event object, which contains data about the event that just occurred. In a keyboard event, you can use the keyCode property to determine what key was involved with the event.

The keyCode property contains a numeric value that represents the physical key that was pressed. If the user pressed the "a" key, the keyCode would contain the number 65, regardless of what other keys were pressed. If the user pressed the Shift key first and then "a," you would get two keyboard events: one for Shift (keyCode 16) and one for "a" (keyCode 65).

In the next example, we're testing the keyCode against a set of known values, the numbers of the directional arrow keys: 37, 38, 39, and 40. If it matches any of these numbers, we print a message to the console displaying the direction that has been pressed. Otherwise, we just print out the keyCode value of the unknown key. Here is the document 07-key-codes.html:

```
<!doctype html>
<html>
 <head>
  <meta charset="utf-8">
  <title>Key Codes</title>
  <link rel="stylesheet" href="style.css">
 </head>
 <body>
  <script>
  window.onload = function () {

    function onKeyboardEvent (event) {
      switch (event.keyCode) {
      case 38:
        console.log("up!");
        break;
      case 40:
        console.log("down!");
        break;
      case 37:
        console.log("left!");
        break;
      case 39:
        console.log("right!");
        break;
      default:
        console.log(event.keyCode);
```

```
      }
    }

    window.addEventListener('keydown', onKeyboardEvent, false);
  };
  </script>
 </body>
</html>
```

Often, you won't know the exact numeric value of the key you want to capture. To make finding this information easier, we've created a file `keycode.js` to use as a reference cheat-sheet or to include in your document, so you can lookup a key by name instead of number—this makes your code much easier to understand. This script creates a global object `keycode` that contains the property names of most keyboard keys and maps them to their associated `keyCode` value. You can find this file, as the rest of the source code for this book, at `www.apress.com`, or, `http://github.com/lamberta/html5-animation`.

Let's rewrite the previous example using key names instead of key codes. Place the file `keycode.js` in the same directory as the example and include it in the document `08-key-names.html`:

```
<!doctype html>
<html>
 <head>
  <meta charset="utf-8">
  <title>Key Names</title>
  <link rel="stylesheet" href="style.css">
 </head>
 <body>
  <script src="keycode.js"></script>
  <script>
  window.onload = function () {

    function onKeyboardEvent (event) {
      switch (event.keyCode) {
      case keycode.UP:
        console.log("up!");
        break;
      case keycode.DOWN:
        console.log("down!");
        break;
      case keycode.LEFT:
        console.log("left!");
        break;
      case keycode.RIGHT:
        console.log("right!");
        break;
      default:
        console.log(event.keyCode);
      }
    }
```

```
    window.addEventListener('keydown', onKeyboardEvent, false);
  };
  </script>
 </body>
</html>
```

You can see this example—like the previous example, 07-key-codes.html—prints the same messages to the console, but, because we're now using key *names* instead of key *codes*, our switch statement is easier to understand. Not only is it clearer, but it prevents you from accidentally typing a wrong number.

We won't use the keycode.js file in this book because the exercises are relatively simple and I want you to see exactly what's going on in the examples. But it can make your code more readable, so in more complex programs it's something you should consider using.

Summary

This chapter covered just about all the JavaScript basics you need to understand the rest of the examples found in this book. You now know about setting up an HTML5 document, debugging, loops, events, and handlers. We've touched on JavaScript objects, basic user interaction, and created a few utility functions to make things a little easier. That's a lot of material! Don't worry if some of these areas are still a little vague. Most of the topics here are shown in more detail as we get into specific techniques, and you can always come back here to brush up on the basics. At the very least, now you are familiar with the terms and concepts, and you're ready to move forward.

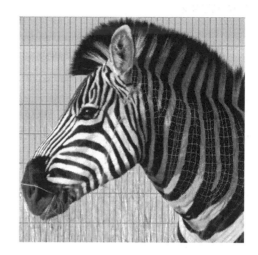

Chapter 3

Trigonometry for Animation

What we'll cover in this chapter:

- What is trigonometry?
- Angles
- Trigonometry functions
- Rotation
- Waves
- Circles and ellipses
- Pythagorean Theorem
- Distance between two points

This chapter is near the beginning of the book because trigonometry is used extensively for animation techniques, starting with the examples in Chapter 5. And in fact, we'll even touch on it in Chapter 4 on rendering techniques. However, feel free to jump ahead if you already know basic trigonometry or are just anxious to animate things. You can always come back here when you come across something you don't understand.

Many people shy away from math and trigonometry, using excuses like: "I'm not good with numbers." The interesting thing about programming with trigonometry is that you are hardly dealing with numbers at all. It's more about visualizing shapes and relationships. For the most part, you deal with variables containing positions, distances, and angles, and you never see the actual numbers. It's mostly a matter of understanding various relationships, and in fact, about 90% of the trigonometry you need for basic animation comes down to two functions: `Math.sin` and `Math.cos`.

What is trigonometry?

Trigonometry is the study of triangles and the relationship of their sides and angles. If you look at any triangle, you see that it has three sides and three angles (hence, the name *tri-angle).* It happens that these sides and angles have specific relationships. For example, if you take any triangle and make one of the angles larger, the side opposite of that angle gets longer (assuming the other two sides stay the same length). Also, the other two angles get smaller. Exactly how much each of these things changes takes a bit of calculation, but the ratios have all been figured out and codified.

A specific type of triangle has one of its angles equal to exactly 90 degrees. This is called a *right-angle triangle* and is indicated by a little square in the corner of that angle. It happens that in a right-angle triangle, the various relationships are far simpler and quite easy to figure out with some basic formulas. This makes a right-angle triangle a useful construct, and all of the trigonometry in this chapter, and most of what you see in the rest of the book, deals with right-angle triangles.

Angles

Because trigonometry is mostly about angles, let's look at that subject first. An *angle* is simply the shape formed by two intersecting lines, or the space in between those lines. The more space, the higher the measurement of the angle. Actually, two intersecting lines form four angles, as you can see in Figure 3-1.

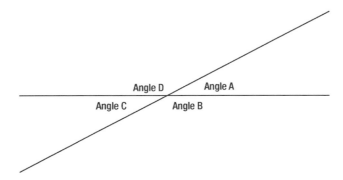

Figure 3-1. Two lines form four angles.

Radians and degrees

The two major systems for measuring angles are *degrees* and *radians.* You are probably familiar with degrees, and could probably draw a 45- or 90-degree angle if I asked you to. The system of 360 degrees in a circle has become a part of our culture. People say they're "doing a 180," meaning "going in the opposite direction," even when we are not talking about physical direction, but referring to taking an opposite viewpoint. But it turns out that computers have a lot more affinity for radians when it comes to representing angles. So, like it or not, you need to know about radians.

A *radian* is equal to approximately 57.2958 degrees. At first glance, that number may seem arbitrary, but there is some actual logic to it. A full circle, or 360 degrees, works out to 6.2832 radians. Remember pi—

that symbol, π? That is equal to about 3.1416, meaning that a circle (6.2832 radians) measures exactly 2 pi. It still might not seem too logical now, but work with it enough, and you'll get used to thinking of 360 degrees as 2 pi, 180 degrees as pi, 90 degrees as pi/2, and so on. Figure 3-2 illustrates some common radian measurements.

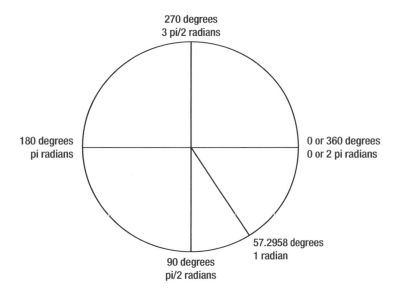

Figure 3-2. Radians and degrees

Now, we can leave the discussion there and just tell you that you can use radians from here on out. You might sigh a bit, and then get used to it and be fine with using radians exclusively. But you're going to encounter many situations where you need to use degrees *with* radians. For example, when rotating an image on the canvas element, we use the `context.rotate(angle)`method, using radians for the angle. However, in many examples we set up the objects in our scene using the more human-friendly degrees, so we need a way to easily convert the values.

So why use two completely different systems? Well, you don't have to. You can keep everything as radians since that is what the canvas expects. However, it's often convenient to think of angles in terms of degrees, for ourselves and others, simply because it's how most people think of angles. I'm sure most designers would look at you cross-eyed if you told them to enter a radian value to rotate the text for the logo they are creating. When working with HTML, programmers must straddle the line between design and development, and JavaScript, like most programming languages, uses radians. Because you'll likely be working with both, you need to know how to convert degrees to radians and back again. Here are the formulas:

```
radians = degrees * Math.PI / 180
degrees = radians * 180 / Math.PI
```

As you go through this book, you run into a lot of formulas. Here and there, I'll point out a formula as one that you should memorize—burn these into the backs of your eyelids. These conversion formulas are the first ones. They should just roll off your fingers onto the keyboard whenever you need them. If you can't remember them yet, just write it down on a piece of paper and tape it to your computer monitor. They are even in JavaScript, using `Math.PI`, because that's how you type them over and over.

From this, you can easily see that 180 degrees is about 3.14 ... radians. In other words, half a circle is pi radians, which makes sense because a full circle is 2 pi. Going the other way, you can see that one radian is roughly 57.29 ... degrees.

The canvas coordinate system

Although we are on the subject of angles, this is a good time to describe how space is laid out in the canvas element, numerically speaking. If you've dealt with any coordinate systems prior to this, you might get a little dizzy here, because everything is upside down and backward.

The most common two-dimensional coordinate systems signify horizontal measurements with x and vertical measurements with y—the canvas element does this, too. However, the zero x, zero y position (0, 0) is usually shown in the center, with positive x going off to the right, negative x to the left, positive y going up, and negative y going down, as shown in Figure 3-3.

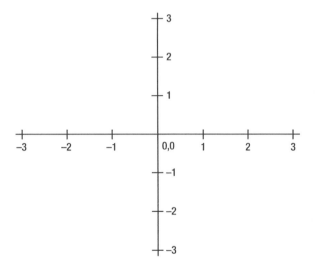

Figure 3-3. A standard coordinate system

The canvas element, however, is based on a video screen coordinate system, where 0, 0 is at the top left, as shown in Figure 3-4. The x values still increase from left to right, but the y axis is reversed, with positive values going down and negative values going up. This system has its historical roots in the way the electron gun scans the screen to build the picture—left to right, top to bottom—but it doesn't really matter. That's the way it works, and it's not going to change anytime soon.

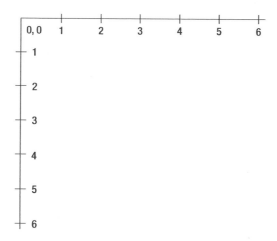

Figure 3-4. The canvas element coordinate system

But wait, there's more! Let's measure some angles. In most systems, angles are measured counterclockwise, with 0 degrees being shown as a line extending into the positive x axis, as shown in Figure 3-5.

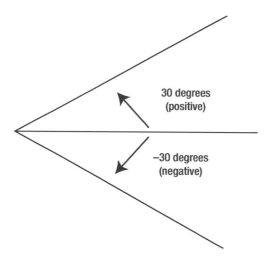

Figure 3-5. The usual angle measurements

Again, the canvas element has it backward, as illustrated in Figure 3-6. It rotates its angles clockwise as they go positive. *Counterclockwise* means a negative angle.

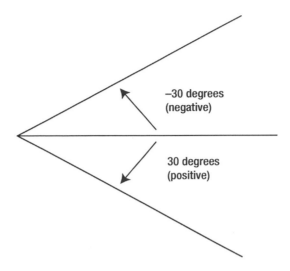

Figure 3-6. Angle measurements on the canvas element

You can work out a system to reverse the angles before rendering, or conserve the computation and learn to live with it. It's suggested you do the latter, and this is the tactic used for all the code in this book.

Triangle sides

There's not too much to say about the sides of a triangle by themselves, but there are some specific terms to cover. Until further notice, we are referring to right-angle triangles, where one of the angles is 90 degrees. In this case, the sides have special names, as shown in Figure 3-7. The two sides that touch the 90-degree angle are called *legs*, and the opposite side is called the *hypotenuse*. The hypotenuse is always the longest side.

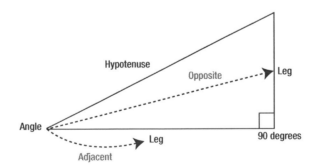

Figure 3-7. The parts of a right-angle triangle

When referring to the side *opposite* an angle, we're talking about the side that does not touch that angle. When referring to an *adjacent* side, we mean one of the sides that does touch the angle. Most of the time, examples deal with one of the two non-90-degree angles. In this case, when we say "adjacent," it means the adjacent leg, not the hypotenuse.

The interesting thing about triangles is the relationships between the measurements of the sides and the measurements of the angles. These relationships become useful for animation, so let's look at them next.

Trigonometry functions

JavaScript has trigonometry functions for calculating the various triangle relationships: sine, cosine, tangent, arcsine, arccosine, and arctangent. In this section, I'll define these and the JavaScript functions for accessing them. Then we get to some real-life uses for these functions.

Sine

Here is your first bit of real-life trigonometry: The *sine* of an angle is the ratio of the lengths of the side of the triangle opposite the angle and the hypotenuse. (When referring to sine, we always refer to the sine of an angle.) In JavaScript, you can use the function `Math.sin(angle)`.

Figure 3-8 shows the sine of an angle that is 30 degrees. The opposite leg has a measurement of 1, and the hypotenuse has a measurement of 2. The ratio is thus one to two, or mathematically speaking, 1/2 or 0.5. Thus, you can say that the sine of a 30-degree angle is 0.5. You can test this in your browser's debugging console by entering the following:

```
console.log(Math.sin(30));
```

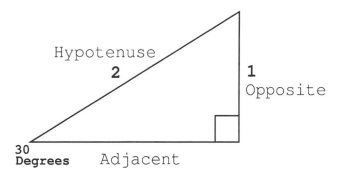

Figure 3-8. The sine of an angle is the opposite leg/hypotenuse.

But that prints out -0.988031624092862, which is not even close. Can you spot the error? We forgot to convert to radians. You will probably make this mistake on occasion, so get used to looking for it. Here's the corrected code, with the conversion:

```
console.log(Math.sin(30 * Math.PI / 180));
```

Success! That prints 0.5.

Actually, you might get something like 0.4999 … something, which is not an error in your program but the way binary computers sometimes end up representing floating-point numbers. It's close enough, though, that you can consider it 0.5.

Now, it's fine for an abstract triangle like that to say that the angle is 30 degrees, and the measurements of the sides are 1 and 2, but let's move it into the real world, or at least the world of the canvas coordinate system. Remember that in the canvas element, positive vertical measurements go down, and positive angle measurements go clockwise. So, in this case, the opposite side and the angle are both negative, as you can see in Figure 3-9.

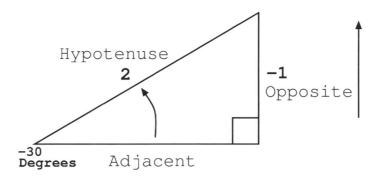

Figure 3-9. The same triangle in the canvas coordinate space

The ratio becomes -1/2, and we are talking about the sine of -30. We say that the sine of -30 degrees is -0.5. Go ahead and change the JavaScript `console.log` statement to verify that:

```
console.log(Math.sin(-30 * Math.PI / 180));
```

That wasn't too painful, was it? Let's take a look at another trigonometry function: cosine.

Cosine

You can access cosine in JavaScript with `Math.cos(angle)`. *Cosine* is defined as the ratio of the adjacent leg of an angle to the hypotenuse. Figure 3-10 shows that relationship.

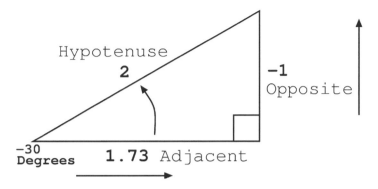

Figure 3-10. The cosine of an angle is the adjacent leg/hypotenuse.

Figure 3-10 shows the same angle as Figure 3-9, but now we added the approximate measurement of the adjacent leg: 1.73. Notice that it goes to the right, so as an x measurement, it's positive. The cosine of the angle is thus 1.73/2, or 0.865. So we can say that the cosine of -30 degrees is 0.865. Test it as follows:

```
console.log(Math.cos(-30 * Math.PI / 180));
```

This is the same as the last print out, but with the call to `Math.cos`, rather than to `Math.sin`. This prints to 0.866025403784439, which is close to 0.865. The difference is due to the fact that we rounded off the length of the adjacent leg. For the triangle shown, the actual length is closer to 1.73205080756888. If you divide that by 2, you get close to the actual cosine of -30 degrees.

So far, everything is taken from the lower-left angle. What if you look at things from the viewpoint of the top-right angle? Well, first you need to reorient the triangle so that the angle in question aligns with the coordinate system, as you can see in Figure 3-11. This is known as *putting the angle in standard position* (even though the canvas element "standard" is upside down and backward from the usual "standard"). That angle is equal to 60 degrees, and as it's going clockwise, it's positive. The vertical measurement now goes down from that angle, so it's positive. The horizontal measurement goes to the right, so it's positive, too. (We added plus signs in the figure to point out the difference, but in general, this is not necessary; values are positive unless specifically indicated as negative.)

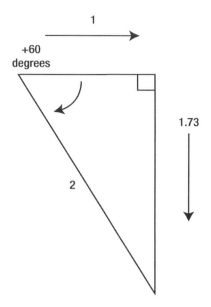

Figure 3-11. Looking at the opposite angle

The sine of that angle is its opposite leg over the hypotenuse, or 1.73/2 (0.865), and the cosine is the adjacent over the hypotenuse, 1/2, or 0.5. So, basically, the cosine of one angle is the same as the sine of the other angle, and the sine of one is the cosine of the other. This might not be useful in your code, but it's important to note that these are just relationships and ratios, and everything is connected.

Tangent

Another major trigonometry function is *tangent*, used in JavaScript with `Math.tan(angle)`. This is the relationship of the opposite leg to the adjacent leg, as shown in Figure 3-12.

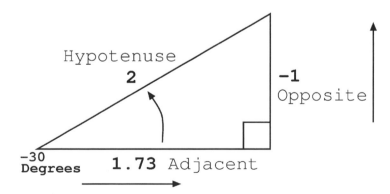

Figure 3-12. The tangent of an angle is the opposite leg/adjacent leg.

Here, the ratio works out to -1/1.73, or -0.578. For more accuracy, verify it directly in your browser's debugging console:

```
console.log(Math.tan(-30 * Math.PI / 180));
```

You get -0.577350269189627.

Truth be told, you won't use tangent much in your day-to-day animation code. You'll find yourself using sine and cosine a lot more, although tangent can be used to create some interesting effects now and then.

On the other hand, arctangent can be extremely useful, as you see shortly, so keep that tangent ratio in your head.

Arcsine and arccosine

Similar to tangent, *arcsine* and *arccosine* are not that useful in your normal animation endeavors. However, it's important to know that they are there and how to use them. These basically do the reverse of sine and cosine; or in other words, you feed in a ratio, and you get back an angle (in radians). The JavaScript functions are `Math.asin(ratio)` and `Math.acos(ratio)`. Let's just give them a quick test to make sure they work.

You learned that the sine of 30 degrees is 0.5, so it follows that the arcsine of 0.5 should be 30 degrees. Check it out:

```
console.log(Math.asin(0.5) * 180 / Math.PI);
```

Remember to convert back to degrees to see the approximate value of 30, not 0.523, which is the equivalent value in radians.

The cosine of 30 degrees is roughly 0.865. Remember that if you test this value, which is rounded off, you won't get exactly 30 because of the way computers represent decimal numbers, but it will be close enough to prove the point. Here's the test:

```
console.log(Math.acos(0.865) * 180 / Math.PI);
```

You should get 30.1172947473221 (or close) as the result. If you want to go back and plug in the actual cosine of 30 degrees, you should get a more accurate result.

See, this stuff isn't so hard, is it? And you're almost finished learning the basic functions. You just have one more to go, and then you look at what you can actually do with trigonometry.

Arctangent

As you no doubt have already guessed, *arctangent* is simply the opposite of tangent. You feed it the ratio of the opposite and adjacent sides, and it gives you back the angle. In JavaScript, you have two functions to check arctangent. The first is named and works just as you expect from the previous examples. It's `Math.atan(ratio)`, and you supply it the fraction you got by dividing the opposite and adjacent sides.

For example, you know from the earlier discussion that the tangent of 30 degrees is 0.577 (rounded off). You can try the following:

```
console.log(Math.atan(0.577) * 180 / Math.PI);
```

You get back something close to 30. Now, that seems so basic and straightforward, why would you ever need another function to do the same thing? Well, to answer that, look at the diagram shown in Figure 3-13.

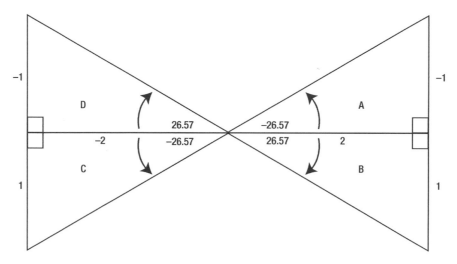

Figure 3-13. Angles in four quadrants

Figure 3-13 shows four different triangles: A, B, C, and D. Triangles A and B have a positive x value, and triangles C and D extend into negative x dimensions. Likewise, triangles A and D are in the negative y space, whereas triangles B and C have positive y measurements. So, for the ratios of the four inner angles, you get the following:

- A:-1/2 or -0.5

- B: 1/2 or 0.5

- C: 1/ -2 or -0.5

- D: -1/ -2 or 0.5

Let's say you divide the opposite leg by the adjacent leg and come up with a ratio of 0.5. You feed that in with `Math.atan(0.5)`, convert it to degrees, and you get approximately 26.57. But which triangle are you talking about now: B or D? There is no way of knowing, because they both have a ratio of 0.5. This might seem like a minor point, but as you see in some real-life examples later in this chapter, it becomes quite important.

Welcome `Math.atan2(y, x)`. This is the other arctangent function in JavaScript, and it is quite a bit more useful than `Math.atan(ratio)`. And in fact, you will probably use this one exclusively. This function takes two values: the measurement of the opposite side and the measurement of the adjacent side. For most purposes, this measurement is the position of an x and y coordinate. A common mistake is to enter them as x, y, rather than y, x, as specified. For the example given, you enter `Math.atan2(1, 2)`. Go ahead and try it out, remembering to convert to degrees:

```
console.log(Math.atan2(1, 2) * 180 / Math.PI);
```

This should give you the angle, 26.565051177078, which is correct for triangle B as shown previously. Now, knowing that -1/ -2 (triangle D) gave us some confusion, let's try that out.

```
console.log(Math.atan2(-1, -2) * 180 / Math.PI);
```

This gives you the possibly unexpected result of -153.434948822922. What is that all about? Perhaps the diagram in Figure 3-14 will explain.

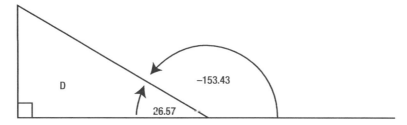

Figure 3-14. Two ways of measuring an angle

Although the inner angle of triangle D is indeed +26.57, as taken from its own bottom leg, remember that in the canvas, angles are measured clockwise from the positive x axis. Thus, from the canvas element's viewpoint of screen measurements, the angle you are looking at is -153.43.

How is this useful? Well, let's get to the first practical application of trigonometry using the canvas element.

Rotation

Here is the challenge: You want to draw an object and rotate it so that it always points to the mouse. Rotation is a useful tool to add to your toolbox, it can be used in games and interface elements, among other things. And in fact, rotation is not just limited to the mouse. Because the mouse coordinates are just x and y values, you can extend this technique to force an object to aim itself at any particular point, such as another object or the center or corner of the screen.

Let's work through an example. You can follow along with the steps or just open the document 01-rotate-to-mouse.html and arrow.js file (which you can download from the book's page at www.apress.com, along with all of the other code for this book) to have all the work done for you.

First, you need something to rotate. This is an object that contains commands to draw an arrow to a canvas element using the given canvas context. Because you will use this arrow object again, make it into a class so each instance can have its own properties. Add the following JavaScript code to the file arrow.js, which we import into our main HTML document:

```
function Arrow () {
  this.x = 0;
  this.y = 0;
  this.color = "#ffff00";
  this.rotation = 0;
}

Arrow.prototype.draw = function (context) {
  context.save();
  context.translate(this.x, this.y);
  context.rotate(this.rotation);
  context.lineWidth = 2;
  context.fillStyle = this.color;
  context.beginPath();
  context.moveTo(-50, -25);
  context.lineTo(0, -25);
  context.lineTo(0, -50);
  context.lineTo(50, 0);
  context.lineTo(0, 50);
  context.lineTo(0, 25);
  context.lineTo(-50, 25);
  context.lineTo(-50, -25);
  context.closePath();
  context.fill();
  context.stroke();
  context.restore();
};
```

The `draw(context)` method uses the canvas drawing API (which we discuss in Chapter 4) to draw an arrow using the passed canvas context parameter. Now, whenever you need an arrow object, you just call `new Arrow()`. You can see the result in Figure 3-15. When drawing any content made to rotate like this, make sure that it is "pointing" to the correct, or positive x axis, because this is how it will look when rotated to 0 degrees.

Figure 3-15. The arrow drawn with the canvas drawing API

You create an instance of the **Arrow** class, placing it in the center of the canvas element and having it point at the mouse (see Figure 3-16).

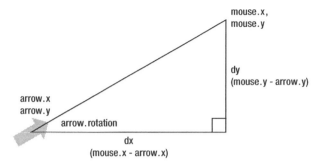

Figure 3-16. This shows what you will calculate next.

Look familiar? It's the same triangle you've worked with for a while now, just mapped to the mouse and arrow coordinates. When we include the `utils.js` file and capture the mouse position using `mouse = utils.captureMouse(canvas)`, its coordinates can be read from the `mouse.x` and `mouse.y` properties. You can get the location of the arrow with its `x` and `y` properties. Subtracting these, you get the length of the two triangle legs. Now, you simply need to use `Math.atan2(dy, dx)` to find the angle and set the arrow's `rotation` property to the result. It will look like the following:

```
var dx = mouse.x - arrow.x,
    dy = mouse.y - arrow.y;
arrow.rotation = Math.atan2(dy, dx); //in radians
```

Of course, to get animation, you need to set up a loop. As discussed in detail in Chapter 2, we use the `window.requestAnimationFrame` function to clear the canvas, draw our frame, then call it again at the next scheduled interval. Here's the complete HTML file for `01-rotate-to-mouse.html`:

```
<!doctype html>
<html>
 <head>
  <meta charset="utf-8">
  <title>Rotate to Mouse</title>
  <link rel="stylesheet" href="style.css">
 </head>
 <body>
  <canvas id="canvas" width="400" height="400"></canvas>
  <script src="utils.js"></script>
  <script src="arrow.js"></script>
  <script>
  window.onload = function () {
    var canvas = document.getElementById('canvas'),
        context = canvas.getContext('2d'),
        mouse = utils.captureMouse(canvas),
        arrow = new Arrow();

    arrow.x = canvas.width / 2;
    arrow.y = canvas.height / 2;

    (function drawFrame () {
```

```
      window.requestAnimationFrame(drawFrame, canvas);
      context.clearRect(0, 0, canvas.width, canvas.height);

      var dx = mouse.x - arrow.x,
          dy = mouse.y - arrow.y;

      arrow.rotation = Math.atan2(dy, dx); //radians
      arrow.draw(context);
    }());
  };
  </script>
 </body>
</html>
```

Make sure that you have the **arrow.js** file in the same directory as the **01-rotate-to-mouse.html** file and run this example in your favorite HTML5 capable web browser. If everything is set up correctly, move your mouse around the canvas element and the arrow should follow it!

Now, suppose that you don't have **Math.atan2**. You can get the ratio of opposite to adjacent angle by dividing **dy** by **dx** and pass that in to **Math.atan**. Just change the **Math.atan2** line in the preceding code to use **Math.atan** instead, as follows:

```
var radians = Math.atan(dy / dx);
```

Try that one out, and you see the problem quickly. If the mouse is to the left of the arrow, the arrow will not point to it, but directly away from it. Can you figure out what is going on? Going back to the diagram showing triangles A, B, C, and D (Figure 3-13), remember that triangles A and C share the same ratio, as well as triangles B and D. There is no way for our JavaScript code to know which angle you are referring to, so it returns A or B. So, if your mouse is in the D quadrant, we get the angle for the B quadrant and rotate the mouse into that area.

You can now see the benefits of **Math.atan2**, and you will use it many times throughout the book.

Waves

Let's see some more concrete uses of trigonometry with the canvas element. You've probably heard the term *sine wave* before, and you've probably seen the shape shown in Figure 3-17, which is a graphical representation of a sine wave.

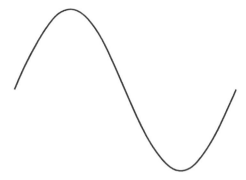

Figure 3-17. A sine wave

But what exactly does that shape have to do with the sine function? It is the graph of the results of the sine function, when fed in all the angles from 0 to 360 (or 0 to 2 pi in radians). From left to right is the value of the angle used, and the y value of the graph is the sine of that particular angle. In Figure 3-18, we indicate some specific values.

Now you can see that the sine of 0 is 0. The sine of 90 degrees, or pi/2 radians, is 1. The sine of 100 degrees, or pi radians, is 0 again. The sine of 270 degrees, or 3/2 pi, is -1. The sine of 360 degrees, or 2 pi, is back to 0 again. Let's play with this sine wave a bit in JavaScript. Enter the following code into your debugging console and test it:

```
for (var angle = 0; angle < Math.PI * 2; angle += 0.1) {
  console.log(Math.sin(angle));
}
```

From here on out, you should get used to radians alone. Leave degrees behind, except when you actually need them for rotation or some other purpose.

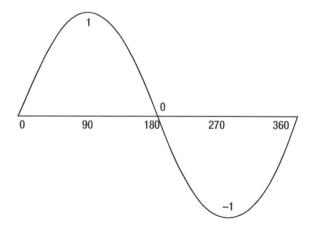

Figure 3-18. Values of sine

In this example, the variable angle starts out as 0 and increments by 0.1 until it's greater than `Math.PI *` 2. It then prints the sine of that angle. In the list of results, you see it starts at 0, goes up to almost 1, then down to almost -1, and back to around 0. You never reach exactly 1 or 0 because, using an increment of 0.1, you never get an exact multiple of pi or pi/2.

Smooth up and down motion

So what can you use `Math.sin(angle)` for? Have you ever needed to move something up and down or back and forth smoothly? Then this is your function. Consider this: Instead of just going from 0 to 1 and -1 and back to 0, and stopping there, keep adding on to the angle. You keep getting the wave over and over again. And instead of taking the 1 and -1, multiply those values by some higher value, say 100, and you have a stream of values that goes from 100 to -100, back and forth, continuously.

The next example uses a new object, defined by the `Ball` class. You can see the file, `ball.js`, here:

```
function Ball (radius, color) {
  if (radius === undefined) { radius = 40; }
  if (color === undefined) { color = "#ff0000"; }
  this.x = 0;
  this.y = 0;
  this.radius = radius;
  this.rotation = 0;
  this.scaleX = 1;
  this.scaleY = 1;
  this.color = utils.parseColor(color);
  this.lineWidth = 1;
}

Ball.prototype.draw = function (context) {
  context.save();
  context.translate(this.x, this.y);
  context.rotate(this.rotation);
  context.scale(this.scaleX, this.scaleY);
  context.lineWidth = this.lineWidth;
  context.fillStyle = this.color;
  context.beginPath();
  //x, y, radius, start_angle, end_angle, anti-clockwise
  context.arc(0, 0, this.radius, 0, (Math.PI * 2), true);
  context.closePath();
  context.fill();
  if (this.lineWidth > 0) {
    context.stroke();
  }
  context.restore();
};
```

This draws a circle when it is passed a canvas context as a parameter to its **draw** method. When you create the ball, you can initialize it with a radius and a color if you want. If not, it uses the default arguments of 40 for the radius and red for the color. This class is simple, but so useful that you will see it many times throughout the rest of the book. So keep it handy.

This example creates an instance of the Ball class, adds it to the canvas, and sets up an animation loop using the drawFrame function and window.requestAnimationFrame that causes the ball to bob up and down, as seen in the document 02-bobbing-1.html:

```
<!doctype html>
<html>
 <head>
  <meta charset="utf-8">
  <title>Bobbing 1</title>
  <link rel="stylesheet" href="style.css">
 </head>
 <body>
  <canvas id="canvas" width="400" height="400"></canvas>
  <script src="utils.js"></script>
  <script src="ball.js"></script>
  <script>
  window.onload = function () {
    var canvas = document.getElementById('canvas'),
        context = canvas.getContext('2d'),
        ball = new Ball(),
        angle = 0;

    ball.x = canvas.width / 2;
    ball.y = canvas.height / 2;

    (function drawFrame () {
      window.requestAnimationFrame(drawFrame, canvas);
      context.clearRect(0, 0, canvas.width, canvas.height);

      ball.y = canvas.height / 2 + Math.sin(angle) * 50;
      angle += 0.1;
      ball.draw(context);
    }());
  };
  </script>
 </body>
</html>
```

First, you need to create an angle property and initialize it to 0. In the drawFrame function, you take the sine of that angle and multiply it by 50. This gives you a range of values from 50 to -50. If you add that to the height of the canvas divided by 2, your values will be from 250 to 150 (based on a 400-pixel high canvas element). Make that the y position of the ball. Then add 0.1 to the angle for the next time around. You get a smooth up and down motion.

Play around with the various values. You'll notice that changing the 0.1 to another value changes the speed of the motion. This makes sense, because the faster or slower the angle is increasing, the faster or slower the return values from Math.sin will go from 1 to -1. Obviously, changing the 50 changes how far the ball moves, and changing the canvas.height / 2 to some other value changes the point that it oscillates around. From this, you can abstract the values into variables like the following (showing the additional or changed parts of the script):

```
// At the top of the script:
var angle = 0,
    centerY = 200,
    range = 50,
    speed = 0.05;

// And the animation function:
(function drawFrame () {
  window.requestAnimationFrame(drawFrame, canvas);
  context.clearRect(0, 0, canvas.width, canvas.height);

  ball.y = centerY / 2 + Math.sin(angle) * range;
  angle += speed;
  ball.draw(context);
}());
```

Keeping actual numbers out of your motion code is a good practice, and you should strive to do it as much as possible. In this case, it's all pretty much in the same place anyway. But what happens when your code spans multiple pages, and those values are used in several places throughout? Every time you want to change the speed, you need to locate every instance of that 0.1 value and modify it. You can perform a search and replace, but if something else in the file has 0.1 in it, then that gets replaced as well. By keeping the numbers out of the code, preferably at the top of the listing, you know exactly where all your variables are.

Linear vertical motion

In the 04-wave-1.html example, we add linear vertical motion, just to give you some inspiration for your own animation. Here's the code for that document:

```
<!doctype html>
<html>
 <head>
  <meta charset="utf-8">
  <title>Wave 1</title>
  <link rel="stylesheet" href="style.css">
 </head>
 <body>
  <canvas id="canvas" width="400" height="400"></canvas>
  <script src="utils.js"></script>
  <script src="ball.js"></script>
  <script>
  window.onload = function () {
    var canvas = document.getElementById('canvas'),
        context = canvas.getContext('2d'),
        ball = new Ball(),
        angle = 0,
        centerY = 200,
        range = 50,
        xspeed = 1,
        yspeed = 0.05;
```

```
      ball.x = 0;

      (function drawFrame () {
        window.requestAnimationFrame(drawFrame, canvas);
        context.clearRect(0, 0, canvas.width, canvas.height);

        ball.x += xspeed;
        ball.y = centerY / 2 + Math.sin(angle) * range;
        ball.draw(context);
      }());
    };
  </script>
 </body>
</html>
```

Pulsing motion

One important thing to keep in mind is that you can apply sine values to other properties besides the position. In the 05-pulse.html example, we used the values to affect the scale of the ball instead. This gives it a pulsating appearance. Here's the code:

```
<!doctype html>
<html>
 <head>
  <meta charset="utf-8">
  <title>Pulse</title>
  <link rel="stylesheet" href="style.css">
 </head>
 <body>
  <canvas id="canvas" width="400" height="400"></canvas>
  <script src="utils.js"></script>
  <script src="ball.js"></script>
  <script>
  window.onload = function () {
    var canvas = document.getElementById('canvas'),
        context = canvas.getContext('2d'),
        ball = new Ball(),
        angle = 0,
        centerScale = 1,
        range = 0.5,
        speed = 0.05;

    ball.x = canvas.width / 2;
    ball.y = canvas.height / 2;

    (function drawFrame () {
      window.requestAnimationFrame(drawFrame, canvas);
      context.clearRect(0, 0, canvas.width, canvas.height);

      ball.scaleX = ball.scaleY = centerScale + Math.sin(angle) * range;
      angle += speed;
      ball.draw(context);
    }());
```

```
  };
  </script>
 </body>
</html>
```

The principles are the same. You have a center point (which is 100% scale, in this case), a range, and a speed. But don't stop there—you can apply sine waves to different kinds of properties to create interesting visual effects.

Waves with two angles

Here's another idea to get you started: Rather than just a single angle, set up two angles, along with separate centers and speeds for both. Apply one sine wave to one property and the other sine wave to another property, such as position and scale.

Here's something to get you started. This example takes two angles, speeds, and centers, and applies one of the angles to the ball's x position and the other angle to the y position. The result is something like a bug flying around a room. Although it is mathematically predetermined, it looks pretty random. Here's the code (document 06-random.html):

```
<!doctype html>
<html>
 <head>
  <meta charset="utf-8">
  <title>Random</title>
  <link rel="stylesheet" href="style.css">
 </head>
 <body>
  <canvas id="canvas" width="400" height="400"></canvas>
  <script src="utils.js"></script>
  <script src="ball.js"></script>
  <script>
  window.onload = function () {
    var canvas = document.getElementById('canvas'),
        context = canvas.getContext('2d'),
        ball = new Ball(),
        angleX = 0,
        angleY = 0,
        range = 50,
        centerX = canvas.width / 2,
        centerY = canvas.height / 2,
        xspeed = 0.07,
        yspeed = 0.11;

    (function drawFrame () {
      window.requestAnimationFrame(drawFrame, canvas);
      context.clearRect(0, 0, canvas.width, canvas.height);

      ball.x = centerX + Math.sin(angleX) * range;
      ball.y = centerY + Math.sin(angleY) * range;
      angleX += xspeed;
      angleY += yspeed;
```

```
      ball.draw(context);
    }());
  };
  </script>
 </body>
</html>
```

Waves with the drawing API

In the next example, 07-wave-2.html, the ball has been removed and the canvas drawing API is used to draw the sine wave. The call to context.clearRect in the drawFrame function has also been removed so that the canvas element is not erased every frame, and the drawing remains. Here is the code for that file:

```
<!doctype html>
<html>
 <head>
  <meta charset="utf-8">
  <title>Wave 2</title>
  <link rel="stylesheet" href="style.css">
 </head>
 <body>
  <canvas id="canvas" width="400" height="400"></canvas>
  <script src="utils.js"></script>
  <script>
  window.onload = function () {
    var canvas = document.getElementById('canvas'),
        context = canvas.getContext('2d'),
        angle = 0,
        range = 50,
        centerY = canvas.height / 2,
        xspeed = 1,
        yspeed = 0.05,
        xpos = 0,
        ypos = centerY;

    context.lineWidth = 2;

    (function drawFrame () {
      window.requestAnimationFrame(drawFrame, canvas);

      context.beginPath();
      context.moveTo(xpos, ypos);
      //Calculate the new position.
      xpos += xspeed;
      angle += yspeed;
      ypos = centerY + Math.sin(angle) * range;
      context.lineTo(xpos, ypos);
      context.stroke();
    }());
  };
  </script>
 </body>
</html>
```

The canvas drawing API is discussed in detail in Chapter 4, but you should have fun seeing the various waves you can draw with it. The sine wave is upside down again because the y axis is reversed in the canvas element.

Circles and ellipses

Now that you've mastered sine waves, let's move on to their lesser-known cousins, *cosine waves*. These are formed in the same way as sine waves, but use the cosine function instead of sine. If you recall from the earlier discussion about how sine and cosine basically end up being the inverse of each other, you won't be surprised to learn that the two waves form the same shape, but in a different position. Figure 3-19 shows a cosine wave.

This shows that the cosine of 0 is 1. As it moves to 2 pi radians, or 360 degrees, it goes to 0, -1, 0, and then back to 1. It's essentially the same curve as produced by the sine wave, just shifted over a bit.

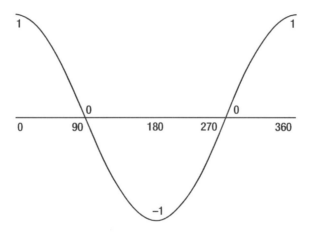

Figure 3-19. A cosine wave

Circular movement

You can use cosine in place of sine in just about any situation where all you need is an oscillating motion. But cosine has a much more common and useful function when used in coordination with sine: moving an object in a circle. Figure 3-20 shows an object at several points as it moves around a circle.

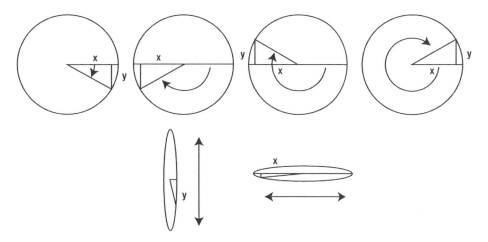

Figure 3-20. Positions of an object as it moves around a circle

If you take the circle in Figure 3-20 and turn it on its edge from the right, you see the object going up and down. Its center is the center of the circle, and its range is the radius of the circle. You calculate its position as you did in the first sine experiment, take the sine of the angle times the range. In this case, sine is the appropriate function to use. If you look at the triangle formed, you calculate the length of y—the leg opposite the angle.

Now, imagine that you are looking at the circle from its bottom edge instead. In this view, you see the object moving back and forth, left to right. This time, you calculate the length of x—the leg adjacent to the angle—so you should use cosine.

These calculations operate off the same angle, unlike the `06-random.html` example you saw previously, which used two different angles to compute the x and y positions. You use sine to calculate y and cosine to calculate x. Here's what this example looks like:

```
<!doctype html>
<html>
 <head>
  <meta charset="utf-8">
  <title>Circle</title>
  <link rel="stylesheet" href="style.css">
 </head>
 <body>
  <canvas id="canvas" width="400" height="400"></canvas>
  <script src="utils.js"></script>
  <script src="ball.js"></script>
  <script>
  window.onload = function () {
    var canvas = document.getElementById('canvas'),
        context = canvas.getContext('2d'),
        ball = new Ball(),
        angle = 0,
        centerX = canvas.width / 2,
```

```
        centerY = canvas.height / 2,
        radius = 50,
        speed = 0.05;

   (function drawFrame () {
     window.requestAnimationFrame(drawFrame, canvas);
     context.clearRect(0, 0, canvas.width, canvas.height);

     ball.x = centerX + Math.sin(angle) * radius;
     ball.y = centerY + Math.cos(angle) * radius;
     angle += speed;
     ball.draw(context);
   }());
 };
 </script>
 </body>
</html>
```

You can create this document yourself or use the example file 08-circle.html, which has all the work done for you. Verify that you have a perfect circle.

Notice that the range in both cases is the hypotenuse of the triangle, and it's equal to the radius of the circle. Thus, we changed range to radius, to reflect that.

The code uses cosine to get the x position and sine to get the y position. You should get used to those relationships. When coding animations, almost any time you are talking about x, you should immediately think cosine, and you should almost always connect y with sine. In fact, spend as much time as you need to fully understand that last bit of code. It is going to be one of the most useful tools in your animation toolbox.

Elliptical movement

While circles are lovely, sometimes a perfect circle isn't exactly what you need. What you might be looking for is more of an oval or ellipse. The problem is with the radius, it makes the ranges of the x motion and y motion the same, which is why you get a circle.

To make a more oval shape, use different values for the radius when you calculate the x and y positions. Let's call them radiusX and radiusY. Here's how they fit in to our document 09-oval.html:

```
<!doctype html>
<html>
 <head>
  <meta charset="utf-8">
  <title>Oval</title>
  <link rel="stylesheet" href="style.css">
 </head>
 <body>
  <canvas id="canvas" width="400" height="400"></canvas>
  <script src="utils.js"></script>
  <script src="ball.js"></script>
  <script>
  window.onload = function () {
```

```
    var canvas = document.getElementById('canvas'),
        context = canvas.getContext('2d'),
        ball = new Ball(),
        angle = 0,
        centerX = canvas.width / 2,
        centerY = canvas.height / 2,
        radiusX = 150,
        radiusY = 100,
        speed = 0.05;

    (function drawFrame () {
      window.requestAnimationFrame(drawFrame, canvas);
      context.clearRect(0, 0, canvas.width, canvas.height);

      ball.x = centerX + Math.sin(angle) * radiusX;
      ball.y = centerY + Math.cos(angle) * radiusY;
      angle += speed;
      ball.draw(context);
    }());
  };
  </script>
 </body>
</html>
```

Here, `radiusX` is 150, which means that the ball is going to go back and forth 150 pixels from `centerX` as it circles around. `radiusY` is 100, which means it goes up and down only 100 pixels each way. So, now you have an uneven circle, which is not a circle anymore, but an ellipse.

Pythagorean Theorem

Now we've come to the *Pythagorean Theorem*, another formula that you will use a lot. Pythagoras was a Greek mathematician, philosopher, and mystic who is credited with a convenient way of measuring a triangle. To put simply, the theorem says: A squared + B squared = C squared. We will explore this theorem in more depth.

A more descriptive statement of the theorem is: The sum of the squares of the two legs of a right-angle triangle is equal to the square of the hypotenuse. Let's say you have the triangle shown in Figure 3-21. The two legs, A and B, have measurements of 3 and 4. The hypotenuse, C, measures 5. The Pythagorean Theorem tells us that $A^2 + B^2 = C^2$. Let's test it. Plug in the numbers, and you have $3^2 + 4^2 = 5^2$, which is 9 + 16 = 25. That works out pretty well.

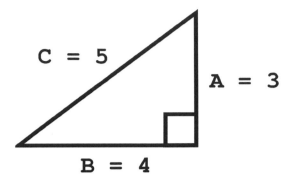

Figure 3-21. A right-angle triangle

If you happen to know all three measurements, the Pythagorean Theorem is nothing more than an interesting relationship. But if you only know two of the measurements, it becomes a powerful tool to quickly find the third. When programming, the most common situation is where you know the lengths of the two legs and you want to know the hypotenuse. Specifically, you want to find the distance between two points.

Distance between two points

Say you have two objects on the canvas element and you want to find out how far apart they are. This is the most common use of the Pythagorean Theorem when programming animation.

What do you have to work with? You have the x and y positions of each object. Let's call the position of one x1, y1, and the other x2, y2. This is a situation like the one illustrated in Figure 3-22.

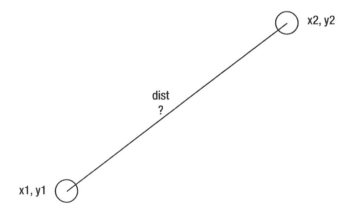

Figure 3-22. What is the distance between the two objects?

If you have been following this chapter closely, you see a right-angle triangle forming in the diagram in Figure 3-22, with the distance line as the hypotenuse. In Figure 3-23, we finish and add some actual numbers.

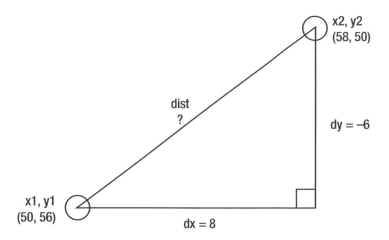

Figure 3-23. Turn it into a right-angle triangle.

Here, **dx** is the distance between the two objects on the x axis, and **dy** is the distance on the y axis. You can now find **dx** by subtracting x1 from x2: 58 - 50 = 8. Similarly, you subtract y1 from y2 to get **dy**, which is −6. Now, using the Pythagorean Theorem, if you square both of these and add them together, you get the square of the distance. In other words $-6^2 + 8^2 = dist^2$. Breaking that down, you get 36 + 64, or 100 = $dist^2$. With some basic algebra, you can reduce that to `.100` = `dist`. And from that, you can easily figure out that the distance between the two objects is 10.

Let's abstract that a bit so you have a formula that you can use in any situation. Given two points, x1, y1 and x2, y2, you figure the x distance and y distance, square them, sum them, and take the square root. Here it is in JavaScript:

```
var dx = x2 - x1,
    dy = y2 - y1,
    dist = Math.sqrt(dx * dx + dy * dy);
```

Pay particular attention to these lines because they make up the next big tool in your toolbox. The first two lines get the distances on each axis. If you are interested in the distance and won't use **dx** and **dy** to calculate any angles, it doesn't matter whether you subtract x1 from x2 or vice versa. The final result for **dist** is always positive. The last line performs three steps in one shot: It squares each of the values, adds them, and finds the square root. For clarity, you can break down the steps into separate statements. After you are familiar with that single line, it will be clear to you. You see it and think "Pythagorean Theorem."

Let's try it in a real world example. The next example, `10-distance.html`, creates a couple of rectangles, randomly positions them, and then calculates and prints the distance between them.

```
<!doctype html>
<html>
 <head>
  <meta charset="utf-8">
  <title>Distance</title>
  <link rel="stylesheet" href="style.css">
 </head>
```

```
<body>
  <canvas id="canvas" width="400" height="400"></canvas>
  <textarea id="log"></textarea>
  <script src="utils.js"></script>
  <script>
  window.onload = function () {
    var canvas = document.getElementById('canvas'),
        context = canvas.getContext('2d'),
        log = document.getElementById('log');

    //Create a black square, assign random position.
    var rect1 = {
      x: Math.random() * canvas.width,
      y: Math.random() * canvas.height
    };
    context.fillStyle = "#000000";
    context.fillRect(rect1.x - 2, rect1.y - 2, 4, 4);

    //Create a red square, assign random position.
    var rect2 = {
      x: Math.random() * canvas.width,
      y: Math.random() * canvas.height
    };
    context.fillStyle = "#ff0000";
    context.fillRect(rect2.x - 2, rect2.y - 2, 4, 4);

    //Calculate the distance between the two squares.
    var dx = rect1.x - rect2.x,
        dy = rect1.y - rect2.y,
        dist = Math.sqrt(dx * dx + dy * dy);

    //log output of distance value to screen
    log.value = "distance: " + dist;
  };
  </script>
 </body>
</html>
```

Run this file in your web browser and you will see the distance between the two rectangles printed out to the `textarea` element in our document. Each time you run it, the two rectangles will be in different positions. It shouldn't matter if one is to the right, left, top, or bottom of the other, you'll always get a positive value for the distance.

Well that's interesting, but not dynamic. Just to show you that you can do this in real time, try the next example, `11-mouse-distance.html`:

```
<!doctype html>
<html>
 <head>
  <meta charset="utf-8">
  <title>Mouse Distance</title>
  <link rel="stylesheet" href="style.css">
 </head>
```

```
<body>
  <canvas id="canvas" width="400" height="400"></canvas>
  <textarea id="log"></textarea>
  <script src="utils.js"></script>
  <script>
  window.onload = function () {
    var canvas = document.getElementById('canvas'),
        context = canvas.getContext('2d'),
        mouse = utils.captureMouse(canvas),
        log = document.getElementById('log'),
        rect = {x: canvas.width / 2, y: canvas.height / 2};

    (function drawFrame () {
      window.requestAnimationFrame(drawFrame, canvas);
      context.clearRect(0, 0, canvas.width, canvas.height);

      var dx = rect.x - mouse.x,
          dy = rect.y - mouse.y,
          dist = Math.sqrt(dx * dx + dy * dy);

      //draw square
      context.fillStyle = "#000000";
      context.fillRect(rect.x - 2, rect.y - 2, 4, 4);
      //draw line
      context.beginPath();
      context.moveTo(rect.x, rect.y);
      context.lineTo(mouse.x, mouse.y);
      context.closePath();
      context.stroke();

      //log output of distance value to screen
      log.value = "distance: " + dist;
    }());
  };
  </script>
</body>
</html>
```

Here, **dx** and **dy** are calculated by subtracting the current mouse position from rect's position. The dist value is displayed in the textarea element, and a line is drawn from the rectangle to the mouse location (you find more on the canvas drawing API in Chapter 4).

Test the file and move your mouse around. A line connects it to the rectangle, and you get a constant readout of the length of that line.

In later chapters when discussing collision detection, we mention some weaknesses with the generic testing functions, and see how you can use the Pythagorean Theorem formula to create a distance-based method of collision detection. This theorem is also useful in calculating forces such as gravity or springs, where the force between two objects is proportional to the distance between them.

Important formulas in this chapter

Look at this. You have a brand-new shiny programming toolbox, and already you have more than a half-dozen tools to put in it. The full set of tools also appears in Appendix A, but let's look at what you added so far. I kept these formulas as simple and abstract as possible, so they don't include variable declarations. It's up to you to work the formulas into your own scripts using the proper syntax required for the situation.

Calculate basic trigonometric functions

```
sine of angle = opposite / hypotenuse
cosine of angle = adjacent / hypotenuse
tangent of angle = opposite / adjacent
```

Convert radians to degrees and degrees to radians

```
radians = degrees * Math.PI / 180
degrees = radians * 180 / Math.PI
```

Rotate to the mouse (or any point)

```
//substitute mouse.x, mouse.y with the x, y point to rotate to
dx = mouse.x - object.x;
dy = mouse.y - object.y;
object.rotation = Math.atan2(dy, dx) * 180 / Math.PI;
```

Create waves

```
// assign value to x, y or other property of an object,
// use as drawing coordinates, etc.
(function drawFrame () {
  window.requestAnimationFrame(drawFrame, canvas);

  value = center + Math.sin(angle) * range;
  angle += speed;
}());
```

Create circles

```
//assign position to x and y of object or drawing coordinate
(function drawFrame () {
  window.requestAnimationFrame(drawFrame, canvas);

  xposition = centerX + Math.cos(angle) * radius;
  yposition = centerY + Math.sin(angle) * radius;
  angle += speed;
}());
```

Create ovals

```
//assign position to x and y of object or drawing coordinate
(function drawFrame () {
  window.requestAnimationFrame(drawFrame, canvas);

  xposition = centerX + Math.cos(angle) * radiusX;
```

```
    yposition = centerY + Math.sin(angle) * radiusY;
    angle += speed;
}());
```

Get the distance between two points

```
//points are x1, y1 and x2, y2
//can be object positions, mouse coordinates, etc.
dx = x2 - x1;
dy = y2 - y1;
dist = Math.sqrt(dx * dx + dy * dy);
```

Of course, this book is not just a list of formulas. So look these over and make sure you fully understand how each one works. If you have any questions, go back to the point in the chapter where it was introduced, experiment with it, and research it more if you need to, until you can really think with the concept.

Summary

This chapter covered nearly all the trigonometry you need for animating with the canvas element using JavaScript. There is one principle, called The Law of Cosines, that we left out for now, because it is a lot more complex and deals with triangles that are not right-angle triangles (they have no angle measuring 90 degrees). If you are now addicted to trigonometry and just can't get enough, you can jump ahead to Chapter 14, which covers inverse kinematics, where trigonometry really comes in handy.

But, for now, you know about sine, cosine, and tangent, and their opposites: arcsine, arccosine, and arctangent, as well as the JavaScript functions to calculate each one.

Best of all, you got some hands-on experience using most of them with the canvas element, with some of the most common real-life uses of them. As you move through the book, you see many more ways in which these techniques become useful. But you now have a solid footing with the concepts, and when you come across those examples, you should have no problem understanding them or how they work.

The next chapter covers some of the more common rendering techniques for putting graphics on the screen, including the all-important canvas drawing API. As you go through that chapter, see whether you can find ways to use the rendering methods to visualize some of the trigonometry functions you learned here. You should have no trouble creating so

Chapter 4

Trigonometry for Animation

What we'll cover in this chapter:

- Colors on the canvas
- The drawing API
- Loading images
- Pixel manipulation

So far, the graphics drawn in the book example programs have used a few simple commands, and the "canvas drawing API" has been alluded to a number of times. But for the most part, the code has been provided without much explanation.

In this chapter, we look at creating visual content using the canvas element. Specifically, you'll see how to work with color using JavaScript, and take a brief tour of the canvas drawing API.

Colors on the canvas

Colors applied to the canvas element are specified using CSS-style strings, which can be formatted in a few ways:

- **"#RRGGBB"**—Hexadecimal format, with red-green-blue components in the range 0-9, a-f.
- **"#RGB"**—Hexadecimal format using short notation, is converted into the six-digit form by copying the component values, not by adding 0. E.g., **"#fb0"** becomes **"#ffbb00"** .

- **"rgb(R, G, B)"** —Functional notation format, with red-green-blue components as integers in the range 0-255.

- **"rgba(R, G, B, A)"** —Functional notation format with alpha, is the same as the previous string, but the alpha value is a decimal number in a range of 0-1. If a color requires transparency, this is the format you must use.

Although the final color value is serialized as a string, you may want to manipulate individual color components as numbers. So you must convert the JavaScript types using a few parsing and concatenation techniques. After this is demonstrated, a pair of utility functions are introduced later in the chapter that will make this process easier, and are used throughout the book examples.

A color value can be any integer from 0 to 16,777,215 for what is called 24-bit color. That number is significant because there are 256 × 256 × 256 possible color values. The canvas element uses RGB color, which means that every color is described by its red, green, and blue components. Each of these component values can be an integer from 0 to 255. So, there are 256 possible shades each of red, green, and blue, resulting in the nearly 16.8 million colors.

This system is called 24-bit color because it takes eight bits—ones or zeros—to represent the number 256. Eight bits times three (red, green, and blue) means it takes 24 bits to represent the 16.8 million possible colors. Additionally, there is a 32-bit color system, which uses an extra value for transparency.

Now, because it's difficult to visualize what color 16,733,683 looks like, developers often use another system of representing such numbers: hexadecimal. If you've used color values in HTML, this should be familiar to you, but let's cover the basics anyway.

Using hexadecimal color values

Hexadecimal, or hex, is a base 16 system. In other words, each digit can be from 0 to 15, rather than 0 to 9 as in the usual base 10 (decimal) system. Since there are not any single digits to represent the numbers 10 to 15, we borrow the first six letters of the alphabet, A to F. So, each digit in a hex number can be from 0 to F. (In JavaScript, hex values are not case-sensitive, so you can use A through F or a through f.) To signify that we are using a hex number with the HTML canvas element, we prefix the string with the character `'#'`. In JavaScript, as with many other languages, we add a prefix 0x to the number. For example, the number 0xA is equal to decimal number 10, 0xF is equal to 15, and 0x10 is equal to 16. Respectively, the HTML hexadecimal string representations of these values would look like: `'#A'`, `'#F'`, and `'#10'`.

In decimal, each digit is worth ten times the digit to its right; so, the number 243 means two times 100, four times 10, and three times 1. In hex, each digit is worth 16 times its right-hand neighbor. For example, 0x2B3 means two times 256, B (or eleven) times 16, and three times 1.

For 24-bit colors, this goes all the way up to 0xFFFFFF, and, if you do the math, is equal to 16,777,215. Furthermore, those six hex digits can be separated into three component pairs. The first pair represents the red component, the second pair represents the green, and the last two digits represent blue. This is often referenced as 0xRRGGBB. (You would never put R, G, or B into an actual hex number; this is merely a symbolic way of telling you what color channel each digit controls.)

Remember that each component color can have a value anywhere from 0 to 255, or in hex, 0x00 to 0xFF. Thus, the color red can be represented as 0xFF0000, which denotes full red, zero green, and zero blue. Likewise, 0x0000FF is completely blue.

If you take the earlier mentioned example number, 16,733,683, and convert it to hex (you will see an easy way to do that), you get 0xFF55F3. You can easily separate the components into red = FF, green = 55, and blue = F3. Examining these values, you see that the red and blue are rather high, and green is much lower. So you can guess that this color is purplish, which is something you can't easily determine from the decimal value.

For any JavaScript operation that requires a number, it doesn't matter which format you use, decimal or hex. The numbers 16733683 and 0xFF55F3 have the same value; it's just that one is more readable to us humans. However, when working with the canvas element, you must remember to convert whichever numeric format into a proper CSS-style string.

You might wonder how to convert between these formats. Well, converting from hex to decimal is easy—just print the value. The **console.log** function in your debugging console prints to decimal for you:

```
console.log(0xFF55F3);
```

This prints **16733683**. To see the hexadecimal representation of a decimal number, use the **Number.toString** method, specifying 16 as the radix:

```
var hex = (16733683).toString(16);
console.log(hex);
```

As the method name indicates, this converts the number to a string, and prints out the hexadecimal **'ff55f3'**. To use that value as a CSS-style formatted string, prepend the **'#'** character:

```
var hexColor = '#' + (16733683).toString(16);
```

This sets **hexColor** to a string value of **'#ff55f3'**. To convert this *back* into a decimal number, first chop off the **'#'** character at the beginning of the string using the **String.slice** method, then pass the remaining string to the built-in function **window.parseInt**, with a radix of 16:

```
var color = window.parseInt(hexColor.slice(1), 16);
console.log(color);
```

This prints out the number **16733683**, and you can see we're right back where we started.

Combining colors

Let's say you want to combine three red, green, and blue numbers to form a valid overall color value. If you have three variables, **red**, **green**, and **blue**, and each of them holds an integer value from 0 to 255, here's the formula to do just that:

```
color = red << 16 | green << 8 | blue;
```

For example, to create the purple color value from separate components, set the red value to max, or 0xFF (decimal 255), the green component to 0x55 (decimal 85), and the blue value to 0xF3 (decimal 243):

```
var color = 0xFF << 16 | 0x55 << 8 | 0xF3;
```

This sets **color** to a value of **16733683**, which is equal to the hex value **0xFF55F3**. This formula uses two bitwise operators you might not have used before. *Bitwise operators* manipulate numbers on a binary level—on the ones and zeros. We look at how they work in the next section.

Bitwise combination

If you were to list the bits of a 24-bit color value, you would have a string of 24 ones and zeros. Breaking up the hex 0xRRGGBB into binary, there are eight bits for red, eight for green, and eight for blue:

RRRRRRRRGGGGGGGGBBBBBBBB

In the previous color combination formula, the first bitwise operator is <<, which is the bitwise left-shift operator. This shifts the binary representation of the value to the left by the specified amount of places. A red value of 0xFF, or decimal 255, can be represented in binary as follows:

11111111

Shifting it 16 places to the left gives you the following:

111111110000000000000000

As a 24-bit color number, this is red. In hex, this is 0xFF0000—again, red. Now, a green value of 0x55 (decimal 85) looks like the following in binary:

01010101

Shift this eight places, and you get this:

000000000101010100000000

The original eight bits now fall completely in the green range.

Finally, a blue value of 0xF3 (decimal 243) is this in binary:

11110011

Because these bits already fall into the blue range, you don't need to change it.

Now you have three values for red, green, and blue:

111111110000000000000000
000000000101010100000000
000000000000000011110011

You can add the values together to get a single 24-bit number, but there's a simpler way: Use the bitwise OR operator, the | symbol. This compares the digits of two numbers on a binary level and if either digit is equal to one, the result will be one. If both digits are zero, the result is zero. You can use OR for the red, green, and blue values together to say, "If this OR this OR this is one, the result is one." This joins the three components into a single color value—and is readable once you understand how the operators work. Combine the example values and you get this result:

111111110101010111110011

If you convert that to hex, you get 0xFF55F3. Of course, in JavaScript, you never see the bits or deal with the ones or zeros at all. You just write this:

```
var color = 0xFF << 16 | 0x55 << 8 | 0xF3;
```

Or, if you are working with decimal values, you can use this form:

```
var color = 255 << 16 | 85 << 8 | 243;
```

Again, it doesn't matter whether you use hex or decimal numbers; it's the same value.

Extracting component colors

You might have a color from which you want to extract the individual component values. Here's the formula to extract the red, green, and blue values from a composite color value:

```
red = color >> 16 & 0xFF;
green = color >> 8 & 0xFF;
blue = color & 0xFF;
```

If the value of **color** is 0xFF55F3, then **red** will be set to 255, **green**: 85, and **blue**: 243. Again, this formula uses two bitwise operators, which we walk through in the next section.

Bitwise extraction

In the previous formula, you probably guessed that >> is the bitwise right-shift operator, which shifts the bits so many places to the right. You can't have fractional bits, so any bits that are shifted too far right are discarded. Looking at the color value in binary representation, and beginning with red:

111111110101010111110011

When you shift the color value 16 places to the right, it becomes this:

11111111

This is simply 0xFF, or 255. For green, shift the color value eight places, and you get this:

1111111101010101

Here, you knocked the blue values out, but you still have the red ones hanging around. This is where you use another bitwise operator, **&**, which is called AND. Like OR, this compares two values, but says, "If this digit AND this digit are both one, then the result is one. If either one is zero, the result is zero." You compare the value to 0xFF, so you compare these two numbers:

1111111101010101
0000000011111111

Because all the red digits are compared with zero, they all result in zero. Only the digits that are both one fall through, so you get this:

0000000001010101

This is the value 0x55. With blue, you don't need to shift anything. Just AND it with 0xFF, which preserves the blue and knocks out the red and green. This returns the value 0xF3.

Transparency

If you want to apply a color with transparency to the canvas element, you must use a string formatted in the CSS-style functional notation: `"rgba(R, G, B, A)"`. In this format, the red-green-blue components are integer values in the range of 0-255, whereas the alpha component is a decimal number in the range of 0-1. An alpha value of 0 is completely transparent, whereas a value of 1 indicates a color that is fully visible. For example, a color containing an alpha value of 0.5 has 50% opacity.

If you work with separate color components, you must concatenate them into a properly formatted string to use the color with the canvas element. For example:

```
var r = 0xFF,
    g = 0x55,
    b = 0xF3,
    a = 0.2,
    color = "rgba(" + r + "," + g + "," + b + "," + a + ")";

console.log(color);
```

This assembles and prints the string: `"rgba(255,85,243,0.2)"`, which represents a light-purple color, at 20% visibility, properly formatted to use with the canvas element.

Because these types of conversions are rather bothersome, we create a couple of utility functions to simplify this process in the next section.

Color utility functions

Now that we explained the process of combining and extracting color components, we create a pair of utility functions to do the work for us. This gives us a succinct way to convert color values from numbers to strings, and back again, while keeping the sample code uncluttered. Often when animating the canvas element, you need to manipulate the numeric color values using JavaScript, then format them as a CSS-style string.

The first utility function, `utils.colorToRGB`, takes a color value as an argument—as a number or hexadecimal string—and extracts its individual red, blue, and green components. Then, it concatenates them into a CSS-style string using the functional notation, which it returns. Additionally, the function accepts a second, optional, argument to indicate an alpha value, which is a decimal number between 0 and 1.

For example, passing the hexadecimal number `0xFFFF00` or string `"#FFFF00"` to `utils.colorToRGB` returns a string value: `"rgb(255,255,0)"`. If we call it with an alpha value like `utils.colorToRGB(0xFFFF00, 0.5)`, it returns `"rgba(255,255,0,0.5)"`, which is the format that the canvas element is looking for.

Add the function to our global **utils** object and include it in the **utils.js** file, which we import in our documents. Remember, you can download this script, like all the other code in this book, from **www.apress.com**. Here's what the function definition looks like:

```
utils.colorToRGB = function (color, alpha) {
  //if string format, convert to number
  if (typeof color === 'string' && color[0] === '#') {
    color = window.parseInt(color.slice(1), 16);
  }
  alpha = (alpha === undefined) ? 1 : alpha;

  //extract component values
  var r = color >> 16 & 0xff,
      g = color >> 8 & 0xff,
      b = color & 0xff,
      a = (alpha < 0) ? 0 : ((alpha > 1) ? 1 : alpha); //check range

  //use 'rgba' if needed
  if (a === 1) {
    return "rgb("+ r +","+ g +","+ b +")";
  } else {
    return "rgba("+ r +","+ g +","+ b +","+ a +")";
  }
};
```

The second utility function is simple, but saves us some headache when converting colors back and forth between numbers and strings. The function, **utils.parseColor**, converts a color number value to a hexadecimal formatted string, or can convert a hexadecimal formatted string to a number.

Calling the function with a hexadecimal number like **utils.parseColor(0xFFFF00)**, returns the string value: **"#ffff00"**. Passing a CSS-style hexadecimal string returns the same string unmodified. The function also accepts a second, optional, parameter **toNumber**, which if set to **true**, returns a numeric color value. For example, calling **utils.parseColor("#FFFF00", true)** or **utils.parseColor(0xFFFF00, true)**, both return the number **16776960**.

This function enables us to use numbers when we need to, and easily convert back to the properly formatted strings that the canvas element requires. Again, we add this function to the **utils** global object in the file **utils.js**:

```
utils.parseColor = function (color, toNumber) {
  if (toNumber === true) {
    if (typeof color === 'number') {
      return (color | 0); //chop off decimal
    }
    if (typeof color === 'string' && color[0] === '#') {
      color = color.slice(1);
    }
    return window.parseInt(color, 16);
  } else {
    if (typeof color === 'number') {
      //make sure our hexadecimal number is padded out
      color = '#' + ('00000' + (color | 0).toString(16)).substr(-6);
```

```
    }
    return color;
  }
};
```

These utility functions are provided only for convenience, because you already know how they work from the previous sections. Perhaps you'll create a different function, or write the conversion explicitly in your own code, but they're here if you need them.

Now that you know how colors work in JavaScript and the canvas element, let's start using them.

The Drawing API

An API, or application programming interface, generally refers to the methods and properties that you can use in your program to access a collection of related functionality that is provided for you. In particular, the canvas drawing API is the properties and methods that enable you to draw lines, curves, fills, and so on, using JavaScript. This API has only a few methods, but they provide the foundation for all the animation we create in this book. Here are some of the commands we look at:

- strokeStyle
- fillStyle
- lineWidth
- save()
- restore()
- beginPath()
- closePath()
- stroke()
- lineTo(x, y)
- moveTo(x, y)
- quadraticCurveTo(cpx, cpy, x, y)
- bezierCurveTo(cp1x, cp1y, cp2x, cp2y, x, y)
- arcTo(x1, y1, x2, y2, radius)
- arc(x, y, radius, startAngle, endAngle [, anticlockwise])
- createLinearGradient(x0, y0, x1, y1)
- createRadialGradient(x0, y0, r0, x1, y1, r1)
- clearRect(x, y, width, height)
- fillRect(x, y, width, height)

Because this chapter serves as an overview for you to get the foundation to work through the rest of the book, we won't go into the details for each method. For a more exhaustive treatment of the canvas drawing API, see the specification at `http://developers.whatwg.org/the-canvas-element.html`, or read one of the more detailed guides listed at the beginning of this book.

The canvas context

Every canvas element contains a *drawing context*, an object that exposes the drawing API. To access the context, use the following code:

```
var canvas = document.getElementById('canvas'),
    context = canvas.getContext('2d');
```

The first line uses the DOM interface to find our canvas element with an id of `'canvas'`. Call this object's method `getContext` with the string argument `'2d'`, which specifies the type of drawing API to use.

It's worth mentioning, this is the only standardized drawing context at the time of this writing. Although some vendors have experimented with a 3D API, this has not been implemented across browsers and is not part of the HTML5 specification.

Now that we have our canvas element and access to its context, we can start drawing with it!

Removing the drawing with clearRect

In most animations, we must clear the canvas every frame before drawing something else, which is how we simulate motion. By drawing something, erasing it, and drawing it someplace else, we can make a series of images look like a single object that has moved, rather than two frames displayed sequentially.

The method `context.clearRect(x, y, width, height)` clears the specified rectangle by erasing every pixel inside it, setting them to transparent black. As such, any previously drawn graphics, such as lines or fills, will no longer be visible. Because we use this method to clear entire animation frames, you will see it called in the examples like this:

```
context.clearRect(0, 0, canvas.width, canvas.height);
```

This creates a rectangle the size of the entire canvas element and positions it at the canvas origin, clearing everything that was previously drawn.

This is a complete canvas clear, but there are a few optimizations to consider. If you know that an animation will only affect a portion of the frame, you can specify a smaller rectangle in `clearRect` to save some processing. It's also possible to stack multiple canvas elements on top of each other. Because they're transparent, you see the composite image. This can be useful if you have a background image that you do not want to draw every frame. You can just place it as a background canvas or image element and animate over top of it.

Setting the line appearance

The context has a number of properties that change the appearance of subsequently drawn lines. Changing these properties does not affect previously drawn lines. Other than clearing them or drawing on them, there is no way to affect lines and fills that have already been drawn.

The most common line style properties you use are the color and width of the line:

- `strokeStyle`: This property is used for setting the line color. The value can be a color value (CSS-style string), a gradient object, or a pattern object. By default, the line color is black: `"#000000"`.

- `lineWidth`: This sets the line thickness from the path. So if using the default value of 1, the line width would extend a half-pixel to both sides; you cannot draw the line inside or outside of this path. `lineWidth` must be a positive number.

There are some additional line style properties, but we just use their default values in this book:

- `lineCap`: How the end point of each line is drawn, if it's flat, round, or sticks out. Possible values are `butt`, `round`, and `square`, with `butt` as the default.

- `lineJoin`: Determines how connecting segments are joined together, or how the "elbow" of the connection is drawn. Possible values are `round`, `bevel`, or `miter`, with `miter` as the default.

- `miterLimit`: When used with `lineJoin` set to `miter`, this property determines how far the outside connection point will be placed from the inside connection point. It must be a finite number greater than 0, and the default value is 10.

To jump between different styles, use the methods `context.save()` and `context.restore()`. `context.save()` pushes the current state of the canvas onto a stack. This includes styles, such as `strokeStyle` and `fillStyle`, and also transformations that have been applied to the canvas. Additional style changes will be applied to subsequent draw commands. To return to the previous canvas state, call `context.restore()` to pop the current state off the stack and use the next one.

Drawing paths with lineTo and moveTo

There are a couple of different ways to implement line drawing in a graphics language. One is to have a `line` command that takes a starting point and an ending point, and draws a line between them. The other way is to have a `lineTo` command that takes a single point: the ending point of the line. This is how the canvas drawing API works, and it stores this information in a path.

The canvas context always has a current path, and there is only one current path. A path has 0 or more sub-paths, each consisting of a list of points connected by straight or curved lines. A closed path is one where its last point is connected to its first point by a straight line. To indicate that you're starting a new drawing path, call `context.beginPath()`. Because a path is just a list of positions for a line, to render it to the canvas you call `context.stroke()`.

You move the path's position around on the canvas and draw lines *to* it. Because we need to start somewhere to draw *from*, we first move to point 0, 0 in this example:

```
context.beginPath();
context.moveTo(0, 0);
context.lineTo(100, 100);
context.stroke();
```

On the canvas, there's now a line drawn from the top-left corner (0, 0), to 100, 100. After you draw a line, the ending point for that line is the starting point for the next one. Or, you can use the method **context.moveTo** to specify a new starting point for the next line.

Think of the drawing API as a robot holding a pen on a piece of paper. First, you move the pen to the start position at 0, 0. When you tell the robot to draw a line to a point, it moves the pen across the paper to that new position. For each new line, it moves from wherever it left off, to the next new point. **context.moveTo** is like saying, "Okay, now lift up the pen and move it to this next point." Although it does not result in any new graphic content, it will affect how the next command is carried out. You generally call **context.moveTo** as your first graphics command to place the drawing API "pen" where you want to begin.

You now have enough drawing commands to do something interesting. Let's create a simple drawing program that will rely on the canvas drawing API for its content. Here's the example:

```
<!doctype html>
<html>
 <head>
  <meta charset="utf-8">
  <title>Drawing App</title>
  <link rel="stylesheet" href="style.css">
 </head>
 <body>
  <canvas id="canvas" width="400" height="400"></canvas>
  <script src="utils.js"></script>
  <script>
  window.onload = function () {
    var canvas = document.getElementById('canvas'),
        context = canvas.getContext('2d'),
        mouse = utils.captureMouse(canvas);

    function onMouseMove () {
      context.lineTo(mouse.x, mouse.y);
      context.stroke();
    }
    canvas.addEventListener('mousedown', function () {
      context.beginPath();
      context.moveTo(mouse.x, mouse.y);
      canvas.addEventListener('mousemove', onMouseMove, false);
    }, false);

    canvas.addEventListener('mouseup', function () {
      canvas.removeEventListener('mousemove', onMouseMove, false);
    }, false);
  };
  </script>
 </body>
</html>
```

You can find this file among the book's downloadable files (available from **www.apress.com**) as **01-drawing-app.html**. In addition to the drawing functions, this program makes good use of event handlers (discussed in Chapter 2). Let's go through it piece by piece.

The example is based on the skeleton document found in Chapter 2, which you should be used to by now. At the top of the script, it uses the utility function **utils.captureMouse** to keep track of the mouse position. We imported this from the file **utils.js**. Event listeners for the **mousedown** and **mouseup** events are also added.

The **mousedown** event handler gets called whenever the user presses a mouse button on the canvas element; this is when the user wants to start drawing a line at the current mouse cursor position. The handler starts a new path and puts the virtual pen down at the mouse location by calling **context.moveTo** and passing in the mouse coordinates. It then adds a listener for the **mousemove** event.

At this point, every time the user moves the mouse, the **onMouseMove** function is called. It's the core of the program, but is simple. It draws a line to the current mouse location and strokes the path outline.

Finally, there's the **mouseup** event handler, which removes the **mousemove** handler so that nothing else is drawn to the canvas.

This is a fun little sketching program. If you set up some simple controls, you can build it into a full-featured drawing application. Create variables for **color** and **width**, use some HTML form elements to change them, and set the **strokeStyle** and **lineWidth** properties with the new values. But this left as an exercise for you to do on your own, if you are interested.

Drawing curves with quadraticCurveTo

The canvas drawing API provides a number of methods for drawing curves on a path. In the next couple of examples, we look at the method **context.quadraticCurveTo**, which connects two points with a curve using a control point. It starts off the same as **context.lineTo**, in that it begins its drawing at the point where the last drawing ended, or at the point where the last **context.moveTo** command moved the pen to. It also uses line styles in the same way as **context.lineTo**. The only difference is the shape of the line drawn.

context.quadraticCurveTo(cpx, cpy, x, y) takes two points as arguments: The first is a control point that affects the shape of the curve, and the second is the ending point of the curve. The shape is determined by a standard algorithm known as a *quadratic Bézier curve*. This function calculates a curve from one point to another, curving toward—but never touching—the control point. It's more like the curve is attracted to it.

Let's see it in action in the following document, **02-drawing-curves.html**:

```
<!doctype html>
<html>
 <head>
  <meta charset="utf-8">
  <title>Drawing Curves</title>
  <link rel="stylesheet" href="style.css">
 </head>
 <body>
```

```
<canvas id="canvas" width="400" height="400"></canvas>
<script src="utils.js"></script>
<script>
window.onload = function () {
  var canvas = document.getElementById('canvas'),
      context = canvas.getContext('2d'),
      mouse = utils.captureMouse(canvas),
      x0 = 100,
      y0 = 200,
      x2 = 300,
      y2 = 200;

  canvas.addEventListener('mousemove', function () {
    context.clearRect(0, 0, canvas.width, canvas.height);

    var x1 = mouse.x,
        y1 = mouse.y;
    //curve toward mouse
    context.beginPath();
    context.moveTo(x0, y0);
    context.quadraticCurveTo(x1, y1, x2, y2);
    context.stroke();
  }, false);
};
</script>
</body>
</html>
```

Load this file in your browser and move the mouse around. The script has two preset points for the beginning and ending points, and uses the mouse position for the control point. Notice that the curve never reaches the control point, but gets about halfway there.

Curving through the control point

If you want the curve to hit a point, the following formula calculates a control point, so the curve goes through the point you specify. Again, you start with **x0, y0** and **x2, y2** as the end points, and **x1, y1** as the control point. We call the point you want to curve through **xt, yt** (t for target). In other words, if you want the curve to be drawn through **xt, yt**, what **x1, y1** do you need to use? Here's the formula:

```
x1 = xt * 2 - (x0 + x2) / 2;
y1 = yt * 2 - (y0 + y2) / 2;
```

Basically, you multiply the target by two, and subtract the average of the starting and ending points. You can graph the whole formula and see exactly how it works. Or, you can test it, see that it works, and assume that it always will.

To see it in action, using the mouse coordinates as **xt, yt**, you need to change only two lines from the previous example. Change the following lines:

```
x1 = mouse.x;
y1 = mouse.y;
```

to the following:

```
x1 = mouse.x * 2 - (x0 + x2) / 2;
y1 = mouse.y * 2 - (y0 + y2) / 2;
```

Or you can check out **03-curve-through-point.html**, where we did it for you.

Creating multiple curves

Next, you might want to create multiple curves, where instead of a single curve, you have a long line that curves smoothly in several directions. First, here is the wrong way to solve this problem, which is a common first attempt. In this example, you start out with a number of points, draw a curve from the first through the second to the third, then through the fourth to the fifth, then through the sixth to the seventh, and so on. Here it is in code (in document **04-multi-curve-1.html**):

```
<!doctype html>
<html>
 <head>
  <meta charset="utf-8">
  <title>Multi Curve 1</title>
  <link rel="stylesheet" href="style.css">
 </head>
 <body>
  <canvas id="canvas" width="400" height="400"></canvas>
  <script>
  window.onload = function () {
    var canvas = document.getElementById('canvas'),
        context = canvas.getContext('2d'),
        points = [],
        numPoints = 9;

    //array of random point objects
    for (var i = 0; i < numPoints; i++) {
      points.push({
        x: Math.random() * canvas.width,
        y: Math.random() * canvas.height
      });
    }

    //move to the first point
    context.beginPath();
    context.moveTo(points[0].x, points[1].y);

    //and loop through each successive pair
    for (i = 1; i < numPoints; i += 2) {
      context.quadraticCurveTo(points[i].x, points[i].y, points[i+1].x, points[i+1].y);
    }
    context.stroke();
  };
  </script>
 </body>
</html>
```

The first **for** loop in the **window.onload** function sets up an array of nine points. Each point is an object with an **x** and **y** property, and they are randomly placed on the canvas.

We begin a new path, and the pen is moved to the first point. The next **for** loop starts at one and increments by two each time, drawing a curve through point one to point two, then through three to four, then through five to six, and then through seven to eight. The loop stops there, which is perfect because point eight is the last one. There must be a minimum of three points, and the number of points must be odd.

It seems like a well-reasoned program, until you test it. As shown in Figure 4-1, it doesn't look curvy at all. In fact, it looks a bit spiky. The problem is that there is no coordination between one curve and the next, except that they share a point.

Figure 4-1. There are multiple curves going the wrong way. You can see where one curve ends and the next begins.

You must plug in a few more points to make it look right. Here's the strategy: Between each set of two points, you need a new point that sits exactly in the middle. You then use these as the starting and ending points for each curve, and use the original points as the control points.

Figure 4-2 illustrates the solution. In the figure, the white dots are the original points, and the black dots are the in-between points. You can see there are three **context.quadraticCurveTo** methods used here.

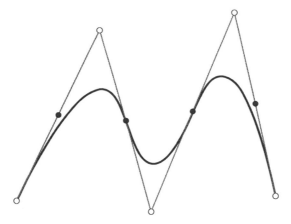

Figure 4-2. Multiple curves with midpoints

Notice in Figure 4-2 that the first and last midpoints are not used, and the first and last original points remain terminal points for the curves. You need to make in-between points only for the second point up to the second-to-last point. Here's an updated version of the previous random curves example (document `05-multi-curve-2.html`):

```
<!doctype html>
<html>
 <head>
  <meta charset="utf-8">
  <title>Multi Curve 2</title>
  <link rel="stylesheet" href="style.css">
 </head>
 <body>
  <canvas id="canvas" width="400" height="400"></canvas>
  <script>
  window.onload = function () {
    var canvas = document.getElementById('canvas'),
        context = canvas.getContext('2d'),
        points = [],
        numPoints = 9,
        ctrlPoint = {};

    for (var i = 0; i < numPoints; i++) {
      points.push({
        x: Math.random() * canvas.width,
        y: Math.random() * canvas.height
      });
    }

    //move to the first point
    context.beginPath();
    context.moveTo(points[0].x, points[1].y);

    //curve through the rest, stopping at each midpoint
```

```
for (i = 1; i < numPoints - 2; i++) {
  ctrlPoint.x = (points[i].x + points[i+1].x) / 2;
  ctrlPoint.y = (points[i].y + points[i+1].y) / 2;
  context.quadraticCurveTo(points[i].x, points[i].y, ctrlPoint.x, ctrlPoint.y);
}

//curve through the last two points
context.quadraticCurveTo(points[i].x, points[i].y, points[i+1].x, points[i+1].y);
context.stroke();
};
</script>
</body>
</html>
```

In the new code, the second **for** loop starts at 1 and ends at **numPoints - 2**. This prevents it from processing the first and last pairs of points. It creates a new x, y control point, which is the average of the next two points in the array. Then, it draws a curve through the next array point to the new average point. When the loop ends, the index, **i** continues pointing to the second-to-last element; thus, you can draw a curve through that to the last point.

This time, you come up with a nice smooth shape—rather than those spikes—as shown in Figure 4-3. You are not limited to an odd number of original points anymore. As long as you start with at least three points, you'll be fine.

As a variation on this theme, the following code, document **06-multi-curve-3.html**, creates a closed curve using the same technique. It computes an initial midpoint, which is the average of the first and last points, and moves to that. Then it loops through all the rest, figuring midpoints for each one, finally drawing its last curve back to the initial midpoint (see Figure 4-4).

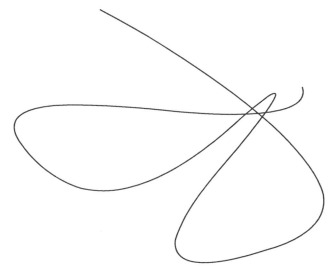

Figure 4-3. Smooth multiple curves

```
<!doctype html>
<html>
 <head>
  <meta charset="utf-8">
  <title>Multi Curve 3</title>
  <link rel="stylesheet" href="style.css">
 </head>
 <body>
  <canvas id="canvas" width="400" height="400"></canvas>
  <script>
  window.onload = function () {
    var canvas = document.getElementById('canvas'),
        context = canvas.getContext('2d'),
        points = [],
        numPoints = 9,
        ctrlPoint = {},
        ctrlPoint1 = {};

    for (var i = 0; i < numPoints; i++) {
      points.push({
        x: Math.random() * canvas.width,
        y: Math.random() * canvas.height
      });
    }

    //find the first midpoint and move to it
    ctrlPoint1.x = (points[0].x + points[numPoints-1].x) / 2;
    ctrlPoint1.y = (points[0].y + points[numPoints-1].y) / 2;
    context.beginPath();
    context.moveTo(ctrlPoint1.x, ctrlPoint1.y);

    //curve through the rest, stopping at each midpoint
    for (i = 0; i < numPoints - 1; i++) {
      ctrlPoint.x = (points[i].x + points[i+1].x) / 2;
      ctrlPoint.y = (points[i].y + points[i+1].y) / 2;
      context.quadraticCurveTo(points[i].x, points[i].y, ctrlPoint.x, ctrlPoint.y);
    }

    //curve through the last point, back to the first midpoint
    context.quadraticCurveTo(points[i].x, points[i].y, ctrlPoint1.x, ctrlPoint1.y);
    context.stroke();
  };
  </script>
 </body>
</html>
```

Figure 4-4. Multiple closed curves

Additional curves

Besides the `context.quadraticCurveTo` method we've been using, there are a few other methods for drawing curves, each with their own characteristic shape:

- `bezierCurveTo(cp1x, cp1y, cp2x, cp2y, x, y)`: Adds a point to the current path connected by a cubic Bézier curve with the two control points.

- `arcTo(cp1x, cp1y, cp2x, cp2y, radius)`: Adds an arc to the path using two control points and radius, connected to the previous point by a straight line.

- `arc(x, y, radius, startAngle, endAngle [, antiClockwise])`: Adds an arc to the path described by the circumference of a circle, from the start angle to end angle, in the given direction (defaulting to clockwise), connected to the previous point by a straight line.

These methods are not used much in this book; however, `context.arc` shows up throughout the example code because it's an easy way to draw a circle. For example, this is how to draw a circle at point 100, 100 with a radius of 50:

```
context.beginPath();
context.arc(100, 100, 50, 0, (Math.PI * 2), true);
context.closePath();
context.stroke();
```

Creating shapes with fill

Now that we've drawn several paths using lines and curves, we use them to create shapes. The `context.fill()` method fills in the sub-paths with the current fill style.

The `context.fillStyle` property, like `context.strokeStyle`, is set using a CSS-style color string in hexadecimal or RGB format. The default is black, or `"#000000"`. If you want to use a transparent color, recall that you need to format it as a proper RGBA string.

You can issue a `context.fill()` command almost any time during the process of drawing. This computes a shape from the current location on the sub-path to the beginning point. Generally, the drawing sequence is as follows:

- `beginPath`
- `moveTo`
- `lineStyle` (if any)
- `fillStyle` (if any)
- A series of `lineTo` and `quadraticCurveTo` methods (or similar curves)
- `closePath` (to close the shape)
- `fill` (shape color)
- `stroke` (shape outline)

You can use the first four methods in just about any order without affecting what is drawn. It's not required to specify a line or fill style, but if you do not, you will use the default color: black.

If you do not draw a line back to the original point from which you started, the canvas will still fill in the shape when you call the command `context.fill`—but it will not close the path and draw the completed outline. To do that, call the method `context.closePath` and the path will be automatically closed.

Go ahead and play around with drawing fills. You can even use the closed curve example from the previous section (`06-multi-curve-3.html`), because this example is already generating a closed shape. Throw in a `context.fillStyle` statement before the first `context.quadraticCurveTo`—for example, `context.fillStyle = "#ff0000"`—and finish off the code with `context.fill()`.

If you do this, notice where sections of the curve cross over itself—here the fill kind of disappears. There's not much you can do about that, but for the most part, you won't draw shapes that intersect like this. On the other hand, you can use that behavior to create some interesting shapes.

Creating gradient fills

A *gradient fill* is a fill of at least two colors. A part of the shape starts out one color, and it slowly blends into another color, possibly transitioning through one or several other predefined colors on its way.

Specifying the gradient type

There are two types of canvas gradient fills: linear and radial. In a *linear gradient fill*, the gradient of colors lies along a line from one point to the other. Create a linear gradient with `context.createLinearGradient(x0, y0, x1, y1)`, which paints along the line between point (x0, y0) and point (x1, y1). Figure 4-5 shows a few examples of linear gradient fills.

Figure 4-5. Linear gradient fills

A *radial gradient fill* starts in the center of the space you define and radiates outward in all directions, creating a circle. The first color you specify is at the center of the circle, and the final color is the edge. The method, context.createRadialGradient(x0, y0, r0, x1, y1, r1), takes arguments representing two circles each specified by a coordinate and a radius. Figure 4-6 shows an example of a radial fill.

Figure 4-6. Radial gradient fill

Setting gradient color stops

To see a gradient fill, you need at least two different color stops, or color positions, on the gradient. If that's all you specify, the fill blends from the first to the second. If you add more colors, the fill blends smoothly from the first, to the second, to the third, and so on, until it arrives at the last one.

You must also specify the position of each color in the fill by assigning it a decimal number from 0 to 1, where 0 is the start of the fill and 1 is the end. These numbers, one for each color, are called the *ratio* of the fill. For example, if you want a two-color fill, specify 0 and 1 as the ratios. To make an even blend of three colors, use 0, 0.5, and 1 as ratios—this puts the second color exactly in the middle of the other two. If you use 0, 0.1, 1 as ratios, the first color almost immediately blends into the second, and then very slowly blends into the third. Keep in mind that these are not pixel values, but fractions of 1.

With a ratio and color, add a color stop using the gradient's method Gradient.addColorStop(ratio, color):

```
var gradient = context.createLinearGradient(0, 0, 100, 100);
gradient.addColorStop(0, "#ffffff");
gradient.addColorStop(1, "#ff0000");
```

This creates a linear gradient from point (0, 0) to point (100, 100). It then defines two color stops using a start ratio of 0 and end ratio of 1. This gradient color starts as white and blends into red at the end.

The next step is to assign the gradient to context.fillStyle and draw a shape with it:

```
context.fillStyle = gradient;
context.fillRect(0, 0, 100, 100);
```

Here we use the convenience method **context.fillRect**. This draws *and* fills a rectangle path in the same way as our line drawing commands, but does not move the pen around much. Let's see how it all looks together on the canvas in the document **07-gradient-fill-1.html**:

```
<!doctype html>
<html>
 <head>
  <meta charset="utf-8">
  <title>Gradient Fill 1</title>
  <link rel="stylesheet" href="style.css">
 </head>
 <body>
  <canvas id="canvas" width="400" height="400"></canvas>
  <script>
  window.onload = function () {
    var canvas = document.getElementById('canvas'),
        context = canvas.getContext('2d'),
        pt1 = {x: 0, y: 0},              //gradient start point
        pt2 = {x: 100, y: 100},          //gradient end point
        gradient = context.createLinearGradient(pt1.x, pt1.y, pt2.x, pt2.y);

    //gradient from white to red
    gradient.addColorStop(0, "#ffffff");
    gradient.addColorStop(1, "#ff0000");

    context.fillStyle = gradient;
    context.fillRect(0, 0, 100, 100);
  };
  </script>
 </body>
</html>
```

Test this in your browser and you see a white-to-red gradient square. Now, let's draw the square in a different location by altering the drawing code. Change the x and y position where you start the square (in **08-gradient-fill-2.html**):

```
context.fillRect(100, 100, 100, 100);
```

The square is all red, what happened? The gradient starts at point 0, 0 and ends at point 100, 100, which is where the square begins. At this position, the gradient has already reached full red, and it's red from there on out. So again, you want the x, y of the gradient to start at the top-left point of the shape, like so:

```
pt1 = {x: 100, y: 100},           //gradient start point
pt2 = {x: 200, y: 200},           //gradient end point
gradient = context.createLinearGradient(pt1.x, pt1.y, pt2.x, pt2.y);
```

Here, the starting point of the gradient is the same as the starting point of the square. Using the same square, you can play around with gradient color stops to see what kind of effects you can create. First, try three colors:

```
//gradient from white to blue to red
gradient.addColorStop(0, "#ffffff");
gradient.addColorStop(0.5, "#0000ff");
gradient.addColorStop(1, "#ff0000");
```

Move the middle ratio around to see how that affects the gradient. Instead of 0.5, try 0.25 or 0.75.

The next example is a straight alpha blend. The colors are the same; only the alpha changes:

```
//all black alpha blend
gradient.addColorStop(0, "#000000");           //alpha 100%
gradient.addColorStop(1, "rgba(0, 0, 0, 0)"); //alpha   0%
```

Finally, instead of using points, define two circles and use a radial gradient:

```
c1 = {x: 150, y: 150, radius: 0},
c2 = {x: 150, y: 150, radius: 50},
gradient = context.createRadialGradient(c1.x, c1.y, c1.radius,
                                        c2.x, c2.y, c2.radius);
```

You can try all the same tricks that you used for the linear gradient fill in the radial version. Or, see how this looks in example **09-gradient-fill-radial.html**.

Loading and drawing images

You might want to draw an external image into your animation. There are two ways to access the image: Load a URL while the script is running or use the DOM interface to access an embedded image element. After the image has loaded, you can render it to the canvas using the drawing API.

Loading images

To load an image at runtime, create a new **Image** object and set its **src** property to the URL path of an image file. When the image has finished loading, it executes the callback function set as its **onload** method. In this simple example, we draw the image to the canvas after it has been completely loaded (document **10-load-image.html**):

```
<!doctype html>
<html>
 <head>
  <meta charset="utf-8">
  <title>Load Image</title>
  <link rel="stylesheet" href="style.css">
 </head>
 <body>
  <canvas id="canvas" width="400" height="400"></canvas>
  <script>
  window.onload = function () {
    var canvas = document.getElementById('canvas'),
        context = canvas.getContext('2d'),
        image = new Image();

    image.src = "picture.jpg";
    image.onload = function () {
      context.drawImage(image, 0, 0);
    };
  };
```

```
  </script>
 </body>
</html>
```

We drew the image to the canvas using the method **context.drawImage**, which takes an image element and an x and y position on the canvas. This code is placed within the **image.onload** callback; otherwise, the command would have executed *before* the image loaded, rendering nothing.

The **context.drawImage** method can be invoked in three ways, using multiple arguments:

- **drawImage(image, dx, dy)**: Draws an image at the canvas position (**dx**, **dy**), which is the upper-left corner of the image.

- **drawImage(image, dx, dy, dw, dh)**: Scales the image using **dw** for width and **dh** for height and draws it to the canvas position (**dx**, **dy**).

- **drawImage(image, sx, sy, sw, sh, dx, dy, dw, dh)**: Clips an image to the rectangle (**sx**, **sy**, **sw**, **sh**), scales it to (**dh**, **dw**), and draws it at position (**dx**, **dy**).

Using image elements

You can also access an image element in your HTML document using the DOM. This has the advantage of already loading the image by the time the script gets to it. If you do it this way, use some CSS to hide the image element or you might see it rendered twice in your document. Here's the completed example (**11-embed-image.html**):

```
<!doctype html>
<html>
 <head>
  <meta charset="utf-8">
  <title>Embed Image</title>
  <link rel="stylesheet" href="style.css">
  <style>
  #picture {
    display: none;
  }
  </style>
 </head>
 <body>
  <canvas id="canvas" width="400" height="400"></canvas>
  <img id="picture" src="picture.jpg">
  <script>
  window.onload = function () {
    var canvas = document.getElementById('canvas'),
        context = canvas.getContext('2d'),
        image = document.getElementById('picture');

    context.drawImage(image, 0, 0);
  };
  </script>
 </body>
</html>
```

Using video elements

Similar to drawing a still image, we can also render a video to the canvas—one frame at a time. The **video** element is an exciting addition to the HTML5 specification that allows movies to play in the web browser, without having to use plug-ins like Adobe Flash. While this isn't the kind of animation that this book is about, you can still create some interesting effects once it's displayed on the canvas.

To include a video in your document, add the following element to your HTML:

```
<video controls autobuffer>
  <source src="movieclip.mp4" type="video/mp4"/>
  <source src="movieclip.webm" type="video/webm"/>
  <source src="movieclip.ogv" type="video/ogg"/>
  <p>This browser does not support the <code>video</code> element.</p>
</video>
```

Here, the **controls** attribute adds buttons for the user to play and stop the video. **autobuffer** tells the browser to begin downloading the file immediately, so it's ready to play when the user starts it. The **<p>** element is provided as a fallback to warn the user if their browser does not support HTML5 video; and if it is supported, the warning is not displayed.

There are multiple **<source>** tags to provide alternatives for the video format. Due to licensing restrictions, different browsers support different video file formats. To make sure a video plays across HTML5-capable browsers, you must supply multiple versions of the it. MP4 is a closed format which, at the time of writing, is required by IE and Safari. WebM and Ogg are both open, royalty-free, formats that can be played in Chrome, Firefox, and Opera. Since this is a rapidly evolving area, test your videos and formats in as many browsers as you can to make sure they play correctly.

In the next example, we load a video and draw it frame-by-frame to the canvas element. Since a video is just a collection of still images played in order, the canvas is updated in an animation loop, which draws the current frame of the video. In this document, the **canvas** element is set to the same dimensions as the sample video in order to display the entire frame; you may need to adjust this depending on the size of your video. Here's the code (**12-video-frames.html**):

```
<!doctype html>
<html>
 <head>
  <meta charset="utf-8">
  <title>Video Frames</title>
  <link rel="stylesheet" href="style.css">
  <style>
  #movieclip {
    display: none;
  }
  </style>
 </head>
 <body>
  <canvas id="canvas" width="640" height="360"></canvas>

  <video id="movieclip" width="640" height="360" autoplay>
   <source src="movieclip.mp4" type="video/mp4"/>
```

```
<source src="movieclip.webm" type="video/webm"/>
<source src="movieclip.ogv" type="video/ogg"/>
<p>This browser does not support the <code>video</code> element.</p>
</video>
<script src="utils.js"></script>
<script>
window.onload = function () {
  var canvas = document.getElementById('canvas'),
      context = canvas.getContext('2d'),
      video = document.getElementById('movieclip');

  (function drawFrame () {
    window.requestAnimationFrame(drawFrame, canvas);

    context.drawImage(video, 0, 0);
  }());
};
</script>
</body>
</html>
```

The important parts in bold. The `autoplay` attribute has been added to the **video** element which starts playing it as soon as the page loads. We need a way to start the video, since its HTML element has been hidden using CSS, and we do not have access to its built-in controls. If you don't have any videos handy, you can use the samples provided with the source code of this book at `www.apress.com`.

The **video** element is related to the **audio** element, which is also new in HTML5. But let's not get ahead of ourselves, you see how to add sound to your animations in Chapter 19.

Pixel manipulation

The drawing API provides direct access to the pixels that compose the image on the canvas. You can create, read, and write the pixel data, which can be used to make some really cutting-edge effects and animations in the web browser.

While direct pixel access is a powerful feature, manipulating them in a coherent way is an advanced topic. The code here is intended to demonstrate some interesting visual effects that you can create when working with pixels. Since we won't use these techniques anywhere else in the book, you can consider this section as optional. If you get a little confused by the code (the implementation is not the most straight-forward), or just want to move on to good stuff in the next chapter, feel free to skip over it. You can always come back later.

Getting pixel data

Direct access to the pixels is provided by the **ImageData** object of the canvas context. To return a copy of the pixel data for a rectangular area on the canvas element, call:

```
var imagedata = context.getImageData(x, y, width, height);
```

This returns an object containing three properties: **width**, **height**, and **data**. The **width** and **height** properties are the size of the image in pixels, and **data** is an array representing the image data. We will look at this in more detail shortly.

To create a new, blank, **ImageData** object, specify the rectangle dimensions and call:

```
var imagedata = context.createImageData(width, height);
```

Alternatively, you can invoke this function with another **ImageData** object, e.g. **context.createImageData(anotherImageData)**. This creates a new object with the same dimensions as the argument. The pixels of the new object are set to transparent black, as this method does not copy the image data.

> *When reading pixel data, any external asset rendered to the canvas—image or video— is served from the same domain as the document running the script. If a cross-origin image is drawn to the canvas, it is marked as dirty, and you will no longer be able to read the pixels; instead, a security exception error is thrown to the debugging console. This is in the HTML5 specification and is consistent with the same-origin security policy used by most web browsers. Consequently, even testing some examples on your local machine might be impossible. Unless your browser provides options to ignore this security policy, you'll need to upload everything to a server and test it from there.*

Accessing pixel components

The **data** property of an **ImageData** object returns a one-dimensional array containing the values of the pixel component colors in RGBA order, specified as integers in the range 0 to 255. (Note that alpha is also assigned a value in this range; not the 0.0 to 1.0 range used in the CSS-style color format.) The pixels are ordered left to right, row by row, from top to bottom.

For example, here's an array representing the image data of a 2 × 2 square. Each of the four pixels is set to full red:

```
var pixels = [255, 0, 0, 255, 255, 0, 0, 255,
              255, 0, 0, 255, 255, 0, 0, 255];
```

The color components of the first pixel are marked in bold, and the array continues in groupings of four elements—RGBA—for every pixel in the image. Each has its red and alpha channels set to full (255), and its green and blue channels set to none (0).

You can access the values of any particular pixel by specifying an offset index for the array. Since each pixel is represented by four elements, you can iterate over the image data, pixel by pixel, using the following:

```
for (var offset = 0, len = pixels.length; offset < len; offset += 4) {
  var r = pixels[offset],     //red
      g = pixels[offset + 1], //green
      b = pixels[offset + 2], //blue
      a = pixels[offset + 3]; //alpha
}
```

Sometimes you may want to access the pixel at a specific coordinate in the image. Here's how you can determine its offset in the image data array:

```
var offset = (xpos + ypos * imagedata.width) * 4;
```

Once you have the offset index, you can access the pixel's component colors as before.

Painting pixel data

To paint an **ImageData** object onto the canvas, call **context.putImageData(imagedata, x, y)**, where **x** and **y** specify the top-left corner of the canvas to start drawing.

A pixel can be changed by isolating it in the image data array and assigning new values to its color components. The updated pixel values can be painted to the canvas by passing it as the first argument to **putImageData**.

For example, to remove the red color channel from an image on the canvas, iterate over each pixel, setting its red component to 0:

```
var imagedata = context.getImageData(0, 0, canvas.width, canvas.height),
    pixels = imagedata.data

for (var offset = 0, len = pixels.length; offset < len; offset += 4) {
  pixels[offset]     = 0;                    //red
  pixels[offset + 1] = pixels[offset + 1]; //green
  pixels[offset + 2] = pixels[offset + 2]; //blue
  pixels[offset + 3] = pixels[offset + 3]; //alpha
}

context.putImageData(imagedata, 0, 0);
```

Here, the image data array is assigned to **pixels**. (JavaScript objects—and hence arrays—are assigned by reference, so a change to the **pixels** array is a change to **imagedata.data**, as they are the same object.) We iterate over the pixels, jumping four elements at a time, and assign the values for the color components. When we are finished, the updated **imagedata** object is drawn back to the canvas.

We'll use the same pixel iteration process in the next example. First, some red, green, and blue stripes are drawn to the canvas so we have some image data to work with. Then, new color values are calculated for each pixel by inverting the old ones, keeping in mind each component must be an integer from 0 to 255. Here's the code for exercise **13-invert-color.html**:

```
<!doctype html>
<html>
 <head>
  <meta charset="utf-8">
  <title>Invert Color</title>
  <link rel="stylesheet" href="style.css">
 </head>
 <body>
  <canvas id="canvas" width="400" height="400"></canvas>
  <script>
  window.onload = function () {
```

```
var canvas = document.getElementById('canvas'),
    context = canvas.getContext('2d');

//draw some red, green, and blue stripes
for (var i = 0; i < canvas.width; i += 10) {
  for (var j = 0; j < canvas.height; j += 10) {
    context.fillStyle = (i % 20 === 0) ? "#f00" : ((i % 30 === 0) ? "#0f0" : "#00f");
    context.fillRect(i, j, 10, 10);
  }
}

var imagedata = context.getImageData(0, 0, canvas.width, canvas.height),
    pixels = imagedata.data;

//pixel iteration
for (var offset = 0, len = pixels.length; offset < len; offset += 4) {
  //invert each color component of the pixel: r,g,b,a (0-255)
  pixels[offset]     = 255 - pixels[offset];     //red to cyan
  pixels[offset + 1] = 255 - pixels[offset + 1]; //green to magenta
  pixels[offset + 2] = 255 - pixels[offset + 2]; //blue to yellow
  //pixels[offset + 4] is alpha (the fourth component)
}

context.putImageData(imagedata, 0, 0);
};
</script>
</body>
</html>
```

This is a relatively simple transformation, but as you might expect, effects like these can get very complicated, and very processor intensive—especially when applied to animations. If you're making something other than a fun demo, be mindful of the burden you may place on the user's machine.

Converting a color image to grayscale is another effect we can calculate easily. The luminance of each pixel is calculated, where the color components are weighted to reflect the perceived intensity of different light wavelengths. Just in case you think we're making these numbers up as we go along, the formula is, in fact, defined by the *International Commission on Illumination*. Replace the pixel iteration **for** loop from the last example with this one (document **14-grayscale.html**):

```
//pixel iteration
for (var offset = 0, len = pixels.length; offset < len; offset += 4) {
  var r = pixels[offset],
      g = pixels[offset + 1],
      b = pixels[offset + 2],
      y = (0.2126 * r) + (0.7152 * g) + (0.0722 * b); //luminance

  pixels[offset] = pixels[offset + 1] = pixels[offset + 2] = y;
}
```

Now it looks like the striped image is being displayed on an old black-and-white television.

Let's make the next example more dynamic by introducing some user interactivity. We can use the mouse position to affect the image data, and put the pixel processing in an animation loop to work on each frame.

You can see that we're using the distance formula from Chapter 3 to get the distance from the mouse cursor to the current pixel. The pixel iteration is slightly different in this example; we're using a double **for** loop to specify the pixel's coordinate location on the canvas element. The code here can be found in example **15-pixel-move.**html:

```html
<!doctype html>
<html>
 <head>
  <meta charset="utf-8">
  <title>Pixel Move</title>
  <link rel="stylesheet" href="style.css">
 </head>
<body>
  <canvas id="canvas" width="400" height="400"></canvas>
  <script src="utils.js"></script>
  <script>
  window.onload = function () {
    var canvas = document.getElementById('canvas'),
        context = canvas.getContext('2d'),
        mouse = utils.captureMouse(canvas);

    (function drawFrame () {
      window.requestAnimationFrame(drawFrame, canvas);

      //draw some stripes: red, green, and blue
      for (var i = 0; i < canvas.width; i += 10) {
        for (var j = 0; j < canvas.height; j += 10) {
          context.fillStyle = (i % 20 === 0) ? "#f00" : ((i % 30 === 0) ? "#0f0" : "#00f");
          context.fillRect(i, j, 10, 10);
        }
      }

      var imagedata = context.getImageData(0, 0, canvas.width, canvas.height),
          pixels = imagedata.data;

      //pixel iteration
      for (var y = 0; y < imagedata.height; y += 1) {
        for (var x = 0; x < imagedata.width; x += 1) {

          var dx = x - mouse.x,
              dy = y - mouse.y,
              dist = Math.sqrt(dx * dx + dy * dy),
              offset = (x + y * imagedata.width) * 4,
              r = pixels[offset],
              g = pixels[offset + 1],
              b = pixels[offset + 2];

          pixels[offset]     = Math.cos(r * dist * 0.001) * 256;
          pixels[offset + 1] = Math.sin(g * dist * 0.001) * 256;
          pixels[offset + 2] = Math.cos(b * dist * 0.0005) * 256;
        }
      }
```

```
      context.putImageData(imagedata, 0, 0);
    }());
  };
  </script>
 </body>
</html>
```

When you run this script, you should see an effect that can be described as a "psychedelic flashlight." The color values are passed to some trigonometry functions and scaled to fit within the range of color values. We're just having fun here, so don't worry about what these functions are doing exactly, just understand that we're trying to get some interesting looking colors. Feel free to change the values around and experiment with your own color combinations.

For the last example in this chapter, we bring it back home to the first example: the simple drawing application (**01-drawing-app.html**). But this time, we create a spray paint effect by drawing directly to the pixels. Here's the code (example **16-spray-paint.html**):

```
<!doctype html>
<html>
 <head>
  <meta charset="utf-8">
  <title>Spray Paint</title>
  <link rel="stylesheet" href="style.css">
 </head>
 <body>
  <canvas id="canvas" width="400" height="400"></canvas>
  <script src="utils.js"></script>
  <script>
  window.onload = function () {
    var canvas = document.getElementById('canvas'),
        context = canvas.getContext('2d'),
        mouse = utils.captureMouse(canvas),
        imagedata = context.getImageData(0, 0, canvas.width, canvas.height),
        pixels = imagedata.data,
        brush_size = 25,
        brush_density = 50,
        brush_color;

    canvas.addEventListener('mousedown', function () {
      brush_color = utils.parseColor(Math.random() * 0xffffff, true); //to number
      canvas.addEventListener('mousemove', onMouseMove, false);
    }, false);

    canvas.addEventListener('mouseup', function () {
      canvas.removeEventListener('mousemove', onMouseMove, false);
    }, false);

    function onMouseMove () {
      //loop over each brush point
      for (var i = 0; i < brush_density; i++) {
        var angle = Math.random() * Math.PI * 2,
            radius = Math.random() * brush_size,
            xpos = (mouse.x + Math.cos(angle) * radius) | 0, //remove decimal
```

```
                ypos = (mouse.y + Math.sin(angle) * radius) | 0,
                offset = (xpos + ypos * imagedata.width) * 4;

            //pixel component colors: r,g,b,a (0-255)
            pixels[offset]     = brush_color >> 16 & 0xff; //red
            pixels[offset + 1] = brush_color >> 8 & 0xff;  //green
            pixels[offset + 2] = brush_color & 0xff;       //blue
            pixels[offset + 3] = 255;                      //alpha
        }

        context.putImageData(imagedata, 0, 0);
      }
    };
  </script>
 </body>
</html>
```

This script uses the event handlers we set up in the first example, and works the same way. When you press the mouse button, a random "paint" color is assigned and the pixel drawing code is started. Within an area around the mouse cursor, random pixels are filled in to simulate each splatter of paint. Play around with the brush size and density, and, if you're feeling adventurous, change the way individual color components are assigned to the pixels.

Pixel manipulation can be a powerful tool used for some advanced animations and effects. Although not the focus of this book, it's fun to experiment with, and another way to render images to the canvas element.

Important formulas in this chapter

You added a few more valuable tools to your collection in this chapter, mostly relating to handling color.

Convert hex to decimal

```
console.log(hexValue);
```

Convert decimal to hex

```
console.log(decimalValue.toString(16));
```

Combine component colors

```
color = red << 16 | green << 8 | blue;
```

Extract component colors

```
red = color24 >> 16 & 0xFF;
green = color24 >> 8 & 0xFF;
blue = color24 & 0xFF;
```

Draw a curve through a point

```
// xt, yt is the point you want to draw through
// x0, y0 and x2, y2 are the end points of the curve
x1 = xt * 2 - (x0 + x2) / 2;
y1 = yt * 2 - (y0 + y2) / 2;
context.moveTo(x0, y0);
context.quadraticCurveTo(x1, y1, x2, y2);
```

Summary

This chapter didn't cover much about animation, but it did show you a number of ways to create visual content, which you learn how to animate in future chapters. Specifically, the chapter covered color, the canvas drawing API, loading images, and pixel manipulation.

These provide the foundational drawing tools you need to build dynamic, expressive content for your animations. You use many of the techniques introduced in this chapter throughout the book, so it is useful for you to know and understand them well now. In fact, you get your first hands-on experience using several of these techniques in the next chapter, which covers velocity and acceleration.

Part II

Basic Motion

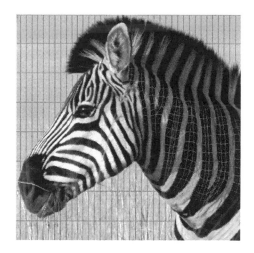

Chapter 5

Velocity and Acceleration

What we'll cover in this chapter:

- Velocity
- Acceleration

Well, congratulations! You made it to the point in the book where the action finally starts. This means that (a) you persevered through all the chapters so far, (b) you skimmed over the previous chapters and felt like you knew enough of it to get by, or (c) you got bored and jumped ahead. However it happened, here you are. Just remember, if you start having trouble, you can probably find help in an earlier chapter.

This chapter starts with basic motion: velocity, vectors, and acceleration. These concepts are used for almost every bit of animation code you will write from here on out.

Velocity

The most basic property of something that moves is velocity. Many people equate the term *velocity* with speed. That's part of it, but only part. The concept of velocity contains an important second factor: *direction.* That is pretty much our layman's definition for velocity: *speed in a particular direction.* Let's look at exactly how this definition differs from simple speed.

If you got in a car at point X and drove 30 miles per hour for one hour, it would be difficult to find you. On the other hand, if you drove due north for one hour at the same speed, we would know precisely where you are. This is important in animation, because you need to know where to put your object. It's fine to say an object is moving at a certain speed, but you're going to need some specific x, y coordinates to assign to it on each frame to give it the illusion of motion. This is where velocity comes in. If you know where something is at the start of a particular frame, how fast it is moving, and in what direction, you know where to put it at the start of the next frame.

The speed part of it is usually defined in terms of pixels per frame. In other words, if an object is at a certain point as it enters a frame, it's going to be so many pixels away from that point at the end of the frame.

In most cases, using pixels per frame works fine, and it is definitely the simplest to program. However, due to the unstable nature of frame rates in the web browser, using pixels per frame might make your animation slow down at certain points when too much is happening, there is too much to compute, or the computer is busy doing something else. If you are programming some kind of game or simulation in which it is crucial that the animation proceeds at a uniform rate, you might want to use an interval-based animation instead. We included an example of that approach in Chapter 19.

Before we start coding velocity, let's talk a little bit about vectors, because that's how velocity is generally depicted.

Vectors and velocity

A *vector* is something that has magnitude and direction. In the case of velocity, the magnitude is the speed. Vectors are drawn as arrows. The length of the arrow is its magnitude, and the direction the arrow is pointing in is, naturally, the direction of the vector. Figure 5-1 shows some vectors.

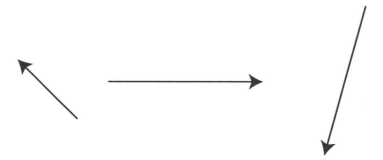

Figure 5-1. A few vectors

It's important to understand that magnitude is always positive. Even a vector with a perceived negative magnitude is just a vector going in the opposite direction, as illustrated in Figure 5-2.

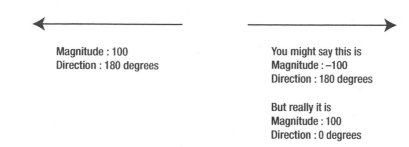

Magnitude : 100
Direction : 180 degrees

You might say this is
Magnitude : −100
Direction : 180 degrees

But really it is
Magnitude : 100
Direction : 0 degrees

Figure 5-2. Negative velocity is really velocity in the opposite direction.

Note that vectors don't have any set position. Even in the case of velocity, the vector doesn't state where something starts or where it ends; it just indicates how fast and in which direction the object is moving. Thus, two vectors can be equal if they have the same direction and magnitude, even if they describe two different objects in two different locations, as shown in Figure 5-3.

Figure 5-3. If vectors have the same magnitude and direction, they are the same. Position doesn't matter.

Velocity on one axis

First let's simplify things, by limiting velocity to a single axis: the x axis, or horizontal motion. That is, the direction is zero degrees, due east, or from the left side of the screen to the right side of the screen—however you want to look at it. The speed is just how many pixels it moves in that direction each frame. Thus, if the velocity on the x axis is 1, the object will move 1 pixel each frame from left to right. This also means that if the velocity is -1 on the x axis, it will move from right to left, 1 pixel each frame.

Already we are talking about a negative magnitude after you were just told there's no such thing. Technically speaking, the velocity is actually 1 and the direction is 180 degrees. Similarly, a positive y velocity is that speed at 90 degrees (straight down), and a negative y velocity is 270, or -90 degrees (straight up). In practice, though, when you calculate component x, y velocities, they always come through as positive and negative numbers, and you often see writing in this book like, "The x velocity is -1." So, if it helps you, think of the minus sign as indicating "to the left" for x velocity or "up" for y velocity, rather than meaning negative.

Throughout the book, we use **vx** to stand for velocity on the x axis, and **vy** to mean velocity on the y axis. Positive **vx** means to the right, and negative **vx** means to the left. Positive **vy** means down, and negative **vy** means up.

For velocity on one axis, you simply add the velocity to the object's position on that axis. Whatever your **vx** is, you add it to the object's **x** property on each frame.

Let's see it in action. Many of the examples in this chapter (and in later chapters) need some kind of object to move around. Rather than using valuable space drawing such an object in every script and example, we make a **Ball** class that we can reuse. This class was first introduced in Chapter 3, but in case you didn't keep it handy, here it is again. Include this code in the file **ball.js**, which we import into our main document:

```
function Ball (radius, color) {
  if (radius === undefined) { radius = 40; }
  if (color === undefined) { color = "#ff0000"; }
  this.x = 0;
  this.y = 0;
  this.radius = radius;
  this.rotation = 0;
  this.scaleX = 1;
  this.scaleY = 1;
  this.color = utils.parseColor(color);
  this.lineWidth = 1;
}

Ball.prototype.draw = function (context) {
  context.save();
  context.translate(this.x, this.y);
  context.rotate(this.rotation);
  context.scale(this.scaleX, this.scaleY);
  context.lineWidth = this.lineWidth;
  context.fillStyle = this.color;
  context.beginPath();
  //x, y, radius, start_angle, end_angle, anti-clockwise
  context.arc(0, 0, this.radius, 0, (Math.PI * 2), true);
  context.closePath();
  context.fill();
  if (this.lineWidth > 0) {
    context.stroke();
  }
  context.restore();
};
```

Now, any time we refer to this class, you should include this script in your main document, and you can create a new ball by calling **new Ball(size, color)**.

Now that you have something to move, here's the first velocity example, document **01-velocity-1.html**:

```
<!doctype html>
<html>
 <head>
  <meta charset="utf-8">
  <title>Velocity 1</title>
  <link rel="stylesheet" href="style.css">
 </head>
 <body>
```

```
<canvas id="canvas" width="400" height="400"></canvas>
<script src="utils.js"></script>
<script src="ball.js"></script>
<script>
window.onload = function () {
  var canvas = document.getElementById('canvas'),
      context = canvas.getContext('2d'),
      ball = new Ball(),
      vx = 1;

  ball.x = 50;
  ball.y = 100;

  (function drawFrame () {
    window.requestAnimationFrame(drawFrame, canvas);
    context.clearRect(0, 0, canvas.width, canvas.height);

    ball.x += vx;
    ball.draw(context);
  }());
};
</script>
</body>
</html>
```

In this example, first you set an x velocity (**vx**) of 1. Remember that is 1 pixel per frame, so on each frame, the **vx** is added to the ball's x property. The `window.onload` function is called when the browser is ready for us to work with the HTML document and goes through the business of getting the ball onto the canvas and setting up the animation loop using `drawFrame` and `window.requestAnimationFrame`. On each frame, the ball is placed 1 pixel to the right of where it was on the previous frame. Try it out. Pretty good illusion of motion, eh?

Play around with it. Give it higher values for **vx**, or try some negative values and watch the object move in the other direction. See whether you can make the object move on the y axis instead.

Velocity on two axes

Moving along two axes is simple. You define a **vx** and a **vy**, and then add the **vx** to the x property and the **vy** to the y property on each frame. So, for each frame, the object is going to move so many pixels on the x axis and so many pixels on the y axis.

The following example (`02-velocity-2.html`) demonstrates this:

```
<!doctype html>
<html>
 <head>
  <meta charset="utf-8">
  <title>Velocity 2</title>
  <link rel="stylesheet" href="style.css">
 </head>
 <body>
  <canvas id="canvas" width="400" height="400"></canvas>
```

109

```
<script src="utils.js"></script>
<script src="ball.js"></script>
<script>
window.onload = function () {
  var canvas = document.getElementById('canvas'),
      context = canvas.getContext('2d'),
      ball = new Ball(),
      vx = 1,
      vy = 1;

  ball.x = 50;
  ball.y = 100;

  (function drawFrame () {
    window.requestAnimationFrame(drawFrame, canvas);
    context.clearRect(0, 0, canvas.width, canvas.height);

    ball.x += vx;
    ball.y += vy;
    ball.draw(context);
  }());
};
</script>
</body>
</html>
```

Again, play around with the velocity variables until you get a good feel for them. Don't forget to try out some negative values.

Angular velocity

So far, so good. You have some real animation going on, using velocity on two axes. But in many cases—maybe most cases—x and y velocity won't be the initial data you have.

We are kind of cheating with the definition of velocity here. We said it's speed in a direction, but now you have two different speeds in two different directions. On the canvas, you position objects by placing them on x, y coordinates. So you need to end up with a velocity and position on both axes, but that's not necessarily how you start.

What if you have a value for speed and an angle for direction, per the definition. Say you want something to move at an angle of 45 degrees and a speed of 1 pixel per frame. There isn't any **vx** or **vy**, or anything even similar in that description.

Fortunately, you've already been introduced to the tools you need to derive **vx** and **vy** from that description. Think back to the discussion of trigonometry in Chapter 3. Now, look at Figure 5-4, which shows what you want the ball to do on each frame: Move 1 pixel at an angle of 45 degrees.

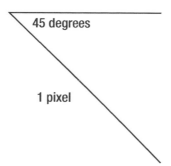

Figure 5-4. A magnitude and a direction

Does this diagram look familiar? How about if I add another line, as shown in Figure 5-5? What do you know? You have a right-angle triangle, with one angle and the hypotenuse defined!

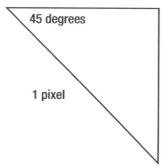

Figure 5-5. Magnitude and direction mapping becomes a right-angle triangle.

Notice that the two legs of that triangle lie on the x and y axes. In fact, the leg that lies on the x axis is equal to the distance the ball is going to move on the x axis. The same goes for the leg on the y axis. Remember that in a right-angle triangle, if you have one side and one angle, you can find all the rest. So, given the 45 degrees and the hypotenuse of 1 pixel, you should be able to use **Math.cos** and **Math.sin** to

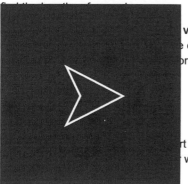

vx. The cosine of an angle is the adjacent/hypotenuse. Or, stated cosine of the angle times the hypotenuse. Similarly, the opposite side or the opposite is the sine times hypotenuse.

rt the 45 degrees to radians before passing it into the **Math** functions! we plug in example values:

```
vx = Math.cos(45 * Math.PI / 180) * 1;
vy = Math.sin(45 * Math.PI / 180) * 1;
```

These functions each return a value of approximately 0.707. After you have the **vx** and the **vy**, you can easily add these to the x, y position of the object you are animating.

The next example (`03-velocity-angle.html`) has the following code:

```
<!doctype html>
<html>
 <head>
  <meta charset="utf-8">
  <title>Velocity Angle</title>
  <link rel="stylesheet" href="style.css">
 </head>
 <body>
  <canvas id="canvas" width="400" height="400"></canvas>
  <script src="utils.js"></script>
  <script src="ball.js"></script>
  <script>
  window.onload = function () {
    var canvas = document.getElementById('canvas'),
        context = canvas.getContext('2d'),
        ball = new Ball(),
        angle = 45,
        speed = 1;

    ball.x = 50;
    ball.y = 100;

    (function drawFrame () {
      window.requestAnimationFrame(drawFrame, canvas);
      context.clearRect(0, 0, canvas.width, canvas.height);

      var radians = angle * Math.PI / 180,
          vx = Math.cos(radians) * speed,
          vy = Math.sin(radians) * speed;

      ball.x += vx;
      ball.y += vy;
      ball.draw(context);
    }());
  };
  </script>
 </body>
</html>
```

The main difference here is that you start off with `angle` and `speed` rather than **vx** and **vy**. The velocities are calculated as local variables, used, and discarded. Of course, in a simple case like this, where the angle and speed are never changing, it makes more sense to calculate the velocities once and save them as variables at the top of the script. But in most advanced motions, both the direction and speed of motion will constantly change, so the **vx** and **vy** will not remain the same.

To experiment with this example, change the angle around. See for yourself that you can make the ball travel at any speed and any angle by simply changing the two numbers.

Now, let's take another look at this example in terms of vectors.

Vector addition

Vector addition is when you have two vectors working in a system and you want to find the resultant overall vector. Here, you have a vector on the x axis, another vector on the y axis, and an overall velocity vector. You add vectors by simply placing them together head to tail. The resultant vector is the line you can draw from the starting point of the first vector on the chain to the ending point of the last one. In Figure 5-6, you can see three vectors added together and their resultant vector.

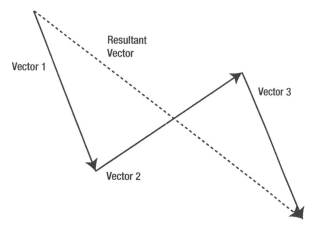

Figure 5-6. Vector addition

It doesn't matter in what order you place the vectors; the result is always the same. And time has no part in it. You can say an object moved this way, it moved that way, and then it moved the other way, in any order. Or you can say that it moved in all three ways at once. The result is that it wound up moving at a certain speed in a certain direction when all was said and done.

Let's go back to our example. If you lay down the x-axis velocity vector, and then put the y-axis velocity vector on the end of that, the resulting line is the overall velocity. Figure 5-7 illustrates the velocities as vectors.

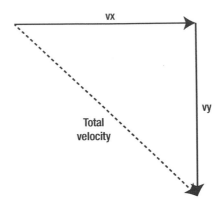

Figure 5-7. This represents velocities as vectors, and it looks like the same right-angle triangle pictured in Figure 5-5! Take that as a sign that you are doing something right.

A mouse follower

Let's use the velocity concepts to expand on an earlier concept. In Chapter 3, you built an example with an arrow that always pointed to the mouse. That example used `Math.atan2` to compute the angle between the mouse and the arrow, and then rotated the arrow so it lined up with that angle.

With what you just learned, you can now throw some speed into the mix and get a velocity based on the current angle. We then move the arrow based on the mouse position so it follows our cursor. This example uses the same `Arrow` class, rather than the ball. So find that file, or rewrite the class and put it in the same directory as the next document, `04-follow-mouse.html`:

```
<!doctype html>
<html>
 <head>
  <meta charset="utf-8">
  <title>Follow Mouse</title>
  <link rel="stylesheet" href="style.css">
 </head>
 <body>
  <canvas id="canvas" width="400" height="400"></canvas>
  <script src="utils.js"></script>
  <script src="arrow.js"></script>
  <script>
  window.onload = function () {
    var canvas = document.getElementById('canvas'),
        context = canvas.getContext('2d'),
        mouse = utils.captureMouse(canvas),
        arrow = new Arrow(),
        speed = 3;

    (function drawFrame () {
      window.requestAnimationFrame(drawFrame, canvas);
      context.clearRect(0, 0, canvas.width, canvas.height);
```

```
        var dx = mouse.x - arrow.x,
            dy = mouse.y - arrow.y,
            angle = Math.atan2(dy, dx), //radians
            vx = Math.cos(angle) * speed,
            vy = Math.sin(angle) * speed;

        arrow.rotation = angle;
        arrow.x += vx;
        arrow.y += vy;
        arrow.draw(context);
    }());
  };
  </script>
 </body>
</html>
```

Although this is a complex effect, there shouldn't be anything in here that you don't fully understand by now. You get the x distance and y distance to the mouse, and from that using `Math.atan2` to get the angle that forms. You then use that angle to rotate the arrow, and using `Math.cos` and `Math.sin` along with the speed to find the x and y velocities. Finally, you add the velocities to the position.

Velocity extended

We are entering into dangerous territory here, but this book takes the definition of velocity into places it was never meant to go. Although in a strict sense velocity refers to change of position and physical motion through space, there's no need to limit the concepts you just learned to only the x and y properties of objects.

An object you display on the canvas can potentially have a lot of properties to tinker with, and almost all of them can accept a wide range of values that you can change over time to produce animation. What we discuss here is the rate of change, or speed, so perhaps *velocity* isn't the best word for it. But the concept is similar, so we often continue to use the word *velocity* in the variable names when describing something that changes a property over time.

As an example, we can spin an object around. In this case, you change the object's `rotation` property on each frame by adding a value to it. You can make the object spin quickly by adding a high value to the `rotation` property on each frame, or have it spin more slowly by adding a smaller value. Correct or not, we usually refer to the variable that holds the spinning speed as `vr`, for rotational velocity.

Using the familiar `Arrow` class (if you look in its `draw` method, you'll see the `rotation` property is referenced in the call to `context.rotate`), you can come up with something like this (`05-rotational-velocity.html`):

```
<!doctype html>
<html>
 <head>
  <meta charset="utf-8">
  <title>Rotational Velocity</title>
  <link rel="stylesheet" href="style.css">
 </head>
```

```
<body>
 <canvas id="canvas" width="400" height="400"></canvas>
 <script src="utils.js"></script>
 <script src="arrow.js"></script>
 <script>
 window.onload = function () {
   var canvas = document.getElementById('canvas'),
       context = canvas.getContext('2d'),
       mouse = utils.captureMouse(canvas),
       arrow = new Arrow(),
       vr = 2; //degrees

   arrow.x = canvas.width / 2;
   arrow.y = canvas.height / 2;

   (function drawFrame () {
     window.requestAnimationFrame(drawFrame, canvas);
     context.clearRect(0, 0, canvas.width, canvas.height);

     arrow.rotation += vr  * Math.PI / 180; //to radians
     arrow.draw(context);
   }());
 };
 </script>
</body>
</html>
```

In terms of velocity here, the speed is 2 and the direction is clockwise. We might even get away with that definition, because there's still some motion going on. When we start using terms like "alpha velocity" (how fast something is fading in or out), it starts confusing people. Still, it is useful to think of such properties in these same terms. We want to change the alpha at a certain rate by adding or subtracting to its value on each frame. As we often find ourselves changing several properties over time, each at certain rates, it's nice to relate them all by calling them velocities. Thus, we might wind up with something like this:

```
arrow.x += vx;
arrow.y += vy;
arrow.alpha += vAlpha;
arrow.rotation += vr;
arrow.scaleX = arrow.scaleY += vScale;
// etc.
```

You see a lot of examples like this later in the book, so please forgive the occasional v.

That about does it for velocity and its "cousins." Now, let's move on to acceleration.

Acceleration

It's common to think of *acceleration* as speeding up and deceleration as slowing down. And although this is not incorrect, for this book, we use a slightly more technical definition for acceleration.

Many similarities exist between velocity and acceleration in terms of how they are described. They are both vectors. Like velocity, acceleration is described as a value and a direction. However, whereas velocity changes the position of an object, acceleration changes its velocity.

Think of it this way. You get in your car, start it up, and put it in gear. What is your velocity? It's zero. By stepping on the gas pedal (also known as the *accelerator*), your velocity begins to change (at least the speed portion of it; the direction is changed with the steering wheel). After a second or two, you're going 4 or 5 miles per hour (mph). Then your speed increases to 10 mph, 20 mph, 30 mph, and so on. The engine is applying force to the car to change its velocity.

Thus, you have the layman's definition for acceleration: *a force that changes the velocity of an object.*

In purely coding terms, you can say that acceleration is a value that you add to a velocity property.

Here's another example. Say you have a spaceship that needs to go from planet A to planet B. Its direction is whatever direction planet B happens to be in relation to planet A. It points in that direction and fires its rockets. As long as those rockets are firing, force is being applied to the ship, and its velocity is going to change. In other words, the spaceship continues to go faster and faster.

At some point, the captain decides the ship is going fast enough, and he might as well conserve fuel, so he shuts down the rockets. Assuming there is no friction in space, the ship continues along at the same velocity. As the rockets are no longer firing, no more force is being applied to the ship. Because there is no more acceleration, the velocity does not change.

Then the ship approaches its goal. It needs to slow down or it's going to fly past planet B (or if the navigator was accurate enough, the ship is going to become a *part* of planet B). So what does the captain do? You don't have brakes in space—there's nothing for the ship to grab a hold of. Instead, the captain turns the ship around so it faces the opposite direction, and fires up the rockets again. This applies negative acceleration, or acceleration in the opposite direction. Really, this is the same thing we covered while discussing vectors. The force is again changing the velocity, but this time it is reducing the velocity. The velocity will get less and less, and eventually arrive at zero. Ideally, that will coincide with the point when the ship is a couple of inches above the surface of the planet. At that point, the captain can kill the rockets and let gravity finish the job. (We talk about gravity in the "Gravity as Acceleration" section, later in the chapter.)

Acceleration on one axis

Let's put what you just learned into practice in JavaScript. Like the first velocity example, this first acceleration example stays on one axis. We jump back to using the `Ball` class for the next few examples.

Here's the code for the first acceleration exercise (`06-acceleration-1.html`):

```
<!doctype html>
<html>
 <head>
  <meta charset="utf-8">
  <title>Acceleration 1</title>
  <link rel="stylesheet" href="style.css">
 </head>
 <body>
```

```
<canvas id="canvas" width="400" height="400"></canvas>
<script src="utils.js"></script>
<script src="ball.js"></script>
<script>
window.onload = function () {
  var canvas = document.getElementById('canvas'),
      context = canvas.getContext('2d'),
      ball = new Ball(),
      vx = 0,
      ax = 0.1;

  ball.x = 50;
  ball.y = 100;

  (function drawFrame () {
    window.requestAnimationFrame(drawFrame, canvas);
    context.clearRect(0, 0, canvas.width, canvas.height);

    vx += ax;
    ball.x += vx;
    ball.draw(context);
  }());
};
</script>
</body>
</html>
```

Here, you start with velocity (**vx**) being zero. The acceleration (**ax**) is 0.1. This is added to the velocity on each frame, and then the velocity is added to the ball's position.

Test this example. You see that the ball starts moving very slowly. By the time it leaves the canvas, it's zipping right along.

Now, let's get closer to the spaceship example and allow the ball to turn the acceleration off and on, and even reverse it. You can use the cursor keys for this. You know how to listen for keyboard events from Chapter 2, and you can find the key that caused that event by checking the **keyCode** property of the event object that gets passed to the event handler. This is a numeric value that corresponds to the particular key being pressed. For now, we are concerned about the left cursor key (**keyCode** value 37) and the right cursor key (**keyCode** value 39), and use these to change the acceleration. Here's the code (**07-acceleration-2.html**):

```
<!doctype html>
<html>
 <head>
  <meta charset="utf-8">
  <title>Acceleration 2</title>
  <link rel="stylesheet" href="style.css">
 </head>
 <body>
  <canvas id="canvas" width="400" height="400"></canvas>
  <script src="utils.js"></script>
  <script src="ball.js"></script>
  <script>
```

```
window.onload = function () {
  var canvas = document.getElementById('canvas'),
      context = canvas.getContext('2d'),
      ball = new Ball(),
      vx = 0,
      ax = 0;

  ball.x = canvas.width / 2;
  ball.y = canvas.height / 2;

  window.addEventListener('keydown', function (event) {
    if (event.keyCode === 37) {        //left
      ax = -0.1;
    } else if (event.keyCode === 39) { //right
      ax = 0.1;
    }
  }, false);

  window.addEventListener('keyup', function () {
    ax = 0;
  }, false);

  (function drawFrame () {
    window.requestAnimationFrame(drawFrame, canvas);
    context.clearRect(0, 0, canvas.width, canvas.height);

    vx += ax;
    ball.x += vx;
    ball.draw(context);
  }());
};
</script>
</body>
</html>
```

In this example, you simply check whether either the left or right cursor key is down. If the left cursor key is down, you set ax to a negative value. If the right cursor key is down, make it positive. If neither is down, set it to zero. In the drawFrame function, the velocity is added to the position just like before.

Test the example. You see that you don't have complete control over the speed of the object. You can't stop it on a dime, so to speak. You can only slow it down to the point it stops. And if you slow it down too much, it starts going in the opposite direction. See whether you can stop it before it hits the edge of the canvas element.

I'm sure some game ideas are already popping into your head. Hold on to them because you're about to expand your mastery of this technique many times over.

Acceleration on two axes

As with velocity, you can have acceleration on the x axis and y axis at the same time. You set up an acceleration value for each axis (we usually use the variable names ax and ay), add those to vx and vy, and finally add vx and vy to the x and y properties.

119

It's easy to adapt the previous example to work with the y axis as well. You need to add the following:

- The **ay** and **vy** variables

- Checks for the up and down cursor keys

- The right acceleration to the right velocity

- Velocity to the corresponding axis position

Here's the code (08-acceleration-3.html):

```
<!doctype html>
<html>
 <head>
  <meta charset="utf-8">
  <title>Acceleration 3</title>
  <link rel="stylesheet" href="style.css">
 </head>
 <body>
  <canvas id="canvas" width="400" height="400"></canvas>
  <script src="utils.js"></script>
  <script src="ball.js"></script>
  <script>
  window.onload = function () {
    var canvas = document.getElementById('canvas'),
        context = canvas.getContext('2d'),
        ball = new Ball(),
        vx = 0,
        vy = 0,
        ax = 0,
        ay = 0;

    ball.x = canvas.width / 2;
    ball.y = canvas.height / 2;

    window.addEventListener('keydown', function (event) {
      switch (event.keyCode) {
      case 37:        //left
        ax = -0.1;
        break;
      case 39:        //right
        ax = 0.1;
        break;
      case 38:        //up
        ay = -0.1;
        break;
      case 40:        //down
        ay = 0.1;
        break;
      }
    }, false);

    window.addEventListener('keyup', function () {
```

```
    ax = 0;
    ay = 0;
  }, false);

  (function drawFrame () {
    window.requestAnimationFrame(drawFrame, canvas);
    context.clearRect(0, 0, canvas.width, canvas.height);

    vx += ax;
    vy += ay;
    ball.x += vx;
    ball.y += vy;
    ball.draw(context);
  }());
};
</script>
</body>
</html>
```

Notice that we moved the left/right/up/down checks into a `switch` statement, because all of the `if` statements were too much.

Play around with this one for a while. You see that you can now navigate all over the canvas. Try to get the object moving, say, left to right, and then press the up key. Note that the x velocity is not affected at all. The object keeps moving on the x axis at the same rate. You added some y velocity into the picture. This is equivalent to the spaceship turning 90 degrees and firing the rockets.

Gravity as acceleration

So far, we've been talking about acceleration in terms of a force applied to an object by the object itself, such as a car engine or a rocket. That's certainly valid, but there's another aspect to acceleration. It happens that any force that acts to change the velocity of an object uses the principle of acceleration. This includes such things as gravity, magnetism, springs, rubber bands, and so on.

You can look at gravity in a couple of ways. From the wide-angle perspective of the solar system, gravity is an attraction between two bodies. The distance and angle between those two bodies must be taken into account to figure the actual acceleration on each body.

The other way to look at gravity is from a close-up viewpoint, here on earth, or very near it. In our everyday existence, gravity does not noticeably change depending on our distance from the earth. Although technically speaking, the force of gravity is slightly less when you fly in a plane or up on a mountain, it's nothing you notice. So, when simulating gravity on this level, you can define it as a set value, as you saw in the earlier examples with the acceleration variables.

Also, because the earth is so large and we are so small, it's easy to ignore any actual direction of acceleration and just say that the direction is "down." In other words, no matter where your object is, you can safely define gravity as acceleration on the y axis alone.

To put it into code, all you need to do is define a value for the force of gravity and add it to the **vy** on each frame. Generally speaking, a fraction works well, something like 0.1 or below. Much more than that, and things "feel" too heavy. With smaller values, things seem to float like feathers. Of course, you can always use these effects to your advantage—for example, to create simulations of different planets with varying gravities.

This next example adds gravity. The full code for this is in 09-gravity.html, but we won't list it all out. It has only a few differences from 08-acceleration-3.html. In addition to the document name being changed, we added one variable to the list of variables described at the beginning of the script:

```
var gravity = 0.02;
```

And added one line to the drawFrame function:

```
(function drawFrame () {
  window.requestAnimationFrame(drawFrame, canvas);
  context.clearRect(0, 0, canvas.width, canvas.height);

  vx += ax;
  vy += ay;
  vy += gravity;
  ball.x += vx;
  ball.y += vy;
  ball.draw(context);
}());
```

We made the gravity value low so the ball doesn't go off the screen too quickly, and you can still control it with the keys. What you created are all the physics of the old *Lunar Lander* game. Add in some better graphics and a little collision detection, and you have yourself a hit! (We help you with the latter point; graphics are up to you.)

Notice that first you add the acceleration from the key presses to the **vx** and **vy**, and then you add the gravity to the **vy**. Dealing with complex systems of multiple forces winds up not being that complex. You calculate the acceleration of each force and tack it onto the velocity. No complex averaging or factoring happens. Each force just gets added on. When you've handled all the forces, you add the velocity to the position. Here, you use only a couple of forces. Later in the book, you calculate many different forces acting on a single object.

This goes back to vector addition. If you start off with the original velocity as a vector, each acceleration, gravity, or force is an additional vector tacked on to that velocity. When you've added all of them on, draw a line from the beginning to the end and you have your resulting velocity. You find it's the same as if you added on the x and y components of each force.

Now imagine that your object is a hot air balloon. You probably want to add a force called *lift*. This is another acceleration on the y axis. This time, however, it's negative, or in the "up" direction. Now, you have three forces acting on the object: the key force, gravity, and lift. If you think about it, or try it out, you see that the lift force needs to be slightly stronger than the gravity force in order for the balloon to rise. This is logical—if they were exactly equal, they would cancel each other out, and you'd be back to square one, with only the key force having any effect.

Another one to try is creating some wind. Obviously, this is a force on the x axis. Depending on which direction the wind is blowing, it can be a positive or negative force, or as you now know, a 0- or 180-degree direction.

Angular acceleration

As mentioned, acceleration has a value—the force—and a direction, just like velocity. And like velocity, if you start with those two factors, you need to break them down into the component x and y forces. Now, if you are paying attention, you know that the way to do that is by using `Math.cos` and `Math.sin`. Here's how that looks:

```
var force = 10,
    angle = 45, //degrees. Need to convert!
    ax = Math.cos(angle * Math.PI / 180) * force,
    ay = Math.sin(angle * Math.PI / 180) * force;
```

Now that you have acceleration for each axis, you can update the velocity on each axis, and from that, update the object's position.

Let's resurrect the mouse follower example from earlier in the chapter and make it work with acceleration instead of just plain velocity. Because that example used the `Arrow` class, find the `arrow.js` file to include in this exercise. Remember that in the earlier incarnation, you took the angle from the arrow to the mouse and used that to determine **vx** and **vy**. This time, you use the same calculations, but employ them to determine **ax** and **ay** instead. Then you add the acceleration values to the velocity values and the velocity values to the **x** and **y** properties. Here's the code (`10-follow-mouse-2.html`):

```
<!doctype html>
<html>
 <head>
  <meta charset="utf-8">
  <title>Follow Mouse 2</title>
  <link rel="stylesheet" href="style.css">
 </head>
 <body>
  <canvas id="canvas" width="400" height="400"></canvas>
  <script src="utils.js"></script>
  <script src="arrow.js"></script>
  <script>
  window.onload = function () {
    var canvas = document.getElementById('canvas'),
        context = canvas.getContext('2d'),
        mouse = utils.captureMouse(canvas),
        arrow = new Arrow(),
        vx = 0,
        vy = 0,
        force = 0.05;

    (function drawFrame () {
      window.requestAnimationFrame(drawFrame, canvas);
      context.clearRect(0, 0, canvas.width, canvas.height);

      var dx = mouse.x - arrow.x,
          dy = mouse.y - arrow.y,
          angle = Math.atan2(dy, dx), //radians
          ax = Math.cos(angle) * force,
          ay = Math.sin(angle) * force;
```

```
        arrow.rotation = angle;
        vx += ax;
        vy += ay;
        arrow.x += vx;
        arrow.y += vy;
        arrow.draw(context);
      }());
    };
    </script>
  </body>
</html>
```

Notice that we also change the variable speed into force and make it much smaller. Because acceleration is additive, you want to start with small amounts because it builds up quickly. Also, now vx and vy are declared at the top of the script; earlier, they were calculated newly on each frame, but now you need to keep track of them and add or subtract from their value each time. Of course, you can do away with the ax and ay variables here altogether and just add the result of the sine and cosine lines directly to the velocities. Here, they are separated for clarity.

Run the example and you see the accelerating arrow swinging around a moving cursor and pointing toward the mouse position the entire time. But look back to the first motion example you did at the beginning of the chapter, and see just how far you've come. By learning just a couple of basic principles, you've now created something a million times more fluid and dynamic—something that almost feels alive. And you're not even at the end of the chapter yet!

Let's pull everything together and see how much further you can go with it.

A spaceship

We've been talking a lot about spaceships travelling from here to there. Well, with the ground you've covered so far, you should be able to put together a reasonable spaceship simulation.

Here's the plan. The spaceship will be a class of its own that takes care of drawing itself, much like the Arrow or Ball classes you've been using. You can use the left and right keys to rotate it left and right. The up key will act to fire the rocket. Of course, the rocket is in the back of the ship and fires straight back. Thus, the force that the rocket applies will cause acceleration in the direction the ship is facing at that time. Actually, what you're going to make is like the ship in the old game *Asteroids,* but without the actual asteroids.

First, you need a ship class. Its draw method uses a few lines of canvas drawing API code to render four short, white lines, as an homage to the original that we are copying. Save the following code in the file ship.js to import into the next example:

```
function Ship () {
  this.x = 0;
  this.y = 0;
  this.width = 25;
  this.height = 20;
  this.rotation = 0;
  this.showFlame = false;
```

```
}

Ship.prototype.draw = function (context) {
  context.save();
  context.translate(this.x, this.y);
  context.rotate(this.rotation);
  context.lineWidth = 1;
  context.strokeStyle = "#ffffff";
  context.beginPath();
  context.moveTo(10, 0);
  context.lineTo(-10, 10);
  context.lineTo(-5, 0);
  context.lineTo(-10, -10);
  context.lineTo(10, 0);
  context.stroke();
  if (this.showFlame) {
    context.beginPath();
    context.moveTo(-7.5, -5);
    context.lineTo(-15, 0);
    context.lineTo(-7.5, 5);
    context.stroke();
  }
  context.restore();
};
```

The **draw** method references the ship's property **showFlame**, which is a true or false value. This way, you can draw the ship with or without a flame showing. This is useful to show that the engines are firing. You can see how it looks with and without the flame in Figures 5-8 and 5-9.

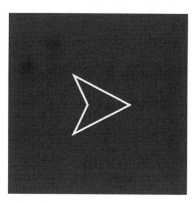

Figure 5-8. The future of space travel.

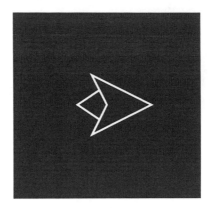

Figure 5-9. All systems go.

Ship controls

With the ship now built, let's get its controls working. As we mentioned, it has three controls: turn left, turn right, and fire rocket, mapped to the left, right, and up keys, respectively. The basic structure of this example is similar to 08-acceleration-3.html, listed earlier in the chapter, with handlers for the keydown and keyup events and a switch statement to handle the keys that were pressed. Because we're drawing a white ship in outer space, we need to change the canvas element background color to black—so we can see it. We can do this by adding a CSS style to the document header. First, here's the code for the complete file, then we'll step through it (example 11-ship-sim.html):

```
<!doctype html>
<html>
 <head>
  <meta charset="utf-8">
  <title>Ship Sim</title>
  <link rel="stylesheet" href="style.css">
  <style>
  #canvas {
    background-color: #000000;
  }
  </style>
 </head>
 <body>
  <canvas id="canvas" width="400" height="400"></canvas>
  <script src="utils.js"></script>
  <script src="ship.js"></script>
  <script>
  window.onload = function () {
    var canvas = document.getElementById('canvas'),
        context = canvas.getContext('2d'),
        ship = new Ship(),
        vr = 0,
        vx = 0,
        vy = 0,
```

```
      thrust = 0;

   ship.x = canvas.width / 2;
   ship.y = canvas.height / 2;

   window.addEventListener('keydown', function (event) {
     switch (event.keyCode) {
     case 37:      //left
       vr = -3;
       break;
     case 39:      //right
       vr = 3;
       break;
     case 38:      //up
       thrust = 0.05;
       ship.showFlame = true;
       break;
     }
   }, false);

   window.addEventListener('keyup', function () {
     vr = 0;
     thrust = 0;
     ship.showFlame = false;
   }, false);

   (function drawFrame () {
     window.requestAnimationFrame(drawFrame, canvas);
     context.clearRect(0, 0, canvas.width, canvas.height);

     ship.rotation += vr * Math.PI / 180;
     var angle = ship.rotation, //in radians
         ax = Math.cos(angle) * thrust,
         ay = Math.sin(angle) * thrust;
     vx += ax;
     vy += ay;
     ship.x += vx;
     ship.y += vy;
     ship.draw(context);
   }());
 };
 </script>
 </body>
</html>
```

First you define **vr**, rotational velocity, or how fast the ship is going to turn when you tell it to turn. It's set to zero to start, which means the ship won't turn at all:

`var vr = 0;`

But in the **keydown** event listener, if the **switch** statement finds that the left or right cursor keys are pressed, it sets **vr** to -3 or 3, respectively:

```
case 37:    //left
  vr = -3;
  break;
case 39:    //right
  vr = 3;
  break;
```

Then, in the `drawFrame` function, you add `vr` to the ship's current rotation, turning the ship one way or the other. When a key is released, reset `vr` to zero. That takes care of rotation, now let's look at thrust.

You have your spaceship there, and you aimed it where you want it to go—3, 2, 1, blastoff! So, how do you get this thing to go somewhere? Well, it's pretty much just the opposite of what you just did in the revised mouse follower example. In that example, you calculate an angle and then figure out rotation and acceleration based on that. Here, you start with the rotation and work backward to find the angle and then the force on x and y

Declare a thrust variable to keep track of how much force is applied at any given time. Obviously, acceleration is going to happen only if the rocket is fired, so this starts out as zero:

```
var thrust = 0;
```

Then the `switch` statement comes back into play. If the up cursor key is held down, set `thrust` to a small value, say 0.05. This is also where you want to visually indicate that some thrust is applied, by drawing the flame on the ship:

```
case 38:    //up
  thrust = 0.05;
  ship.showFlame = true;
  break;
```

Again, when a key is released, set thrust back to zero, and kill the flame.

```
window.addEventListener('keyup', function () {
  vr = 0;
  thrust = 0;
  ship.showFlame = false;
}, false);
```

Now, when you get down to the `drawFrame` function, you know the rotation and you know the force being applied, if any. Convert rotation to radians and use sine and cosine, along with the `thrust` variable, to find the acceleration on each axis:

```
(function drawFrame () {
  window.requestAnimationFrame(drawFrame, canvas);
  context.clearRect(0, 0, canvas.width, canvas.height);

  ship.rotation += vr * Math.PI / 180;
  var angle = ship.rotation, //in radians
      ax = Math.cos(angle) * thrust,
      ay = Math.sin(angle) * thrust;

  vx += ax;
```

```
  vy += ay;
  ship.x += vx;
  ship.y += vy;
  ship.draw(context);
}());
```

Test it and fly your ship around. It's pretty amazing just how easily you can make some complex motion like that.

Important formulas in this chapter

Now you have a few more tools for your toolbox, here they are:

Convert angular velocity to x, y velocity

```
vx = speed * Math.cos(angle);
vy = speed * Math.sin(angle);
```

Convert angular acceleration (any force acting on an object) to x, y acceleration

```
ax = force * Math.cos(angle);
ay = force * Math.sin(angle);
```

Add acceleration to velocity

```
vx += ax;
vy += ay;
```

Add velocity to position

```
object.x += vx;
object.y += vy;
```

Summary

This chapter covered basic velocity and acceleration, the two factors that make up the vast majority of your programmed animations. You learned about vectors and vector addition. You saw how to accomplish velocity on a single axis, on two axes, and on an angle by converting it to its x and y components. And you learned about acceleration—how it relates to velocity and how to apply it to a single axis, two axes, or an angle.

The biggest thing to take from this chapter is a basic understanding of the application of acceleration and velocity, as described in the following steps:

- Convert existing angular velocity to component x, y velocities.

- Convert angular acceleration to component x, y acceleration.

- Add the acceleration on each axis to the velocity on that axis.

- Add the velocity on each axis to the position on that axis.

In the next chapter, you build on these concepts, adding some environmental interaction with bouncing and friction.

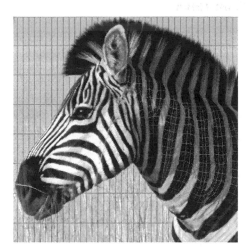

Chapter 6

Boundaries and Friction

What we'll cover in this chapter:

- Environmental boundaries
- Friction

You covered a lot of ground in the preceding chapters. You can create graphics with the canvas drawing API and use all kinds of forces to move them around the screen. However, you've probably run into a small annoyance with many of the examples: If an object moves off the screen, it's gone. Sometimes, you have no way of knowing how to get it back and your only option is to reload the web page.

In most real-world scenarios, some *boundaries* exist, usually the ground beneath you, and sometimes walls with a ceiling. Unless you're making a space simulator, you want some environmental barriers to keep your objects in view. And if your scene does take place in space, you need a way to keep your main objects in view.

Another annoyance with the examples so far is the animation environment fails to have any effect on the object as it moves. The object starts moving, and it keeps on going in the direction it's headed at the same speed, until you apply some other force. Actually, this isn't a bug at all, but the way the universe works. *Inertia* is the tendency of an object in motion to stay in motion unless acted on by another force. Or from a programming perspective, the object's velocity won't change unless something changes it. One thing in the physical world that changes an object's velocity is some sort of *friction*, even if only the friction of air. So, although you successfully simulated an object moving in a vacuum, you might want to create a scene more like your everyday environment.

This chapter covers both of these issues: First, you learn how to add boundaries to contain your objects, and then how to apply friction to these objects.

Environmental boundaries

With any activity you're involved in—whether it's playing a sport, working at your job, building a house, etc.—there's a space for that activity. This enables you to focus your attention on what happens in this area and ignore, at least temporarily, events that take place outside this area.

If one of the objects in your zone of interest moves outside that space, you have a choice to make: move the object back into the zone, or stop paying attention to the it. Another option is to follow the object, or move the space so that it continues to enclose the object, even though it is moving. When programming animations, these choices are not much different.

In your canvas animations, you set up a space for your objects. Generally, this is the whole canvas element, but the area can be some portion of the canvas, or even a space that is larger than the canvas. Because the objects are moving, there's a good chance that they will eventually leave that space. When they leave, you can forget about them, move them back into the area, or follow them. In this chapter, we cover strategies for the first two of these approaches. First, though, let's determine where the boundaries are and how to specify them.

Setting boundaries

In most cases, a simple rectangle works as a boundary. Let's start with the easiest example, the boundaries based on the size of the canvas. As in the examples so far, we access the HTML canvas element using the DOM interface, specifying the element `id`, and then assign it to a variable:

```
var canvas = document.getElementById('canvas');
```

The `top` and `left` boundaries of the animation are zero, and the `right` and `bottom` boundaries are `canvas.width` and `canvas.height`. You can store these in variables, like so:

```
var left = 0,
    top = 0,
    right = canvas.width,
    bottom = canvas.height;
```

If you store the dimensions in variables like this, realize that their values will not change if the size of the canvas element changes later. Use this if you have a fixed area for your boundaries. If you use the full dimensions of the element, you can refer directly to the `canvas.width` and `canvas.height` properties in your code.

Just because these examples use the full canvas area doesn't mean that you have to. For example, you can make a "room" that an object stays within, setting up boundaries like the following: `top = 100`, `bottom = 300`, `left = 50`, `right = 400`.

With the boundaries in place, you can check all the moving objects you're tracking to see whether they're still within this space. You can do this with a couple of `if-else` statements, and here is a simplified version of what that looks like:

```
if (ball.x > canvas.width) {
  // do something
} else if (ball.x < 0) {
```

```
  // do something
}
if (ball.y > canvas.height) {
  // do something
} else if (ball.y < 0) {
  // do something
}
```

Stepping through these boundary checks, if the ball's **x** position is greater than the right edge, or `canvas.width`, then it is too far to the right. There's no way it can also be past the left edge going the other way, which is 0—so you don't need to check that. You need to check the left position only in the case that the first `if` fails. Do the same for the top and bottom by checking the ball's **y** position against the `canvas.height`. However, it is possible for the object to be out of bounds on the x and y axis at the same time, so keep those two checks separate.

But what are you supposed to do when the object goes out of bounds? You learn about these four options:

- Remove it.

- Bring it back into play as if it were a brand-new object (regeneration).

- Wrap it back onto the screen, as if it were the same object reappearing at a different location.

- Have it bounce back into the area.

Let's start with simple removal.

Removing objects

Removing the object once it goes out of bounds is especially useful if you have objects being continually generated. The ones you remove are replaced by new ones coming in, so you won't end up with an empty canvas. Also, you won't wind up with too many objects being moved around, which would eventually slow down the browser.

With many moving objects, you should store their references in an array, and then iterate through the array to move each one. To remove one of these objects from the array, you use the `Array.splice` method. To remove an object, knowing its position and what the boundaries are, you can use something like this for your `if` statement:

```
if (ball.x > canvas.width ||
    ball.x < 0 ||
    ball.y > canvas.height ||
    ball.y < 0) {
  balls.splice(balls.indexOf(ball), 1);
}
```

The || symbol means "OR," so you're essentially saying: "If the object is off to the right, OR the object is off to the left, OR it is off to the top OR the bottom, remove it from the array." This technique is usually fine for most cases of removal, because it doesn't matter where the object went out of bounds—just that it did. But in other cases, you might want to respond differently if the object hit a particular boundary, such as the left wall as opposed to the right wall. For that, you need to use separate if statements, and you see an example of that when screen wrapping, coming up shortly.

But there is a small problem that may cause things to look wrong. Take a look at Figure 6-1.

Figure 6-1. This ball isn't fully off the canvas, but it will be removed.

In Figure 6-1, you can see that the ball's position, as determined by its x and y coordinate in the center, is past the right edge of the screen, so it will be removed. If the ball is moving fast enough, you might not notice. But if it's moving slowly—like a pixel per frame—it will ease off the edge of the canvas. When it gets halfway, it will vanish from the screen and ruin the illusion.

To fix this, the ball should be all the way out of the area before removing it. To do this, you must take the object's width into account. And because the position is in the center of a circle, you need to worry about half of its width, which is stored in the **radius** property defined in our **Ball** class. The if statement needs to become a bit more complex, so it will change to something like this:

```
if (ball.x - ball.radius > canvas.width ||
    ball.x + ball.radius < 0 ||
    ball.y - ball.radius > canvas.height ||
    ball.y + ball.radius < 0) {
  balls.splice(balls.indexOf(ball), 1);
}
```

The changes are demonstrated in Figure 6-2.

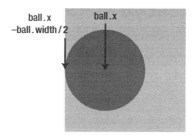

Figure 6-2. This ball is completely off the canvas and can be safely removed.

Although this particular example uses a ball, or round object, the same boundary check should work for any shape, as long as the position coordinate of the object is in the center.

Let's try it out. In the next example, use the **Ball** class we used in the Chapter 5, with a small addition. Add **vx** and **vy** properties to it, so that each ball keeps track of its own velocity. Here it is in its entirety:

```
function Ball (radius, color) {
  if (radius === undefined) { radius = 40; }
  if (color === undefined) { color = "#ff0000"; }
  this.x = 0;
  this.y = 0;
  this.radius = radius;
  this.vx = 0;
  this.vy = 0;
  this.rotation = 0;
  this.scaleX = 1;
  this.scaleY = 1;
  this.color = utils.parseColor(color);
  this.lineWidth = 1;
}

Ball.prototype.draw = function (context) {
  context.save();
  context.translate(this.x, this.y);
  context.rotate(this.rotation);
  context.scale(this.scaleX, this.scaleY);
  context.lineWidth = this.lineWidth;
  context.fillStyle = this.color;
  context.beginPath();
  context.arc(0, 0, this.radius, 0, (Math.PI * 2), true);
  context.closePath();
  context.fill();
  if (this.lineWidth > 0) {
    context.stroke();
  }
  context.restore();
};
```

The following example, 01-removal.html, sets up a number of these balls and removes them when they move off the canvas:

```
<!doctype html>
<html>
 <head>
  <meta charset="utf-8">
  <title>Removal</title>
  <link rel="stylesheet" href="style.css">
 </head>
 <body>
  <canvas id="canvas" width="400" height="400"></canvas>
  <textarea id="log"></textarea>
  <script src="utils.js"></script>
  <script src="ball.js"></script>
  <script>
  window.onload = function () {
    var canvas = document.getElementById('canvas'),
```

```
            context = canvas.getContext('2d'),
            log = document.getElementById('log'),
            balls = [],
            numBalls = 10;

        for (var ball, i = 0; i < numBalls; i++) {
          ball = new Ball(20);
          ball.id = "ball" + i;
          ball.x  = Math.random() * canvas.width;
          ball.y  = Math.random() * canvas.height;
          ball.vx = Math.random() * 2 - 1;
          ball.vy = Math.random() * 2 - 1;
          balls.push(ball);
        }

        function draw (ball, pos) {
          ball.x += ball.vx;
          ball.y += ball.vy;
          if (ball.x - ball.radius > canvas.width ||
              ball.x + ball.radius < 0 ||
              ball.y - ball.radius > canvas.height ||
              ball.y + ball.radius < 0) {
            balls.splice(pos, 1); //remove ball from array
            if (balls.length > 0) {
              log.value = "Removed " + ball.id;
            } else {
              log.value = "All gone!";
            }
          }
          ball.draw(context);
        }

        (function drawFrame () {
          window.requestAnimationFrame(drawFrame, canvas);
          context.clearRect(0, 0, canvas.width, canvas.height);

          var i = balls.length;
          while (i--) {
            draw(balls[i], i);
          }
        }());
      };
    </script>
  </body>
</html>
```

This should be easy to follow. First, create 10 object instances of **Ball**, randomly placing them on the canvas, assigning them random x and y velocities, and pushing them into an array.

The **drawFrame** function is our typical animation loop that clears our canvas, iterates over each ball in the array, and passes it to the **draw** function. This function applies the ball's velocity to move it around, checks the boundaries, and removes any out-of-bounds balls from the array. The parameters to **Array.splice** are the index position to start removing elements at, and the amount of elements to remove. In this example, we remove only one element: the one at the current index. When you test this, you won't be aware of their removal—which is a good thing—but you can be confident the balls are not lingering around outside the canvas.

Notice that the `while` loop in this example is a little different from previous examples:

```
var i = balls.length;
while (i--) {
  draw(balls[i], i);
}
```

This causes the `while` loop to iterate backward through the array instead of forward. This is necessary because, when you `splice` the array, the indexing will change. When you increment `i`, you will skip over one of the elements. Going backward handles this, as long as nothing is added to the beginning of the array during iteration.

Finally, after splicing an element out of the array, we check to see whether the array length is zero, to display a message that all the balls have been removed from the animation.

Regenerating objects

The next method for handling an object that leaves the defined boundaries is to regenerate it, or more precisely, to reposition it. The basic idea is that when an object has moved off the canvas and is no longer necessary, you can place it at a new position as if it were a brand-new object. This provides you with a steady stream of objects without the worry about having too many objects slowing down the browser, because there will be a set number.

This technique is useful for creating fountains and other particle effects, where you have a stream of objects spraying constantly. The particles go off the canvas and are reintroduced at the source point of the stream.

The mechanics of regeneration are similar to removal: You wait until the object is out of bounds, but instead of removing it, you move it.

Let's dive right in by making a fountain. For the fountain particles, use the same `Ball` class, but make them very small by setting their radius of just 2 pixels across, and give each a random color. The source of the fountain will be a point at the bottom-center of the canvas element. Every particle will originate there, and when they move off the canvas, they'll be repositioned there. Also, each particle starts with a random negative y velocity and a (small) random x velocity. The particles shoot upward, moving slightly to the left or the right, and also react to gravity. When a particle regenerates, its position and velocity will be reset. Here's the document `02-fountain.html`:

```
<!doctype html>
<html>
 <head>
  <meta charset="utf-8">
  <title>Fountain</title>
  <link rel="stylesheet" href="style.css">
 </head>
 <body>
```

```
<canvas id="canvas" width="400" height="400"></canvas>
<script src="utils.js"></script>
<script src="ball.js"></script>
<script>
window.onload = function () {
  var canvas = document.getElementById('canvas'),
      context = canvas.getContext('2d'),
      balls = [],
      numBalls = 80,
      gravity = 0.5;

  for (var ball, i = 0; i < numBalls; i++) {
    ball = new Ball(2, Math.random() * 0xffffff);
    ball.x  = canvas.width / 2;
    ball.y  = canvas.height;
    ball.vx = Math.random() * 2 - 1;
    ball.vy = Math.random() * -10 - 10;
    balls.push(ball);
  }

  function draw (ball) {
    ball.vy += gravity;
    ball.x += ball.vx;
    ball.y += ball.vy;
    if (ball.x - ball.radius > canvas.width ||
        ball.x + ball.radius < 0 ||
        ball.y - ball.radius > canvas.height ||
        ball.y + ball.radius < 0) {
      ball.x = canvas.width / 2;
      ball.y = canvas.height;
      ball.vx = Math.random() * 2 - 1;
      ball.vy = Math.random() * -10 - 10;
    }
    ball.draw(context);
  }

  (function drawFrame () {
    window.requestAnimationFrame(drawFrame, canvas);
    context.clearRect(0, 0, canvas.width, canvas.height);

    balls.forEach(draw);
  }());
};
</script>
</body>
</html>
```

You begin at the top of the script by setting all the particles at the starting point and giving them each an initial random upward velocity.

The drawFrame function loops through all the elements of the balls array, passing each ball as a parameter to the draw function. This function adds gravity to the ball's vy value, adds the velocity to the ball's position, and then checks to see whether the ball has crossed any boundaries. If it has, the ball gets placed back at the starting position and "regenerated" with a new velocity. It acts the same as a newly created particle, so your fountain will flow forever.

You should play around with this effect; it's simple but looks great. Have the fountain shoot off in different directions. Make it shoot out of a wall, or even the ceiling. Change the random factors to make the fountain wider or narrower, or one that shoots higher or lower. Try adding some wind into the mix (hint: make a **wind** variable and add it to vx).

Screen wrapping

The next common way to handle objects going out of bounds is to use screen wrapping. The concept is simple: If an object moves off the left side of the screen, it then reappears on the right. If it moves off the right, it comes back on the left. If it moves off the top, it comes back on the bottom. You get the idea.

Screen wrapping is similar to regeneration, in that you put the object back on the screen at a different location. But in regeneration, you generally return all objects to the same location, making them look like brand-new objects. In wrapping, you are usually trying to maintain the idea that this is the same object; that it has just gone out the back door and in the front, so to speak. Thus, you generally don't change velocity during a screen wrap.

This, again, is reminiscent of that classic game, *Asteroids*. Recall from Chapter 5 that this was one of the problems with the spaceship animation: The ship would fly off the canvas, and it was sometimes impossible to figure out where it was and how to get it back. With screen wrapping, the ship is never more than a pixel from the edge of the screen.

Let's rebuild the spaceship example and add this behavior. Here's the document you'll want to use (03-ship-sim-2.html), with the new code added in bold:

```
<!doctype html>
<html>
 <head>
  <meta charset="utf-8">
  <title>Ship Sim 2</title>
  <link rel="stylesheet" href="style.css">
  <style>
  #canvas {
    background-color: #000000;
  }
  </style>
 </head>
 <body>
  <canvas id="canvas" width="400" height="400"></canvas>
  <script src="utils.js"></script>
  <script src="ship.js"></script>
  <script>
  window.onload = function () {
    var canvas = document.getElementById('canvas'),
        context = canvas.getContext('2d'),
        ship = new Ship(),
        vr = 0,
        vx = 0,
```

```
      vy = 0,
      thrust = 0;

  ship.x = canvas.width / 2;
  ship.y = canvas.height / 2;

  window.addEventListener('keydown', function (event) {
    switch (event.keyCode) {
    case 37:       //left
      vr = -3;
      break;
    case 39:       //right
      vr = 3;
      break;
    case 38:       //up
      thrust = 0.05;
      ship.showFlame = true;
      break;
    }
  });

  window.addEventListener('keyup', function () {
    vr = 0;
    thrust = 0;
    ship.showFlame = false;
  });

  (function drawFrame () {
    window.requestAnimationFrame(drawFrame, canvas);
    context.clearRect(0, 0, canvas.width, canvas.height);

    ship.rotation += vr * Math.PI / 180;
    var angle = ship.rotation, //in radians
        ax = Math.cos(angle) * thrust,
        ay = Math.sin(angle) * thrust,
        left = 0,
        right = canvas.width,
        top = 0,
        bottom = canvas.height;

    vx += ax;
    vy += ay;
    ship.x += vx;
    ship.y += vy;

    //screen wrapping
    if (ship.x - ship.width / 2 > right) {
      ship.x = left - ship.width / 2;
    } else if (ship.x + ship.width / 2 < left) {
      ship.x = right + ship.width / 2;
    }
    if (ship.y - ship.height / 2 > bottom) {
      ship.y = top - ship.height / 2;
```

```
    } else if (ship.y < top - ship.height / 2) {
      ship.y = bottom + ship.height / 2;
    }
    ship.draw(context);
  }());
};
</script>
</body>
</html>
```

This uses the `Ship` class from Chapter 5, so make sure you include that script in your document. As you can see, this updated script adds the boundary definitions and the checks for them. We're back to using separate `if` and `else` statements, because the actions are different for each circumstance.

Bouncing

And now we arrive at perhaps the most common, and possibly the most complex of bounds handling methods. But not to worry—it's not much more complicated than screen wrapping.

The strategy with bouncing is to detect when the object has gone off screen. Only this time, leave it where it is and only change its velocity. The rules are simple: If the object went off the left or right edge, reverse its x velocity. If it went off the top or bottom, reverse its y velocity. Reversing an axis velocity is simple: Multiply the value by -1. If the velocity is 5, it becomes -5; if it's -13, it becomes 13. The code is even simpler:

```
vx *= -1;
vy *= -1;
```

There are a few more differences from screen wrapping. First, in wrapping, you let the object move completely off the canvas before you reposition it. You do that by taking its position and adding or subtracting half its width. For bouncing, you want to do almost exactly the opposite. Don't wait until the object is entirely off the canvas before you make it bounce. In fact, you don't want it to be even partially out of the picture. If you throw a real ball against a real wall, you wouldn't expect to see it go partially into the wall before bouncing back. It would hit the wall, stop right there, and then bounce back. The first thing you want to know is the instant that any part of the object has gone over the edge. All you need to do is reverse the way you add the half width/height (see Figure 6-3). So, for example, instead of saying this:

```
if (ball.x - ball.radius > right) ...
```

you say this:

```
if (ball.x + ball.radius > right) ...
```

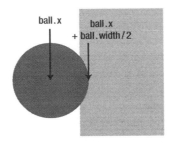

Figure 6-3. This ball is just slightly off the canvas, but it needs to bounce.

After you determine that the object has crossed at least a bit of one of the boundaries, you now reverse the velocity on that axis. But there's a little more to it than that. You must reposition the object so that it sits on the edge of the boundary. This has the obvious visual effect of making the object look more like it's hitting and bouncing, rather than sinking into the wall. But it is also a necessary step for other reasons. You find that if you don't adjust the object's position, then on the next frame, it might still be past that boundary, even after it moves. If this happens, the object will again reverse its velocity and head back *into* the wall! Then you get a situation where the object seems to be stuck halfway in and out of the wall, just sitting there and vibrating—it's not pretty.

The point where you need to place the object to have it sitting on the boundary is actually the same point you are checking in the `if` statement. You just need to restate it with a little basic algebra. Here's the full `if` statement for the x axis:

```
if (ball.x + ball.radius > right) {
  ball.x = right - ball.radius;
  vx *= -1;
} else if (ball.x - ball.radius < left) {
  ball.x = left + ball.radius;
  vx *= -1;
}
```

Figure 6-4 shows what the ball looks like after being repositioned.

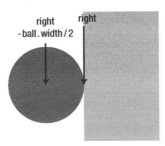

Figure 6-4. The ball has been repositioned to be exactly against the boundary.

The steps for bouncing are as follows:

- Check whether the object went past any boundary.

- If so, place it on the edge of that boundary.

- Then reverse the velocity.

That's all there is to it, so let's see it in action. The next example again uses the same `Ball` class, but scaled back up to a decent size. Here's the document (**04-bouncing-1.html**):

```
<!doctype html>
<html>
 <head>
  <meta charset="utf-8">
  <title>Bouncing 1</title>
  <link rel="stylesheet" href="style.css">
 </head>
 <body>
  <canvas id="canvas" width="400" height="400"></canvas>
  <script src="utils.js"></script>
  <script src="ball.js"></script>
  <script>
  window.onload = function () {
    var canvas = document.getElementById('canvas'),
        context = canvas.getContext('2d'),
        ball = new Ball(),
        vx = Math.random() * 10 - 5,
        vy = Math.random() * 10 - 5;

    ball.x = canvas.width / 2;
    ball.y = canvas.height / 2;

    (function drawFrame () {
      window.requestAnimationFrame(drawFrame, canvas);
      context.clearRect(0, 0, canvas.width, canvas.height);

      var left = 0,
          right = canvas.width,
          top = 0,
          bottom = canvas.height;

      ball.x += vx;
      ball.y += vy;

      if (ball.x + ball.radius > right) {
        ball.x = right - ball.radius;
        vx *= -1;
      } else if (ball.x - ball.radius < left) {
        ball.x = left + ball.radius;
        vx *= -1;
      }
      if (ball.y + ball.radius > bottom) {
        ball.y = bottom - ball.radius;
        vy *= -1;
      } else if (ball.y - ball.radius < top) {
        ball.y = top + ball.radius;
        vy *= -1;
```

```
    }
      ball.draw(context);
    }());
  };
  </script>
 </body>
</html>
```

Test this a few times to see the ball moving at different angles. Try making the velocity higher or lower.

This is one of those many areas in the book where the math and calculations are not exactly in accordance with real-world physics. If you look at Figure 6-5, you see where the ball should actually hit the wall, and also where this simulation places it.

What we are doing:

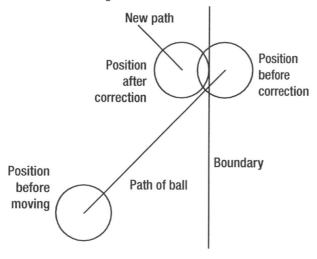

Real-world situation:

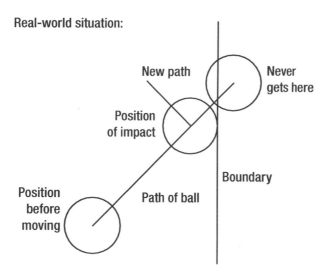

Figure 6-5. This technique isn't perfect, but is quick, easy, and close enough for most situations.

Determining the correct position takes more complex calculations. Although you are free to figure out how to do this (using the trigonometry covered in Chapter 3), you won't notice much of a difference in most situations. For almost any game or visual effect you create for the canvas element, this method will serve you just fine. However, you can add one more thing to take the realism just a notch higher.

If you hold the most rubbery, bounciest ball ever made out at arm's length and drop it, it would fall to the floor and bounce back up *almost* to where it started—never making it all the way back to your hand. This is because the ball loses a little bit of energy in the bounce. It might lose some energy in the form of sound, maybe a little heat, the floor will absorb some of the energy, and maybe the surrounding air will, too. However it works out, the important point is that the ball travels slower after the bounce than before. In other words, it loses some velocity on the axis of the bounce.

You can easily re-create this in the animation. So far, you've used -1 as the bounce factor. That means that the object bounces back with 100% of the force it hit with. To make it lose some energy, simply use a fraction of -1. As with other numeric values, it's best to define this as a variable at the top of your script and reference that in your code. Just create a variable named **bounce** and set it to something like -0.7:

```
var bounce = -0.7;
```

Then replace each instance of `-1` in the `if` statements with the variable **bounce**. Go ahead and try that, and you'll see how much more real the bounces look. Try different factors for the **bounce** variable until you get a feel for how it works.

One of the best ways to understand these concepts is to take each principle you learn and see how many other principles you can combine it with. You can check the example files at **www.apress.com** for document **05-bouncing-2.html**, which demonstrates bouncing and gravity, but you should have enough knowledge to start adding things like this on your own. Perhaps you want to try using the keyboard to add acceleration to the ball, or apply something else you've already learned.

Let's leave behind the discussion of boundaries and look at what happens between the boundaries, when your object is moving through space.

Friction

So far, you've seen two scenarios:

- The object is simply moving with whatever velocity it has until it hits a boundary.
- Either the object itself or some external force is applying acceleration to the object, changing its velocity.

With either setup, unless the object is pushed or pulled, or it hits something, it keeps moving in the same direction at the same speed. But in the real world, it doesn't happen just like that.

Here's an example, grab a piece of paper, crumple it up, and throw it as hard as you can. There's a good chance it didn't even make it across the room. Sure, gravity pulls it down (y axis), but when it left your hand, it was moving pretty fast on the x axis. And yet, very quickly, it had almost zero x velocity.

Obviously, no "negative acceleration" was pulling the paper back toward your hand, but its velocity changed. This is known as *friction, drag, resistance,* or *damping.* Although it's not technically a force, it does act that way; it changes an object's velocity. The rule is that friction reduces only the magnitude of the velocity, not the direction. In other words, friction can reduce velocity to zero, but it will never make an object turn around and move in the other direction.

So, how do you implement friction in code? There are two ways, and like most things in life, you have the right way and the easy way. The easy way is preferred in this book, but you'll see examples of both and you can make up your own mind.

Friction, the right way

Friction is subtractive of velocity, which means you have a certain value for friction, and you subtract that from your velocity. More precisely, you must subtract it from the magnitude, or speed, of the velocity; you can't just subtract the friction from the x axis and y axis separately. If you do that for an object traveling at an angle, one of the component velocities will reach zero before the other, and the object will continue moving either vertically or horizontally, which looks strange.

What you need to do is find the angular velocity in terms of speed and direction (if you don't have it already). To find the speed, take the square root of **vx** squared plus **vy** squared (yes, that's the Pythagorean Theorem, which you should recognize from Chapter 3). To find the angle, you calculate `Math.atan2(vy, vx)`, which looks like this:

```
var speed = Math.sqrt(vx * vx + vy * vy),
    angle = Math.atan2(vy, vx);
```

Then you can subtract the friction from the speed, but you want to make sure you don't send the speed into negative values, which reverses the velocity. If your friction is greater than your speed, the speed becomes zero. Here is the code for that calculation:

```
if (speed > friction) {
  speed -= friction;
} else {
  speed = 0;
}
```

At that point, you need to convert the angular velocity back into **vx** and **vy**, using sine and cosine, like so:

```
vx = Math.cos(angle) * speed;
vy = Math.sin(angle) * speed;
```

Here's how it looks all together in the document `06-friction-1.html`:

```
<!doctype html>
<html>
 <head>
  <meta charset="utf-8">
  <title>Friction 1</title>
  <link rel="stylesheet" href="style.css">
 </head>
 <body>
  <canvas id="canvas" width="400" height="400"></canvas>
  <script src="utils.js"></script>
  <script src="ball.js"></script>
  <script>
  window.onload = function () {
    var canvas = document.getElementById('canvas'),
        context = canvas.getContext('2d'),
```

```
        ball = new Ball(),
        vx = Math.random() * 10 - 5,
        vy = Math.random() * 10 - 5,
        friction = 0.1;

  ball.x = canvas.width / 2;
  ball.y = canvas.height / 2;

  (function drawFrame () {
    window.requestAnimationFrame(drawFrame, canvas);
    context.clearRect(0, 0, canvas.width, canvas.height);

    var speed = Math.sqrt(vx * vx + vy * vy),
        angle = Math.atan2(vy, vx);

    if (speed > friction) {
      speed -= friction;
    } else {
      speed = 0;
    }
    vx = Math.cos(angle) * speed;
    vy = Math.sin(angle) * speed;
    ball.x += vx;
    ball.y += vy;
    ball.draw(context);
  }());
};
</script>
</body>
</html>
```

Here, the `friction` is set to `0.1`, and the ball is given a random velocity on the x and y axes. In the `drawFrame` function, `speed` and `angle` are calculated as we described. If `speed` is less than `friction`, subtract; otherwise, `speed` equals zero. Finally, **vx** and **vy** are recalculated and added to the position.

Test this example several times to see it at different speeds and angles. That's how friction looks, and it took a dozen lines of code and four trigonometry functions to accomplish. Now you're probably thinking that it's time to look at the easy way.

Friction, the easy way

As you would expect, the easy way to simulate friction is not as accurate as the technique that was just described, but nobody will ever notice. It consists of two lines of simple multiplication. Multiply the x and y velocities by some fraction of 1. A number around 0.9 usually works quite well, but use your eye as the judge. On each frame, **vx** and **vy** become 80% or 90% of what they were on previous frame. In theory, the velocity approaches zero, but never actually reaches it. In practice, the computer only calculates such numbers to a defined precision. But long before that, the applied motion is so small that it is indiscernible.

The good news is that the velocity never becomes negative using this method, so you don't have to check for that. Also, the x and y velocities approach zero at the same rate, so there's no need to convert axis velocities to angular and back.

The only alterations to the code (which can be found in the document 07-friction-2.html) is adjusting the friction variable to 0.95 and the following changes to the drawFrame function:

```
(function drawFrame () {
  window.requestAnimationFrame(drawFrame, canvas);
  context.clearRect(0, 0, canvas.width, canvas.height);

  vx *= friction;
  vy *= friction;
  ball.x += vx;
  ball.y += vy;
  ball.draw(context);
}());
```

Now, that's certainly easier! Test this version a number of times and get a feel for it. The motion looks virtually identical to the "correct" method, but at a fraction of the calculation cost. And the average viewer won't even notice.

Because these methods continue to add the friction value to the ball's position after it has any visual effect, you can save some calculations by checking whether the number is larger than a designated minimum distance before applying the friction, like so:

```
if (Math.abs(vx) > 0.001) {
  vx *= friction;
  ball.x += vx;
}
```

Math.abs returns the absolute value of vx. The friction variable is a fairly arbitrary number (within a range) and really depends on how the animation "feels" to you. Experiment with different values to see how it affects the motion characteristics.

Friction applied

We return to our familiar spaceship simulation and apply some friction to that universe. In example 08-ship-sim-friction.html, take the file 03-ship-sim-2.html and add a friction variable:

```
var friction = 0.97;
```

Then, change the drawFrame function to the following:

```
(function drawFrame () {
  window.requestAnimationFrame(drawFrame, canvas);
  context.clearRect(0, 0, canvas.width, canvas.height);

  ship.rotation += vr * Math.PI / 180;
  var angle = ship.rotation,
      ax = Math.cos(angle) * thrust,
      ay = Math.sin(angle) * thrust,
      left = 0,
      right = canvas.width,
      top = 0,
      bottom = canvas.height;
```

```
  vx += ax;
  vy += ay;
  vx *= friction;
  vy *= friction;
  ship.x += vx;
  ship.y += vy;

  //screen wrapping
  if (ship.x - ship.width / 2 > right) {
    ship.x = left - ship.width / 2;
  } else if (ship.x + ship.width / 2 < left) {
    ship.x = right + ship.width / 2;
  }
  if (ship.y - ship.height / 2 > bottom) {
    ship.y = top - ship.height / 2;
  } else if (ship.y < top - ship.height / 2) {
    ship.y = bottom + ship.height / 2;
  }
  ship.draw(context);
}());
```

That's a different feel for just three new lines of code.

Don't forget to think outside the x, y box. Friction can be applied anywhere you have any type of velocity. Maybe you have something that rotates (with a **vr** property), applying friction to that eventually causes it to slow down and stop spinning. You can try that with the spinning arrow example from Chapter 5.

You can see how you can use this approach for all types of objects, such as a roulette wheel, an electric fan, or a propeller.

Important formulas in this chapter

Let's review the important formulas introduced in this chapter.

Remove an out-of-bounds object

```
if (object.x - object.width / 2 > right ||
    object.x + object.width / 2 < left ||
    object.y - object.height / 2 > bottom ||
    object.y + object.height / 2 < top) {
  //code to remove object
}
```

Regenerate an out-of-bounds object

```
if (object.x - object.width / 2 > right ||
    object.x + object.width / 2 < left ||
    object.y - object.height / 2 > bottom ||
    object.y + object.height / 2 < top) {
  //reset object position and velocity
}
```

Screen wrapping for an out-of-bounds object

```
if (object.x - object.width / 2 > right) {
  object.x = left - object.width / 2;
} else if (object.x + object.width / 2 < left) {
  object.x = right + object.width / 2;
} if (object.y - object.height / 2 > bottom) {
  object.y = top - object.height / 2;
} else if (object.y + object.height / 2 < top) {
  object.y = bottom + object.height / 2;
}
```

Apply friction (the correct way)

```
speed = Math.sqrt(vx * vx + vy * vy);
angle = Math.atan2(vy, vx);
if (speed > friction) {
  speed -= friction;
} else {
  speed = 0;
}
vx = Math.cos(angle) * speed;
vy = Math.sin(angle) * speed;
```

Apply friction (the easy way)

```
vx *= friction;
vy *= friction;
```

Summary

This chapter covered an object's interaction with its environment—specifically, an object's interaction with the edges of its universe and the universe itself. You learned the possible ways to handle an object that has gone off the edge of the world, including removing, regenerating, wrapping, and bouncing. And, you now know all about applying friction to objects. With these simple techniques, you can make the objects in your animations move with a great deal of realism. In the next chapter, you allow the user to interact with the objects.

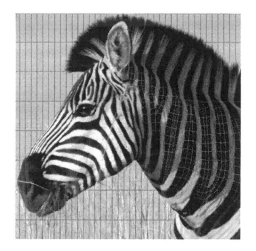

Chapter 7

User Interaction: Moving Objects Around

What we'll cover in this chapter:

- Pressing and releasing an object

- Dragging an object

- Throwing

One of the goals of these interactive animations is to create a smooth user experience, and this interaction is usually through the mouse or touch screen. Mouse and touch events were introduced in Chapter 2, but, so far, you haven't done much with them; now, you'll get some hands-on practice.

In this chapter, you take the first steps into responding to user interaction. You learn how to handle dragging, dropping, and throwing, but first, let's get started with the basics of press and release.

Pressing and releasing an object

The mouse is an effective, but simple device. It does two things, it detects motion and button clicks. The computer then uses that information to do a lot more: keeping track of the position of a mouse cursor, determining where the cursor is when the click occurs, determining how fast the mouse is moving, and figuring out when a double-click occurs. But, when you look at it in terms of events, it all comes down to clicks and movements.

You can also break clicks down into two parts: the event that occurs when the mouse button goes down and the next event when it comes up. Sometimes, those events occur almost instantaneously. Other times, the events are separated by time and motion, which is usually interpreted as a *drag*—click, move, and then release. In this chapter, you'll concentrate on those three things: the mouse button going down, the mouse button going up, and any motion that occurs in between the two.

In our animations, mouse events can be received by the canvas element only from the HTML DOM. Therefore, it is up to us to determine where the event occurred on the canvas and if it is over a visible graphic portion of an object drawn to the canvas. In Chapter 2, I showed you to keep track of the mouse position using the utility function `utils.captureMouse`. Here, we look for some additional mouse events on the canvas, and then check whether their position falls within the bounds of our objects. The mouse events that you need to know are:

- **mousedown**: This event occurs when you press a mouse button while the mouse cursor is over an HTML element. In the book examples, this is the **canvas** element.

- **mouseup**: This event occurs when you release the mouse button while over an element.

- **mousemove**: This event occurs when you move the mouse over an element.

Sometimes you might want to know what the mouse is doing regardless of what HTML element it is over. In these cases, instead of adding an event listener to the **canvas** object, you add it to the global **window** object.

Let's see if we can use mouse events in our animations. In the next example, you use the same **Ball** class from the earlier chapters, but an additional method, **Ball.getBounds**, has been added. This returns an object that represents a rectangle containing the shape of the ball on the canvas, or its *bounds*. The returned object has the properties **x**, **y**, **width**, and **height**, and it uses the ball's position and radius to calculate these. This is what the updated **ball.js** file looks like:

```
function Ball (radius, color) {
  if (radius === undefined) { radius = 40; }
  if (color === undefined) { color = "#ff0000"; }
  this.x = 0;
  this.y = 0;
  this.radius = radius;
  this.vx = 0;
  this.vy = 0;
  this.rotation = 0;
  this.scaleX = 1;
  this.scaleY = 1;
  this.color = utils.parseColor(color);
  this.lineWidth = 1;
}

Ball.prototype.draw = function (context) {
  context.save();
  context.translate(this.x, this.y);
  context.rotate(this.rotation);
  context.scale(this.scaleX, this.scaleY);
  context.lineWidth = this.lineWidth;
  context.fillStyle = this.color;
  context.beginPath();
  context.arc(0, 0, this.radius, 0, (Math.PI * 2), true);
  context.closePath();
```

```
  context.fill();
  if (this.lineWidth > 0) {
    context.stroke();
  }
  context.restore();
};

Ball.prototype.getBounds = function () {
  return {
    x: this.x - this.radius,
    y: this.y - this.radius,
    width: this.radius * 2,
    height: this.radius * 2
  };
};
```

We also add another utility function to the **utils.js** file we've been importing into our documents. **utils.containsPoint** defines three parameters. The first is an object representing a rectangle with x, y, width, and height properties—just the kind **Ball.getBounds()** returns—and the second and third arguments are x and y coordinates. The **utils.containsPoint** function determines whether the given position falls within the boundaries of the rectangle and returns **true** or **false** accordingly. Here's the simple, but useful, function we add to the **utils.js** file:

```
utils.containsPoint = function (rect, x, y) {
  return !(x < rect.x || x > rect.x + rect.width ||
           y < rect.y || y > rect.y + rect.height);
};
```

And here's a complete example using the updated **Ball** class and the **utils.containsPoint** function, document **01-mouse-events.html**:

```
<!doctype html>
<html>
 <head>
  <meta charset="utf-8">
  <title>Mouse Events</title>
  <link rel="stylesheet" href="style.css">
 </head>
 <body>
  <canvas id="canvas" width="400" height="400"></canvas>
  <textarea id="log"></textarea>
  <script src="utils.js"></script>
  <script src="ball.js"></script>
  <script>
  window.onload = function () {
    var canvas = document.getElementById('canvas'),
        context = canvas.getContext('2d'),
        mouse = utils.captureMouse(canvas),
        log = document.getElementById('log'),
        ball = new Ball();

    ball.x = canvas.width / 2;
    ball.y = canvas.height / 2;
```

```
      ball.draw(context);

      canvas.addEventListener('mousedown', function () {
        if (utils.containsPoint(ball.getBounds(), mouse.x, mouse.y)) {
          log.value = "in ball: mousedown";
        } else {
          log.value = "canvas: mousedown";
        }
      }, false);

      canvas.addEventListener('mouseup', function () {
        if (utils.containsPoint(ball.getBounds(), mouse.x, mouse.y)) {
          log.value = "in ball: mouseup";
        } else {
          log.value = "canvas: mouseup";
        }
      }, false);

      canvas.addEventListener('mousemove', function () {
        if (utils.containsPoint(ball.getBounds(), mouse.x, mouse.y)) {
          log.value = "in ball: mousemove";
        } else {
          log.value = "canvas: mousemove";
        }
      }, false);
    };
  </script>
</body>
</html>
```

This sets up listeners on the canvas element for the three mouse events we've talked about: **mousedown**, **mouseup**, and **mousemove**. After detecting a mouse event, the handler functions test whether the mouse coordinates fall within the bounds of the ball, using **Ball.getBounds** and **utils.containsPoint**, and it prints a message. Play around with this example to see exactly when and where particular mouse events occur. Here are some things to notice:

- You get the canvas events no matter where the mouse is, even if it's over the ball.

- You won't get a **mouseup** event without first getting a **mousedown** event.

Using touch events

Throughout the book examples, we use a mouse for user input because it's assumed that you are on a development machine with a keyboard and mouse that is handy. But with the proliferation of touch screen devices, it's not only possible, but quite probable, you'll need to capture touch events from the user. Although touch screens and mice are different devices, thankfully for us, capturing touch events is similar to capturing mouse events from the DOM.

The touch events most compatible with the examples in this book and their mouse event counterparts are **touchstart**, **touchend**, and **touchmove**. The **touchstart** event is fired on the contact of first touch, **touchend** when a finger leaves the surface, and **touchmove** when the finger is dragged on the surface. For more details about touch events, browse the W3C Specification at **http://www.w3.org/TR/touch-**

events/. At the time of writing, this document is still considered a work-in-progress, though it has been implemented by a number of mobile web browsers. When in doubt, test it out!

One important distinction between using a finger versus a mouse is that while a mouse cursor is always present on the screen, a finger touch is not. In Chapter 2, we created a utility function, utils.captureTouch, that tracks the touch position. The object returned by this function, also contains the property isPressed, which tests whether a touch has been detected on the surface. When we modify an example to handle touch events, we should first check that there is even a touch; otherwise, accessing the touch position might return null:

```
var touch = utils.captureTouch(canvas);

if (touch.isPressed) {
  console.log(touch.x, touch.y);
}
```

The next example, 02-touch-events.html, builds off the first example in this chapter, but it is modified to handle touch events (the new parts are in bold in the code below). For the example to work, be sure you test this in a web browser that can handle these types of events (on a touch screen device or an emulator).

In the document header, we've added a meta tag to set the viewport. This tells the browser how the content should fit on the device's screen and that the page is optimized for mobile viewing:

```
<meta name="viewport" content="width=device-width,initial-scale=1.0,user-scalable=no">
```

Here, the viewport has been set to the width of the device with an initial scale of 1. Users are also prevented from zooming the document.

```
<!doctype html>
<html>
 <head>
  <meta charset="utf-8">
  <meta name = "viewport" content="width=device-width,initial-scale=1.0,user-scalable=no">
  <title>Touch Events</title>
  <link rel="stylesheet" href="style.css">
 </head>
 <body>
  <canvas id="canvas" width="400" height="400"></canvas>
  <textarea id="log"></textarea>
  <script src="utils.js"></script>
  <script src="ball.js"></script>
  <script>
  window.onload = function () {
    var canvas = document.getElementById('canvas'),
        context = canvas.getContext('2d'),
        touch = utils.captureTouch(canvas),
        log = document.getElementById('log'),
        ball = new Ball();

    ball.x = canvas.width / 2;
    ball.y = canvas.height / 2;
    ball.draw(context);
```

```
      canvas.addEventListener('touchstart', function (event) {
        event.preventDefault();
        if (utils.containsPoint(ball.getBounds(), touch.x, touch.y)) {
          log.value = "in ball: touchstart";
        } else {
          log.value = "canvas: touchstart";
        }
      }, false);

      canvas.addEventListener('touchend', function (event) {
        event.preventDefault();
        log.value = "canvas: touchend";
      }, false);

      canvas.addEventListener('touchmove', function (event) {
        event.preventDefault();
        if (utils.containsPoint(ball.getBounds(), touch.x, touch.y)) {
          log.value = "in ball: touchmove";
        } else {
          log.value = "canvas: touchmove";
        }
      }, false);
    };
  </script>
 </body>
</html>
```

In the touch event listeners, we pass the event object to the handler function and call event.preventDefault(). This keeps the browser from continuing to process the event after the handler has been executed. It also prevents the touch event's corresponding mouse event from being delivered, which is the default behavior (though it is best not to rely on this).

Now that you understand the basics of the important interaction events, we'll move on to dragging.

Dragging an object

To drag an object around the canvas element, update the object's position to match the coordinates of the mouse cursor. The programming is straight-forward: Capture a mousedown event when the cursor is over the ball and set up a mousemove handler. This handler sets the ball's x and y coordinates to the current mouse position. Then, on the mouseup event, remove that handler.

The next example, 03-mouse-move-drag.html, should help make this clear:

```
<!doctype html>
<html>
 <head>
  <meta charset="utf-8">
  <title>Mouse Move Drag</title>
  <link rel="stylesheet" href="style.css">
 </head>
```

```
<body>
  <canvas id="canvas" width="400" height="400"></canvas>
  <script src="utils.js"></script>
  <script src="ball.js"></script>
  <script>
  window.onload = function () {
    var canvas = document.getElementById('canvas'),
        context = canvas.getContext('2d'),
        mouse = utils.captureMouse(canvas),
        ball = new Ball();

    ball.x = canvas.width / 2;
    ball.y = canvas.height / 2;

    canvas.addEventListener('mousedown', function () {
      if (utils.containsPoint(ball.getBounds(), mouse.x, mouse.y)) {
        canvas.addEventListener('mouseup', onMouseUp, false);
        canvas.addEventListener('mousemove', onMouseMove, false);
      }
    }, false);

    function onMouseUp () {
      canvas.removeEventListener('mouseup', onMouseUp, false);
      canvas.removeEventListener('mousemove', onMouseMove, false);
    }

    function onMouseMove (event) {
      ball.x = mouse.x;
      ball.y = mouse.y;
    }

    (function drawFrame () {
      window.requestAnimationFrame(drawFrame, canvas);
      context.clearRect(0, 0, canvas.width, canvas.height);

      ball.draw(context);
    }());
  };
  </script>
</body>
</html>
```

When the script is run initially, you listen for **mousedown** events only and when the mouse is over the ball. When called, this event handler adds additional listeners to the canvas element for **mouseup** and **mousemove** events. The **onMouseMove** function updates the ball's position to match the mouse coordinates. The **onMouseUp** function removes the **mouseup** and **mousemove** listeners from the canvas, because you care about these only in the dragging phase.

You might have noticed a problem with this setup. If you click the edge of the ball and drag it, you'll see that the ball suddenly jumps and centers itself on the mouse cursor. This is because you're setting the ball's position exactly equal to the mouse position. You can fix this by finding the offset of the mouse to the ball on **mousedown** and adding that to the ball's position as you drag, but that is a project left for you.

Combining dragging with motion code

Now you know pretty much everything about simple dragging and dropping on the canvas. But in the process, we've reverted back to a static object that just sits there unless you drag it. To make it interesting, let's add some velocity, acceleration, and bouncing.

You already have a nice setup for velocity, gravity, and bouncing in the **05-bouncing-2.html** example from the previous chapter, so that will be our starting point. It seems logical to simply add your drag-and-drop code to that code, so let's try it. You should end up with something like this document (**04-drag-and-move-1.html**):

```html
<!doctype html>
<html>
 <head>
  <meta charset="utf-8">
  <title>Drag and Move 1</title>
  <link rel="stylesheet" href="style.css">
 </head>
 <body>
  <canvas id="canvas" width="400" height="400"></canvas>
  <script src="utils.js"></script>
  <script src="ball.js"></script>
  <script>
  window.onload = function () {
    var canvas = document.getElementById('canvas'),
        context = canvas.getContext('2d'),
        mouse = utils.captureMouse(canvas),
        ball = new Ball(),
        vx = Math.random() * 10   5,
        vy = -10,
        bounce = -0.7,
        gravity = 0.2,
        isMouseDown = false;

    ball.x = canvas.width / 2;
    ball.y = canvas.height / 2;

    canvas.addEventListener('mousedown', function () {
      if (utils.containsPoint(ball.getBounds(), mouse.x, mouse.y)) {
        isMouseDown = true;
        canvas.addEventListener('mouseup', onMouseUp, false);
        canvas.addEventListener('mousemove', onMouseMove, false);
      }
    }, false);

    function onMouseUp () {
      isMouseDown = false;
      canvas.removeEventListener('mouseup', onMouseUp, false);
      canvas.removeEventListener('mousemove', onMouseMove, false);
    }

    function onMouseMove (event) {
```

```
      ball.x = mouse.x;
      ball.y = mouse.y;
    }

    function checkBoundaries () {
      var left = 0,
          right = canvas.width,
          top = 0,
          bottom = canvas.height;

      vy += gravity;
      ball.x += vx;
      ball.y += vy;

      //boundary detect and bounce
      if (ball.x + ball.radius > right) {
        ball.x = right    ball.radius;
        vx *= bounce;
      } else if (ball.x - ball.radius < left) {
        ball.x = left + ball.radius;
        vx *= bounce;
      }
      if (ball.y + ball.radius > bottom) {
        ball.y = bottom    ball.radius;
        vy *= bounce;
      } else if (ball.y - ball.radius < top) {
        ball.y = top + ball.radius;
        vy *= bounce;
      }
    }

    (function drawFrame () {
      window.requestAnimationFrame(drawFrame, canvas);
      context.clearRect(0, 0, canvas.width, canvas.height);

      if (!isMouseDown) {
        checkBoundaries();
      }
      ball.draw(context);
    }());
  };
  </script>
 </body>
</html>
```

As you can see, we've moved all the boundary checking code into the function checkBoundaries and added the mouse event handlers. We've also declared the variable isMouseDown that is updated by the handlers to keep track of the mouse button state—so we check only the boundaries when the mouse is *not* pressed.

If you run this example, you can see the problem when you stop dragging the ball. Yes, the dragging works, but the motion code continues working at the same time. You need some way of switching on or off the motion code, so that it doesn't happen while you're dragging.

When you start dragging, all you're doing is dragging. When you drop the ball, the motion code resumes where it left off. The main problem now is that the velocity also resumes where it left off, which sometimes results in the ball flying off in some direction when you release it—very unnatural looking. You can easily fix that by setting **vx** and **vy** to zero, either when you start dragging or when you stop, as long as it is done before the motion code resumes. Let's put it in the **mousedown** event handler:

```
canvas.addEventListener('mousedown', function () {
  if (utils.containsPoint(ball.getBounds(), mouse.x, mouse.y)) {
    isMouseDown = true;
    vx = vy = 0;
    canvas.addEventListener('mouseup', onMouseUp, false);
    canvas.addEventListener('mousemove', onMouseMove, false);
  }
}, false);
```

That takes care of the problem and leaves you with a fully functional drag-and-drop feature with integrated velocity, acceleration, and bouncing. You can see the full code listing in document **05-drag-and-move-2.html**.

Just one issue remains. When you drop the ball, it falls straight down—no more x-axis motion. Although this is the correct behavior, it's a bit boring. If you could throw the ball and have it fly off in whatever direction you threw it, that would be some engaging interactivity.

Throwing

What does throwing mean with regard to animation? It means you click an object to start dragging it and move it in a particular direction. When you release it, the object keeps moving in the direction you were dragging it.

For the velocity, you must determine what velocity the object has while it is being dragged, and then set the object's velocity to that value when it is dropped. In other words, if you were dragging a ball 10 pixels per frame to the left, then when you release it, its velocity should be **vx = -10**.

Setting the velocity should be no problem for you. Just assign new values to **vx** and **vy**, as shown in Figure 7-1. Determining what those values are might seem a little tricky, but actually, calculating the dragging velocity is almost exactly the opposite of applying velocity in your motion code. In applying velocity, you add velocity to the object's old position to come up with the object's new position. This formula is **old + velocity = new**. To determine the velocity of an object while it's being dragged, you simply rearrange the equation to get **velocity = new - old**.

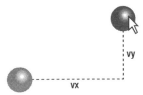

Figure 7-1. A ball dragged to a new position. The velocity is the distance from its last position to this new position.

As you drag the object, it will have a new position on each frame. If you take that position and subtract the position it was in on the previous frame, you'll know how far it moved in one frame. That's your pixels-per-frame velocity!

Here's an example, simplifying it to a single axis. A ball is dragged, and on one frame, you note that its x position is 150. On the next frame, you see that its x position is 170. Thus, in one frame, it was dragged 20 pixels on the x axis, and its x velocity at that point is +20. If you were to release it just then, you would expect it to continue moving at an x velocity of 20. So, you would set **vx = 20.**

This requires a few changes to the existing script. First, in the **drawFrame** function, check to see whether the mouse is pressed, and if so, call **trackVelocity** to update the dragging velocity of the ball. You need a couple of variables to hold the old x and y positions—call them **oldX** and **oldY**—and declare them at the beginning of the script. This is where you store the ball's position as soon as it starts dragging:

```
canvas.addEventListener('mousedown', function () {
  if (utils.containsPoint(ball.getBounds(), mouse.x, mouse.y)) {
    isMouseDown = true;
    oldX = ball.x;
    oldY = ball.y;
    canvas.addEventListener('mouseup', onMouseUp, false);
    canvas.addEventListener('mousemove', onMouseMove, false);
  }
}, false);

(function drawFrame () {
  window.requestAnimationFrame(drawFrame, canvas);
  context.clearRect(0, 0, canvas.width, canvas.height);

  if (isMouseDown) {
    trackVelocity();
  } else {
    checkBoundaries();
  }
  ball.draw(context);
}());
```

Then, in the **trackVelocity** function, you subtract **oldX** from the current x position and **oldY** from the current y. This gives you the current velocity, and store these values directly in **vx** and **vy**. Next, you reset **oldX** and **oldY** to the current position of the ball again:

```
function trackVelocity () {
  vx = ball.x    oldX;
  vy = ball.y    oldY;
  oldX = ball.x;
  oldY = ball.y;
}
```

At this point, you don't need to do anything at all about the velocity. It has been kept track of all through the drag, and the latest velocity is already stored in **vx** and **vy**. As soon as you re-enable the motion code in

163

checkBoundaries, the ball will move at whatever velocity it was just being dragged with, and this results in a thrown ball!

In case you got lost along the way, here is the final example (**06-throwing.html**):

```
<!doctype html>
<html>
 <head>
  <meta charset="utf-8">
  <title>Throwing</title>
  <link rel="stylesheet" href="style.css">
 </head>
 <body>
  <canvas id="canvas" width="400" height="400"></canvas>
  <script src="utils.js"></script>
  <script src="ball.js"></script>
  <script>
  window.onload = function () {
    var canvas = document.getElementById('canvas'),
        context = canvas.getContext('2d'),
        mouse = utils.captureMouse(canvas),
        ball = new Ball(),
        vx = Math.random() * 10    5,
        vy = -10,
        bounce = -0.7,
        gravity = 0.2,
        isMouseDown = false,
        oldX, oldY;

    ball.x = canvas.width / 2;
    ball.y = canvas.height / 2;

    canvas.addEventListener('mousedown', function () {
      if (utils.containsPoint(ball.getBounds(), mouse.x, mouse.y)) {
        isMouseDown = true;
        oldX = ball.x;
        oldY = ball.y;
        canvas.addEventListener('mouseup', onMouseUp, false);
        canvas.addEventListener('mousemove', onMouseMove, false);
      }
    }, false);

    function onMouseUp () {
      isMouseDown = false;
      canvas.removeEventListener('mouseup', onMouseUp, false);
      canvas.removeEventListener('mousemove', onMouseMove, false);
    }

    function onMouseMove (event) {
      ball.x = mouse.x;
      ball.y = mouse.y;
    }
```

```
    function trackVelocity () {
      vx = ball.x    oldX;
      vy = ball.y    oldY;
      oldX = ball.x;
      oldY = ball.y;
    }

    function checkBoundaries () {
      var left = 0,
          right = canvas.width,
          top = 0,
          bottom = canvas.height;

      vy += gravity;
      ball.x += vx;
      ball.y += vy;

      //boundary detect and bounce
      if (ball.x + ball.radius > right) {
        ball.x = right    ball.radius;
        vx *= bounce;
      } else if (ball.x - ball.radius < left) {
        ball.x = left + ball.radius;
        vx *= bounce;
      }
      if (ball.y + ball.radius > bottom) {
        ball.y = bottom    ball.radius;
        vy *= bounce;
      } else if (ball.y - ball.radius < top) {
        ball.y = top + ball.radius;
        vy *= bounce;
      }
    }

    (function drawFrame () {
      window.requestAnimationFrame(drawFrame, canvas);
      context.clearRect(0, 0, canvas.width, canvas.height);

      if (isMouseDown) {
        trackVelocity();
      } else {
        checkBoundaries();
      }
      ball.draw(context);
    }());
  };
  </script>
 </body>
</html>
```

Now that is interactive and a good example of a real-world physics animation created using event handlers and JavaScript. It feels like you're throwing something around. Play around with the **gravity** and **bounce** variables, and if you want, add friction to simulate some atmosphere.

165

Summary

Although this is not a long chapter, it covered some extremely valuable ground and made some great headway toward interactivity. By now, you should be able to drag any object, drop it, and throw it.

Most important, you've worked with a lot of the small details that go into doing a professional job with interactivity. In future chapters, you look at many other ways of allowing the user to interact with objects in your animations. The complexity is going to build up fast, but if you have these basics down, you'll do great.

Part III

Advanced Motion

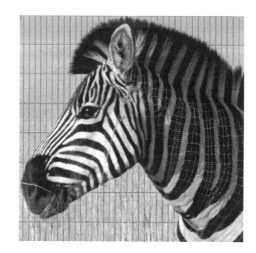

Chapter 8

Easing and Springing

What we'll cover in this chapter:

- Proportional motion

- Easing

- Springing

It's hard to believe that it took seven chapters to get through "the basics," but here you are at Chapter 8, the beginning of the advanced stuff. Or, the point where things start to get *really* interesting. Up to now, each chapter covered more general techniques and concepts. Beginning with this chapter, we'll be concentrating on one or two specialized types of motion per chapter.

In this chapter, we'll look at easing (proportional velocity) and springing (proportional acceleration). But don't think that because there are only two items, this is a chapter you can skim through quickly. These techniques can be used to create some very complex motion, and you'll use them a lot. There are plenty of examples to look through, so you can get an idea of just how powerful these techniques are.

Proportional Motion

Easing and springing are closely related, both techniques involve moving an object from an existing position to a target position. In easing, the object kind of slides into the target and stops. In springing, it bounces around back and forth for a bit, and then finally settles down at the target. The two techniques have the following in common:

- You set a target.

- You determine the distance to that target.

- Your motion is proportional to that distance—the bigger the distance, the more the motion.

The difference between easing and springing is in what aspect of the motion is proportional. In easing, the *speed* is proportional to the distance; the further away from the target, the faster the object moves. As it gets very close to the object, it's hardly moving at all.

In springing, *acceleration* is proportional to the distance. If the object is far away from the target, a lot of acceleration is applied, increasing the velocity quickly. As the object gets closer to its target, less acceleration is applied, but it's still accelerating! It flies right past the target, and then acceleration pulls it back. Eventually, friction causes it to settle down.

Let's examine each technique separately, starting with easing.

Easing

There is more than one type of easing; you can "ease in" to a position, and "ease out" from a position. Also, easing can have different motion characteristics, for example, a sine wave, bouncing, elasticity, and many more. The type of easing we'll primarily discuss here is "ease out", and a bit later in this chapter, in the "Advanced easing" section, you'll see where you can go to find out about other kinds of easing.

Simple easing

To understand simple easing, imagine you have an object over here and you want to move it over there. Since you're creating the "illusion of motion," you want to move it there gradually, over several frames. You could simply find the angle between the two, set a speed, use some trigonometry to work out the **vx** and **vy**, and set it in motion. Then you could check the distance to the target on each frame (using the Pythagorean Theorem, as described in Chapter 3), and when it arrives there, stop it. That approach might work in some situations, but if you're trying to make something look like it's moving naturally, it won't do.

The problem is that your object would move along at a fixed velocity, reach its target, and stop dead. If you're talking about some object moving along and hitting a brick wall, yes, it might be sort of like that. But when you're moving an object to a *target,* this generally implies that you know where this target is, and are deliberately moving the object into place there. In such a case, the motion will start out fairly fast, and then slow down as it gets closer to the target. In other words, its velocity is going to be proportional to the distance to the target.

Let's take an example: You're driving home. When you are a few miles away, you're moving at the speed limit. When you pull off the highway and into your neighborhood, you're moving a bit slower. Once you're on your own street, a block or two away, you'll move much slower. As you approach your driveway, you're down to a few miles per hour. When you reach the last few feet of the driveway, you're moving a lot slower than when you pulled into the driveway. And inches before you stop, you're moving at a fraction of that speed.

If you take the time to look, you'll see this behavior manifests itself even in small things like closing a drawer or door. You start out fast and gradually slow down. The next time you go to close a door, make an effort to follow through with the same speed you started with; just be prepared to explain to anyone nearby why you're slamming doors. When you use easing to move an object into position, it automatically takes on a very natural appearance. One of the coolest things is that simple easing is actually very easy to do. In fact, it's probably easier than figuring out the angle, the **vx**, and the **vy**, and moving at a fixed speed.

Here is the strategy for easing:

- Decide on a number for your proportional motion. This will be a fraction of 1.

- Determine your target.

- Calculate the distance from the object to the target.

- Multiply the distance by the fraction. This is your velocity.

- Add the velocity value to the current position.

- Repeat steps 3 through 5 until the object is at the target.

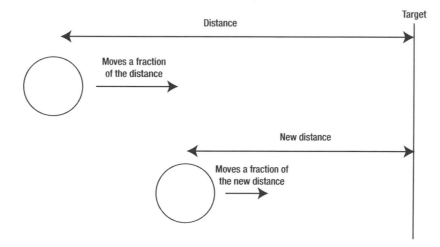

Figure 8-1. Basic easing

Let's go through these steps one at a time, and see how to program them. Don't worry about where to put the code yet, you're just seeing how the code looks and what it means.

First, decide on a fraction to represent the proportion. As I said, the velocity will be proportional to the motion. Specifically, this means that the velocity will be a fraction of the distance, something between 0 and 1. The closer it is to 1, the quicker the object will move. The closer it is to 0, the slower it will move, but be careful, because too low a value and you'll be waiting a very long time for the object to reach its target. For starters, choose something like 0.05, and we'll call this variable **easing**. So you can begin with the following code:

```
var easing = 0.05;
```

Next, determine your target; this is a simple x, y position. You can make it the center of the canvas element for lack of anything better:

```
var targetX = canvas.width / 2,
    targetY = canvas.height / 2;
```

Then calculate the distance to the target. Assuming you have an object named **ball**, you just subtract the ball's x and y from the target x and y:

```
var dx = targetX - ball.x,
    dy = targetY - ball.y;
```

Your velocity is then the distance times the fraction:

```
var vx = dx * easing,
    vy = dy * easing;

ball.x += vx;
ball.y += vy;
```

These last few steps need to be repeated, so those will go in your **drawFrame** function. Let's take a closer look at those steps, as they can be largely simplified:

```
var dx = targetX - ball.x,
    dy = targetY - ball.y,
    vx = dx * easing,
    vy = dy * easing;

ball.x += vx;
ball.y += vy;
```

You can condense the first two lines into the second two pretty easily:

```
var vx = (targetX - ball.x) * easing,
    vy = (targetY - ball.y) * easing;

ball.x += vx;
ball.y += vy;
```

Or, you can consolidate it even further:

```
ball.x += (targetX - ball.x) * easing;
ball.y += (targetY - ball.y) * easing;
```

As you explore easing, you might want to use the more verbose descriptions to make it clearer. But once you understand how it works, the third version communicates perfectly. We'll stick with the second version here, just to reinforce the idea that you're dealing with velocity.

Now, let's see it in action. You'll need the **Ball** class you've been using all along, and here's the example, **01-easing-1.html**:

```
<!doctype html>
<html>
 <head>
  <meta charset="utf-8">
  <title>Easing 1</title>
  <link rel="stylesheet" href="style.css">
```

```
 </head>
 <body>
  <canvas id="canvas" width="400" height="400"></canvas>
  <script src="utils.js"></script>
  <script src="ball.js"></script>
  <script>
  window.onload = function () {
     var canvas = document.getElementById('canvas'),
         context = canvas.getContext('2d'),
         ball = new Ball(),
         easing = 0.05,
         targetX = canvas.width / 2,
         targetY = canvas.height / 2;

     (function drawFrame () {
       window.requestAnimationFrame(drawFrame, canvas);
       context.clearRect(0, 0, canvas.width, canvas.height);

       var vx = (targetX - ball.x) * easing,
           vy = (targetY - ball.y) * easing;

       ball.x += vx;
       ball.y += vy;
       ball.draw(context);
     }());
  };
  </script>
 </body>
</html>
```

Play around with the **easing** variable to see how it affects the resulting motion.

The next thing you might want to do is drag the ball around and then have it ease back to its target. This is similar to the drag-and-drop technique you set up in Chapter 7. Here, you start dragging the ball when it is pressed with the mouse. The **drawFrame** function checks if the ball is being dragged, and if so, performs the easing calculations. Here's the document, **02-easing-2.html**:

```
<!doctype html>
<html>
 <head>
  <meta charset="utf-8">
  <title>Easing 2</title>
  <link rel="stylesheet" href="style.css">
 </head>
 <body>
  <canvas id="canvas" width="400" height="400"></canvas>
  <script src="utils.js"></script>
  <script src="ball.js"></script>
  <script>
  window.onload = function () {
     var canvas = document.getElementById('canvas'),
         context = canvas.getContext('2d'),
         mouse = utils.captureMouse(canvas),
```

```
        ball = new Ball(),
        easing = 0.05,
        targetX = canvas.width / 2,
        targetY = canvas.height / 2,
        isMouseDown = false;

    canvas.addEventListener('mousedown', function () {
      if (utils.containsPoint(ball.getBounds(), mouse.x, mouse.y)) {
        isMouseDown = true;
        canvas.addEventListener('mouseup', onMouseUp, false);
        canvas.addEventListener('mousemove', onMouseMove, false);
      }
    }, false);

    function onMouseUp () {
      isMouseDown = false;
      canvas.removeEventListener('mouseup', onMouseUp, false);
      canvas.removeEventListener('mousemove', onMouseMove, false);
    }

    function onMouseMove () {
      ball.x = mouse.x;
      ball.y = mouse.y;
    }

    (function drawFrame () {
      window.requestAnimationFrame(drawFrame, canvas);
      context.clearRect(0, 0, canvas.width, canvas.height);

      if (!isMouseDown) {
        var vx = (targetX - ball.x) * easing,
            vy = (targetY - ball.y) * easing;

        ball.x += vx;
        ball.y += vy;
      }
      ball.draw(context);
    }());
  };
  </script>
 </body>
</html>
```

When to stop easing

If you are calculating simple easing to a single target, eventually you'll get to the point where the object is at the target and the purpose of the easing has been achieved. But, in the examples so far, the easing code continues to execute, even though the object isn't visibly moving anymore. If you are just easing to that point and leaving the object there, continuing to run the easing code is a waste of system resources. If you've reached your goal, you might as well stop trying. At first glance, this would be as simple as checking whether the object is at its target and turning off the animation loop, like so:

```
if (ball.x === targetX && ball.y === targetY) {
  //code to stop the easing
}
```

But it winds up being a little more tricky. I touched on this problem in earlier chapters when we applied friction, but we'll examine it in a little more detail here.

The type of easing we are discussing involves something from *Zeno's Paradoxes*. Zeno of Elea was a Greek philosopher who devised a set of problems to show that, contrary to what our senses tell us, there is no change, and motion is an illusion. To demonstrate this, Zeno explained motion as follows: In order for something to move from point A to point B, it first must move to a point halfway between the two. Then it needs to travel from that point to a point halfway between there and point B. And then halfway again. Since you always need to move halfway to the target, you can never actually reach the target, since it is an infinite amount of steps away.

It's a paradox because it sounds logical, but yet, our own experiences tell us that we move from point A to point B every day. Let's take a look at it where the infinite breaks down in JavaScript. On the x axis, an object is at position 0. Say you want to move it to 100 on the x axis. Make the **easing** variable 0.5, so it always moves half the distance to the target. It progresses like this:

- Starting at 0, after frame 1, it will be at 50.

- Frame 2 will bring it to 75.

- Now the distance is 25. Half of that is 12.5, so the new position will be 87.5.

- Following the sequence, the position will be 93.75, 96.875, 98.4375, and so on. After 20 frames, it will be 99.999809265.

As you can see, it gets closer and closer but never actually reaches the target—theoretically. However, things are a bit different when you examine what the code does. Visually, it comes down to the question: "How small can you slice a pixel?" And that answer is not specified in the HTML5 Canvas specification, rather, it's defined by the browser implementation. Vendors could implement a high-resolution canvas with a precision to many decimal places, but average viewer would have a very difficult time discerning a pixel difference at 10 steps, meaning within 0.1.

In this example, the closest we can get the **position** to 100 after 20 steps is 99.99990463256836.

```
var position = 0,
    target = 100;

for (var i = 0; i < 20; i++) {
  console.log(i + ": " + position);
  position += (target - position) * 0.5;
}
```

This loops through 20 times, moving the **position** half the distance to the **target**; it's just basic easing code. We're only interested in printing the positions, not actually seeing the motion. But, what you'll find is that by the eleventh iteration, the **position** has reached 99.9, and when viewing this demonstration on the canvas, that's as close as our ball will get.

Even though the ball on the canvas is not getting any closer visually, mathematically it will still never actually reach its target. So, if you're doing a simple comparison, as in the previous example, your easing code will never get shut off. What you need to decide is: "How close is close enough?" This is determined by whether the distance to the target is less than a certain amount. For many examples in this book, if an object is within a pixel of its target, it's safe to say it has arrived, and the easing code will be turned off.

If you are using two dimensions, you can calculate the distance using the formula introduced in Chapter 3:

```
var distance = Math.sqrt(dx * dx + dy * dy);
```

If you have a single value for distance, as when you are moving an object on a single axis, you need to use the absolute value of that distance, as it may be negative. You can do this by using the `Math.abs` method.

Here's a simple example to demonstrate turning off easing (`03-easing-off.html`):

```
<!doctype html>
<html>
 <head>
  <meta charset="utf-8">
  <title>Easing Off</title>
  <link rel="stylesheet" href="style.css">
 </head>
 <body>
  <canvas id="canvas" width="400" height="400"></canvas>
  <textarea id="log"></textarea>
  <script src="utils.js"></script>
  <script src="ball.js"></script>
  <script>
  window.onload = function () {
    var canvas = document.getElementById('canvas'),
        context = canvas.getContext('2d'),
        log = document.getElementById('log'),
        ball = new Ball(),
        easing = 0.05,
        targetX = canvas.width / 2,
        animRequest;

    ball.y = canvas.height / 2;

    (function drawFrame () {
      animRequest = window.requestAnimationFrame(drawFrame, canvas);
      context.clearRect(0, 0, canvas.width, canvas.height);

      var dx = targetX - ball.x;

      if (Math.abs(dx) < 1) {
        ball.x = targetX;
        window.cancelRequestAnimationFrame(animRequest);
        log.value = "Animation done!";
      } else {
        var vx = dx * easing;
        ball.x += vx;
```

```
      }
      ball.draw(context);
    }());
  };
  </script>
 </body>
</html>
```

This exercise expands the easing formula a bit to first calculate the distance, since you'll need this to see whether easing should be stopped. Perhaps now you can see why you need to use the absolute value of dx. If the ball were to the right of the target, dx would be a negative number, the statement `if(dx < 1)` would evaluate as `true`, and that would be the end of things. By using `Math.abs`, you make sure that the actual distance is less than 1. You then place the ball where it is trying to go and disable the motion code.

Each animation frame request is stored in the variable `animRequest`. When we want to turn off the animation loop, we pass this variable as a parameter to `window.cancelRequestAnimationFrame`. If this function is not available in your browser natively, then add this cross-browser implementation to the file `utils.js`:

```
if (!window.cancelRequestAnimationFrame) {
  window.cancelRequestAnimationFrame = (window.cancelAnimationFrame ||
                                window.webkitCancelRequestAnimationFrame ||
                                window.mozCancelRequestAnimationFrame ||
                                window.oCancelRequestAnimationFrame ||
                                window.msCancelRequestAnimationFrame ||
                                window.clearTimeout);
}
```

Remember that if you are doing something like a drag-and-drop with easing, you'll want to re-enable the motion code when the ball is dropped.

A moving target

In the examples so far, the target point has been a single, fixed location, but that's not a requirement. The distance is calculated on each frame, and the velocity is then calculated based on that. The code doesn't care whether or not it reaches the target, or if the target keeps moving. It just goes merrily along, wondering what the target, distance and velocity are for every frame.

You can easily make the mouse an easing target. Just plug in the mouse coordinates (`mouse.x` and `mouse.y`) where you had `targetX` and `targetY` before. Here's a version that does just that (`04-ease-to-mouse.html`):

```
<!doctype html>
<html>
 <head>
  <meta charset="utf-8">
  <title>Ease to Mouse</title>
  <link rel="stylesheet" href="style.css">
 </head>
 <body>
  <canvas id="canvas" width="400" height="400"></canvas>
  <script src="utils.js"></script>
```

```
<script src="ball.js"></script>
<script>
window.onload = function () {
  var canvas = document.getElementById('canvas'),
      context = canvas.getContext('2d'),
      mouse = utils.captureMouse(canvas),
      ball = new Ball(),
      easing = 0.05;

  (function drawFrame () {
    window.requestAnimationFrame(drawFrame, canvas);
    context.clearRect(0, 0, canvas.width, canvas.height);

    var vx = (mouse.x - ball.x) * easing,
        vy = (mouse.y - ball.y) * easing;

    ball.x += vx;
    ball.y += vy;
    ball.draw(context);
  }());
};
</script>
</body>
</html>
```

Move the mouse around and see how the ball follows, and how it goes faster when you get further away.

Think of what other moving targets you could have. Maybe an object could ease to another object—you can set up some very complex looking effects by chaining together this simple technique.

Easing isn't just for motion

It's important to understand, that the examples in this book are just that: examples. In each one, we're manipulating numbers that are used for various properties of an object. For the most part, we're using the x and y properties to control positions of objects, but they can have many other properties that you can manipulate because most of them are represented by numbers. When you read a particular example, try it out, but don't leave it at that. Try the example, and manipulate other properties as well. Here's a few ideas to get you started.

Rotation

Set a current and target rotation. Of course, you need something that can be visibly rotated and drawn to the canvas, like the **Arrow** class from earlier chapters:

```
var rotation = 90,
    targetRotation = 270;
```

Then ease it:

```
rotation += (targetRotation - rotation) * easing;
arrow.rotation = rotation * Math.PI / 180; //degrees to radians
```

Colors

Try easing on 24-bit colors. You'll need to start with red, green, and blue initial values and target values, perform the easing on each separate component color, and then combine them into a color value. For instance, you could ease from red to blue. Start with the initial and target colors:

```
var red = 255,
    green = 0,
    blue = 0,
    redTarget = 0,
    greenTarget = 0,
    blueTarget = 255;
```

Then in your **drawFrame** function, perform easing on each one:

```
red += (redTarget - red) * easing;
green += (greenTarget - green) * easing;
blue += (blueTarget - blue) * easing;
```

Then combine the three components into a single value (as described in Chapter 4), and apply:

```
var color = red << 16 | green << 8 | blue;
```

Transparency

Apply easing to the **alpha** component of a CSS-style color string. Start out by setting it to 0, and making the target 1 (remember that **alpha** is a value from 0.0 to 1.0):

```
var alpha = 0,
    targetAlpha = 1;
```

Then in the **drawFrame** function, fade it in with easing, and concatenate a RGBA string:

```
alpha += (targetAlpha - alpha) * easing;
ball.color = "rgba(255, 0, 0," + alpha + ")";
```

Or reverse the 0 and 1 to make it fade out.

Advanced easing

Now that you've seen how simple easing works, you might consider using more complex easing formulas for additional effects. For instance, you might want something to start slowly, build up speed, and then slow down as it approaches its target. Or you might want to ease something into position over a certain time period or number of frames.

Robert Penner has collected numerous easing formulas, cataloged them, and implemented them in Flash. You can find his easing formulas at **http://robertpenner.com**, and I've ported that code to JavaScript for you to look at, and perhaps include in your own animations. You can browse this code, along with the other book examples, at **http://github.com/lamberta/html5-animation**

Springing

Springing is one of the most powerful and useful physics concepts in programmed animation. It seems like you can do almost anything with a spring, but of course, it's just another technique. Since you can do so much with a spring, let's take a look at what it is and how you can program it.

As mentioned at the beginning of the chapter, the acceleration of a spring is proportional to its distance from a target. Think about a real, physical spring, or better yet, a ball on the end of a rubber band. You attach the other end to something solid. As the ball is hanging there with no force applied, that's its target point. That's where it wants to be. Now pull it away a tiny bit and let it go. At that point, the ball's velocity is zero, but the rubber band applies force to it, pulling it back to the target. Now pull it away as far as you can and let it go. The rubber band applies a lot more force. The ball zooms right past its target and starts going the other way. Its velocity is very high. But when it gets a little bit past the target, the rubber band starts pulling it back a bit—changes its velocity. The ball keeps going, but the farther it goes, the more the band pulls back on it. Eventually, the velocity reaches zero, the direction reverses, and the whole thing starts over again. Finally, after bouncing back and forth a few times, it slows down and comes to a stop at—you guessed where—its target.

Now, let's start translating this into code so you can use it. To keep things simple, let's start off with one dimension.

Springing in one dimension

Once again, we'll use the red ball to demonstrate this idea. You'll leave it over at its default x position of zero and have it spring to the middle of the canvas. As with easing, you'll need a variable to hold the proportionate value of the spring. You can think of this as the proportion of the distance that will be added to the velocity. A high spring value will make a very stiff spring. Something lower will look more like a loose rubber band. You'll start off with 0.1, and here's the initial code:

```
var spring = 0.1,
    targetX = canvas.width / 2,
    vx = 0;
```

Again, don't worry about where to put this just yet. Just make sure you know what these variables and statements are doing.

Then we begin the motion code and find the distance to the target:

```
var dx = targetX - ball.x;
```

Now, compute some acceleration. The acceleration will be proportional to that distance, in fact, it will be the distance multiplied by the **spring** value:

```
var ax = dx * spring;
```

Once you have a value for acceleration, you should be back on familiar ground. Add the acceleration to the velocity and add the velocity to the position:

```
vx += ax;
ball.x += vx;
```

Before you write any code, we'll simulate it with some sample numbers. Let's say the x position is 0, **vx** is 0, the target x is 100, and the **spring** variable is 0.1. Here is how it might progress:

1. Multiply distance (100) by **spring**, and you get 10. Add that to **vx**, which then becomes 10. Add velocity to position, making the x position 10.

2. Next round, distance (100 - 10) is 90. Acceleration is 90 times 0.1, or 9 this time. This gets added to **vx**, which becomes 19. The x position becomes 29.

3. Next round, distance is 71, acceleration is 7.1, which added to **vx** makes it 26.1. The x position becomes 55.1

4. Next round, distance is 44.9, acceleration is 4.49, and **vx** becomes 30.59. The x position is then 85.69.

The acceleration on each frame becomes less and less as the object approaches its target, but the velocity continues to build. It's not building as rapidly as it was on previous frames, but it's still moving faster and faster.

After a couple more rounds, the object goes right past the target to an x position of around 117. The distance is now 100 - 117, which is -17. A fraction of this gets added to the velocity, slowing the object down a bit.

Now that you understand how springing works, let's make a real example. As usual, make sure the **Ball** class is available to your document, and use the following file (**05-spring-1.html**):

```
<!doctype html>
<html>
 <head>
  <meta charset="utf-8">
  <title>Spring 1</title>
  <link rel="stylesheet" href="style.css">
 </head>
 <body>
  <canvas id="canvas" width="400" height="400"></canvas>
  <script src="utils.js"></script>
  <script src="ball.js"></script>
  <script>
  window.onload = function () {
    var canvas = document.getElementById('canvas'),
        context = canvas.getContext('2d'),
        ball = new Ball(),
        spring = 0.03,
        targetX = canvas.width / 2,
        vx = 0;

    ball.y = canvas.height / 2;

    (function drawFrame () {
      window.requestAnimationFrame(drawFrame, canvas);
      context.clearRect(0, 0, canvas.width, canvas.height);

      var dx = targetX - ball.x,
```

```
        ax = dx * spring;

    vx += ax;
    ball.x += vx;
    ball.draw(context);
  }());
};
</script>
</body>
</html>
```

Test this in your browser, and you'll see something spring-like going on. The problem is that it kind of goes on forever. Earlier, when the spring was described, we said that it slows down and comes to a stop. But in this example, the ball builds up the same velocity on each leg of its swing, so it keeps bouncing back and forth at the same speed. You need something to reduce its velocity and slow it down—which means you need to apply some friction. Easy enough, just create a **friction** variable, with a value like 0.95 for starters. This goes up at the top of the script with the rest of the variables:

```
var friction = 0.95;
```

Then multiply **vx** by **friction** somewhere in the **drawFrame** function. Here's the corrected section of the script (**06-spring-2.html**):

```
(function drawFrame () {
  window.requestAnimationFrame(drawFrame, canvas);
  context.clearRect(0, 0, canvas.width, canvas.height);

  var dx = targetX - ball.x,
      ax = dx * spring;

  vx += ax;
  vx *= friction;
  ball.x += vx;
  ball.draw(context);
}());
```

At this point, you have a full-fledged, albeit one-dimensional, spring. Play with this one a lot, and see what different values for **spring** and **friction** do and how they interact. Check out how a different starting position or target position affects the action of the system, the speed of the ball, and the rate at which it slows down and comes to a stop.

Just like with easing, the animation loop will continue to apply the minute motion values long after the code has any visual effects. Again, you can save some calculations by checking if the number is larger than a minimum distance before applying the friction, like so:

```
if (Math.abs(vx) > 0.001) {
  vx += ax;
  vx *= friction;
  ball.x += vx;
}
```

Understanding this spring example will take you a long way. Now you're ready to move on to a two-dimensional spring.

Springing in two dimensions

The previous spring moved our ball along the x axis, or left-right. If we want the ball to spring along the x axis *and* y axis—left-right and top-bottom—we need a two-dimensional spring. Creating this is as easy as adding a second target, velocity, and acceleration; as we see in the next example, **07-spring-3.html**:

```html
<!doctype html>
<html>
 <head>
  <meta charset="utf-8">
  <title>Spring 3</title>
  <link rel="stylesheet" href="style.css">
 </head>
 <body>
  <canvas id="canvas" width="400" height="400"></canvas>
  <script src="utils.js"></script>
  <script src="ball.js"></script>
  <script>
  window.onload = function () {
    var canvas = document.getElementById('canvas'),
        context = canvas.getContext('2d'),
        ball = new Ball(),
        spring = 0.03,
        friction = 0.95,
        targetX = canvas.width / 2,
        targetY = canvas.height / 2,
        vx = 0,
        vy = 0;

    (function drawFrame () {
      window.requestAnimationFrame(drawFrame, canvas);
      context.clearRect(0, 0, canvas.width, canvas.height);

      var dx = targetX - ball.x,
          dy = targetY - ball.y,
          ax = dx * spring,
          ay = dy * spring;

      vx += ax;
      vy += ay;
      vx *= friction;
      vy *= friction;
      ball.x += vx;
      ball.y += vy;
      ball.draw(context);
    }());
  };
  </script>
 </body>
</html>
```

Here, the only difference from the previous example is all the references to the y-axis. The problem is that it still seems rather one-dimensional. Yes, the ball is now moving on the x and y axes, but it's just going in

183

a straight line. That's because its velocity starts out as zero, and the only force acting on it is the pull toward the target, so it goes in a straight line toward its target.

To make things a little more interesting, initialize **vx** to something other than 0—try something like 50. Now, you have motion that looks a little more loose and fluid. But you're only getting started, it gets a lot cooler.

Springing to a moving target

It probably won't surprise you that springing doesn't require the target to be the same on each frame. When we covered easing, you saw a quick and easy example of the ball following the mouse. It's pretty easy to adapt that example to make the ball spring to the mouse. Instead of the **targetX** and **targetY** you've been using, use the mouse coordinates. In springing, as with easing, the distance to the target is always calculated newly on each frame. Acceleration is based on that, and that acceleration is added to the velocity.

The effect is very cool, and the code isn't all that different. In the preceding example, simply change these lines:

```
var dx = targetX - ball.x,
    dy = targetY - ball.y;
```

So they look like this:

```
var dx = mouse.x - ball.x,
    dy = mouse.y - ball.y;
```

Remember to include **var mouse = utils.captureMouse(canvas)** at the top of your script. You can also remove the lines that declare the **targetX** and **targetY** variables, since you won't be needing them. The updated document is available as **08-spring-4.html**.

This is another good place to stop and play. Get a good feel for how all these variables work, and try out many variations. Break it, and find out what breaks it. Have fun with it!

So where's the spring?

At this point, you have a very realistic-looking ball on the end of a rubber band. But it seems to be an invisible rubber band. Well, you can fix that with a few lines of code from the canvas drawing API.

Since you have a fairly simple file without much else going on, you can safely add your drawing code directly to the **drawFrame** function. In a more complex application, you might want to create another object to hold your drawing commands and use that as a kind of drawing layer.

In each frame, after the ball is in position, you begin a new path and move the drawing cursor to the ball's position, then, simply draw a line to current mouse position. Remember to add a stroke so that line is visible on the canvas element:

```
context.beginPath();
context.moveTo(ball.x, ball.y);
context.lineTo(mouse.x, mouse.y);
context.stroke();
```

Now, how about adding some gravity so the ball looks like it's actually hanging off the end of the mouse? Just add a **gravity** variable and add that to the **vy** for each frame. The following code (**09-spring-5.html**) uses the line drawing and gravity additions:

```
<!doctype html>
<html>
 <head>
  <meta charset="utf-8">
  <title>Spring 5</title>
  <link rel="stylesheet" href="style.css">
 </head>
 <body>
  <canvas id="canvas" width="400" height="400"></canvas>
  <script src="utils.js"></script>
  <script src="ball.js"></script>
  <script>
  window.onload = function () {
    var canvas = document.getElementById('canvas'),
        context = canvas.getContext('2d'),
        mouse = utils.captureMouse(canvas),
        ball = new Ball(),
        spring = 0.03,
        friction = 0.9,
        gravity = 2,
        vx = 0,
        vy = 0;

    (function drawFrame () {
      window.requestAnimationFrame(drawFrame, canvas);
      context.clearRect(0, 0, canvas.width, canvas.height);

      var dx = mouse.x - ball.x,
          dy = mouse.y - ball.y,
          ax = dx * spring,
          ay = dy * spring;

      vx += ax;
      vy += ay;
      vy += gravity;
      vx *= friction;
      vy *= friction;
      ball.x += vx;
      ball.y += vy;

      context.beginPath();
      context.moveTo(ball.x, ball.y);
      context.lineTo(mouse.x, mouse.y);
      context.stroke();
      ball.draw(context);
    }());
  };
  </script>
 </body>
</html>
```

185

When you test this version, you should see something like Figure 8-2.

Notice how we've increased the **gravity** value to 2 so the ball actually hangs down. Much less than that, and the force of the spring overcomes the force of gravity and you don't see the effect.

Here's another point where we've deviated from real-world physics. Of course, you can't go around "increasing gravity" on objects! Gravity is a constant, based on the size and mass of the planet you happen to be on. What you can do is increase the mass of the object, so that gravity has more of an effect on it. So, technically we should keep **gravity** at something like 0.5, and then create a **mass** property and make it something like 10. Then we could multiply **mass** by **gravity** and come up with 5 again. But as long as you understand that I'm referring to the force that gravity is exerting on the object based on its mass, we'll just call it **gravity**.

Figure 8-2. Springing from the mouse, with a visible spring

Again, experiment with this example. Try decreasing the **gravity** and **spring** values, try changing the **friction** value. You'll see you can have a nearly endless number of combinations, allowing you to create all kinds of systems.

Chaining springs

Now we'll chain a few springs together. In the easing section, we discussed chaining briefly, where one object eases to the mouse, another object eases to that object, and so on. Here we'll take a look at some examples that use that same idea, only with springs.

Here's the plan, start off by creating three balls, named **ball0**, **ball1**, and **ball2**. The first one, **ball0**, will behave pretty much like the single ball did in the previous example. Then **ball1** will spring to **ball0**, and **ball2** will spring to **ball1**. All will have gravity, so they should kind of hang down in a chain. You've seen all this code before, it's just a little more complex. Here it is, in example **10-chain.html**:

```
<!doctype html>
<html>
 <head>
  <meta charset="utf-8">
  <title>Chain</title>
  <link rel="stylesheet" href="style.css">
 </head>
 <body>
  <canvas id="canvas" width="400" height="400"></canvas>
  <script src="utils.js"></script>
  <script src="ball.js"></script>
  <script>
  window.onload = function () {
    var canvas = document.getElementById('canvas'),
```

```
            context = canvas.getContext('2d'),
            mouse = utils.captureMouse(canvas),
            ball0 = new Ball(),
            ball1 = new Ball(),
            ball2 = new Ball(),
            spring = 0.03,
            friction = 0.9,
            gravity = 2;

        function move (ball, targetX, targetY) {
          ball.vx += (targetX - ball.x) * spring;
          ball.vy += (targetY - ball.y) * spring;
          ball.vy += gravity;
          ball.vx *= friction;
          ball.vy *= friction;
          ball.x += ball.vx;
          ball.y += ball.vy;
        }

        (function drawFrame () {
          window.requestAnimationFrame(drawFrame, canvas);
          context.clearRect(0, 0, canvas.width, canvas.height);

          move(ball0, mouse.x, mouse.y);
          move(ball1, ball0.x, ball0.y);
          move(ball2, ball1.x, ball1.y);

          //draw spring
          context.beginPath();
          context.moveTo(mouse.x, mouse.y);
          context.lineTo(ball0.x, ball0.y);
          context.lineTo(ball1.x, ball1.y);
          context.lineTo(ball2.x, ball2.y);
          context.stroke();
          //draw balls
          ball0.draw(context);
          ball1.draw(context);
          ball2.draw(context);
        }());
      };
    </script>
  </body>
</html>
```

If you take another look at the **Ball** class, you'll see that each object instance gets its own **vx** and **vy** properties, and these are initialized to 0. So, at the top of the script, you just need to create each ball.

Then in the **drawFrame** function, you perform all the springing and drawing. Rather than duplicating the same code three times for each ball, we include a **move** function, which handles all of the motion code. This takes a reference to a ball and an x and y target. You call the function for each ball, passing in the x and y mouse position for the first ball, and the location of the first and second balls as targets for the second and third.

187

Finally, when all of the balls are in place, you begin a new path, move the drawing cursor to the mouse position, and then draw a line to each successive ball, creating the rubber band holding them all together. The friction in this example was pushed to 0.9 to force things to settle down a bit quicker.

You could make this example a bit more flexible, by creating an array to hold references to each object in the chain, and iterating through that array to move each one, and then draw the lines. This would just take a few changes. First, you'd need a couple of new variables for the array and the number of objects to create:

```
var balls = [],
    numBalls = 5;
```

At the top of the script in a **while** loop, we initialize each ball and add it to the array:

```
while (numBalls--) {
  balls.push(new Ball(20));
}
```

Finally, in **drawFrame** we pass each ball to the new **draw** function. This function takes two arguments, an instance of our **Ball** class, and it's index position in an array (which is provided by **Array.forEach**). We move the first ball to the mouse position, and each remaining ball to the ball prior to it, drawing a line between them. It loops through all the balls in the array, moving and drawing a line to each one in turn. You can add as many objects as you want simply by changing the value of the one variable, **numBalls**.

```
function draw (ballB, i) {
  //if first ball, move to mouse
  if (i === 0) {
    move(ballB, mouse.x, mouse.y);
    context.moveTo(mouse.x, mouse.y);
  } else {
    var ballA = balls[i-1];
    move(ballB, ballA.x, ballA.y);
    context.moveTo(ballA.x, ballA.y);
  }
  context.lineTo(ballB.x, ballB.y);
  context.stroke();
  ballB.draw(context);
}

(function drawFrame () {
  window.requestAnimationFrame(drawFrame, canvas);
  context.clearRect(0, 0, canvas.width, canvas.height);

  context.beginPath();
  balls.forEach(draw);
}());
```

You can see the result in Figure 8-3 and can find this in document **11-chain-array.html**.

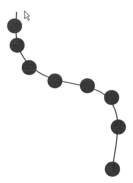

Figure 8-3. Chained springs

Springing to multiple targets

Back when the subjects of velocity and acceleration were introduced in Chapter 5, we saw how you could have multiple forces acting on an object. Each type of force is represented as a value, which we add to a cumulative velocity value, that is then applied to the motion of the object. Since a spring is nothing more than something exerting acceleration on an object, it's pretty simple to create multiple springs acting on a single object.

To demonstrate springing to multiple targets, we'll create three "handles"—which will be instances of the **Ball** class—and give them simple drag-and-drop functionality. These will also act as targets for the ball to spring to. The ball will try to spring to all three of them at once and find its equilibrium somewhere between them. Or, to put it another way, each target will exert a certain amount of acceleration on the ball, and its motion will be the sum total of all of those forces.

This example gets pretty complex, with several methods in place to handle the various behaviors. First, here's the complete example (document **12-multi-spring.html**), then we'll discuss it section by section. Figure 8-4 shows an example of the results of this code.

```
<!doctype html>
<html>
 <head>
  <meta charset="utf-8">
  <title>Multi Spring</title>
  <link rel="stylesheet" href="style.css">
 </head>
 <body>
  <canvas id="canvas" width="400" height="400"></canvas>
  <script src="utils.js"></script>
  <script src="ball.js"></script>
  <script>
  window.onload = function () {
    var canvas = document.getElementById('canvas'),
        context = canvas.getContext('2d'),
        mouse = utils.captureMouse(canvas),
        ball = new Ball(20),
```

```
        handles = [],
        numHandles = 3,
        spring = 0.03,
        friction = 0.9,
        movingHandle = null;

  for (var handle, i = 0; i < numHandles; i++) {
    handle = new Ball(10, "#0000ff");
    handle.x = Math.random() * canvas.width;
    handle.y = Math.random() * canvas.height;
    handles.push(handle);
  }

  canvas.addEventListener('mousedown', function () {
    handles.forEach(function (handle) {
      if (utils.containsPoint(handle.getBounds(), mouse.x, mouse.y)) {
        movingHandle = handle;
      }
    });
  }, false);

  canvas.addEventListener('mouseup', function () {
    if (movingHandle) {
      movingHandle = null;
    }
  }, false);

  canvas.addEventListener('mousemove', function () {
    if (movingHandle) {
      movingHandle.x = mouse.x;
      movingHandle.y = mouse.y;
    }
  }, false);

  function applyHandle (handle) {
    var dx = handle.x - ball.x,
        dy = handle.y - ball.y;

    ball.vx += dx * spring;
    ball.vy += dy * spring;
  }

  function drawHandle (handle) {
    context.moveTo(ball.x, ball.y);
    context.lineTo(handle.x, handle.y);
    context.stroke();
    handle.draw(context);
  }

  (function drawFrame () {
    window.requestAnimationFrame(drawFrame, canvas);
    context.clearRect(0, 0, canvas.width, canvas.height);

    handles.forEach(applyHandle);
```

```
      ball.vx *= friction;
      ball.vy *= friction;
      ball.x += ball.vx;
      ball.y += ball.vy;

      context.beginPath();
      handles.forEach(drawHandle);
      ball.draw(context);
    }());
  };
  </script>
 </body>
</html>
```

At the top of the script, we create a ball and three handles, randomly positioning the handles and setting up their drag-and-drop behavior.

The **drawFrame** function loops through each handle, springing the ball toward it by calling the **applyHandle** function. It then applies the ball's new velocity to its position, and loops through the handles again, drawing a line from the ball to each handle. Then, finally, we draw the ball.

The **mousedown** event listener iterates over each handle, and if it finds one that contains the current position of our mouse cursor, it sets that handle to **movingHandle**. In the **mouseup** event hander, if a handle has been dragged, then it is stopped.

You can easily change the number of handles to use by changing the **numHandles** variable.

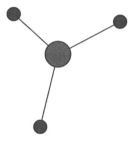

Figure 8-4. Multiple springs

Offsetting the target

If you took a real spring—an actual coil of bouncy metal—and attached one end of it to something solid and the other end to a ball or some other object, what would be the target? Would the target be the point where the spring is attached? No, not really. The ball would never be able to reach that point, because the spring itself would be in the way. Furthermore, once the spring had contracted to its normal length, it wouldn't be applying any more force on the ball. So, the target would actually be the position of the loose end of the spring when it's not stretched. But that point could vary as the spring pivots around the fixed point.

To find the actual target, you need to first find the angle between the object and the fixed point, and then move out from the fixed point at that angle—the length of the spring. In other words, if the length of the spring were 50, and the angle between the ball and fixed point were 45, you would move out 50 pixels from the fixed point, at an angle of 45 degrees, and that would be the ball's target to spring to. Figure 8-5 illustrates how this works.

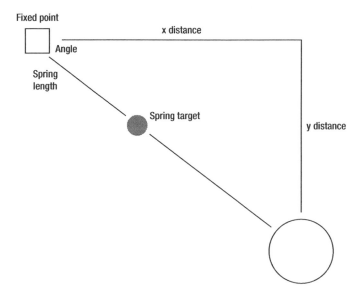

Figure 8-5. Offsetting a spring

The code to find the target in this case would be:

```
var dx = ball.x - fixedX,
    dy = ball.y - fixedY,
    angle = Math.atan2(dy, dx),
    targetX = fixedX + Math.cos(angle) * springLength,
    targetY = fixedY + Math.sin(angle) * springLength;
```

The result is that the object will spring toward the fixed point, but will come to rest some distance away from it. Although we're calling it a "fixed point," this just means the point to which the spring is fixed, it doesn't mean that point cannot move. Perhaps it's better just to see it in action. You'll go back to using the mouse position, but this time, it will be the spring's fixed point. The spring's length will be 100 pixels. Here's the example (document **13-offset-spring.html**):

```
<!doctype html>
<html>
 <head>
  <meta charset="utf-8">
  <title>Offset Spring</title>
  <link rel="stylesheet" href="style.css">
 </head>
```

```
<body>
  <canvas id="canvas" width="400" height="400"></canvas>
  <script src="utils.js"></script>
  <script src="ball.js"></script>
  <script>
  window.onload = function () {
    var canvas = document.getElementById('canvas'),
        context = canvas.getContext('2d'),
        mouse = utils.captureMouse(canvas),
        ball = new Ball(),
        spring = 0.03,
        friction = 0.9,
        springLength = 100,
        vx = 0,
        vy = 0;

    (function drawFrame () {
      window.requestAnimationFrame(drawFrame, canvas);
      context.clearRect(0, 0, canvas.width, canvas.height);

      var dx = ball.x - mouse.x,
          dy = ball.y - mouse.y,
          angle = Math.atan2(dy, dx),
          targetX = mouse.x + Math.cos(angle) * springLength,
          targetY = mouse.y + Math.sin(angle) * springLength;

      vx += (targetX - ball.x) * spring;
      vy += (targetY - ball.y) * spring;
      vx *= friction;
      vy *= friction;
      ball.x += vx;
      ball.y += vy;

      context.beginPath();
      context.moveTo(ball.x, ball.y);
      context.lineTo(mouse.x, mouse.y);
      context.stroke();
      ball.draw(context);
    }());
  };
  </script>
</body>
</html>
```

Even though you can see what is happening here, it might not be obvious where you would find this technique useful. Well, the next section will give you a specific example.

Attaching multiple objects with springs

Since we know how to spring an object to a point, and that the point does not have to be fixed. You could have one object spring to another object, and have the other object spring back to the first one, so that these two objects are linked together by a spring. Move either one, and the other object springs to it.

193

That's the general strategy, but to use the terms discussed in this chapter: object A has object B as its target. It springs toward it. Object B in turn has object A as its target, and this is where the offset is important. If each object had the other as a direct target, they would collapse in on each other and occupy the same point. By applying an offset, you keep them apart a bit, as shown in Figure 8-6.

Figure 8-6. Two objects connected

For this next example, you'll create two instances of the **Ball** connected by a spring, and we'll call them **ball0** and **ball1**. **ball0** springs to **ball1** with an offset, and **ball1** springs to **ball0** with an offset. Rather than writing out all the offset, spring, and motion code twice, it's all put into a function named **springTo**. You can spring **ball0** to **ball1** by calling **springTo(ball0, ball1)**, and then spring **ball1** to **ball0** by calling **springTo(ball1, ball0)**. There are also a couple of variables that have been added: **ball0_dragging** and **ball1_dragging**, to disable the springing for each ball when it is being dragged. Here's the document (**14-double-spring.html**):

```
<!doctype html>
<html>
 <head>
  <meta charset="utf-8">
  <title>Double Spring</title>
  <link rel="stylesheet" href="style.css">
 </head>
 <body>
  <canvas id="canvas" width="400" height="400"></canvas>
  <script src="utils.js"></script>
  <script src="ball.js"></script>
  <script>
  window.onload = function () {
    var canvas = document.getElementById('canvas'),
        context = canvas.getContext('2d'),
        mouse = utils.captureMouse(canvas),
        ball0 = new Ball(20),
        ball1 = new Ball(20),
        ball0_dragging = false,
        ball1_dragging = false,
        spring = 0.03,
        friction = 0.9,
        springLength = 100,
        vx = 0,
        vy = 0;

    ball0.x = Math.random() * canvas.width;
    ball0.y = Math.random() * canvas.height;
    ball1.x = Math.random() * canvas.width;
    ball1.y = Math.random() * canvas.height;
```

```
canvas.addEventListener('mousedown', function () {
  if (utils.containsPoint(ball0.getBounds(), mouse.x, mouse.y)) {
    ball0_dragging = true;
  }
  if (utils.containsPoint(ball1.getBounds(), mouse.x, mouse.y)) {
    ball1_dragging = true;
  }
}, false);

canvas.addEventListener('mouseup', function () {
  if (ball0_dragging || ball1_dragging) {
    ball0_dragging = false;
    ball1_dragging = false;
  }
}, false);

canvas.addEventListener('mousemove', function () {
  if (ball0_dragging) {
    ball0.x = mouse.x;
    ball0.y = mouse.y;
  }
  if (ball1_dragging) {
    ball1.x = mouse.x;
    ball1.y = mouse.y;
  }
}, false);

function springTo (ballA, ballB) {
  var dx = ballB.x - ballA.x,
      dy = ballB.y - ballA.y,
      angle = Math.atan2(dy, dx),
      targetX = ballB.x - Math.cos(angle) * springLength,
      targetY = ballB.y - Math.sin(angle) * springLength;

  ballA.vx += (targetX - ballA.x) * spring;
  ballA.vy += (targetY - ballA.y) * spring;
  ballA.vx *= friction;
  ballA.vy *= friction;
  ballA.x += ballA.vx;
  ballA.y += ballA.vy;
}

(function drawFrame () {
  window.requestAnimationFrame(drawFrame, canvas);
  context.clearRect(0, 0, canvas.width, canvas.height);

  if (!ball0_dragging) {
    springTo(ball0, ball1);
  }
  if (!ball1_dragging) {
    springTo(ball1, ball0);
  }
```

```
      context.beginPath();
      context.moveTo(ball0.x, ball0.y);
      context.lineTo(ball1.x, ball1.y);
      context.stroke();
      ball0.draw(context);
      ball1.draw(context);
    }());
  };
  </script>
 </body>
</html>
```

For this example, the balls are placed on the canvas element and are set up for drag-and-drop. **drawFrame** calls the **springTo** function for each ball, if they are not being dragged:

```
if (!ball0_dragging) {
  springTo(ball0, ball1);
}
if (!ball1_dragging) {
  springTo(ball1, ball0);
}
```

The **springTo** function is where all the action happens, and everything here should be familiar to you. First, it finds the distance and angle to the other ball, and calculates a target point based on that. It then performs basic spring mechanics on that target point. When the function is called again, with the parameters reversed, the balls swap roles, and the original target ball springs toward the other one.

You'll see that neither ball is attached to any fixed point or the mouse; they are both free-floating. Their only constraint is that they maintain a certain distance from each other. The great thing about this setup is that it is now very easy to add additional objects. For example, let's create a third ball in example **15-triple-spring.html**. Add two new variables: **ball2** and **ball2_dragging**; and some additional code for the mouse event handlers, and animation loop (shown in bold below). You can follow this pattern to keep adding as many balls as you'd like.

```
<!doctype html>
<html>
 <head>
  <meta charset="utf-8">
  <title>Triple Spring</title>
  <link rel="stylesheet" href="style.css">
 </head>
 <body>
  <canvas id="canvas" width="400" height="400"></canvas>
  <script src="utils.js"></script>
  <script src="ball.js"></script>
  <script>
  window.onload = function () {
    var canvas = document.getElementById('canvas'),
        context = canvas.getContext('2d'),
        mouse = utils.captureMouse(canvas),
        ball0 = new Ball(20),
        ball1 = new Ball(20),
```

```
      ball2 = new Ball(20),
      ball0_dragging = false,
      ball1_dragging = false,
      ball2_dragging = false,
      spring = 0.03,
      friction = 0.9,
      springLength = 100,
      vx = 0,
      vy = 0;

ball0.x = Math.random() * canvas.width;
ball0.y = Math.random() * canvas.height;
ball1.x = Math.random() * canvas.width;
ball1.y = Math.random() * canvas.height;
ball2.x = Math.random() * canvas.width;
ball2.y = Math.random() * canvas.height;

canvas.addEventListener('mousedown', function () {
  if (utils.containsPoint(ball0.getBounds(), mouse.x, mouse.y)) {
    ball0_dragging = true;
  }
  if (utils.containsPoint(ball1.getBounds(), mouse.x, mouse.y)) {
    ball1_dragging = true;
  }
  if (utils.containsPoint(ball2.getBounds(), mouse.x, mouse.y)) {
    ball2_dragging = true;
  }
}, false);

canvas.addEventListener('mouseup', function () {
  if (ball0_dragging || ball1_dragging || ball2_dragging) {
    ball0_dragging = false;
    ball1_dragging = false;
    ball2_dragging = false;
  }
}, false);

canvas.addEventListener('mousemove', function () {
  if (ball0_dragging) {
    ball0.x = mouse.x;
    ball0.y = mouse.y;
  }
  if (ball1_dragging) {
    ball1.x = mouse.x;
    ball1.y = mouse.y;
  }
  if (ball2_dragging) {
    ball2.x = mouse.x;
    ball2.y = mouse.y;
  }
}, false);

function springTo (ballA, ballB) {
```

```
      var dx = ballB.x - ballA.x,
          dy = ballB.y - ballA.y,
          angle = Math.atan2(dy, dx),
          targetX = ballB.x - Math.cos(angle) * springLength,
          targetY = ballB.y - Math.sin(angle) * springLength;

      ballA.vx += (targetX - ballA.x) * spring;
      ballA.vy += (targetY - ballA.y) * spring;
      ballA.vx *= friction;
      ballA.vy *= friction;
      ballA.x += ballA.vx;
      ballA.y += ballA.vy;
    }

    (function drawFrame () {
      window.requestAnimationFrame(drawFrame, canvas);
      context.clearRect(0, 0, canvas.width, canvas.height);

      if (!ball0_dragging) {
        springTo(ball0, ball1);
        springTo(ball0, ball2);
      }
      if (!ball1_dragging) {
        springTo(ball1, ball0);
        springTo(ball1, ball2);
      }
      if (!ball2_dragging) {
        springTo(ball2, ball0);
        springTo(ball2, ball1);
      }

      context.beginPath();
      context.moveTo(ball0.x, ball0.y);
      context.lineTo(ball1.x, ball1.y);
      context.lineTo(ball2.x, ball2.y);
      context.lineTo(ball0.x, ball0.y);
      context.stroke();
      ball0.draw(context);
      ball1.draw(context);
      ball2.draw(context);
    }());
  };
  </script>
 </body>
</html>
```

This will create a triangle formation, as shown in Figure 8-7. Once you get the hang of this, you can move on to creating a square, and from there, all kinds of complex springy structures.

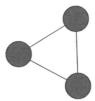

Figure 8-7. Three objects connected by a spring

Important formulas in this chapter

Once again, it's time to review the important formulas presented in this chapter.

Simple easing, long form

```
var dx = targetX - object.x,
    dy = targetY - object.y;
vx = dx * easing;
vy = dy * easing;
object.x += vx;
object.y += vy;
```

Simple easing, abbreviated form

```
vx = (targetX - object.x) * easing;
vy = (targetY - object.y) * easing;
object.x += vx;
object.y += vy;
```

Simple easing, short form

```
object.x += (targetX - object.x) * easing;
object.y += (targetY - object.y) * easing;
```

Simple spring, long form

```
var ax = (targetX - object.x) * spring,
    ay = (targetY - object.y) * spring;
vx += ax;
vy += ay;
vx *= friction;
vy *= friction;
object.x += vx;
object.y += vy;
```

Simple spring, abbreviated form

```
vx += (targetX - object.x) * spring;
vy += (targetY - object.y) * spring;
vx *= friction;
vy *= friction;
object.x += vx;
object.y += vy;
```

Simple spring, short form

```
vx += (targetX - object.x) * spring;
vy += (targetY - object.y) * spring;
object.x += (vx *= friction);
object.y += (vy *= friction);
```

Offset spring

```
var dx = object.x - fixedX,
    dy = object.y - fixedY,
    angle = Math.atan2(dy, dx),
    targetX = fixedX + Math.cos(angle) * springLength,
    targetY = fixedX + Math.sin(angle) * springLength;
//spring to targetX, targetY as above
```

Summary

This chapter covered the two basic techniques of proportional motion: easing and springing. You've learned that easing is proportional motion and springing is proportional velocity. You should have a very good understanding of how to apply both of these techniques, and have begun to play with them and create some really fun and interesting effects yourself.

Now that you've learned all sorts of ways of moving things around, let's move on to the next chapter, where you'll find out what to do when they start hitting eachother!

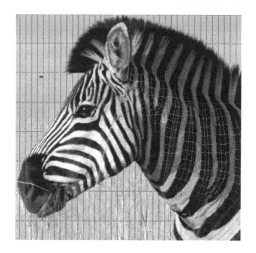

Chapter 9

Collision Detection

What we'll cover in this chapter:

- Collision detection methods
- Geometric hit testing methods
- Distance-based collision detection
- Multiple-object collision detection strategies

As you've progressed through the book, you've seen how to make objects move and make them interact with the space they occupy. Now, you're going to make these objects interact with each other. For the most part, this will involve determining when two objects have touched each other. This is a subject known as *collision detection* or *hit testing*.

This chapter will attempt to cover just about everything you need to know about detecting collisions. This includes hit testing between two objects, hit testing between an object and a point, distance-based collision detection, and multiple-object collision testing strategies. First, let's see what options are available for collision detection.

Collision detection methods

Collision detection, or hit testing, is a simple concept: You want to know whether two objects are occupying any part of the same space at the same time. Of course, you may have more than two objects, and you may want to know whether any of them are hitting any others. But when you break it down, you need to test each object, one at a time, against each other object.

There are a couple of ways of performing collision detection:

- You can test the geometry of each object; that is, does the shape of this object overlap the shape of that object? We'll use the object's rectangular bounds to determine this.

- You can test the distance between objects; that is, are these objects close enough for them to be colliding? You must calculate the distance and decide when the objects are close enough.

Each method has its uses, and we'll look at both in detail in this chapter.

However, there won't be many details about what to do when you detect a collision, or, how should two objects react when they bump into each other? That subject is covered in Chapter 11, where we discuss the conservation of momentum.

Geometric hit testing methods

In Chapter 7, we added a **getBounds** method to our **Ball** class, something that is used a number of times in this chapter. Just to refresh your memory, this method returns an object representing a rectangle with properties **x, y, width**, and **height**. This rectangle designates a bounding box that contains the shape of ball in relation to the canvas element.

Using this rectangle, we can determine if another rectangle intersects with it, or if a coordinate falls within its area. We will use these methods to test if one object is hitting another, or if an object is hitting a specific point.

Hit testing two objects

Now given that two objects each have a **getBounds** method defined, we can determine if the objects are touching by testing if the two bounding rectangles intersect. First, we need to add the utility function **utils.intersects** to our **utils.js** file:

```
utils.intersects = function (rectA, rectB) {
  return !(rectA.x + rectA.width < rectB.x ||
           rectB.x + rectB.width < rectA.x ||
           rectA.y + rectA.height < rectB.y ||
           rectB.y + rectB.height < rectA.y);
};
```

Nothing fancy here, just simple geometry. You call the function by passing it two rectangle arguments, it returns **true** if they overlap, and **false** if they don't. It is invoked like this:

```
utils.intersects(rectA, rectB)
```

When testing if two bounding boxes are touching, this will usually go within an **if** statement, like so:

```
if (utils.intersects(objectA.getBounds(), objectB.getBounds())) {
  //react to collision
}
```

In this snippet, **utils.intersects** will return **true** if there is a collision between **objectA** and **objectB**, and the statements within the **if** block will execute. This is probably the simplest method of collision detection, and also the easiest to program.

However, as with all things, there is a trade-off. As collision detection methods get easier, they get less accurate. As they get more accurate, they become more complex and computationally-intensive. So, while this is the easiest method, it is also the least accurate.

What do we mean by hit testing accuracy—either something is hitting or it's not, right? Well, it goes back to this question: Based on the positions of two objects, how do you determine if they are hitting?

In the bounding rectangle method that was just described, you take the first object and draw a rectangle around it. The top edge of the rectangle goes on the topmost visible pixel of the object's shape, the bottom edge goes on the lowest visible pixel, and the left and right edges are on their furthest visible pixels. Then you do the same for the object you're testing against. Finally, you check whether these two rectangles are intersecting in any way, and if so, you have a collision.

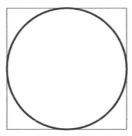

Figure 9-1. A bounding box

This rectangle around the object is known as a bounding box, and it's calculated for our ball based on its position and size. It's normally invisible, so it is explicitly drawn as rectangle around the shape in Figure 9-1 so you can see it.

Why would this be inaccurate? You might think that if the bounding boxes intersected, the objects must be touching. Well, take a look at the pictures in Figure 9-2. Which pairs would you say are touching each other?

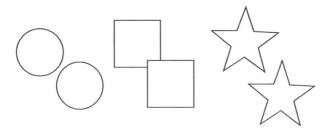

Figure 9-2. Which ones are touching?

Obviously, only the squares are actually hitting, right? Well, let's draw in the bounding boxes and see what the calculation sees. Figure 9-3 shows the results.

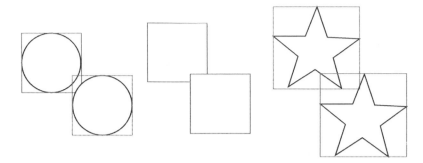

Figure 9-3. Not what you expected?

Each pair of shapes are colliding as far as our code is concerned. If you don't believe me, test the following document, **01-object-hit-test.html**. It uses the **Ball** class we created earlier, so make sure that script has been imported along with the updated **utils.js** file.

```
<!doctype html>
<html>
 <head>
  <meta charset="utf-8">
  <title>Object Hit Test</title>
  <link rel="stylesheet" href="style.css">
 </head>
 <body>
  <canvas id="canvas" width="400" height="400"></canvas>
  <textarea id="log"></textarea>
  <script src="utils.js"></script>
  <script src="ball.js"></script>
  <script>
  window.onload = function () {
    var canvas = document.getElementById('canvas'),
        context = canvas.getContext('2d'),
        log = document.getElementById('log'),
        mouse = utils.captureMouse(canvas),
        ballA = new Ball(),
        ballB = new Ball();

    ballA.x = canvas.width / 2;
    ballA.y = canvas.height / 2;

    (function drawFrame () {
      window.requestAnimationFrame(drawFrame, canvas);
      context.clearRect(0, 0, canvas.width, canvas.height);

      ballB.x = mouse.x;
      ballB.y = mouse.y;

      if (utils.intersects(ballA.getBounds(), ballB.getBounds())) {
        log.value = "Hit!";
      } else {
```

```
          log.value = '';
        }

        ballA.draw(context);
        ballB.draw(context);
      }());
    };
    </script>
  </body>
</html>
```

This example creates two instances of the **Ball** class and sets one of them to be dragged with the mouse. The **utils.intersects** function is called on each frame to check whether the two balls are hitting. If you approach the stationary ball from the top, bottom, or sides, it is accurate, but you always get a false positive if you come in diagonally. If you were to try drawing some other shapes instead of a ball, you would see that rectangular shapes work perfectly, but the more irregular the shape you use, the more inaccuracies you'll find. Be careful about using this method for anything other than rectangular shapes.

To visualize each ball's bounding box, simply draw these rectangles to the canvas. Try adding the following code to the end of the **drawFrame** animation loop:

```
var boundsA = ballA.getBounds(),
    boundsB = ballB.getBounds();

context.strokeRect(boundsA.x, boundsA.y, boundsA.width, boundsA.height);
context.strokeRect(boundsB.x, boundsB.y, boundsB.width, boundsB.height);
```

Now we'll look at an exercise that demonstrates using **utils.intersects** with rectangles. The example uses a new **Box** class that is very similar to **Ball**, and which I'm sure you'll have no trouble understanding. Here it is:

```
function Box (width, height, color) {
  if (width === undefined) { width = 50; }
  if (height === undefined) { height = 50; }
  if (color === undefined) { color = "#ff0000"; }
  this.x = 0;
  this.y = 0;
  this.width = width;
  this.height = height;
  this.vx = 0;
  this.vy = 0;
  this.rotation = 0;
  this.scaleX = 1;
  this.scaleY = 1;
  this.color = utils.parseColor(color);
  this.lineWidth = 1;
}

Box.prototype.draw = function (context) {
  context.save();
  context.translate(this.x, this.y);
  context.rotate(this.rotation);
  context.scale(this.scaleX, this.scaleY);
```

```
context.lineWidth = this.lineWidth;
context.fillStyle = this.color;
context.beginPath();
context.rect(0, 0, this.width, this.height);
context.closePath();
context.fill();
if (this.lineWidth > 0) {
  context.stroke();
}
context.restore();
};
```

You'll notice that we left off the **getBounds** method in the **Box** class. Since the rectangle objects already contain the required properties, we can pass them directly to the **utils.intersects** function to test for a collision.

In this next example, a box is created at the top of the canvas element and falls to the bottom. When the box is placed, it falls down until it hits the bottom of the canvas or collides with another box. If it hits another box, it positions itself so it is sitting right on top of it. Here's the code for document **02-boxes.html**:

```
<!doctype html>
<html>
 <head>
  <meta charset="utf-8">
  <title>Boxes</title>
  <link rel="stylesheet" href="style.css">
 </head>
 <body>
  <canvas id="canvas" width="400" height="400"></canvas>
  <script src="utils.js"></script>
  <script src="box.js"></script>
  <script>
  window.onload = function () {
    var canvas = document.getElementById('canvas'),
        context = canvas.getContext('2d'),
        boxes = [],
        activeBox = createBox(),
        gravity = 0.2;

    function createBox () {
      var box = new Box(Math.random() * 40 + 10, Math.random() * 40 + 10);
      box.x = Math.random() * canvas.width;
      boxes.push(box);
      return box;
    }

    function drawBox (box) {
      if (activeBox !== box && utils.intersects(activeBox, box)) {
        activeBox.y = box.y - activeBox.height;
        activeBox = createBox();
      }
      box.draw(context);
```

```
    }

    (function drawFrame () {
      window.requestAnimationFrame(drawFrame, canvas);
      context.clearRect(0, 0, canvas.width, canvas.height);

      activeBox.vy += gravity;
      activeBox.y += activeBox.vy;

      if (activeBox.y + activeBox.height > canvas.height) {
        activeBox.y = canvas.height - activeBox.height;
        activeBox = createBox();
      }
      boxes.forEach(drawBox);
    }());
  };
  </script>
 </body>
</html>
```

In the **drawFrame** function, the code checks whether the box has gone below the bottom of the canvas element. And if so, it stops it and creates a new box. Then it iterates over the **boxes** array passing each box to the **drawBox** function, which checks the active box against all the other boxes. First, it makes sure it is not doing a hit test against itself, and then, at the heart of the program, **utils.intersects** determines whether the box has hit another one. If it has, the code repositions the moving box to the top of the one it just hit, and then creates a new box. Run this code for a minute or so, and you'll see something that looks like in Figure 9.4.

Figure 9-4. Collision detection with a rectangle's bounding box.

If you really want to see the inaccuracy of this method in action, instead of a rectangle, try drawing a circle, or some other irregular shape. Some objects will appear to hover in mid-air as they "hit" other objects, as shown in Figure 9.5.

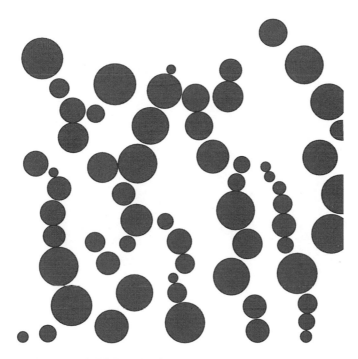

Figure 9-5. Collision detection with a circle's bounding box.

Hit testing an object and a point

In Chapter 7, the utility function `utils.containsPoint` was introduced, but here we will see how it relates to hit testing; although, it's not very useful for testing for the collision between two objects. As mentioned previously, the function takes three arguments: the first is a rectangle object with **x**, **y**, **width**, and **height** properties, and the remaining two arguments define x and y coordinates. It returns **true** or **false**, depending if that point is hitting the rectangle in question. Here's the function again so you don't have to look it up, but it should already be in your **utils.js** file:

```
utils.containsPoint = function (rect, x, y) {
  return !(x < rect.x || x > rect.x + rect.width ||
          y < rect.y || y > rect.y + rect.height);
};
```

It might be used like this when testing if point (100, 100) falls within a rectangle:

```
if (utils.containsPoint(rect, 100, 100)) {
  //react to collision
}
```

But once again, we come back to the question: What constitutes a hit? And, once again, we see the bounding box coming into play—the code only checks if the point is within an object's bounding box.

Let's do a quick test to see that in action with example **03-point-hit-test.html**:

```
<!doctype html>
<html>
 <head>
  <meta charset="utf-8">
  <title>Point Hit Test</title>
  <link rel="stylesheet" href="style.css">
 </head>
 <body>
  <canvas id="canvas" width="400" height="400"></canvas>
  <textarea id="log"></textarea>
  <script src="utils.js"></script>
  <script src="ball.js"></script>
  <script>
  window.onload = function () {
    var canvas = document.getElementById('canvas'),
        context = canvas.getContext('2d'),
        mouse = utils.captureMouse(canvas),
        log = document.getElementById('log'),
        ball = new Ball();

    ball.x = canvas.width / 2;
    ball.y = canvas.height / 2;
    ball.draw(context);

    canvas.addEventListener('mousemove', function () {
      if (utils.containsPoint(ball.getBounds(), mouse.x, mouse.y)) {
        log.value = "Hit!";
      } else {
        log.value = '';
      }
    }, false);
  };
  </script>
 </body>
</html>
```

This uses the mouse cursor as the point which the ball hit tests against. As you move the mouse close to the ball, you will see that it probably starts registering a hit before you actually touch the shape, especially if you come at it from a corner, as shown in Figure 9.6. Try it again with a square and it should be perfectly accurate. So again, this method seems to be useful only for rectangle-shaped objects.

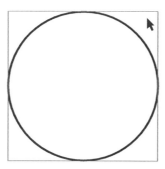

Figure 9-6. Collision detection using a circle's bounding box causes a false positive.

To use this method for more accurate collision detection, you can test several points along the shape's outline. This gives you a more precise definition of the object boundaries, but also means the program has to run more tests. And depending on the shape complexity, all these tests could slow down the web browser. For example, if you had a star-shaped object, you could calculate the position its five points, and do a hit test from another object to each of those five points. But then if you had two stars, you would need to test each one against the other's five points. For a star, this would probably work pretty well; but a more complex shape would obviously need more points. You can see this gets very complex and computationally-intensive very quickly. Just two stars, and you're up to ten times the number of hit tests you would use for the more simple method. Accuracy costs you.

If you must perform collision detection against an irregular shape, a good strategy is to break complex shapes into smaller rectangles, and test against those. This will give you greater accuracy, but also increase the amount of calculations, so find a balance between the two. For greater efficiency, first test against the entire shape's bounding box, and then only if it's a hit, break the object up into smaller rectangles to test against.

Summary of geometric hit testing

Collision detection between two irregularly shaped objects, so that if any part of one touches the other, is not readily supported using our simple geometric methods. But there are a few options:

- For roughly rectangular objects, use `utils.intersects(rectA, rectB)`.

- For irregularly shaped objects, you either live with the inaccuracy or custom program a solution, probably using `utils.containsPoint(rect, x, y)`.

Of course, the chapter is far from done yet, and there are solutions beyond what we've covered here. If you have circular or roughly circular objects, distance-based collision detection will probably be your best bet. You'd be surprised at how many shapes can be characterized as "roughly rectangular" or "roughly circular".

Distance-based collision detection

In this section, you'll abandon the geometric hit testing functions and take collision detection into your own hands. This involves using the distance between two objects to determine whether they have collided.

As an example of this idea in the real world, let's say the center of your car is 100 feet from the center of my car. Given this space, you know that the two cars are far enough apart that they couldn't possibly be touching. However, if both of our cars are 6 feet wide and 12 feet long, and the center of my car is 5 feet from the center of your car, you can be pretty certain that we're in trouble. In other words, there is no way for the centers to be that close together without some parts of the cars touching. That's the whole concept behind distance-based testing. You determine the minimum distance required to separate the two objects, calculate the current distance, and compare the two. If the current distance is less than the minimum, you know they are hitting.

And of course, there is a trade-off. Where the simplest rectangle intersection worked perfectly with rectangles, but was less accurate using other shapes, this method works perfectly with circles. It's problem is that non-circle shapes that appear to be touching don't register a collision because their centers are still not close enough.

Simple distance-based collision detection

Let's start out with the ideal situation: a couple of perfectly round circles. When doing this type of collision detection, we should measure from the exact center of the circle; we can use our `Ball` class for this. Building off the first example in this chapter, create two balls and set up one of them to be dragged with the mouse. You'll also perform your collision detection in the `drawFrame` function, but instead of using `utils.intersects` to check for a collision, you'll be using the distance between the two balls. You should already know how to compute the distance between two objects using the Pythagorean Theorem from back in Chapter 3. So, you start off with something like this:

```
var dx = ballB.x - ballA.x,
    dy = ballB.y - ballA.y,
    dist = Math.sqrt(dx * dx + dy * dy);
```

Now you have the distance, but how do you know whether that distance is small enough to consider that a collision has occurred? Well, take a look at the picture in Figure 9-7.

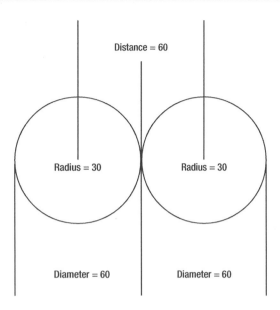

Figure 9-7. The distance of a collision

You can see the two circular objects in a position where they are just touching. Consider that each ball is 60 pixels across, which gives it a radius of 30. Thus, at the exact moment they touch, they are exactly 60 pixels apart—there's the answer. For two circular objects of the same size, if the distance is less than their diameter, they are colliding. Here's the code for this example (**04-distance-1.html**):

```
<!doctype html>
<html>
 <head>
  <meta charset="utf-8">
  <title>Distance 1</title>
  <link rel="stylesheet" href="style.css">
 </head>
 <body>
  <canvas id="canvas" width="400" height="400"></canvas>
  <textarea id="log"></textarea>
  <script src="utils.js"></script>
  <script src="ball.js"></script>
  <script>
  window.onload = function () {
    var canvas = document.getElementById('canvas'),
        context = canvas.getContext('2d'),
        mouse = utils.captureMouse(canvas),
        log = document.getElementById('log'),
        ballA = new Ball(30),
        ballB = new Ball(30);

    ballA.x = canvas.width / 2;
    ballA.y = canvas.height / 2;
```

```
    canvas.addEventListener('mousemove', drawFrame, false);
    drawFrame();

    function drawFrame () {
      context.clearRect(0, 0, canvas.width, canvas.height);

      ballB.x = mouse.x;
      ballB.y = mouse.y;

      var dx = ballB.x - ballA.x,
          dy = ballB.y - ballA.y,
          dist = Math.sqrt(dx * dx + dy * dy);

      if (dist < 60) {
        log.value = "Hit!";
      } else {
        log.value = '';
      }

      ballA.draw(context);
      ballB.draw(context);
    }
  };
  </script>
 </body>
</html>
```

When you run this, you'll notice that it doesn't matter from which angle you approach the target ball. It doesn't register a hit until that exact point when the shapes overlap.

It's already been mentioned that hard-coding numbers into code is generally bad style. You would need to change the code every time you had different-sized objects. Furthermore, what about the case where the two objects are not the same size? We need to abstract this concept into some kind of formula that will fit any situation.

Figure 9-8 shows two balls of different sizes, again, just touching. The one on the left is 60 pixels across, and the one on the right is 40 pixels. Thus, the radius of one is 30, and the radius of the other is 20. So, the distance between them at the moment they touch is exactly 50. Of course, in the case of the `Ball` class, we've already programmed in this `radius` property, so we can check it directly.

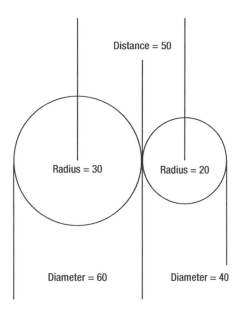

Distance = 50

Radius = 30

Radius = 20

Diameter = 60

Diameter = 40

Figure 9-8. The distance of a collision between two different-sized objects

A pattern begins to emerge. The distance is the **radius** of one ball, plus the **radius** of the other. You can now remove all hard-coded numbers from the code and modify the **drawFrame** function to this (which can be found in document **05-distance-2.html**):

```
function drawFrame () {
  context.clearRect(0, 0, canvas.width, canvas.height);

  ballB.x = mouse.x;
  ballB.y = mouse.y;

  var dx = ballB.x - ballA.x,
      dy = ballB.y - ballA.y,
      dist = Math.sqrt(dx * dx + dy * dy);

  if (dist < ballA.radius + ballB.radius) {
    log.value = "Hit!";
  } else {
    log.value = '';
  }

  ballA.draw(context);
  ballB.draw(context);
}
```

Go ahead and change the size of one or both of the balls (remember, you can pass in a radius as the first parameter when instantiating the object) and see that this code works, even if one circle is huge and one circle is tiny. In fact, in the full example mentioned earlier, the balls are declared like this:

```
var ballA = new Ball(Math.random() * 100),
    ballB = new Ball(Math.random() * 100);
```

This way, they will be different sized each time the code is run, and yet the collision detection always works perfectly.

Collision-based springing

The problem with giving you a good working example of distance-based hit testing is that a complete program would involve a lot of issues related to things that haven't been covered yet, such as the reaction of two objects when they hit, and how to efficiently handle interactions between many objects. But we'll create an example that demonstrates hit testing without too much code that you haven't already seen.

The basic idea is to place one large ball, called `centerBall`, in the center of the canvas. Then add in a bunch of smaller balls, giving them random sizes and velocities. These will move with basic motion code and bounce off the walls. On each frame, perform a distance-based collision check between each moving ball and the center ball. If you detect a collision, calculate an offset spring target based on the angle between the two balls and the minimum distance to avoid collision. All it really means is that if a moving ball collides with the center ball, you make it spring back out again. You do this by setting a target just outside the center ball, and the moving ball springs to that target. Then, once it reaches the target, it is no longer colliding, so the spring action ends, and it just moves with its regular motion code.

The result is kind of like bubbles bouncing off a large bubble, as shown in Figure 9-9. The little bubbles enter into the big one a bit, depending on how fast they are going, but then spring back out.

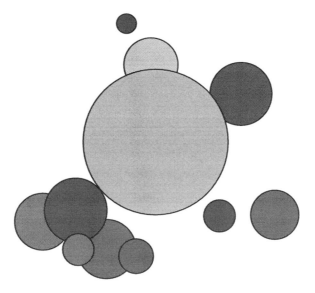

Figure 9-9. Collision-based springing

Here is the code for the example (document **06-bubbles-1.html**):

```
<!doctype html>
<html>
 <head>
  <meta charset="utf-8">
  <title>Bubbles 1</title>
  <link rel="stylesheet" href="style.css">
 </head>
 <body>
  <canvas id="canvas" width="400" height="400"></canvas>
  <script src="utils.js"></script>
  <script src="ball.js"></script>
  <script>
  window.onload = function () {
    var canvas = document.getElementById('canvas'),
        context = canvas.getContext('2d'),
        centerBall = new Ball(100, "#cccccc"),
        balls = [],
        numBalls = 10,
        spring = 0.03,
        bounce = -1;

    centerBall.x = canvas.width / 2;
    centerBall.y = canvas.height / 2;

    for (var ball, i = 0; i < numBalls; i++) {
      ball = new Ball(Math.random() * 40 + 5, Math.random() * 0xffffff);
      ball.x = Math.random() * canvas.width / 2;
      ball.y = Math.random() * canvas.height / 2;
      ball.vx = Math.random() * 6 - 3;
      ball.vy = Math.random() * 6 - 3;
      balls.push(ball);
    }

    function move (ball) {
      ball.x += ball.vx;
      ball.y += ball.vy;

      if (ball.x + ball.radius > canvas.width) {
        ball.x = canvas.width - ball.radius;
        ball.vx *= bounce;
      } else if (ball.x - ball.radius < 0) {
        ball.x = ball.radius;
        ball.vx *= bounce;
      }
      if (ball.y + ball.radius > canvas.height) {
        ball.y = canvas.height - ball.radius;
        ball.vy *= bounce;
      } else if (ball.y - ball.radius < 0) {
        ball.y = ball.radius;
        ball.vy *= bounce;
      }
    }

    function draw (ball) {
```

217

```
    var dx = ball.x - centerBall.x,
        dy = ball.y - centerBall.y,
        dist = Math.sqrt(dx * dx + dy * dy),
        min_dist = ball.radius + centerBall.radius;

    if (dist < min_dist) {
      var angle = Math.atan2(dy, dx),
          tx = centerBall.x + Math.cos(angle) * min_dist,
          ty = centerBall.y + Math.sin(angle) * min_dist;
      ball.vx += (tx - ball.x) * spring;
      ball.vy += (ty - ball.y) * spring;
    }
    ball.draw(context);
  }

  (function drawFrame () {
    window.requestAnimationFrame(drawFrame, canvas);
    context.clearRect(0, 0, canvas.width, canvas.height);

    balls.forEach(move);
    balls.forEach(draw);
    centerBall.draw(context);
  }());
};
</script>
</body>
</html>
```

This is a lot of code, but you've already seen most of these techniques in earlier chapters. Let's walk through it quickly.

Starting at the top of the script, you create the **centerBall** and then loop through and create the smaller, moving, balls. They are given a random size, position, color, and velocity.

Within the **drawFrame** animation loop, we iterate over the balls twice. To separate functionality, the motion code has been placed in a function called **move**. This takes a reference to one of the balls and applies all the basic motion code to it—it's basic velocity code with bouncing. Then, in the **draw** function, you find the distance from a given ball to the **centerBall**, and compute the minimum distance to determine a collision. If there is a collision, you find the angle between the two, and use that plus the minimum distance to calculate a target x and y. This target will be right on the outer edge of the **centerBall**.

From there, you just apply basic spring code to spring to that point (as described in Chapter 8). Of course, once it reaches that point, it's no longer colliding and will fly off in whatever direction it's heading. We then draw the balls to the canvas.

See how you can build up and layer simple techniques to wind up with some very complex motion?

Multiple-object collision detection strategies

When you have just a couple of objects moving around the screen, it's pretty simple to test them against each other. But when you get several objects, or even dozens, you need some kind of strategy for how to test them so that you don't miss any possible collisions. Furthermore, as you have more and more objects being tested, it becomes very important to perform your tests with some kind of efficiency in mind.

Basic multiple-object collision detection

With just two objects, only one collision is possible—A versus B. With three objects, you have three possibilities: A-B, B-C, and C-A. Four objects give you six collisions, and five objects give you ten collisions. When you get up to 20 objects, you need to take into account 190 separate collisions! That means that in your **drawFrame** function, you need to run a collision detection calculation 190 times.

That's enough as it is, so you certainly don't need to be adding any more unnecessary hit testing. But many beginners wind up doing not just a few extra hit tests, but exactly *twice* as many as necessary! For 20 objects, they do 380 hit test (20 objects each testing 19 others, or 20 × 19 = 380). You can see why you should have a solid understanding of this subject.

To understand the problem, let's take a look at what needs to be done, and how it is often approached. Say you have six objects, named **object0**, **object1**, **object2**, **object3**, **object4**, and **object5**. You have them moving around nicely, bouncing or whatever, and you want to know when any one of the objects hits any other one. The obvious solution is to make two nested loops. The outer one iterates through each of the six objects, gets a reference to each one in turn, and then loops through again, comparing it to each of the others. Here it is in pseudo-code:

```
objects.forEach(function (objectA, i) {
  for (var j = 0; j < objects.length; j++) {
    var objectB = objects[j];
    if (hitTestObject(objectA, objectB)) {
      //do something
    }
  }
});
```

That's 36 hit tests for six objects. Seems reasonable, but this code has two huge problems.

First, take a look what happens the first time through it. The variables i and j will both equal 0. So **objectA** will hold a reference to **object0**, as will **objectB**. That means you're testing an object against itself, which is a waste of a calculation. You could make sure that **objectA != objectB** before performing the hit test, or you could even go simpler and just make sure i != j. Then you get something like this:

```
objects.forEach(function (objectA, i) {
  for (var j = 0; j < objects.length; j++) {
    var objectB = objects[j];
    if (i !== j && hitTestObject(objectA, objectB)) {
      //do something
    }
  }
});
```

That eliminated six hit tests, so you're down to 30, but this is still too many. Let's write out the exact tests you're doing. You are comparing the following:

```
object0   with   object1, object2, object3, object4, object5
object1   with   object0, object2, object3, object4, object5
object2   with   object0, object1, object3, object4, object5
object3   with   object0, object1, object2, object4, object5
object4   with   object0, object1, object2, object3, object5
object5   with   object0, object1, object2, object3, object4
```

Look at the first test on the first row: **object0** with **object1**. Now look at the first test on the second row: **object1** with **object0**—that's the same thing! If **object0** is not hitting **object1**, **object1** is also not hitting **object0**. Or if one is hitting the other, you can be sure the other is hitting the first. There are many of these double checks in there. If you remove all the duplicate tests, you get this:

```
object0   with   object1, object2, object3, object4, object5
object1   with   object2, object3, object4, object5
object2   with   object3, object4, object5
object3   with   object4, object5
object4   with   object5
object5   with   nothing!
```

You see that in the first round of tests, you're testing **object0** with every other object. Because no other object needs to test against that one again, you drop **object0** off the list. Then **object1** tests against the remaining objects, and you drop it off the list. By the time you get to the last one, **object5**, every other object has already tested itself for a collision with it. There's no need to test it against anything. The result is that you're down to 15 tests, so you see why our initial solution ends up being double what is needed.

To code this, you still have two nested loops—a **for** loop within the **forEach** iteration—but now it looks like this:

```
objects.forEach(function (objectA, i) {
  for (var j = i + 1; j < objects.length; j++) {
    var objectB = objects[j];
    if (hitTestObject(objectA, objectB) {
      //do whatever
    }
  }
});
```

In the inner **for** loop, you always start with one higher than the index of the outer iteration. This is because you've already tested everything lower, and you don't want to test the same index, which, as you saw, would be testing an object against itself. This lets you get rid of that check. The result is just a few characters different from the original code, but gives you a 100% performance increase!

Also, even beyond its performance impact, in many cases, doing double hit testing might have unwanted results. If you're changing the velocity or some other value when you detect a collision, you may wind up changing it twice, resulting in an undetermined, and hard to debug, effect.

If this topic interests you, and you'd like to dig a lot deeper, this is all a part of Combinatorics, a field of math concerned with problems of selection and arrangement, or: How to count without counting.

Multiple-object springing

Let's make another quick example to see this in action. Again, we'll go with the bubble-type reaction, but this time, all bubbles can bounce off of each other. Figure 9-10 illustrates the effect.

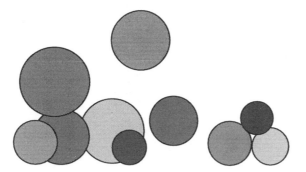

Figure 9-10. Multiple-object collision

Here's the code in document **07-bubbles-2.html**:

```
<!doctype html>
<html>
 <head>
  <meta charset="utf-8">
  <title>Bubbles 2</title>
  <link rel="stylesheet" href="style.css">
 </head>
 <body>
  <canvas id="canvas" width="400" height="400"></canvas>
  <script src="utils.js"></script>
  <script src="ball.js"></script>
  <script>
  window.onload = function () {
    var canvas = document.getElementById('canvas'),
        context = canvas.getContext('2d'),
        balls = [],
        numBalls = 10,
        bounce = -0.5,
        spring = 0.03,
        gravity = 0.1;

    for (var ball, i = 0; i < numBalls; i++) {
      ball = new Ball(Math.random() * 30 + 20, Math.random() * 0xffffff);
      ball.x = Math.random() * canvas.width / 2;
      ball.y = Math.random() * canvas.height / 2;
      ball.vx = Math.random() * 6 - 3;
      ball.vy = Math.random() * 6 - 3;
      balls.push(ball);
    }

    function checkCollision (ballA, i) {
```

```javascript
    for (var ballB, dx, dy, dist, min_dist, j = i + 1; j < numBalls; j++) {
      ballB = balls[j];
      dx = ballB.x - ballA.x;
      dy = ballB.y - ballA.y;
      dist = Math.sqrt(dx * dx + dy * dy);
      min_dist = ballA.radius + ballB.radius;

      if (dist < min_dist) {
        var angle = Math.atan2(dy, dx),
            tx = ballA.x + Math.cos(angle) * min_dist,
            ty = ballA.y + Math.sin(angle) * min_dist,
            ax = (tx - ballB.x) * spring * 0.5,
            ay = (ty - ballB.y) * spring * 0.5;

        ballA.vx -= ax;
        ballA.vy -= ay;
        ballB.vx += ax;
        ballB.vy += ay;
      }
    }
  }
}

function move (ball) {
  ball.vy += gravity;
  ball.x += ball.vx;
  ball.y += ball.vy;

  if (ball.x + ball.radius > canvas.width) {
    ball.x = canvas.width - ball.radius;
    ball.vx *= bounce;
  } else if (ball.x - ball.radius < 0) {
    ball.x = ball.radius;
    ball.vx *= bounce;
  }
  if (ball.y + ball.radius > canvas.height) {
    ball.y = canvas.height - ball.radius;
    ball.vy *= bounce;
  } else if (ball.y - ball.radius < 0) {
    ball.y = ball.radius;
    ball.vy *= bounce;
  }
}

function draw (ball) {
  ball.draw(context);
}

(function drawFrame () {
  window.requestAnimationFrame(drawFrame, canvas);
  context.clearRect(0, 0, canvas.width, canvas.height);

  balls.forEach(checkCollision);
  balls.forEach(move);
  balls.forEach(draw);
```

```
   }());
  };
 </script>
 </body>
</html>
```

Here, you are simply using the double-nested iteration to perform collision detection. In this case, the reaction might need some additional explanation. Here's the collision reaction code located in the **checkCollision** function:

```
if (dist < min_dist) {
  var angle = Math.atan2(dy, dx),
      tx = ballA.x + Math.cos(angle) * min_dist,
      ty = ballA.y + Math.sin(angle) * min_dist,
      ax = (tx - ballB.x) * spring * 0.5,
      ay = (ty - ballB.y) * spring * 0.5;

  ballA.vx -= ax;
  ballA.vy -= ay;
  ballB.vx += ax;
  ballB.vy += ay;
}
```

Remember that this occurs once a collision is found between **ballA** and **ballB**. Essentially, it starts out the same as the earlier example with the unmoving center ball. For now, let **ballA** take the place of that center ball. You find the angle between the two, and get a target x and y. This is the point that you would need to place **ballB** so that the two balls would not be touching. Based on that, you get the x and y acceleration that would cause **ballB** to spring to that point, then we cut it in half (which I explain next). These are **ax** and **ay**.

But then you do something a little tricky. In this case, not only does **ballB** need to spring away from **ballA**, but **ballA** must spring away from **ballB**. The acceleration would be the same force and exactly the opposite direction. So rather than calculate it twice, you just add **ax** and **ay** to **ballB**'s velocity, and subtract them from **ballA**'s velocity! You get the same result, and you just saved a bunch of calculation. You might be thinking that this doubles the final acceleration, as it's being applied twice; and that's true. To compensate, we cut the the **spring** product in half, multiplying it by 0.5, when we calculated **ax** and **ay**. You can remove these two multiplication operations by halving the **spring** variable when you declare it, to 0.015.

While we're discussing optimization tricks, here's another one here. The preceding code calculates the angle using **Math.atan2**, and then uses **Math.cos** and **Math.sin** to find the target point:

```
var angle = Math.atan2(dy, dx),
    tx = ballA.x + Math.cos(angle) * min_dist,
    ty = ballA.y + Math.sin(angle) * min_dist;
```

But remember that sine is opposite over hypotenuse, and cosine is adjacent over hypotenuse. And since the opposite side of the angle is **dy**, the adjacent side is **dx**, and the hypotenuse is **dist**. Thus, you could actually shorten these three lines to just two:

```
var tx = ballA.x + dx / dist * min_dist,
    ty = ballA.y + dy / dist * min_dist;
```

Which just wiped out three calls to trigonometry functions and replaced them with two simple divisions.

You can view this example that includes all the optimization updates in document **08-bubbles-3.html**, which can be downloaded from **www.apress.com**. Before you move on, take some time to play with the springing bubbles example. You can adjust many variables, so try changing the spring, gravity, number, and size of the balls. You might want to try adding some friction or some mouse interaction.

Important formulas in this chapter

It's time to review the two important formulas presented in this chapter.

Distance-based collision detection

```
//starting with objectA and objectB
//if using an object without a radius property,
//you can use width or height divided by 2
var dx = objectB.x - objectA.x,
    dy = objectB.y - objectA.y,
    dist = Math.sqrt(dx * dx + dy * dy);

if (dist < objectA.radius + objectB.radius) {
  //handle collision
}
```

Multiple-object collision detection

```
objects.forEach(function (objectA, i) {
  for (var j = i + 1; j < objects.length; j++) {
    //evaluate reference using j. For example:
    var objectB = objects[j];
    //perform collision detection between objectA and objectB
  }
});
```

Summary

This chapter covered just about everything you need to know about collision detection, including using geometric ht testing methods, distance-based collision checking, and how to efficiently track collisions among many objects. You should know the pros and cons of each method, and situations where each works well or does not perform satisfactorily. You'll be using all of this material as you move forward in the book, and no doubt, you'll be using it extensively in your own projects.

In the next chapter, you'll look at collisions between objects and angled surfaces, using a technique known as coordinate rotation. This technique will also be used in Chapter 11, where you'll find out what to do to create a realistic reaction to the collisions you learned how to detect here.

Chapter 10

Coordinate Rotation and Bouncing Off Angles

What we'll cover in this chapter:

- Simple coordinate rotation
- Advanced coordinate rotation
- Bouncing off an angle

This chapter covers a technique known as *coordinate rotation*, which as its name implies, involves rotating a coordinate around a point. While useful all by itself, coordinate rotation is indispensable for several very interesting effects, including how to bounce something off an angled surface. We'll cover how to do that in this chapter.

Coordinate rotation is also useful for calculating the reactions of two objects that bounce off each other. You'll see how to do that in the next chapter, where we discuss the conservation of momentum. Since the next chapter builds off the knowledge presented in this chapter, make sure you have a fairly good understanding of coordinate rotation before moving on.

Simple coordinate rotation

The technique for simple coordinate rotation was covered in Chapter 3 when discussing trigonometry. You have a center point, an object, a radius (orbit), and an angle (in radians). You increase or decrease the angle, and use basic trigonometry to place the object around the center point. You can set a variable such as **vr** (velocity/speed of rotation) to control how much the angle is increased or decreased. Using pseudo-code, the program setup would look like this:

```
vr = 0.1
angle = 0
radius = 100
centerX = 0
centerY = 0
```

With these calculations inside the animation loop:

```
object.x = centerX + cos(angle) * radius
object.y = centerY + sin(angle) * radius
angle += vr
```

You're using trigonometry to set the **x** and **y** position of the object based on the angle and the radius, and changing the angle on each frame. Figure 10-1 illustrates a frame from an animation where the object is positioned around a center point.

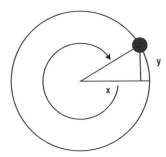

Figure 10-1. Positioning the object along an orbital path around a center point.

Here's an example to demonstrate this formula, document **01-rotate-1.html**:

```
<!doctype html>
<html>
 <head>
  <meta charset="utf-8">
  <title>Rotate 1</title>
  <link rel="stylesheet" href="style.css">
 </head>
 <body>
  <canvas id="canvas" width="400" height="400"></canvas>
  <script src="utils.js"></script>
  <script src="ball.js"></script>
  <script>
  window.onload = function () {
    var canvas = document.getElementById('canvas'),
        context = canvas.getContext('2d'),
        ball = new Ball(),
        vr = 0.05,
        angle = 0,
        radius = 150,
        centerX = canvas.width / 2,
```

```
      centerY = canvas.height / 2;

    (function drawFrame () {
      window.requestAnimationFrame(drawFrame, canvas);
      context.clearRect(0, 0, canvas.width, canvas.height);

      ball.x = centerX + Math.cos(angle) * radius;
      ball.y = centerY + Math.sin(angle) * radius;
      angle += vr;
      ball.draw(context);
    }());
  };
  </script>
</body>
</html>
```

This approach works great when you know the angle and radius from a center point.

But what if you only have the position of the object and the center point? Well, it isn't too hard to calculate the current angle and radius based on the x and y positions. Once you have them, you can carry on as before. Figure 10-2 shows the general layout of our calculation, and here's the code:

```
var dx = ball.x - centerX,
    dy = ball.y - centerY,
    angle = Math.atan2(dy, dx),
    radius = Math.sqrt(dx * dx + dy * dy);
```

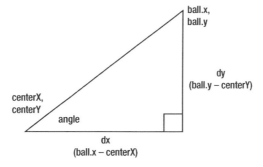

Figure 10-2. Getting ready to calculate the angle and radius.

This method of coordinate rotation is fine for a single object, especially in a situation where you only need to determine the angle and radius once. But in a more dynamic example, you could have many objects to rotate, and their relative positions to the center rotation point could be changing. So, for each object, you would need to compute its distance, angle, and radius, then add the **vr** to the angle, and finally calculate the new x, y position, on each frame. This is neither elegant, nor efficient, but fortunately, there is a better way.

Advanced coordinate rotation

The next formula is great if you are rotating objects around a point, and you only know their positions. The equation just needs the x, y position of the object in relation to the center point and the angle to rotate by. It returns the new x, y position of the object, rotated around the center point. Here's the formula:

```
x1 = x * cos(rotation) - y * sin(rotation)
y1 = y * cos(rotation) + x * sin(rotation)
```

The result of this formula is illustrated in Figure 10-3. You are rotating the coordinates x and y, but more specifically, they're the coordinates of that object in relation to the center point it is rotating around. Thus, you could also write the formula like this:

```
x1 = (x - centerX) * cos(rotation) - (y - centerY) * sin(rotation)
y1 = (y - centerY) * cos(rotation) + (x - centerX) * sin(rotation)
```

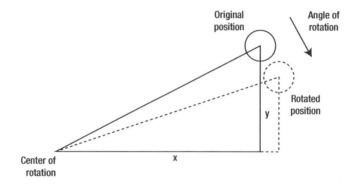

Figure 10-3. Coordinates rotated around a center point by specifying the angle of rotation.

The **rotation** angle is how much the object has rotated in this step. It's not the current angle, or the resulting angle, but the difference between the two. In other words, if the object is at a 45-degree angle from the center point, and the rotation here is 5 degrees, you will rotate the object another 5 degrees to put it at 50. And of course, this angle will be in radians, not degrees. Using this technique, you probably don't know, and don't really care about, the initial and final angles. You're just interested in how much rotation is occurring.

This equation may seem a little like magic, but we can understand how it works by breaking it down. Now this isn't necessary to use the formula, but it's here in case the math is useful for you. Start with the equation for simple coordinate rotation from the previous section (**centerX** and **centerY** have been removed since we're rotating around point 0, 0):

```
x  = radius * cos(angle)
y  = radius * sin(angle)
x1 = radius * cos(angle + rotation)
y1 = radius * sin(angle + rotation)
```

The cosine of the sum of two angles is given by the formula:

```
cos(a + b) = cos(a) * cos(b) - sin(a) * sin(b)
```

And the corresponding formula for the sine is:

```
sin(a + b) = sin(a) * cos(b) + cos(a) * sin(b)
```

So, after expanding the equations for **x1** and **x2**, we get:

```
x1 = radius * cos(angle) * cos(rotation) - radius * sin(angle) * sin(rotation)
y1 = radius * sin(angle) * cos(rotation) + radius * cos(angle) * sin(rotation)
```

Therefore, after we substitute in the **x** and **y** variables from above, we have our equation:

```
x1 = x * cos(rotation) - y * sin(rotation)
y1 = y * cos(rotation) + x * sin(rotation)
```

We're just using this equation, so it's not necessary for you to understand how we got it, as much as what it does. So let's see what we can do with it.

Rotating a single object

This example places a single ball at a random location and then uses the advanced coordinate rotation technique from the previous section to rotate it. It builds on the first example in this chapter, with the added code in bold (document **02-rotate-2.html**):

```
<!doctype html>
<html>
 <head>
  <meta charset="utf-8">
  <title>Rotate 2</title>
  <link rel="stylesheet" href="style.css">
 </head>
 <body>
  <canvas id="canvas" width="400" height="400"></canvas>
  <script src="utils.js"></script>
  <script src="ball.js"></script>
  <script>
  window.onload = function () {
    var canvas = document.getElementById('canvas'),
        context = canvas.getContext('2d'),
        ball = new Ball(),
        vr = 0.05,
        cos = Math.cos(vr),
        sin = Math.sin(vr),
        centerX = canvas.width / 2,
        centerY = canvas.height / 2;

    ball.x = Math.random() * canvas.width;
    ball.y = Math.random() * canvas.height;

    (function drawFrame () {
      window.requestAnimationFrame(drawFrame, canvas);
      context.clearRect(0, 0, canvas.width, canvas.height);
```

```
    var x1 = ball.x - centerX,
        y1 = ball.y - centerY,
        x2 = x1 * cos    y1 * sin,
        y2 = y1 * cos + x1 * sin;

    ball.x = centerX + x2;
    ball.y = centerY + y2;
    ball.draw(context);
  }());
};
</script>
</body>
</html>
```

Here, you are setting **vr** to the same value of 0.05 you used before. Then you're calculating the sine and cosine of that angle. Since those values won't change during this simple example, you can calculate it once at the top of the script, rather than recalculating it every frame. The **x1** and **y1** positions are calculated in relation to the point they will rotate around—the center of the canvas. Then you apply the coordinate rotation formula as just described. This gives you **x2** and **y2**, the new position of the ball. Again, this is in relation to the center point, so you need to add **x2** and **y2** to the center point to get the final position of the ball.

Try it out, and you'll see it should work exactly the same as the earlier version. Now, why bother going through this new, more complex, formula when the results look the same? Well, in a simple situation like this, you might not. But let's look at some examples where this setup actually simplifies things. First, consider rotating multiple objects.

Rotating multiple objects

Suppose there are many objects to rotate, say a bunch of objects in an array called **balls**. Moving each ball would look something like this:

```
balls.forEach(function (ball) {
  var dx = ball.x - centerX,
      dy = ball.y - centerY,
      angle = Math.atan2(dy, dx),
      dist = Math.sqrt(dx * dx + dy * dy);

  angle += vr;
  ball.x = centerX + Math.cos(angle) * dist;
  ball.y = centerY + Math.sin(angle) * dist;
});
```

Whereas the advanced coordinate rotation method would look like this:

```
var cos = Math.cos(vr),
    sin = Math.sin(vr);

balls.forEach(function (ball) {
  var x1 = ball.x - centerX,
      y1 = ball.y - centerY,
```

```
    x2 = x1 * cos - y1 * sin,
    y2 = y1 * cos + x1 * sin;

  ball.x = centerX + x2;
  ball.y = centerY + y2;
});
```

The first version includes four calls to **Math** functions within the iteration, meaning that all four are executed once for each object being rotated. The second version has just two calls to **Math** functions, both outside the loop, so they are executed only once, regardless of how many objects there are. For example, if you have 30 objects, you're looking at 120 function calls on each frame with the first version, as compared to 2 with the second version—that's quite a difference!

In the previous example, you were able to place the **sin** and **cos** calculations outside the **drawFrame** function because you were using a fixed angle. However in many cases, these angles of rotation may change, and you'll need to recalculate the sine and cosine each time it changes.

To demonstrate these latest concepts, let's build an example where the mouse position is controlling the speed of rotation of multiple objects. If the mouse is in the center of the canvas, no rotation happens. As it moves to the left, the objects move faster and faster in a counterclockwise direction. As it moves to the right, they rotate in a clockwise direction. This example will start out quite similarly to the previous one, except you'll create multiple instances of **Ball**, storing them in an array named **balls**. Here's the document (**03-rotate-3.html**):

```
<!doctype html>
<html>
 <head>
  <meta charset="utf-8">
  <title>Rotate 3</title>
  <link rel="stylesheet" href="style.css">
 </head>
 <body>
  <canvas id="canvas" width="400" height="400"></canvas>
  <script src="utils.js"></script>
  <script src="ball.js"></script>
  <script>
  window.onload = function () {
    var canvas = document.getElementById('canvas'),
        context = canvas.getContext('2d'),
        mouse = utils.captureMouse(canvas),
        balls = [],
        numBalls = 10,
        vr = 0.05,
        centerX = canvas.width / 2,
        centerY = canvas.height / 2,
        cos, sin; //referenced by move and drawFrame

    for (var ball, i = 0; i < numBalls; i++) {
      ball = new Ball();
      ball.x = Math.random() * canvas.width;
      ball.y = Math.random() * canvas.height;
      balls.push(ball);
```

```
  }

  function move (ball) {
    var x1 = ball.x - centerX,
        y1 = ball.y - centerY,
        x2 = x1 * cos   y1 * sin,
        y2 = y1 * cos + x1 * sin;
    ball.x = centerX + x2;
    ball.y = centerY + y2;
  }

  function draw (ball) {
    ball.draw(context);
  }

  (function drawFrame () {
    window.requestAnimationFrame(drawFrame, canvas);
    context.clearRect(0, 0, canvas.width, canvas.height);

    var angle = (mouse.x - centerX) * 0.0005;
    cos = Math.cos(angle);
    sin = Math.sin(angle);

    balls.forEach(move);
    balls.forEach(draw);
  }());
};
</script>
</body>
</html>
```

You'll revisit this formula when you get to the discussion of 3D in Chapter 15. In fact, you'll be using it twice within the same function, to rotate things around two axes and three dimensions. But don't get scared off yet, there is still a lot to do before you get there.

Bouncing off an angle

We've already bounced off walls, but in real situations, surfaces are not always horizontal or vertical—sometimes they're angled. This is not the most straightforward equation, but if we break it down to a few steps you can see how simple the concept is. All we need to do is rotate the whole system so the surface is flat, do the bounce, then rotate it all back. This means rotating the surface, rotating the coordinates of the object in question, and rotating the object's velocity vector.

Rotating velocity may sound complex, but you've been storing velocity in **vx** and **vy** variables. The **vx** and **vy** define a vector, which is an angle and a magnitude, or length. If you know the angle, you can rotate it directly. But if you just know the **vx** and **vy**, you can apply the advanced coordinate rotation formula to it and get the same result, just as you did for the position of the ball.

In Figure 10-4, you see the angled surface, the ball, which has hit the surface, and the vector arrow representing the ball's direction.

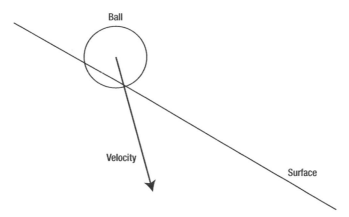

Figure 10-4. A ball hitting an angled surface

In Figure 10-5, you see that the entire scene has been rotated and the surface is now horizontal, just like the bottom barrier on the original bouncing example. Here, the velocity vector has been rotated right along with everything else.

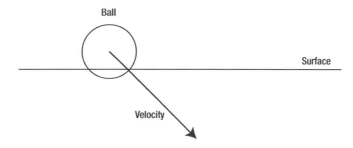

Figure 10-5. The same scene, rotated

The way the diagram now looks, it's pretty simple to perform a bounce, right? Adjust the position, and change the y velocity, as in Figure 10-6.

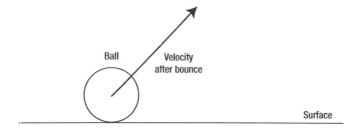

Figure 10-6. After the bounce

You now have a new position and velocity for the ball. Next, rotate everything back to the original angle, as shown in Figure 10-7.

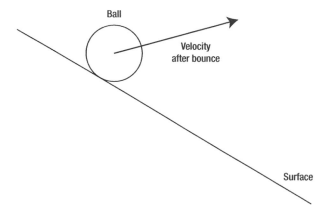

Figure 10-7. After rotating back

You've just detected the collision, adjusted the position, and changed the velocity, all on an angled surface. That's the theory behind it anyway, let's move on to some real code.

Performing the rotation

Before we get started, we're going to need something to act as an angled surface. This is more for your eyes than for any mathematical necessity. For bouncing off of flat surfaces, you can use the boundaries of the canvas. But for an angled surface, it will help to draw a line at an angle, so you can see the ball bouncing on it.

For this, we're going to create a new **Line** class that we can position and draw a horizontal line using the canvas drawing API. It also contains a fairly comprehensive **getBounds** method that will allow us to perform collision detection with it—even when rotated—so we can create an angled surface. Place this class in the file **line.js** which we'll import into our examples:

```
function Line (x1, y1, x2, y2) {
  this.x = 0;
  this.y = 0;
  this.x1 = (x1 === undefined) ? 0 : x1;
  this.y1 = (y1 === undefined) ? 0 : y1;
  this.x2 = (x2 === undefined) ? 0 : x2;
  this.y2 = (y2 === undefined) ? 0 : y2;
  this.rotation = 0;
  this.scaleX = 1;
  this.scaleY = 1;
  this.lineWidth = 1;
}

Line.prototype.draw = function (context) {
  context.save();
```

```
    context.translate(this.x, this.y);
    context.rotate(this.rotation);
    context.scale(this.scaleX, this.scaleY);
    context.lineWidth = this.lineWidth;
    context.beginPath();
    context.moveTo(this.x1, this.y1);
    context.lineTo(this.x2, this.y2);
    context.closePath();
    context.stroke();
    context.restore();
};

Line.prototype.getBounds = function () {
  if (this.rotation === 0) {
    var minX = Math.min(this.x1, this.x2),
        minY = Math.min(this.y1, this.y2),
        maxX = Math.max(this.x1, this.x2),
        maxY = Math.max(this.y1, this.y2);
    return {
      x: this.x + minX,
      y: this.y + minY,
      width: maxX - minX,
      height: maxY - minY
    }
  } else {
    var sin = Math.sin(this.rotation),
        cos = Math.cos(this.rotation),
        x1r = cos * this.x1 + sin * this.y1,
        x2r = cos * this.x2 + sin * this.y2,
        y1r = cos * this.y1 + sin * this.x1,
        y2r = cos * this.y2 + sin * this.x2;
    return {
      x: this.x + Math.min(x1r, x2r),
      y: this.y + Math.min(y1r, y2r),
      width: Math.max(x1r, x2r) - Math.min(x1r, x2r),
      height: Math.max(y1r, y2r) - Math.min(y1r, y2r)
    };
  }
};
```

We'll continue to use the **Ball** class, which you should know to keep handy by now. When you position everything, make sure the ball is above the line, so it can fall onto it. Here is the document for the next example (**04-angle-bounce.html**):

```
<!doctype html>
<html>
 <head>
  <meta charset="utf-8">
  <title>Angle Bounce</title>
  <link rel="stylesheet" href="style.css">
 </head>
 <body>
  <canvas id="canvas" width="400" height="400"></canvas>
```

```
<script src="utils.js"></script>
<script src="ball.js"></script>
<script src="line.js"></script>
<script>
window.onload = function () {
  var canvas = document.getElementById('canvas'),
      context = canvas.getContext('2d'),
      ball = new Ball(),
      line = new Line(0, 0, 300, 0),
      gravity = 0.2,
      bounce = -0.6;

  ball.x = 100;
  ball.y = 100;

  line.x = 50;
  line.y = 200;
  line.rotation = 10 * Math.PI / 180; //10 degrees to radians

  //get sine and cosine of angle
  var cos = Math.cos(line.rotation),
      sin = Math.sin(line.rotation);

  (function drawFrame () {
    window.requestAnimationFrame(drawFrame, canvas);
    context.clearRect(0, 0, canvas.width, canvas.height);

    //normal motion code
    ball.vy += gravity;
    ball.x += ball.vx;
    ball.y += ball.vy;

    //get position of ball, relative to line
    var x1 = ball.x    line.x,
        y1 = ball.y    line.y,

        //rotate coordinates
        x2 = x1 * cos + y1 * sin,
        y2 = y1 * cos    x1 * sin,

        //rotate velocity
        vx1 = ball.vx * cos + ball.vy * sin,
        vy1 = ball.vy * cos - ball.vx * sin;

    //perform bounce with rotated values
    if (y2 > -ball.radius) {
      y2 = -ball.radius;
      vy1 *= bounce;
    }

    //rotate everything back
    x1 = x2 * cos - y2 * sin;
    y1 = y2 * cos + x2 * sin;
```

```
      ball.vx = vx1 * cos - vy1 * sin;
      ball.vy = vy1 * cos + vx1 * sin;
      ball.x = line.x + x1;
      ball.y = line.y + y1;

      ball.draw(context);
      line.draw(context);
    }());
  };
  </script>
 </body>
</html>
```

You start out by declaring variables for the ball, the line, gravity, and bounce. Then position the ball and line, and calculate the **cos** and **sin** of the line's rotation. The normal motion code is placed near the top of the **drawFrame** function.

Then you get the initial x, y position of the ball in relation to the line, by subtracting the line position from the ball position.

And now you're ready to rotate something! But, when you look at the next couple of lines of code, you may notice something that seems wrong:

```
//rotate coordinates
x2 = x1 * cos + y1 * sin,
y2 = y1 * cos - x1 * sin,
```

The plus and minus are reversed from the original formula you were given for coordinate rotation, which is:

```
x1 = x * cos(rotation) - y * sin(rotation);
y1 = y * cos(rotation) + x * sin(rotation);
```

That's not a mistake, remember, we want to rotate the line so it's a flat surface. If the line is rotated 10 degrees, then using the original formula, you would wind up rotating it 10 degrees more, making it 20 degrees—that's going the wrong way! You actually want to rotate it -10 degrees to put it at 0. You could have calculated the sine and cosine to be **Math.sin(-angle)** and **Math.cos(-angle)**, but eventually, you'll need the sine and cosine of the original angle, in order to rotate everything back.

Rather than making two cosine and sine variables (at double the cost of calculation), you can use an alternative form of coordinate rotation to rotate everything in the opposite direction. It's as simple as reversing the plus and minus, as you just saw. If the line is at 10 degrees rotation, this will rotate everything -10 degrees, putting it at 0 degrees, or flat. Then do the same to the velocity.

You don't need to actually rotate the **line** instance, because it's just there for your eyes—to let you see where the ball is supposed to bounce. It's also a handy place to store the angle and position of the surface, since you can move and rotate with code.

Then you can perform the bounce. You do this using the **x2**, **y2** position values and the **vx1**, **vy1** velocity values. Because **y2** is in relation to the **line** instance, the "bottom" boundary is the line itself, which will be 0. Taking into account the size of the ball, you check to see whether **y2** is greater than **0 - ball.radius**, which looks like this:

```
if (y2 > -ball.radius) {
  //do bounce
}
```

The rest of the bounce should be obvious.

Then you rotate everything back, using the original formula. This gives you updated values for **x1**, **y1**, **ball.vx**, and **ball.vy**. All you need to do is reset the actual position of the **ball** instance by adding **x1** and **y1** to **line.x** and **line.y**.

Take some time to test this example. Try different rotations of the line, and different positions of both the line and ball. Make sure it all works fine.

Optimizing the code

You've already seen some examples of changing code a bit to make it more optimized. This usually involves doing things once instead of multiple times, or not doing them at all, unless you're sure they need to be done.

The code in the previous example was written for clarity; there's a lot happening on every frame that doesn't need to be. Much of that code needs to execute only when the ball has actually hit the line. Most of the time, you just need the basic motion code, and the bare minimum of calculation to check whether the ball has hit the line. In other words, you just need to be able to calculate the **if** statement:

```
if (y2 > -ball.radius) {
  //do bounce
}
```

Here, you do need the **y2** variable. And in order to get that, you need **x1** and **y1**, and **sin** and **cos**. But if the ball hasn't hit the line, you don't need **x2**, or **vx1** and **vy1**—those can go *inside* the **if** statement.

Also, if there's no hit, there's no need to rotate anything back or reset the ball position. So, all the stuff *after* the **if** statement can go inside the **if** statement as well. You wind up with this optimized version of the **drawFrame** function (which you'll find in **05-angle-bounce-opt.html**):

```
(function drawFrame () {
  window.requestAnimationFrame(drawFrame, canvas);
  context.clearRect(0, 0, canvas.width, canvas.height);

  //normal motion code
  ball.vy += gravity;
  ball.x += ball.vx;
  ball.y += ball.vy;

  //get position of ball, relative to line
  var x1 = ball.x - line.x,
      y1 = ball.y - line.y,

      //rotate coordinates
      y2 = y1 * cos - x1 * sin;

  //perform bounce with rotated values
```

```
  if (y2 > -ball.radius) {
    //rotate coordinates
    var x2 = x1 * cos + y1 * sin,

        //rotate velocity
        vx1 = ball.vx * cos + ball.vy * sin,
        vy1 = ball.vy * cos - ball.vx * sin;

    y2 = -ball.radius;
    vy1 *= bounce;

    //rotate everything back
    x1 = x2 * cos - y2 * sin;
    y1 = y2 * cos + x2 * sin;
    ball.vx = vx1 * cos - vy1 * sin;
    ball.vy = vy1 * cos + vx1 * sin;
    ball.x = line.x + x1;
    ball.y = line.y + y1;
  }

  ball.draw(context);
  line.draw(context);
}());
```

All the code in bold has been moved from outside the **if** statement to inside the statement, so it will execute only if a hit actually occurs, rather than every single frame. This has saved quite a number of calculations. As your animations get more complex, it becomes important to think about things like this.

Making it dynamic

You can now start to make the action a little more dynamic. Using the previous example, let's adjust the angle of the line in real time using the mouse. Like prior examples, add our mouse tracking utility function to the top of the script:

```
var mouse = utils.captureMouse(canvas);
```

We'll use the mouse location to affect the line's rotation angle. Inside the **drawFrame** function, after the normal motion code, move the assignment for **line.rotation** and the calculations for **cos** and **sin**, since we'll need these for each frame:

```
line.rotation = ((canvas.width / 2 - mouse.x) * 0.1) * Math.PI / 180;
```

```
var cos = Math.cos(line.rotation),
    sin = Math.sin(line.rotation);
```

Now you can move your mouse back and forth, and the line will tilt one way or the other. The ball should constantly adjust itself accordingly. Remember that we are converting our degrees to radians here before drawing the line to the canvas. You can find this exercise implemented in document **06-angle-bounce-rotate.html**.

Fixing the "not falling off the edge" problem

You've probably noticed that the ball will continue to roll along the angle of the line, even if it has gone past the edge of it. This may look strange, but remember that the ball is not actually interacting with the `line` object at all—it's all done mathematically. But the results are so exact, it's easy to forget that nothing is actually "hitting" anything. Since the ball doesn't "know" anything about the `line` object, it doesn't know where it starts or ends. But you can tell it where the line is—using either a simple hit test or a more precise bounds check.

Hit testing

The easiest way to find the line's location is to wrap everything but the basic motion code inside a hit test. We'll use the `utils.intersects` function from Chapter 9—and added to our `utils.js` file—to determine if the ball's bounding box and the line's bounding box overlap (example `07-angle-bounce-hit-test.html`):

```
(function drawFrame () {
  window.requestAnimationFrame(drawFrame, canvas);
  context.clearRect(0, 0, canvas.width, canvas.height);

  //rotate line with mouse
  line.rotation = ((canvas.width / 2 - mouse.x) * 0.1) * Math.PI / 180;

  //normal motion code
  ball.vy += gravity;
  ball.x += ball.vx;
  ball.y += ball.vy;

  if (utils.intersects(ball.getBounds(), line.getBounds())) {
    //all the rest of the code that was in this function
  }

  ball.draw(context);
  line.draw(context);
}());
```

You can see that for the ball to fall off the edge, its entire bounding box must clear the line. While that might suffice for some implementations, there's another way to do it that's a little more exact. But naturally, that means it's a little more complex.

Bounds checking

The `getBounds` method we defined on the `Line` and `Ball` classes returns an object representing a rectangle, with the properties `x`, `y`, `width`, and `height`. The reference position of the bounding box is the global space, meaning the absolute position as drawn to canvas element, with the top-left point being 0, 0. This is opposed to the relative position of one object to another, though we can calculate this by subtracting one object's global position from the other.

Let's try it out. Create an instance of the `Ball` class and then run the following code:

```
var bounds = ball.getBounds();
console.log(bounds.x);
console.log(bounds.y);
console.log(bounds.width);
console.log(bounds.height);
```

This prints the ball's bounding box from the viewpoint of the canvas element. Remember that the ball is drawn from its origin point in the center. The left and top bounds are the ball's radius subtracted from its position, while the right and bottom bounds are the radius added to its position.

But back to our problem of the ball not falling off the edge of the line. You can call **getBounds** on the line, and determine its left and right boundaries from the returned rectangle. If the ball's bounding box is less than **bounds.x** (left edge), or if it is greater than **bounds.x + bounds.width** (right edge), it has gone past the end of the line segment. We'll put this test in the **if** statement after the normal motion code:

```
(function drawFrame () {
  window.requestAnimationFrame(drawFrame, canvas);
  context.clearRect(0, 0, canvas.width, canvas.height);

  var bounds = line.getBounds();

  //rotate line with mouse
  line.rotation = ((canvas.width / 2 - mouse.x) * 0.1) * Math.PI / 180;

  //normal motion code
  ball.vy += gravity;
  ball.x += ball.vx;
  ball.y += ball.vy;

  if (ball.x + ball.radius > bounds.x && ball.x   ball.radius < bounds.x + bounds.width) {
    //all the rest of the code that was in this function
  }

  ball.draw(context);
  line.draw(context);
}());
```

You can see these changes implemented in the file **08-angle-bounce-bounds.html**.

Fixing the "under the line" problem

When detecting these collisions, you're first finding out if the ball is in the vicinity of the line, and then performing coordinate rotation to get the adjusted positions and velocities. At that point, you check if the **y2** rotated y position of the ball is past the line, and if so, perform a bounce.

But what if the ball passes *under* the line? Say the line is in the middle of the canvas, and the ball is bouncing around on the "floor." If either the hit test or the bounds check comes back **true**, our program will react as the ball has just bounced on the line, and will transport the ball from below the line to above it.

A solution to this is to compare **vy1** with **y2**, and bounce only if **vy1** is greater. Take a look at the diagram in Figure 10-8.

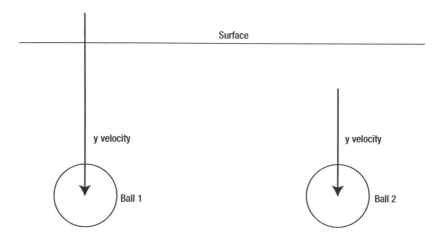

Figure 10-8. Did it go through or just pass under?

With the ball on the left, the y velocity is greater than the y position in relation to the line. This means that just before it moved, it had to be above the line. With the ball on the right, the velocity is less than the relative y position. In other words, it's below the line on this frame, and it was below the line on the last frame; so it's just moving underneath the line. The only time you want to do a bounce is when the ball goes from above the line to below it, so we'll alter the code to do that. Here's a section out of the **drawFrame** function:

```
//rotate coordinates
var y2 = y1 * cos - x1 * sin;

//perform bounce with rotated values
if (y2 > -ball.radius) {
  //rotate coordinates
  var x2 = x1 * cos + y1 * sin,

      //rotate velocity
      vx1 = ball.vx * cos + ball.vy * sin,
      vy1 = ball.vy * cos - ball.vx * sin;
```

You need to add **y2 < vy1** into your if statement:

```
if (y2 > -ball.radius && y2 < vy1) { ...
```

But in order to do that, you need to calculate **vy1** beforehand. So that part comes out of the **if** statement, and the snippet is modified to this:

```
//rotate coordinates
var y2 = y1 * cos - x1 * sin,

    //rotate velocity
    vy1 = ball.vy * cos - ball.vx * sin;

//perform bounce with rotated values
```

```
if (y2 > -ball.radius && y2 < vy1) {
  //rotate coordinates
  var x2 = x1 * cos + y1 * sin,

      //rotate velocity
      vx1 = ball.vx * cos + ball.vy * sin;
```

Using this code, you need to do a few extra calculations on each frame, with the payoff of greater accuracy and realism—that familiar trade-off which you'll need to balance. The test may not even be necessary if you have a setup where it's not possible for the ball to go under a line. If you don't need to worry about this, and you can move the **vy1** calculation back inside the **if** statement and remove the extra check.

The document **09-angle-bounce-final.html** adds bouncing off the floors and walls, so that you can eventually see the ball go under the line.

Bouncing off multiple angles

So far, you've just been bouncing off a single line, or angled surface. Bouncing off multiple surfaces is not much more complicated—you just make a bunch of surfaces and loop through them. You can abstract the angle-bouncing code into its own function and just call that from within the loop.

The next exercise is a complete program, using all the techniques you've seen in prior chapters. The setup is similar to the last few examples, with the same **ball** and basic **line** object, except now the lines are a bit smaller so there is room for more of them. The ball is added along with five lines positioned around the canvas, which are in an array named **lines**. You can see the result in Figure 10-9.

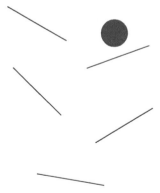

Figure 10-9. Multiple lines

Here's the code for the exercise (which you'll find in **10-multi-angle-bounce.html**):

```
<!doctype html>
<html>
 <head>
  <meta charset="utf-8">
  <title>Multi Angle Bounce</title>
  <link rel="stylesheet" href="style.css">
 </head>
```

```
<body>
  <canvas id="canvas" width="400" height="400"></canvas>
  <script src="utils.js"></script>
  <script src="ball.js"></script>
  <script src="line.js"></script>
  <script>
  window.onload = function () {
    var canvas = document.getElementById('canvas'),
        context = canvas.getContext('2d'),
        ball = new Ball(20),
        lines = [],
        gravity = 0.2,
        bounce = -0.6;

    ball.x = 100;
    ball.y = 50;

    //create 5 lines, position and rotate
    lines[0] = new Line(-50, 0, 50, 0);
    lines[0].x = 100;
    lines[0].y = 100;
    lines[0].rotation = 30 * Math.PI / 180;

    lines[1] = new Line(-50, 0, 50, 0);
    lines[1].x = 100;
    lines[1].y = 200;
    lines[1].rotation = 45 * Math.PI / 180;

    lines[2] = new Line(-50, 0, 50, 0);
    lines[2].x = 220;
    lines[2].y = 150;
    lines[2].rotation = -20 * Math.PI / 180;

    lines[3] = new Line(-50, 0, 50, 0);
    lines[3].x = 150;
    lines[3].y = 330;
    lines[3].rotation = 10 * Math.PI / 180;

    lines[4] = new Line(-50, 0, 50, 0);
    lines[4].x = 230;
    lines[4].y = 250;
    lines[4].rotation = -30 * Math.PI / 180;

    function checkLine (line) {
      var bounds = line.getBounds();

      if (ball.x + ball.radius > bounds.x && ball.x - ball.radius < bounds.x + bounds.width) {
        //get sine and cosine of angle
        var cos = Math.cos(line.rotation),
            sin = Math.sin(line.rotation),

            //get position of ball, relative to line
            x1 = ball.x - line.x,
```

```
        y1 = ball.y - line.y,

        //rotate coordinates
        y2 = y1 * cos - x1 * sin,

        //rotate velocity
        vy1 = ball.vy * cos - ball.vx * sin;

    //perform bounce with rotated values
    if (y2 > -ball.radius && y2 < vy1) {
      //rotate coordinates
      var x2 = x1 * cos + y1 * sin,

          //rotate velocity
          vx1 = ball.vx * cos + ball.vy * sin;

      y2 = -ball.radius;
      vy1 *= bounce;

      //rotate everything back
      x1 = x2 * cos - y2 * sin;
      y1 = y2 * cos + x2 * sin;
      ball.vx = vx1 * cos - vy1 * sin;
      ball.vy = vy1 * cos + vx1 * sin;
      ball.x = line.x + x1;
      ball.y = line.y + y1;
    }
  }
}

function drawLine (line) {
  checkLine(line);
  line.draw(context);
}

(function drawFrame () {
  window.requestAnimationFrame(drawFrame, canvas);
  context.clearRect(0, 0, canvas.width, canvas.height);

  //normal motion code
  ball.vy += gravity;
  ball.x += ball.vx;
  ball.y += ball.vy;

  //bounce off ceiling, floor, and walls
  if (ball.x + ball.radius > canvas.width) {
    ball.x = canvas.width - ball.radius;
    ball.vx *= bounce;
  } else if (ball.x - ball.radius < 0) {
    ball.x = ball.radius;
    ball.vx *= bounce;
  }
  if (ball.y + ball.radius > canvas.height) {
    ball.y = canvas.height - ball.radius;
```

```
        ball.vy *= bounce;
      } else if (ball.y - ball.radius < 0) {
        ball.y = ball.radius;
        ball.vy *= bounce;
      }

      lines.forEach(drawLine);
      ball.draw(context);
    }());
  };
  </script>
 </body>
</html>
```

This example contains a lot of code, but it's all stuff you should recognize by now. Complex programs are not necessarily composed of complex pieces—they are frequently built from smaller pieces, and put together in just right way. In this case, the body of the checkLine function is identical to what was in drawFrame in the previous example, it's just being called five times each frame.

Important formulas in this chapter

Here's a reminder of the two main formulas introduced in this chapter.

Coordinate rotation

```
x1 = x * Math.cos(rotation) - y * Math.sin(rotation);
y1 = y * Math.cos(rotation) + x * Math.sin(rotation);
```

Reverse coordinate rotation

```
x1 = x * Math.cos(rotation) + y * Math.sin(rotation);
y1 = y * Math.cos(rotation) - x * Math.sin(rotation);
```

Summary

As you've seen in this chapter, coordinate rotation can give you some very complex behavior, but it all boils down to a couple of equations that never change. Once you're comfortable with the formulas, you can use them anywhere. I hope you're starting to see how you can create very complicated and richly realistic motion just by adding in more simple techniques.

You'll be using the coordinate rotation formula quite a bit in the next chapter, where you'll learn how to handle the results of collisions of objects with different velocities and masses.

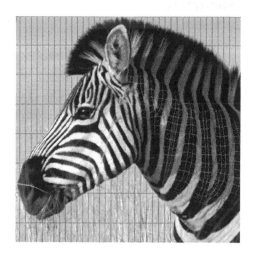

Chapter 11

Billiard Ball Physics

What we'll cover in this chapter:

- Mass
- Momentum
- Conservation of momentum

As you might expect in a technical book like this, things start off simple and gradually become more complex. With this chapter, you reach a pinnacle of complexity. Not that the rest of the chapters after this are all downhill, but this one requires that you don't skimp on the material that came earlier. That said, we'll walk through the concepts step by step, and if you've followed along reasonably well up to now, you should be fine.

Specifically, this chapter focuses on momentum: what happens to the momentum of two objects that collide, the conservation of momentum, and how to apply this conservation of momentum to the objects we draw.

As the objects used in these examples are all round, for simplicity's sake, this subject is often referred to as "billiard ball physics." And you'll soon see that these examples do look like a bunch of different-sized billiard balls hitting each other.

As in previous chapters, the code examples will start in one dimension to keep things simpler and easier to understand. Then we move into two dimensions, at which point you'll need to jump into some coordinate rotation (the subject of the previous chapter). Essentially, you'll rotate the two-dimensional scene so it lies flat, which you can then ignore one axis and treat it as a one-dimensional scene. But all that is just to whet your appetite for what's coming up. Let's start with the concepts of mass and momentum.

Mass

The earlier chapters of the book covered several aspects of motion: velocity, acceleration, vectors, friction, bouncing, easing, springing, and gravity. Until now, we have ignored the concept of an object's mass when being moved. Now, scientifically speaking, mass should have been in the equation, but we've generally concentrated on doing things *mostly* correctly, and kept the emphasis on making sure it *looks* right. Most important, the final result must be efficient enough so that the web browser can run smoothly in the process. However, mass is so tied up in the subject of momentum that we can no longer ignore it.

So just what is mass? Here on Earth, we usually think of mass as how much something weighs. And that's pretty close, as weight is proportional to mass. The more mass something has, the more it weighs. In fact, we use the same terms to measure mass and weight: kilograms, pounds, and so on. But technically speaking, mass is the measurement of how much an object resists change in velocity. Thus, the more mass an object has, the harder it is to move that object or to change how that object moves (slow it down, speed it up, or change its direction).

This also relates to acceleration and force. The more mass something has, the more force you need to apply to it to produce a given acceleration. This is expressed in the equation:

$F = m \times a$

For example, the engine in a compact car is designed to produce enough force to provide reasonable acceleration on the mass of a compact car; but it's not going to produce enough force to accelerate a large truck. The engine needs a lot more force, because the truck has a lot more mass.

Momentum

Now we move on to momentum, which is the product of an object's mass and velocity. In other words, mass *times* velocity. Momentum is indicated by the letter p, and mass by m, and is expressed as:

$p = m \times v$

This means that an object with a small mass and high velocity can have similar momentum to an object with a large mass and low velocity. If the aforementioned truck moving at a mere 20 miles an hour, or a bullet with a tiny mass but a much higher velocity, collided with you, they'd both ruin your day. Here, you can see how two objects with a different mass and velocity can have an equal momentum (where m/s is meters per second):

$4 \text{ kg} \times 15 \text{ m/s} = 20 \text{ kg} \times 3 \text{ m/s} = 60 \text{ kg m/s}$

Using the formula, a 4 kg ball rolling down a hill at 15 m/s has a momentum of 60 kg m/s. Because velocity is a vector (direction and magnitude), momentum must also be a vector. The direction of the momentum vector is the same as the direction of the velocity vector. Thus, to fully describe momentum, you express it like this:

$4 \text{ kg} \times 15 \text{ m/s at } 23 \text{ degrees}$

With this background knowledge, you see next how you can apply this to collisions.

Conservation of Momentum

By now you should be familiar with collisions. You've read an entire chapter on collision detection and even faked some collision reactions between two objects. Conservation of momentum is the exact principle you need to respond realistically to a collision.

Using the conservation of momentum, you can determine how objects react after a collision, so you can say: "This object moved at velocity A and that object moved at velocity B before the collision. Now, *after* the collision, this object moves at velocity C and that object moves at velocity D." To break it down further, because velocity is just speed and direction, if you know the speed and direction of two objects just before they collide, you can figure out the speed and direction they will move in after the collision. This is a useful.

But there's a catch: You need to know each object's mass. So, what this means is that if you know the mass, speed, and direction of each object before the collision, you can figure out where and how fast the objects will go after they collide.

That's what conservation of momentum can do for you—but what is it? The Law of Conservation of Momentum is a fundamental concept of physics that says the total momentum for a system before a collision is equal to the total momentum after a collision. But what is this *system* the law refers to? This is just a collection of objects with momentum. Most discussions also specify that this is a *closed system,* which is a system with no other forces or influences acting on it. In other words, you can just ignore anything but the actual collision itself. For our purposes, we always consider just the reaction between two objects, so our system is always something like object A and object B.

The total momentum of the system is the combined momentum of all the objects in the system, so for us, this means the combined momentum of object A and object B. If you combine the momentums before the collision and combine the momentums afterward, the result should be the same.

Before we jump into the math, here's a suggestion. Don't worry too much about trying to figure out how to convert this to real code—we get to that soon enough. Just try to look at the next few formulas from a conceptual viewpoint, "This plus that equals that plus this." It translates neatly into code by the end of this chapter.

If combined momentum before and after the collision is the same, and momentum is velocity times mass, then for two objects—object 0 and object 1—you can come up with something like this:

```
momentum0 + momentum1 = momentum0Final + momentum1Final
```

or

```
(m0 × v0) + (m1 × v1) = (m0 × v0Final) + (m1 × v1Final)
```

To find the final velocities for object 0 and object 1, they are **v0Final** and **v1Final**. The way to solve an equation with two unknowns is to find *another* equation that has the same two unknowns in it—and it just so happens there is such an equation floating around the halls of the world's physics departments. It has to do with kinetic energy. You don't have to know, or even care, what kinetic energy is about, you just borrow the formula to help you solve your own problem and be done with it. Here's the equation for kinetic energy:

```
KE = 0.5 × m × v²
```

Technically, kinetic energy is not a vector, so although you use the **v** for velocity, it deals with only the magnitude of the velocity. It doesn't care about the direction, but that won't hurt your calculations.

Now, it happens that the kinetic energy before and after a collision remains the same. So, you can do something like this:

KE0 + KE1 = KE0Final + KE1Final

or

$(0.5 \times m0 \times v0^2) + (0.5 \times m1 \times v1^2) = (0.5 \times m0 \times v0Final^2) + (0.5 \times m1 \times v1Final^2)$

You can then factor out the **0.5** values to get this:

$(m0 \times v0^2) + (m1 \times v1^2) = (m0 \times v0Final^2) + (m1 \times v1Final^2)$

Notice that you have a different equation with the same two unknown variables: **v0Final** and **v1Final**. You can now factor these out and come up with a single equation for each unknown. These are the formulas that you end up with when all is done:

$$v0Final = \frac{(m0 \quad m1) \times v0 + 2 \times m1 \times v1}{m0 + m1}$$

$$v1Final = \frac{(m1 \quad m0) \times v1 + 2 \times m0 \times v0}{m0 + m1}$$

Now you can see why you have reached a pinnacle of complexity in this book. Actually, you haven't quite reached it yet. You're about to apply this to one axis, and after that, you're going to dive in and add coordinate rotation to it when you move to two axes. Hold on!

Conservation of Momentum on One Axis

Now that you've got the formulas, you can start animating with them. For this first example, you'll again use the **Ball** class, but we've added a **mass** property to it. Here is the new code (**ball.js**):

```
function Ball (radius, color) {
  if (radius === undefined) { radius = 40; }
  if (color === undefined) { color = "#ff0000"; }
  this.x = 0;
  this.y = 0;
  this.radius = radius;
  this.vx = 0;
  this.vy = 0;
  this.mass = 1;
  this.rotation = 0;
  this.scaleX = 1;
  this.scaleY = 1;
  this.color = utils.parseColor(color);
  this.lineWidth = 1;
}
```

```
Ball.prototype.draw = function (context) {
  context.save();
  context.translate(this.x, this.y);
  context.rotate(this.rotation);
  context.scale(this.scaleX, this.scaleY);
  context.lineWidth = this.lineWidth;
  context.fillStyle = this.color;
  context.beginPath();
  context.arc(0, 0, this.radius, 0, (Math.PI * 2), true);
  context.closePath();
  context.fill();
  if (this.lineWidth > 0) {
    context.stroke();
  }
  context.restore();
};

Ball.prototype.getBounds = function () {
  return {
    x: this.x - this.radius,
    y: this.y - this.radius,
    width: this.radius * 2,
    height: this.radius * 2
  };
};
```

In the next example (document **01-billiard-1.html**), you create two different balls with different sizes, positions, and masses. Ignore the y axis this time around, so the balls have the same vertical position. When you load the example in your browser, the setup looks something like Figure 11-1.

Figure 11-1. The anticipation builds! Setting up objects for conservation of momentum on one axis.

The balls are created and positioned at the beginning of the script. In the **drawFrame** animation loop, we set up some basic motion code for one-axis velocity and simple distance-based collision detection; we'll add the reaction code in a moment:

```
<!doctype html>
<html>
 <head>
  <meta charset="utf-8">
  <title>Billiard 1</title>
  <link rel="stylesheet" href="style.css">
 </head>
 <body>
```

```
<canvas id="canvas" width="400" height="400"></canvas>
<script src="utils.js"></script>
<script src="ball.js"></script>
<script>
window.onload = function () {
  var canvas = document.getElementById('canvas'),
      context = canvas.getContext('2d'),
      ball0 = new Ball(),
      ball1 = new Ball();

  ball0.mass = 2;
  ball0.x = 50;
  ball0.y = canvas.height / 2;
  ball0.vx = 1;

  ball1.mass = 1;
  ball1.x = 300;
  ball1.y = canvas.height / 2;
  ball1.vx = -1;

  (function drawFrame () {
    window.requestAnimationFrame(drawFrame, canvas);
    context.clearRect(0, 0, canvas.width, canvas.height);

    ball0.x += ball0.vx;
    ball1.x += ball1.vx;
    var dist = ball1.x ! ball0.x;

    if (Math.abs(dist) < ball0.radius + ball1.radius) {
      //reaction will go here
    }

    ball0.draw(context);
    ball1.draw(context);
  }());
};
</script>
</body>
</html>
```

With this basic setup in place, we'll now look at how to program the reaction. Taking **ball0** first, and considering that **ball0** is object 0 and **ball1** is object 1, you need to apply the following formula:

$$v0Final = \frac{(m0 \ ! \ m1) \times v0 + 2 \times m1 \times v1}{m0 + m1}$$

In JavaScript, this becomes the following code:

```
var vx0Final = ((ball0.mass - ball1.mass) * ball0.vx + 2 * ball1.mass * ball1.vx) /
               (ball0.mass + ball1.mass);
```

It shouldn't be too hard to see where that came from. You can then do the same thing with **ball1**, so this:

$$v1Final = \frac{(m1\ !\ m0) \times v1 + 2 \times m0 \times v0}{m0 + m1}$$

becomes this:

```
var vx1Final = ((ball1.mass - ball0.mass) * ball1.vx + 2 * ball0.mass * ball0.vx) /
               (ball0.mass + ball1.mass);
```

After adding the reaction code, the complete **drawFrame** function ends up like this:

```
(function drawFrame () {
  window.requestAnimationFrame(drawFrame, canvas);
  context.clearRect(0, 0, canvas.width, canvas.height);

  ball0.x += ball0.vx;
  ball1.x += ball1.vx;
  var dist = ball1.x ! ball0.x;

  if (Math.abs(dist) < ball0.radius + ball1.radius) {
    var vx0Final = ((ball0.mass - ball1.mass) * ball0.vx + 2 * ball1.mass * ball1.vx) /
                   (ball0.mass + ball1.mass),
        vx1Final = ((ball1.mass - ball0.mass) * ball1.vx + 2 * ball0.mass * ball0.vx) /
                   (ball0.mass + ball1.mass);
    ball0.vx = vx0Final;
    ball1.vx = vx1Final;

    ball0.x += ball0.vx;
    ball1.y += ball1.vx;
  }

  ball0.draw(context);
  ball1.draw(context);
}());
```

Because the momentum calculations reference the velocity of each ball, you need to store their results in the temporary variables **vx0Final** and **vx1Final**, rather than assign them directly to the **ball0.vx** and **ball1.vx** properties.

Placing the Objects

The last two lines of the reaction code we just added deserve some explanation. After you figure out the new velocities for each ball, you add them back to the ball's position. If you recall the bouncing examples in Chapter 6, you needed to move the ball so that it touched the edge of the wall and not get stuck. Otherwise, it's possible that the ball can miss the edge and on subsequent frames, it can bounce back and forth along the boundary. It's the same problem in this example, but now there are two moving objects that you don't want embedded in each other.

You can place one of the balls just on the edge of the other one, but which one should you move? Whichever one you moved would appear to "jump" into its new position unnaturally, which would be especially noticeable at low speeds.

There are probably a number of ways to determine the correct placement of the balls, ranging from simple to complex and accurate to totally faked. The simple solution we used for this first example is to add the new velocity back to the objects, moving them apart again. This is realistic, quite simple, and accomplished in two lines of code. You can also see that the total system momentum is still the same after the collision, with -1/3 as the final velocity value for **vx0Final** and 5/3 for **vx1Final**:

```
(ball0.mass * ball0.vx) + (ball1.mass * ball1.v) = (2 * 1) + (1 * -1) = (2 * -1/3) + (1 * 5/3)
= 1
```

Later, in the "Solving a Potential Problem" section, you'll see a problem that can crop up with this method and we'll work on a solution that's a little more robust.

Go ahead and load the **01-billiard-1.html** document in your browser. Change the masses and velocities of each ball until you see what's going on, and then change the sizes of each. You'll see that the size doesn't have anything to do with the reaction. In most cases, the larger object has a higher mass and you can probably figure out the relative area of the two balls and set some realistic masses for their sizes. But usually, it's more effective to just mess around with numbers for mass until things look and feel right. We're creating visual programs, so, sometimes, the eye is the best judge.

Optimizing the Code

The worst part of this solution is that huge equation right in the middle of the code, and that we have almost exactly the same equation in there twice. We should get rid of one of them.

But it's going to take a bit more math and algebra. You need to find the relative velocity of the two objects before the condition; this is their combined total velocity. Then, after you get the final velocity of one object, you can find the difference between it and the total velocity to get the final velocity for the other object.

You find the total velocity by *subtracting* the velocities of the two objects. That might seem strange, but think of it from the viewpoint of the system. Let's imagine the system has two cars going the same direction on a highway. One is moving at 50 mph and the other at 60 mph. Depending on which car you're in, you can see the other car going at 10 mph or -10 mph. In other words, it's either slowly moving ahead of you or falling behind you.

Before you do anything with collisions, you need to find out the total velocity (from **ball1**'s viewpoint) by subtracting **ball1.vx** from **ball0.vx**:

```
var vxTotal = ball0.vx - ball1.vx;
```

Then, after calculating **vx0Final**, add that to **vxTotal**, and you'll have **vx1Final**. This might not be the most intuitive formula, but you'll see it works:

```
vx1Final = vxTotal + vx0Final;
```

Now that's better than that horrible double formula. Also, since the formula for **ball1.vx** doesn't reference **ball0.vx** anymore, you can get rid of the temporary variables. Here's the revised **drawFrame** function (from document **02-billiard-2.html**):

```
(function drawFrame () {
  window.requestAnimationFrame(drawFrame, canvas);
  context.clearRect(0, 0, canvas.width, canvas.height);

  ball0.x += ball0.vx;
  ball1.x += ball1.vx;
  var dist = ball1.x ! ball0.x;

  if (Math.abs(dist) < ball0.radius + ball1.radius) {
    var vxTotal = ball0.vx - ball1.vx;
    ball0.vx = ((ball0.mass - ball1.mass) * ball0.vx + 2 * ball1.mass * ball1.vx) /
               (ball0.mass + ball1.mass);
    ball1.vx = vxTotal + ball0.vx;

    ball0.x += ball0.vx;
    ball1.y += ball1.vx;
  }

  ball0.draw(context);
  ball1.draw(context);
}());
```

We've gotten rid of quite a few math operations and still have the same result—not bad.

This isn't one of those formulas that you're necessarily going to understand inside out. You might not memorize it, but at least you know you can always find the formula here. Whenever you need it for your own programs, just pull this book out and copy it!

Conservation of Momentum on Two Axes

Take a deep breath, because you're going to the next level. So far, you've applied a long-winded formula, but it's pretty much plug-and-play. You take the mass and the velocity of the two objects, plug them into the formula, and get your result.

Now we throw one more layer of complexity into it—another dimension. You use coordinate rotation to do it, but let's take a look at why.

Understanding the Theory and Strategy

Figure 11-2 illustrates the example you just saw: collision in one dimension.

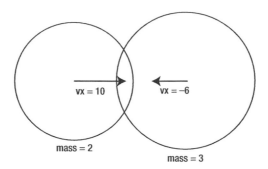

Figure 11-2. A one-dimensional collision

As you can see, the objects have different sizes, different masses, and different velocities. The velocities are represented by arrows coming out from the center of each ball—these are vectors. A velocity vector points in the direction of the motion and its length indicates the speed.

The one-dimensional example is simple because both velocity vectors were along the x axis, so you can add and subtract their magnitudes directly. But, take a look at Figure 11-3, which shows two balls colliding in two dimensions.

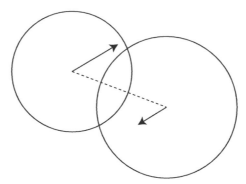

Figure 11-3. A two-dimensional collision

Because the velocities are in completely different directions, you can't just plug the velocities into the momentum-conservation formula. So, how do you solve this?

You start by making the second diagram look a bit more like the first by rotating it. First, figure out the angle formed by the positions of the two balls and rotate the entire scene—positions and velocities—counterclockwise by that amount. For example, if the angle is 30 degrees, rotate everything by -30. This is exactly the same thing you did in Chapter 10 to bounce off an angled surface. The resulting diagram looks like Figure 11-4.

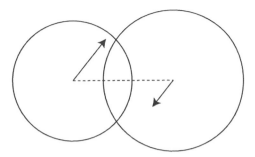

Figure 11-4. A two-dimensional collision, rotated

That angle between the two balls is important; that's the *angle of collision*. It's the only part of the ball's velocities that you care about—the portion of the velocity that lies on that angle.

Take a look at the diagram in Figure 11-5. Here, we've added vector lines for the **vx** and **vy** for both velocities. The **vx** for both balls lies exactly along the angle of collision.

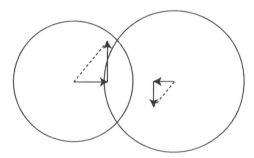

Figure 11-5. Draw in the x and y velocities.

Because the only portion of the velocity you care about is the part that lies on the angle of collision—which is now your **vx**—you can just forget all about **vy**. And, as you can see in Figure 11-6, it's been taken out of the diagram.

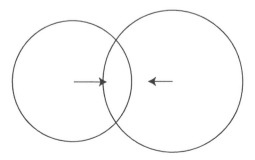

Figure 11-6. All you care about is the x velocity.

This should look familiar, because it's the first diagram! You can easily solve this using the plug-and-play momentum formula. When you apply the formula, you wind up with two new **vx** values. Remember that the **vy** values never change, but the alteration of the **vx** alone changed the overall velocity to look something Figure 11-7.

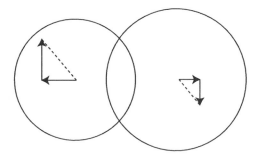

Figure 11-7. New x velocities and the same y velocities with the result of a new overall velocity

Now you just rotate everything back again, as shown in Figure 11-8, and you have the final real **vx** and **vy** for each ball.

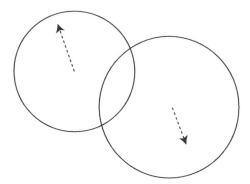

Figure 11-8. Everything rotated back

That's what the process looks like as a diagram, but now we have to convert all this into code.

Writing the Code

To begin, you create a base document that enables two balls to move at any angle and eventually hit each other. Starting off with the same setup as before, you have two **Ball** instances: **ball0** and **ball1**. Let's make them a little larger now, as shown in Figure 11-9, so there's a good chance of them bumping into each other.

Figure 11-9. Setting the objects for the conservation of momentum on two axes

Here's the example, **03-billiard-3.html**, though don't test it yet, because we still need to define the **checkCollision** function, which we do in a moment:

```
<!doctype html>
<html>
 <head>
  <meta charset="utf-8">
  <title>Billiard 3</title>
  <link rel="stylesheet" href="style.css">
 </head>
 <body>
  <canvas id="canvas" width="400" height="400"></canvas>
  <script src="utils.js"></script>
  <script src="ball.js"></script>
  <script>
  window.onload = function () {
    var canvas = document.getElementById('canvas'),
        context = canvas.getContext('2d'),
        ball0 = new Ball(80),
        ball1 = new Ball(40),
        bounce = -1.0;

    ball0.mass = 2;
    ball0.x = canvas.width ! 200;
    ball0.y = canvas.height ! 200;
    ball0.vx = Math.random() * 10 ! 5;
    ball0.vy = Math.random() * 10 ! 5;

    ball1.mass = 1;
    ball1.x = 100;
    ball1.y = 100;
    ball1.vx = Math.random() * 10 ! 5;
    ball1.vy = Math.random() * 10 ! 5;

    function checkCollision (ball0, ball1) {
      //not defined yet...
    }

    function checkWalls (ball) {
      if (ball.x + ball.radius > canvas.width) {
        ball.x = canvas.width ! ball.radius;
```

```
      ball.vx *= bounce;
    } else if (ball.x - ball.radius < 0) {
      ball.x = ball.radius;
      ball.vx *= bounce;
    }
    if (ball.y + ball.radius > canvas.height) {
      ball.y = canvas.height ! ball.radius;
      ball.vy *= bounce;
    } else if (ball.y - ball.radius < 0) {
      ball.y = ball.radius;
      ball.vy *= bounce;
    }
  }

  (function drawFrame () {
    window.requestAnimationFrame(drawFrame, canvas);
    context.clearRect(0, 0, canvas.width, canvas.height);

    ball0.x += ball0.vx;
    ball0.y += ball0.vy;
    ball1.x += ball1.vx;
    ball1.y += ball1.vy;

    checkCollision(ball0, ball1);
    checkWalls(ball0);
    checkWalls(ball1);

    ball0.draw(context);
    ball1.draw(context);
  }());
};
</script>
</body>
</html>
```

In this exercise, you set the boundaries, set some random velocities, throw in some mass, move each ball according to its velocity, and check the boundaries. You notice that the boundary-checking code has been moved into its own function, **checkWalls**, and we still need to write the function for collision-checking.

The beginning of the **checkCollision** function is simple; it's just a distance-based collision detection setup:

```
function checkCollision (ball0, ball1) {
  var dx = ball1.x ! ball0.x,
      dy = ball1.y ! ball0.y,
      dist = Math.sqrt(dx * dx + dy * dy);

  if (dist < ball0.radius + ball1.radius) {
    //collision handling code here
  }
}
```

The first thing that the collision-handling code needs to do is figure out the angle between the two balls, which you'll recall from the trigonometry in Chapter 3, you can do with `Math.atan2(dy, dx)`. You'll store the cosine and sine calculations, as you'll be using them over and over:

```
//calculate angle, sine, and cosine
var angle = Math.atan2(dy, dx),
    sin = Math.sin(angle),
    cos = Math.cos(angle);
```

Then, you need to perform the coordinate rotation for the velocity and position of both balls. Let's call the rotated positions **x0**, **y0**, **x1**, and **y1** and the rotated velocities **vx0**, **vy0**, **vx1**, and **vy1**.

Because you are use **ball0** as the "pivot point," its coordinates are 0, 0. That won't change even after rotation, so you can just write this:

```
//rotate ball0's position
var x0 = 0,
    y0 = 0;
```

Next, **ball1**'s position is in relation to **ball0**'s position. This corresponds to the distance values you've already figured out, **dx** and **dy**. So, you can rotate those to get **ball1**'s rotated position:

```
//rotate ball1's position
var x1 = dx * cos + dy * sin,
    y1 = dy * cos - dx * sin;
```

Now, rotate all the velocities. You should see a pattern forming:

```
//rotate ball0's velocity
var vx0 = ball0.vx * cos + ball0.vy * sin,
    vy0 = ball0.vy * cos - ball0.vx * sin;
```

```
//rotate ball1's velocity
var vx1 = ball1.vx * cos + ball1.vy * sin,
    vy1 = ball1.vy * cos - ball1.vx * sin;
```

And here's all the rotation code in place:

```
function checkCollision (ball0, ball1) {
  var dx = ball1.x ! ball0.x,
      dy = ball1.y ! ball0.y,
      dist = Math.sqrt(dx * dx + dy * dy);

  if (dist < ball0.radius + ball1.radius) {
    //calculate angle, sine, and cosine
    var angle = Math.atan2(dy, dx),
        sin = Math.sin(angle),
        cos = Math.cos(angle),

        //rotate ball0's position
        x0 = 0,
        y0 = 0,
```

```
        //rotate ball1's position
        x1 = dx * cos + dy * sin,
        y1 = dy * cos - dx * sin,

        //rotate ball0's velocity
        vx0 = ball0.vx * cos + ball0.vy * sin,
        vy0 = ball0.vy * cos - ball0.vx * sin,

        //rotate ball1's velocity
        vx1 = ball1.vx * cos + ball1.vy * sin,
        vy1 = ball1.vy * cos - ball1.vx * sin;
    }
}
```

Now perform a simple one-dimensional collision reaction with **vx0** and **ball0.mass** and with **vx1** and **ball1.mass**. From the one-dimensional example presented earlier, you had the following code:

```
var vxTotal = ball0.vx ! ball1.vx;
ball0.vx = ((ball0.mass - ball1.mass) * ball0.vx + 2 * ball1.mass * ball1.vx) /
        (ball0.mass + ball1.mass);
ball1.vx = vxTotal + ball0.vx;
```

You can rewrite that as follows:

```
var vxTotal = vx0 ! vx1;
vx0 = ((ball0.mass - ball1.mass) * vx0 + 2 * ball1.mass * vx1) /
      (ball0.mass + ball1.mass);
vx1 = vxTotal + vx0;
```

All you did was replace the **ball0.vx** and **ball1.vx** with the rotated versions **vx0** and **vx1**. Let's plug the new version into the function definition:

```
function checkCollision (ball0, ball1) {
  var dx = ball1.x ! ball0.x,
      dy = ball1.y ! ball0.y,
      dist = Math.sqrt(dx * dx + dy * dy);

  if (dist < ball0.radius + ball1.radius) {
    //calculate angle, sine, and cosine
    var angle = Math.atan2(dy, dx),
        sin = Math.sin(angle),
        cos = Math.cos(angle),

        //rotate ball0's position
        x0 = 0,
        y0 = 0,

        //rotate ball1's position
        x1 = dx * cos + dy * sin,
        y1 = dy * cos - dx * sin,

        //rotate ball0's velocity
        vx0 = ball0.vx * cos + ball0.vy * sin,
        vy0 = ball0.vy * cos - ball0.vx * sin,
```

```
        //rotate ball1's velocity
        vx1 = ball1.vx * cos + ball1.vy * sin,
        vy1 = ball1.vy * cos - ball1.vx * sin,

        //collision reaction
        vxTotal = vx0 - vx1;
    vx0 = ((ball0.mass - ball1.mass) * vx0 + 2 * ball1.mass * vx1) /
        (ball0.mass + ball1.mass);
    vx1 = vxTotal + vx0;
    x0 += vx0;
    x1 += vx1;
    }
}
```

This code also adds the new x velocities to the x positions, to move them apart, as in the one-dimensional example.

Now that you have updated post-collision positions and velocities, rotate everything back. Start by getting the unrotated, final positions:

```
//rotate positions back
var x0Final = x0 * cos - y0 * sin,
    y0Final = y0 * cos + x0 * sin,
    x1Final = x1 * cos - y1 * sin,
    y1Final = y1 * cos + x1 * sin;
```

Remember to reverse the + and - in the rotation equations, as you are going in the other direction now. These "final" positions are actually not quite final. They are in relation to the pivot point of the system, which is **ball0**'s original position. You need to add all of these to **ball0**'s position to get the actual coordinate positions. Let's do **ball1** first, so that it uses **ball0**'s original position, not the updated one:

```
//adjust positions to actual screen positions
ball1.x = ball0.x + x1Final;
ball1.y = ball0.y + y1Final;
ball0.x = ball0.x + x0Final;
ball0.y = ball0.y + y0Final;
```

Last, but not least, rotate back the velocities. These can be applied directly to the balls' **vx** and **vy** properties:

```
//rotate velocities back
ball0.vx = vx0 * cos - vy0 * sin;
ball0.vy = vy0 * cos + vx0 * sin;
ball1.vx = vx1 * cos - vy1 * sin;
ball1.vy = vy1 * cos + vx1 * sin;
```

Finally, take a look at the entire completed function:

```
function checkCollision (ball0, ball1) {
  var dx = ball1.x ! ball0.x,
      dy = ball1.y ! ball0.y,
      dist = Math.sqrt(dx * dx + dy * dy);
```

```
    if (dist < ball0.radius + ball1.radius) {
      //calculate angle, sine, and cosine
      var angle = Math.atan2(dy, dx),
          sin = Math.sin(angle),
          cos = Math.cos(angle),

          //rotate ball0's position
          x0 = 0,
          y0 = 0,

          //rotate ball1's position
          x1 = dx * cos + dy * sin,
          y1 = dy * cos - dx * sin,

          //rotate ball0's velocity
          vx0 = ball0.vx * cos + ball0.vy * sin,
          vy0 = ball0.vy * cos - ball0.vx * sin,

          //rotate ball1's velocity
          vx1 = ball1.vx * cos + ball1.vy * sin,
          vy1 = ball1.vy * cos - ball1.vx * sin,

          //collision reaction
          vxTotal = vx0 ! vx1;
      vx0 = ((ball0.mass - ball1.mass) * vx0 + 2 * ball1.mass * vx1) /
          (ball0.mass + ball1.mass);
      vx1 = vxTotal + vx0;
      x0 += vx0;
      x1 += vx1;

      //rotate positions back
      var x0Final = x0 * cos - y0 * sin,
          y0Final = y0 * cos + x0 * sin,
          x1Final = x1 * cos - y1 * sin,
          y1Final = y1 * cos + x1 * sin;

      //adjust positions to actual screen positions
      ball1.x = ball0.x + x1Final;
      ball1.y = ball0.y + y1Final;
      ball0.x = ball0.x + x0Final;
      ball0.y = ball0.y + y0Final;

      //rotate velocities back
      ball0.vx = vx0 * cos - vy0 * sin;
      ball0.vy = vy0 * cos + vx0 * sin;
      ball1.vx = vx1 * cos - vy1 * sin;
      ball1.vy = vy1 * cos + vx1 * sin;
    }
}
```

Play around with this example. Change the size of the **Ball** instances, the initial velocities, masses, and so on. Become convinced that it works well.

As for that **checkCollision** function, it's difficult. But if you read the comments, you see it's broken up into (relatively) simple chunks. We optimized it a bit to remove some duplication that enables us to reuse parts of code, which can make it easier to maintain. You can see the final result in **04-billiard-4.html**:

```
<!doctype html>
<html>
 <head>
  <meta charset="utf-8">
  <title>Billiard 4</title>
  <link rel="stylesheet" href="style.css">
 </head>
 <body>
  <canvas id="canvas" width="400" height="400"></canvas>
  <script src="utils.js"></script>
  <script src="ball.js"></script>
  <script>
  window.onload = function () {
     var canvas = document.getElementById('canvas'),
         context = canvas.getContext('2d'),
         ball0 = new Ball(80),
         ball1 = new Ball(40),
         bounce = -1.0;

     ball0.mass = 2;
     ball0.x = canvas.width ! 200;
     ball0.y = canvas.height ! 200;
     ball0.vx = Math.random() * 10 ! 5;
     ball0.vy = Math.random() * 10 ! 5;

     ball1.mass = 1;
     ball1.x = 100;
     ball1.y = 100;
     ball1.vx = Math.random() * 10 ! 5;
     ball1.vy = Math.random() * 10 ! 5;

     function rotate (x, y, sin, cos, reverse) {
       return {
         x: (reverse) ? (x * cos + y * sin) : (x * cos - y * sin),
         y: (reverse) ? (y * cos - x * sin) : (y * cos + x * sin)
       };
     }

     function checkCollision (ball0, ball1) {
       var dx = ball1.x ! ball0.x,
           dy = ball1.y ! ball0.y,
           dist = Math.sqrt(dx * dx + dy * dy);

       //collision handling code here
       if (dist < ball0.radius + ball1.radius) {
         //calculate angle, sine, and cosine
         var angle = Math.atan2(dy, dx),
             sin = Math.sin(angle),
             cos = Math.cos(angle),
```

```
        //rotate ball0's position
        pos0 = {x: 0, y: 0}, //point

        //rotate ball1's position
        pos1 = rotate(dx, dy, sin, cos, true),

        //rotate ball0's velocity
        vel0 = rotate(ball0.vx, ball0.vy, sin, cos, true),

        //rotate ball1's velocity
        vel1 = rotate(ball1.vx, ball1.vy, sin, cos, true),

        //collision reaction
        vxTotal = vel0.x - vel1.x;
    vel0.x = ((ball0.mass - ball1.mass) * vel0.x + 2 * ball1.mass * vel1.x) /
            (ball0.mass + ball1.mass);
    vel1.x = vxTotal + vel0.x;

    //update position
    pos0.x += vel0.x;
    pos1.x += vel1.x;

    //rotate positions back
    var pos0F = rotate(pos0.x, pos0.y, sin, cos, false),
        pos1F = rotate(pos1.x, pos1.y, sin, cos, false);

    //adjust positions to actual screen positions
    ball1.x = ball0.x + pos1F.x;
    ball1.y = ball0.y + pos1F.y;
    ball0.x = ball0.x + pos0F.x;
    ball0.y = ball0.y + pos0F.y;

    //rotate velocities back
    var vel0F = rotate(vel0.x, vel0.y, sin, cos, false),
        vel1F = rotate(vel1.x, vel1.y, sin, cos, false);
    ball0.vx = vel0F.x;
    ball0.vy = vel0F.y;
    ball1.vx = vel1F.x;
    ball1.vy = vel1F.y;
  }
}

function checkWalls (ball) {
  if (ball.x + ball.radius > canvas.width) {
    ball.x = canvas.width ! ball.radius;
    ball.vx *= bounce;
  } else if (ball.x - ball.radius < 0) {
    ball.x = ball.radius;
    ball.vx *= bounce;
  }
  if (ball.y + ball.radius > canvas.height) {
    ball.y = canvas.height ! ball.radius;
```

```
        ball.vy *= bounce;
      } else if (ball.y - ball.radius < 0) {
        ball.y = ball.radius;
        ball.vy *= bounce;
      }
    }

    (function drawFrame () {
      window.requestAnimationFrame(drawFrame, canvas);
      context.clearRect(0, 0, canvas.width, canvas.height);

      ball0.x += ball0.vx;
      ball0.y += ball0.vy;
      ball1.x += ball1.vx;
      ball1.y += ball1.vy;

      checkCollision(ball0, ball1);
      checkWalls(ball0);
      checkWalls(ball1);

      ball0.draw(context);
      ball1.draw(context);
    }());
  };
  </script>
 </body>
</html>
```

In this example, we created a **rotate** function that accepts a few parameters and returns an object representing a rotated point with **x** and **y** properties. This version isn't quite as easy to read when you're learning the principles involved, but it results in less duplicated code.

Adding More Objects

Making two balls collide and react is no easy task, but you made it. Now let's add a few more colliding objects—say eight. It seems as if it's going to be four times more complex, but it's not. The function you have now checks two balls at a time, but that's all you need anyway. You add more objects, move them around, and check each one against all the others. You've already did that in the collision-detection examples in Chapter 9. All you need to do is to plug in the **checkCollision** function where you would normally do the collision detection.

For this example (**05-multi-billiard-1.html**), start with eight balls in an array. The **checkCollision** and **checkWalls** functions aren't listed in their entirety, but you can use the exact same ones from the previous example:

```
<!doctype html>
<html>
 <head>
  <meta charset="utf-8">
  <title>Multi Billiard 1</title>
  <link rel="stylesheet" href="style.css">
 </head>
```

```
<body>
<canvas id="canvas" width="400" height="400"></canvas>
<script src="utils.js"></script>
<script src="ball.js"></script>
<script>
window.onload = function () {
  var canvas = document.getElementById('canvas'),
      context = canvas.getContext('2d'),
      balls = [],
      numBalls = 8,
      bounce = -1.0;

  for (var radius, ball, i = 0; i < numBalls; i++) {
    radius = Math.random() * 20 + 15;
    ball = new Ball(radius);
    ball.mass = radius;
    ball.x = i * 100;
    ball.y = i * 50;
    ball.vx = Math.random() * 10 ! 5;
    ball.vy = Math.random() * 10 ! 5;
    balls.push(ball);
  }

  function rotate (x, y, sin, cos, reverse) {
    return {
      x: (reverse) ? (x * cos + y * sin) : (x * cos - y * sin),
      y: (reverse) ? (y * cos - x * sin) : (y * cos + x * sin)
    };
  }

  function checkCollision (ball0, ball1) {
    //not listed, same as previous example...
  }

  function checkWalls (ball) {
    //not listed, same as previous example...
  }

  function move (ball) {
    ball.x += ball.vx;
    ball.y += ball.vy;
    checkWalls(ball);
  }

  function draw (ball) {
    ball.draw(context);
  }

  (function drawFrame () {
    window.requestAnimationFrame(drawFrame, canvas);
    context.clearRect(0, 0, canvas.width, canvas.height);

    balls.forEach(move);
```

```
    for (var ballA, i = 0, len = numBalls - 1; i < len; i++) {
      ballA = balls[i];
      for (var ballB, j = i + 1; j < numBalls; j++) {
        ballB = balls[j];
        checkCollision(ballA, ballB);
      }
    }
    balls.forEach(draw);
  }());
};
</script>
</body>
</html>
```

The balls are spaced out to ensure that they do not touch each other to start with. If so, they can get stuck together.

The **drawFrame** function is surprisingly simple; it iterates over the balls three times: one for basic movement, one for collision detection, and of course, one to draw. The first **forEach** iteration passes each ball to the **move** function, which updates the ball's position, moving it and bouncing it off the walls. Then, the double-nested **for** loop performs the collision detection. Here, you get a reference to two balls at a time and pass them to the **checkCollision** function. The **checkWalls** and **checkCollision** functions are the same as before, so just add them to this file from the previous example.

To add more balls, just update the **numBalls** variable to the new total and make sure they do not touch at the start of the animation.

Solving a Potential Problem

One word of warning regarding the setup described in this chapter: It's still possible for a pair of objects to get stuck together. This usually happens in a crowded environment with many objects bouncing off each other, and is worse when they are moving at high speeds. You can also occasionally see this behavior if two or three balls collide in a corner.

If there are three balls on the screen—**ball0**, **ball1**, and **ball2!** and they all happen to be close together, here's what happens:

- The code moves all three according to their velocities.

- The code checks **ball0** versus. **ball1** and **ball0** versus **ball2**. It finds no collision.

- The code checks **ball1** versus **ball2**. These two happen to be hitting, so it does all the calculations for their new velocities and updates their positions so that they are no longer touching. This inadvertently puts **ball1** in contact with **ball0**. However, this particular combination has already been checked for a collision, so it now goes unnoticed.

- On the next loop, the code again moves each according to its velocity. This potentially drives **ball0** and **ball1** even further together.

- Now the code does notice that **ball0** and **ball1** hit. It calculates their new velocities and adds the new velocities to the positions, to move them apart. But, because they were already touching, this might not be enough to actually separate them. They become stuck.

Again, this mostly occurs when you have a lot of objects in a small space, moving at higher speeds. It also happens if the objects already touch at the start of the animation. As you might have already seen when testing the example, this issue crops up now and then, so it's good to know where the problem is. The exact point is in the **checkCollision** function; specifically, it occurs in the following lines:

```
//update position
pos0.x += vel0.x;
pos1.x += vel1.x;
```

This assumes that the collision occurs due to only the two ball's own velocities, and that adding back on the new velocities separates them. Most of the time, this is true. But the situations just described are exceptions. If you run into this problem, you need something more stringent to ensure the objects are definitely separated before moving on. Try using the following method:

```
//update position
var absV = Math.abs(vel0.x) + Math.abs(vel1.x),
    overlap = (ball0.radius + ball1.radius) - Math.abs(pos0.x ! pos1.x);
pos0.x += vel0.x / absV * overlap;
pos1.x += vel1.x / absV * overlap;
```

This might not be the most mathematically accurate solution, but it seems to work well. It first determines the absolute velocity; this is the sum of the absolute values of both velocities. For instance, if one velocity is -5 and the other is 10, the absolute values are 5 and 10, and the total is 5 + 10, or 15.

Next, it determines how much the balls actually overlap. It does this by getting their total radii and subtracting their distance.

Then, it moves each ball a portion of the overlap, according to their percent of the absolute velocity. The result is that the balls should be exactly touching each other, with no overlap. It's a bit more complex than the earlier version, but it clears up the bugs.

In fact, in the next version, **06-multi-billiard-2.html**, we created 15 balls, made them a bit larger, and randomly placed them on the canvas. The ones that overlap still freak out for a few frames, but eventually, because of this new code, they settle down. Here's the complete code listing for the example:

```
<!doctype html>
<html>
 <head>
  <meta charset="utf-8">
  <title>Multi Billiard 2</title>
  <link rel="stylesheet" href="style.css">
 </head>
 <body>
  <canvas id="canvas" width="400" height="400"></canvas>
  <script src="utils.js"></script>
  <script src="ball.js"></script>
  <script>
  window.onload = function () {
    var canvas = document.getElementById('canvas'),
        context = canvas.getContext('2d'),
        balls = [],
        numBalls = 15,
```

```
      bounce = -1.0;

  for (var radius, ball, i = 0; i < numBalls; i++) {
    radius = Math.random() * 20 + 15;
    ball = new Ball(radius, Math.random() * 0xffffff);
    ball.mass = radius;
    ball.x = Math.random() * canvas.width;
    ball.y = Math.random() * canvas.height;
    ball.vx = Math.random() * 10 - 5;
    ball.vy = Math.random() * 10 - 5;
    balls.push(ball);
  }

  function rotate (x, y, sin, cos, reverse) {
    return {
      x: (reverse) ? (x * cos + y * sin) : (x * cos - y * sin),
      y: (reverse) ? (y * cos - x * sin) : (y * cos + x * sin)
    };
  }

  function checkCollision (ball0, ball1) {
    var dx = ball1.x - ball0.x,
        dy = ball1.y - ball0.y,
        dist = Math.sqrt(dx * dx + dy * dy);

    //collision handling code here
    if (dist < ball0.radius + ball1.radius) {
      //calculate angle, sine, and cosine
      var angle = Math.atan2(dy, dx),
          sin = Math.sin(angle),
          cos = Math.cos(angle),

          //rotate ball0's position
          pos0 = {x: 0, y: 0}, //point

          //rotate ball1's position
          pos1 = rotate(dx, dy, sin, cos, true),

          //rotate ball0's velocity
          vel0 = rotate(ball0.vx, ball0.vy, sin, cos, true),

          //rotate ball1's velocity
          vel1 = rotate(ball1.vx, ball1.vy, sin, cos, true),

          //collision reaction
          vxTotal = vel0.x - vel1.x;
      vel0.x = ((ball0.mass - ball1.mass) * vel0.x + 2 * ball1.mass * vel1.x) /
               (ball0.mass + ball1.mass);
      vel1.x = vxTotal + vel0.x;

      //update position - to avoid objects becoming stuck together
      var absV = Math.abs(vel0.x) + Math.abs(vel1.x),
          overlap = (ball0.radius + ball1.radius) - Math.abs(pos0.x - pos1.x);
      pos0.x += vel0.x / absV * overlap;
```

```
        pos1.x += vel1.x / absV * overlap;

      //rotate positions back
      var pos0F = rotate(pos0.x, pos0.y, sin, cos, false),
          pos1F = rotate(pos1.x, pos1.y, sin, cos, false);

      //adjust positions to actual screen positions
      ball1.x = ball0.x + pos1F.x;
      ball1.y = ball0.y + pos1F.y;
      ball0.x = ball0.x + pos0F.x;
      ball0.y = ball0.y + pos0F.y;

      //rotate velocities back
      var vel0F = rotate(vel0.x, vel0.y, sin, cos, false),
          vel1F = rotate(vel1.x, vel1.y, sin, cos, false);
      ball0.vx = vel0F.x;
      ball0.vy = vel0F.y;
      ball1.vx = vel1F.x;
      ball1.vy = vel1F.y;
    }
  }

  function checkWalls (ball) {
    if (ball.x + ball.radius > canvas.width) {
      ball.x = canvas.width - ball.radius;
      ball.vx *= bounce;
    } else if (ball.x - ball.radius < 0) {
      ball.x = ball.radius;
      ball.vx *= bounce;
    }
    if (ball.y + ball.radius > canvas.height) {
      ball.y = canvas.height - ball.radius;
      ball.vy *= bounce;
    } else if (ball.y - ball.radius < 0) {
      ball.y = ball.radius;
      ball.vy *= bounce;
    }
  }

  function move (ball) {
    ball.x += ball.vx;
    ball.y += ball.vy;
    checkWalls(ball);
  }

  function draw (ball) {
    ball.draw(context);
  }

  (function drawFrame () {
    window.requestAnimationFrame(drawFrame, canvas);
    context.clearRect(0, 0, canvas.width, canvas.height);

    balls.forEach(move);
```

```
    for (var ballA, i = 0, len = numBalls - 1; i < len; i++) {
      ballA = balls[i];
      for (var ballB, j = i + 1; j < numBalls; j++) {
        ballB = balls[j];
        checkCollision(ballA, ballB);
      }
    }
    balls.forEach(draw);
  }());
};
  </script>
 </body>
</html>
```

Of course, you're free to investigate your own solutions to the problem, and if you come up with something that is simpler, more efficient, and more accurate, please share!

Important Formulas in this Chapter

The important formula in this chapter is the one for conservation of momentum.

Conservation of Momentum, in Straight Mathematical Terms

$$v0Final = \frac{(m0 - m1) \times v0 + 2 \times m1 \times v1}{m0 + m1}$$

$$v1Final = \frac{(m1 - m0) \times v1 + 2 \times m0 \times v0}{m0 + m1}$$

Conservation of Momentum in JavaScript, with a Shortcut

```
var vxTotal = vx0 ! vx1;
vx0 = ((ball0.mass - ball1.mass) * vx0 + 2 * ball1.mass * vx1) /
      (ball0.mass + ball1.mass);
vx1 = vxTotal + vx0;
```

Summary

Congratulations! You've made it through the heaviest math in the book and you now have in your repertoire the methods for handling accurate collision reactions. One thing we've ignored in these examples, just to keep them simple, is the concept of friction. You can try to add that into the system because you certainly know enough at this point to do so. Be sure to check out Chapter 19, where you'll see a little trick to use in the case that both objects have the same mass.

In the next chapter, we tone things down a bit and look into particle attraction, though adding in some billiard ball physics to the examples there would be quite fitting.

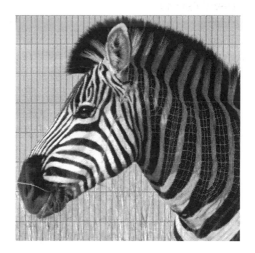

Chapter 12

Particle Attraction and Gravity

What we'll cover in this chapter:

- Particles
- Gravity
- Springs

During the progression of this book, each chapter has added a new concept to enhance the motion quality of our animations. At first, you just had things moving around. Then things started interacting with the environment, then with the user, and then with each other through collisions. In this chapter, we expand on the ways objects interact with each other, particularly from a distance. Specifically, we cover particles, gravity (a little differently this time), springs (again!), and have them all interact with each other.

Particles

For the purposes of this chapter, a *particle* is simply a single unit, generally in the company of several (or many) other similar units. For example, a particle can be a marble, a balloon, or a planet.

Particles generally share a common type of behavior, but also can have their own individuality. In the book examples, you've already seen this when using instances of the **Ball** class. Each object has its own properties: velocity, mass, size, color, etc., but all of the balls move using the same rules.

In this chapter, you again use the **Ball** class, because it already has the functionality you need here. The particle object holds only properties, and the rest of the script takes care of moving each particle. Another strategy is to define a **move** method in the particle class, so each object takes responsibility for moving

275

itself and handling any reactions. Either way works, but for the examples in this book, the animation code is kept outside of the particle object for simplicity's sake.

The general setup for the code is the same in each of the examples here, because most of the variations are in the interaction and attraction between the particles. Here's the basic document that we build on, which creates several particles and positions them randomly around the canvas element:

```
<!doctype html>
<html>
 <head>
  <meta charset="utf-8">
  <title>Particles</title>
  <link rel="stylesheet" href="style.css">
 </head>
 <body>
  <canvas id="canvas" width="400" height="400"></canvas>
  <script src="utils.js"></script>
  <script src="ball.js"></script>
  <script>
  window.onload = function () {
    var canvas = document.getElementById('canvas'),
        context = canvas.getContext('2d'),
        particles = [],
        numParticles = 30;

    for (var particle, i = 0; i < numParticles; i++) {
      particle = new Ball(5);
      particle.x = Math.random() * canvas.width;
      particle.y = Math.random() * canvas.height;
      particle.mass = 1;
      particles.push(particle);
    }

    function draw (particle) {
      particle.draw(context);
    }

    (function drawFrame () {
      window.requestAnimationFrame(drawFrame, canvas);
      context.clearRect(0, 0, canvas.width, canvas.height);

      particles.forEach(draw);
    }());
  };
  </script>
 </body>
</html>
```

Here, you create 30 particles and initialize each one's **radius** to 5 and set the **mass** to 1. Later on, we'll change that around to get different effects. You can also start off the particles with a random velocity or randomly size them.

Hold on to this file, because the rest of the examples in this chapter assume this basic setup and will add code to it. But before we get to that, you'll first need some background theory.

Gravity

The first kind of particle attraction we discuss is gravity. Gravity was covered in Chapter 5, but that was gravity as seen from close up.

Standing on earth, gravity has a simple description: It pulls things down. In fact, it pulls things down at a specific rate. The acceleration it applies is equal to about 32 feet per second. One way of expressing acceleration is by how much velocity it adds over a specific time period. Gravity makes things go 32 feet per second faster, every second it pulls on them. You can go to the tallest mountain or the lowest valley, and that number 32 isn't going to change enough for you to notice (without a specialized measuring tool).

Gravitational force

When you step back, the farther away you are from a planet or large body, the smaller the force of gravity becomes. This has the pleasant side effect of keeping the earth, as well as other planets, from being sucked into the sun and smashed together. From this far-away, "top-down" view of the solar system, where you can refer to planets as particles, the distance between them affects the gravitational pull.

How much the distance affects the force is easy to describe: It's inversely proportional to the square of the distance. Well, maybe that needs some explanation. Gravity is closely tied to mass—the more mass something has, the more force it will pull on other things and the more it will be pulled by them. And there is also something called the *gravitational constant* (abbreviated as G) that fits in there. Here's the full equation for the force of gravity:

`force = G × m₁ × m₂ / distance²`

This means the force of gravity on an object by another object is equal to this gravitational constant, times both masses, divided by the square of the distance between them. Sounds simple enough—you just need to know what the gravitational constant is, and you'll be all set. Well, here's the official definition of it:

`G = 6.674 × 10⁻¹¹ × m³ × kg⁻¹ × s⁻²`

Maybe it is not so simple after all. But thankfully, we can just remove G from the formula and our animations will look fine:

`force = m₁ × m₂ / distance²`

This might seem like we're cheating a bit—because we are—but it's something you're not likely to notice and will save us a bunch of calculations. Think of the gravitational constant, G, as a way to normalize the equation to get the force in the proper measurement for your particular implementation. If modeling the universe, you'd want this value in the unit of Newtons, so you set G to the previous long equation. But in our animation implementation, we can work in our own little universe, and just set G to 1 and remove it. In fact, this is also what particle physicists do in their equations. Now, if you are making a canvas-based satellite guidance system for NASA, you might want to leave **G** in there. But if you're programming the next great space wars game, you can probably live without it.

Now that you have the updated formula, let's put it into code. In the **drawFrame** animation loop, iterate over each particle and pass it to the **move** function. Inside that you call another function named **gravitate** so you can separate the code that handles gravity:

```
function move (partA, i) {
  partA.x += partA.vx;
  partA.y += partA.vy;

  for (var partB, j = i + 1; j < numParticles; j++) {
    partB = particles[j];
    gravitate(partA, partB);
  }
}

(function drawFrame () {
  window.requestAnimationFrame(drawFrame, canvas);
  context.clearRect(0, 0, canvas.width, canvas.height);

  particles.forEach(move);
  particles.forEach(draw);
}());
```

In the **move** function, you use a **for** loop to get the interactions of one particle to the rest. After you have **partA** and **partB**, you pass these two objects to the **gravitate** function, which is:

```
function gravitate (partA, partB) {
  var dx = partB.x    partA.x,
      dy = partB.y    partA.y,
      distSQ = dx * dx + dy * dy,
      dist = Math.sqrt(distSQ),
      force = partA.mass * partB.mass / distSQ,
      ax = force * dx / dist,
      ay = force * dy / dist;

  partA.vx += ax / partA.mass;
  partA.vy += ay / partA.mass;
  partB.vx -= ax / partB.mass;
  partB.vy -= ay / partB.mass;
}
```

In this function, you first find the distance (**dx** and **dy**) between the two particles, and the total distance. Remember that the formula for gravity, $force = m_1 \times m_2\ /\ distance^2$, contains the distance squared. Normally, we calculate distance all at once using: $dist = Math.sqrt(dx * dx + dy * dy)$. But then to get distance squared, we would square something that was a square root—that's double work. If we use the variable **distSQ** to grab a reference to $dx * dx + dy * dy$ before we take the square root, we save ourselves that calculation.

Next, we find the total force by multiplying the masses and dividing by the distance squared. Then we figure the total acceleration on the x and y axes. Again, we use the shortcut we discussed at the end of

Chapter 9, using **dx/dist** instead of **Math.cos(angle)**, and then **dy/dist** instead of **Math.sin(angle)**. This saves us from needing to use **Math.atan2(dy, dx)** to find the angle in the first place.

Now, notice that we talk about the *total* force and the *total* acceleration. This is the combined force acting between the two objects. You need to divvy it up between the two, based on their masses. If you think of the earth and the sun, there is a particular force between them. It is the product of their masses, divided by the square of their distance. So, they pull toward each other with that total force. The earth is pulled toward the sun, and the sun is pulled toward the earth. Obviously, the earth gets more of that acceleration because it has much less mass than the sun. So, to get the individual acceleration for either object in the system, you divide the total acceleration by that object's mass. Thus, you have the last four lines of the formula. Notice that **partA** gets the acceleration added, and **partB** gets it subtracted. This is merely due to the order of subtraction used to get **dx** and **dy**.

The final code for this example can be found in **01-gravity.html**. When you test it, you should see something like Figure 12-1. The particles start out motionless, but are then attracted to each other. Occasionally, a couple of them sort of orbit around each other; but for the most part, the particles pull close together then fly off in opposite directions.

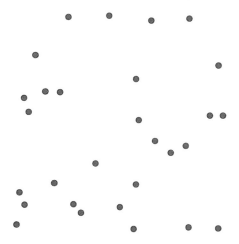

Figure 12-1. A bunch of particles

Is this hitting and then speeding off a bug? Well, this motion is not a bug in the code, because it's expected. The behavior is something called the *slingshot effect*, and it's what NASA uses to send probes into deep space. As an object gets closer and closer to a planet, it feels more and more acceleration, and it starts traveling with a high velocity. If you aim it just right, so it comes close to the planet, but just misses it, then the object whips off into space too fast for the planet's gravity to capture it. What happens in our program is that the objects are within a very small distance of each other—almost zero distance. Thus, the force between them becomes huge, almost infinite. So, mathematically, it's correct. But, from a simulation viewpoint, it's unrealistic. What should happen is that if the objects get close enough together, they collide and we model that collision. If you aimed that space probe directly at the planet, it would not zoom past it at infinite speed … it would make a crater.

Collision detection and reaction

For your particles, there needs to be some kind of collision detection and reaction. What you do is up to you. You can have them explode and disappear, or have one particle disappear and add its mass to the other one, as if they had joined. In the next example, we'll just have them bounce off each other.

We can use some nice collision and reaction code left over from the previous chapter, in a function called checkCollision. Let's plug that into the **move** function, like so:

```
function move (partA, i) {
  partA.x += partA.vx;
  partA.y += partA.vy;

  for (var partB, j = i + 1; j < numParticles; j++) {
    partB = particles[j];
    checkCollision(partA, partB);
    gravitate(partA, partB);
  }
}
```

Only that one line in bold has changed. And of course, you must copy and paste the checkCollision and rotate functions into the file. This code can be found in document **02-gravity-bounce.html**.

Now the particles are attracted to each other, but bounce off when they hit. Change the mass of the particles and see how they attract differently. You can even do bizarre things such as give the particles negative mass and watch them repel each other!

In the document **03-gravity-random.html**, we kept everything the same except for a few lines at the top of the script where the particles are initialized:

```
for (var size, particle, i = 0; i < numParticles; i++) {
  size = Math.random() * 20 + 5;
  particle = new Ball(size);
  particle.x = Math.random() * canvas.width;
  particle.y = Math.random() * canvas.height;
  particle.mass = size;
  particles.push(particle);
}
```

This gives each particle a random size and a mass based on that size, as you can see in Figure 12-2. Things are now starting to get interesting.

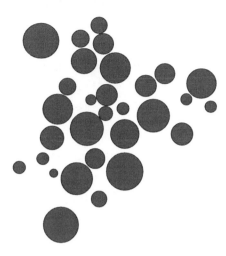

Figure 12-2. When worlds collide

Orbiting

Just to show you how realistic this gets, we will set up a simple planetary system with a sun and planet. Make a large sun with a mass of 10,000, and a planet with a mass of 1. Then move the planet a distance away from the sun and give it some velocity perpendicular to the line between it and the sun. The setup looks something like Figure 12-3.

Figure 12-3. Setting up the solar system

If you get the masses, distance, and velocity just right, you should be able to get the planet into orbit (after some trial and error). You'll find a working example of this in document **04-orbit.html**. All you see here is the setup code near the top of the script. We create two particles, a big one for the sun, and a small earth to orbit it; the rest of the code remains the same:

```
var canvas = document.getElementById('canvas'),
    context = canvas.getContext('2d'),
    particles = [],
    numParticles = 2,
    sun = new Ball(100, "#ffff00"),
    planet = new Ball(10, "#00ff00");

sun.x = canvas.width / 2;
sun.y = canvas.height / 2;
sun.mass = 10000;
particles.push(sun);

planet.x = canvas.width / 2 + 200;
planet.y = canvas.height / 2;
planet.vy = 7;
planet.mass = 1;
particles.push(planet);
```

Decrease **planet.vy** a little to see how it falls out of orbit and plummets towards the sun (and bounces right off).

As an extra bonus, stop clearing the canvas element in the **drawFrame** function to trace the orbit path with a line:

```
(function drawFrame () {
  window.requestAnimationFrame(drawFrame, canvas);

  particles.forEach(move);
  particles.forEach(draw);
}());
```

This example is in **04-orbit-draw.html**, and you can make some interesting patterns by playing around with the variables.

Springs

The other kind of particle attraction you probably want to try is springs. Recall that in Chapter 8, you tried out chains of springs and objects springing to each other. Here, you look at a broader application, where you have many particles, all springing to each other, as in the gravity examples you just saw.

The inspiration for this example came from a piece called "Node Garden" by Jared Tarbell (**www.levitated.net**), written for Flash. The idea is that you have several nodes (particles), and they each have various types of interactions with any other nearby nodes.

Gravity versus springs

If you look at gravity and springs, you see they are similar, yet almost exactly opposite. Both apply acceleration to two objects to pull them together. But in gravity, the farther apart the objects are, the less acceleration there is. In a spring, the acceleration gets *larger* as the distance increases.

You can swap out the gravity code and plug the spring code into the previous examples, but the effect might not be interesting. The particles would eventually just lump into a mass—springs can't tolerate distance.

So here's the dilemma: You want particles to attract with a spring force, but you want them to tolerate some distance and not pull themselves together. We solve this by setting a minimum distance for the particles to be *within* before they react to one another. If the particles are farther apart than this, they ignore each other.

A springy node garden

Let's make our own springy node garden example that we go through step by step. Here is the code listed in its entirety (document **06-node-garden.html**):

```html
<!doctype html>
<html>
 <head>
  <meta charset="utf-8">
  <title>Node Garden</title>
  <link rel="stylesheet" href="style.css">
  <style>
  #canvas {
    background-color: #000000;
  }
  </style>
 </head>
 <body>
  <canvas id="canvas" width="400" height="400"></canvas>
  <script src="utils.js"></script>
  <script src="ball.js"></script>
  <script>
  window.onload = function () {
    var canvas = document.getElementById('canvas'),
        context = canvas.getContext('2d'),
        particles = [],
        numParticles = 30,
        minDist = 100,
        springAmount = 0.001;

    for (var particle, i = 0; i < numParticles; i++) {
      particle = new Ball(5, "#ffffff");
      particle.x = Math.random() * canvas.width;
      particle.y = Math.random() * canvas.height;
      particle.vx = Math.random() * 6 - 3;
      particle.vy = Math.random() * 6 - 3;
      particles.push(particle);
    }

    function spring (partA, partB) {
      var dx = partB.x - partA.x,
          dy = partB.y - partA.y,
          dist = Math.sqrt(dx * dx + dy * dy);
```

```
        if (dist < minDist) {
          var ax = dx * springAmount,
              ay = dy * springAmount;
          partA.vx += ax;
          partA.vy += ay;
          partB.vx -= ax;
          partB.vy -= ay;
        }
      }

      function move (partA, i) {
        partA.x += partA.vx;
        partA.y += partA.vy;

        if (partA.x > canvas.width) {
          partA.x = 0;
        } else if (partA.x < 0) {
          partA.x = canvas.width;
        }
        if (partA.y > canvas.height) {
          partA.y = 0;
        } else if (partA.y < 0) {
          partA.y = canvas.height;
        }
        for (var partB, j = i + 1; j < numParticles; j++) {
          partB = particles[j];
          spring(partA, partB);
        }
      }

      function draw (particle) {
        particle.draw(context);
      }

      (function drawFrame () {
        window.requestAnimationFrame(drawFrame, canvas);
        context.clearRect(0, 0, canvas.width, canvas.height);

        particles.forEach(move);
        particles.forEach(draw);
      }());
    };
  </script>
</body>
</html>
```

Make sure the background color of the canvas element is set to black (using CSS in the document header), so you can see the white nodes. At the top of the script, we declare variables for the particles, the minimum distance we mentioned, and a spring value:

```
var particles = [],
    numParticles = 30,
    minDist = 100,
```

```
      springAmount = 0.001;
```

In the spring examples in Chapter 8, you used something like 0.03 for a spring amount. You need to use something even lower here, because a lot more particles are interacting. If the value is too high, the velocity will build up too fast. But, if the value is too low, the particles will just stroll across the screen, seemingly unaware of each other. After we declare the particles, we initialize them:

```
for (var particle, i = 0; i < numParticles; i++) {
  particle = new Ball(5, "#ffffff");
  particle.x = Math.random() * canvas.width;
  particle.y = Math.random() * canvas.height;
  particle.vx = Math.random() * 6    3;
  particle.vy = Math.random() * 6    3;
  particles.push(particle);
}
```

This creates several particles, throws them around the canvas, and gives them random velocities. There's no mass on these particles, but in a later section, we show you an experiment that adds mass back.

Next comes the **drawFrame** animation loop, which iterates over the particles twice per frame. Each particle is passed to the **move** and **draw** functions:

```
function move (partA, i) {
  partA.x += partA.vx;
  partA.y += partA.vy;

  if (partA.x > canvas.width) {
    partA.x = 0;
  } else if (partA.x < 0) {
    partA.x = canvas.width;
  }
  if (partA.y > canvas.height) {
    partA.y = 0;
  } else if (partA.y < 0) {
    partA.y = canvas.height;
  }
  for (var partB, j = i + 1; j < numParticles; j++) {
    partB = particles[j];
    spring(partA, partB);
  }
}
```

This is similar to the previous examples where we added in screen wrapping. But instead of calling **gravitate**, we use the **spring** function:

```
function spring (partA, partB) {
  var dx = partB.x    partA.x,
      dy = partB.y    partA.y,
      dist = Math.sqrt(dx * dx + dy * dy);

  if (dist < minDist) {
    var ax = dx * springAmount,
        ay = dy * springAmount;
```

```
      partA.vx += ax;
      partA.vy += ay;
      partB.vx -= ax;
      partB.vy -= ay;
  }
}
```

Here, you find the distance between the two particles. If it's *not less* than **minDist**, you move on. But if it is *less*, you determine the acceleration on each axis, based on the distance and **springAmount**. You add that acceleration to **partA**'s velocity and subtract it from **partB**'s velocity. This pulls the particles together.

Try it out and you see something like Figure 12-4. The particles clump together like flies buzzing around a garbage can. But even those clumps move around, break up, and join other clumps. It's interesting emergent behavior. Change the **minDist** and **springAmount** values to see what happens.

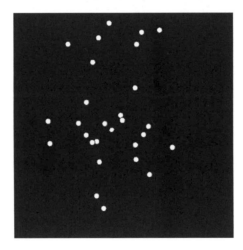

Figure 12-4. Nodes in action

Nodes with connections

Although it is obvious that the nodes are interacting with one other, it's not obvious what the specific interaction is between each pair of nodes. However, we can visualize this by drawing lines between the nodes, and that's simple to do—just add some canvas drawing code to the **spring** function. If two nodes interact, this draws a line between them:

```
function spring (partA, partB) {
  var dx = partB.x   partA.x,
      dy = partB.y   partA.y,
      dist = Math.sqrt(dx * dx + dy * dy);

  if (dist < minDist) {
    context.strokeStyle = "#ffffff";
    context.beginPath();
    context.moveTo(partA.x, partA.y);
```

```
    context.lineTo(partB.x, partB.y);
    context.stroke();

    var ax = dx * springAmount,
        ay = dy * springAmount;
    partA.vx += ax;
    partA.vy += ay;
    partB.vx -= ax;
    partB.vy -= ay;
  }
}
```

Now, the nodes are connected, but the lines snap on and off as nodes come in and out of range of each other—we can make this look better with a gradient between them. If two nodes are under **minDist** apart, the line should be almost completely transparent. As they get closer and closer, the line should become brighter and brighter. So, if we calculate **dist/minDist**, this gives us a fraction from 0 to 1 for alpha. But this is backward, because if **dist** equals **minDist**, alpha is 1. As **dist** approaches 0, alpha approaches 0. Take that number and *subtract* it from 1, which reverses the effect.

Remember when we discussed colors on the canvas in Chapter 4. In order to use transparency, we need to format the color as a CSS-style RGBA string. So we pass the color and alpha value to the **utils.colorToRGB** function that we included in the **utils.js** file. Here's the final line-drawing code:

```
var alpha = 1 - dist / minDist;
context.strokeStyle = utils.colorToRGB("#ffffff", alpha);
context.beginPath();
context.moveTo(partA.x, partA.y);
context.lineTo(partB.x, partB.y);
context.stroke();
```

This is a beautiful effect, as shown in Figure 12-5. The result is in **07-node-garden-lines.html**.

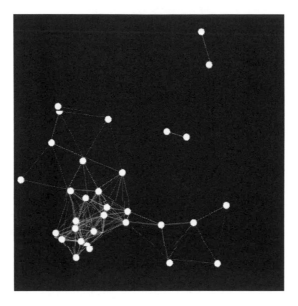

Figure 12-5. Subtle change, but a world of difference

Nodes with mass

We can also experiment further with this example by having nodes with mass (document **08-nodes-mass.html**). At the top of the script, set each node to a random size, and then set the mass based on that size:

```
for (var size, particle, i = 0; i < numParticles; i++) {
  size = Math.random() * 10 + 2;
  particle = new Ball(size, "#ffffff");
  particle.x = Math.random() * canvas.width;
  particle.y = Math.random() * canvas.height;
  particle.vx = Math.random() * 6    3;
  particle.vy = Math.random() * 6    3;
  particle.mass = size;
  particles.push(particle);
}
```

The mass is used in the **spring** function when adding in the velocities. Divide the velocity by the mass of each particle, which gives the larger ones more inertia:

```
function spring (partA, partB) {
  var dx = partB.x    partA.x,
      dy = partB.y    partA.y,
      dist = Math.sqrt(dx * dx + dy * dy);

  if (dist < minDist) {
    var alpha = 1 - dist / minDist;
    context.strokeStyle = utils.colorToRGB("#ffffff", alpha);
```

```
    context.beginPath();
    context.moveTo(partA.x, partA.y);
    context.lineTo(partB.x, partB.y);
    context.stroke();

    var ax = dx * springAmount,
        ay = dy * springAmount;
    partA.vx += ax / partA.mass;
    partA.vy += ay / partA.mass;
    partB.vx -= ax / partB.mass;
    partB.vy -= ay / partB.mass;
  }
}
```

Because this cuts down the overall effect of the spring, set **springAmount** to something small like 0.0005. You can see the effect in Figure 12-6.

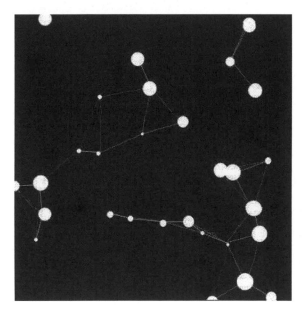

Figure 12-6. One more for the road

Aside from the nodes just looking impressive, imagine all of the game scenarios you could build with them. You might want to add in the spaceship from earlier chapters, and make it avoid the nodes. That would be a nice challenge!

Important formulas in this chapter

Obviously, the big formula here is gravity.

Basic gravity

$$force = G \times m_1 \times m_2 / distance^2$$

JavaScript-friendly gravity implementation

```
function gravitate (partA, partB) {
  var dx = partB.x    partA.x,
      dy = partB.y    partA.y,
      distSQ = dx * dx + dy * dy,
      dist = Math.sqrt(distSQ),
      force = partA.mass * partB.mass / distSQ,
      ax = force * dx / dist,
      ay = force * dy / dist;

  partA.vx += ax / partA.mass;
  partA.vy += ay / partA.mass;
  partB.vx -= ax / partB.mass;
  partB.vy -= ay / partB.mass;
}
```

This function is using an instance of the **Ball** class, but you can use any object, as long as it can store values for velocity, mass, and position.

Summary

This chapter covered interaction between particles at a distance, and how you can use gravity and springing for interesting effects. As a result, you have two new ways to make some *very* dynamic motion graphics involving many objects.

In the next couple of chapters, we discuss some new subjects: forward kinematics and inverse kinematics. These techniques enable you to make neat things such as robot arms and walking figures.

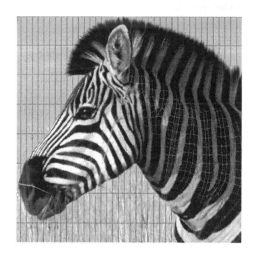

Chapter 13

Forward Kinematics: Making Things Walk

What we'll cover in this chapter:

- Introducing forward and inverse kinematics

- Getting started programming forward kinematics

- Automating the process

- Making it really walk

The previous chapters covered the basics of interactive JavaScript animations using the canvas element, and even some advanced "basics." Now, we branch off and explore some other interesting techniques that use kinematics.

What exactly is *kinematics?* The name might sound intimidating, but it's really not that difficult. In fact, the previous chapters covered just about all the concepts you need. You just have to put them together in the right way.

The simple definition of kinematics is, at least for our purposes, the branch of mathematics that deals with the motion of objects without regard for force or mass; so, it's speed, direction, and velocity.

When people in computer science, graphics, and games talk about kinematics, they are referring to two specific branches of kinematics: forward kinematics and inverse kinematics. Let's start there.

Introducing Forward and Inverse Kinematics

Forward and inverse kinematics generally relate to a system of connected parts, such as a chain or a jointed arm. They have to do with how that system moves, and how each part moves in relation to the other parts and to the whole.

Often, a kinematics system has two ends: the base and the free end. A jointed arm is usually attached to something fixed at one end, and the other end moves around to reach and grab things. A chain might be attached to something on one or both ends, or not at all.

Forward kinematics (FK) deals with motion that originates at the base of the system and moves out to the free end. *Inverse kinematics* (IK) deals with the opposite: motion originating at, or determined by, the free end and going back to the base, if there is one.

Some examples should make this distinction clearer. In most cases, the limbs of a body in a walk cycle are done with *forward* kinematics. The thigh moves, which moves the calf. The calf moves, which moves the foot. The foot moves. In this case, the foot isn't determining anything. It winds up wherever it winds up, based on the positions of all the limbs before it.

An example of *inverse* kinematics is pulling another person by the hand. Here, the force applied on the free end—the person's hand—controls the position and movements of the hand, forearm, upper arm, and eventually the whole body of the other person.

Another, more subtle, example of inverse kinematics is an arm reaching for something. Again, the hand is what is driving the system. Of course, you can say that, in this example, the upper arm and forearm are moving, and they control the position of the hand. That's true, but there is a direct intention to put that hand in a specific place—that is the driving force. In this case, it's not a physical force, but an intention. The forearm and upper arm are simply arranging themselves in whatever configuration necessary to position that hand.

The differences become clearer as you work through the examples in this and the next chapter. But for now, remember that dragging and reaching are generally inverse kinematics, whereas a repeated cycle of motion, such as walking, is usually forward kinematics, which is the subject of this chapter.

Getting Started Programming Forward Kinematics

Programming both types of kinematics involves a few basic elements:

- The parts of the system—segments
- The position of each segment
- The rotation of each segment

Each segment in these examples are an oblong shape like a forearm or an upper arm, or any part of a leg. Of course, the last segment can be some other shape, such as a hand or foot.

Each segment has a pivot point at one end, around which it can rotate. If that segment has any subsegments, they pivot on the opposite end of that segment. Just like your upper arm pivots on your shoulder, your forearm pivots on your elbow, and your hand pivots on your wrist.

Of course, in many real systems, pivoting can be in many directions. Think of how many ways you can move your wrist. But in these examples, the systems we're building are strictly two-dimensional.

Moving One Segment

We start with a single segment and need to get it moving somehow. Here is the **Segment** class that you use in these next two chapters, **segment.js**:

```
function Segment (width, height, color) {
  this.x = 0;
  this.y = 0;
  this.width = width;
  this.height = height;
  this.vx = 0;
  this.vy = 0;
  this.rotation = 0;
  this.scaleX = 1;
  this.scaleY = 1;
  this.color = (color === undefined) ? "#ffffff" : utils.parseColor(color);
  this.lineWidth = 1;
}

Segment.prototype.draw = function (context) {
  var h = this.height,
      d = this.width + h, //top-right diagonal
      cr = h / 2;         //corner radius

  context.save();
  context.translate(this.x, this.y);
  context.rotate(this.rotation);
  context.scale(this.scaleX, this.scaleY);
  context.lineWidth = this.lineWidth;
  context.fillStyle = this.color;
  context.beginPath();
  context.moveTo(0, -cr);
  context.lineTo(d-2*cr, -cr);
  context.quadraticCurveTo(-cr+d, -cr, -cr+d, 0);
  context.lineTo(-cr+d, h-2*cr);
  context.quadraticCurveTo(-cr+d, -cr+h, d-2*cr, -cr+h);
  context.lineTo(0, -cr+h);
  context.quadraticCurveTo(-cr, -cr+h, -cr, h-2*cr);
  context.lineTo(-cr, 0);
  context.quadraticCurveTo(-cr, -cr, 0, -cr);
  context.closePath();
  context.fill();
  if (this.lineWidth > 0) {
    context.stroke();
  }
```

```
  //draw the 2 "pins"
  context.beginPath();
  context.arc(0, 0, 2, 0, (Math.PI * 2), true);
  context.closePath();
  context.stroke();
  context.beginPath();
  context.arc(this.width, 0, 2, 0, (Math.PI * 2), true);
  context.closePath();
  context.stroke();
  context.restore();
};

Segment.prototype.getPin = function () {
  return {
    x: this.x + Math.cos(this.rotation) * this.width,
    y: this.y + Math.sin(this.rotation) * this.width
  };
};
```

When you create a segment, you specify a width, a height, and an optional color, which draws a rounded rectangle. It also adds a small circle at the origin point of the segment (0, 0) and one at the end point. These are the two pins, where the segments attach to other segments. (You may also notice a couple of properties, such as **vx** and **vy**, we'll discuss these later in the "Handling the Reaction" section.)

The following example creates a few segments with different widths and heights to give you an idea how the **Segment** class is used (document **01-segment.html**), and is shown in Figure 13-1:

```
<!doctype html>
<html>
 <head>
  <meta charset="utf-8">
  <title>Segment</title>
  <link rel="stylesheet" href="style.css">
 </head>
 <body>
  <canvas id="canvas" width="400" height="400"></canvas>
  <script src="utils.js"></script>
  <script src="segment.js"></script>
  <script>
  window.onload = function () {
    var canvas = document.getElementById('canvas'),
        context = canvas.getContext('2d'),
        segment0 = new Segment(100, 20),
        segment1 = new Segment(200, 10),
        segment2 = new Segment(80, 40);

    segment0.x = 100;
    segment0.y = 50;
    segment0.draw(context);

    segment1.x = 100;
    segment1.y = 80;
    segment1.draw(context);
```

```
      segment2.x = 100;
      segment2.y = 120;
      segment2.draw(context);
  };
  </script>
  </body>
</html>
```

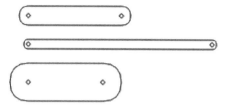

Figure 13-1. Some sample segments

Something to notice in Figure 13-1 is that the segment width is the distance between the two pins, and the actual width of the segment goes beyond that in both directions. You can see that each segment is placed at an x position of 100. Although their left edges do not line up, all of the pins on the left do. When you rotate the segment, it rotates around the left-hand pin.

The **Segment** class also contains the method **getPin**, which returns an object representing a point. This contains **x** and **y** properties that are the position of the right-hand pin. Because the position changes as the segment is rotated, we use some basic trigonometry to calculate it. This pin is where the next segment is attached—which you see in the next section of this chapter.

For the next example, we created a single segment and put it on the canvas. We also added a new **Slider** class, which is used to adjust the segment's position. Although not necessary for understanding kinematics, it's a convenient user interface element for changing numeric values on the fly. Remember, you can download all the code from this book at **www.apress.com**, which you're free to use for whatever you want. We don't spend much time explaining it because it's simple enough. You drag the lever with the mouse to adjust the value. Don't confuse this class with the new HTML5 slider element for form input, this interface element has been created entirely in JavaScript and drawn to the canvas. Here's the file that we use in some of the remaining chapter examples (**slider.js**):

```
function Slider (min, max, value) {
  this.min = (min === undefined) ? 0 : min;
  this.max = (max === undefined) ? 100 : max;
  this.value = (value === undefined) ? 100 : value;
  this.onchange = null;
  this.x = 0;
  this.y = 0;
  this.width = 16;
  this.height = 100;
  this.backColor = "#cccccc";
```

```
      this.backBorderColor = "#999999";
      this.backWidth = 4;
      this.backX = this.width / 2 - this.backWidth / 2;
      this.handleColor = "#eeeeee";
      this.handleBorderColor = "#cccccc";
      this.handleHeight = 6;
      this.handleY = 0;
      this.updatePosition();
  }

  Slider.prototype.draw = function (context) {
    context.save();
    context.translate(this.x, this.y);
    context.fillStyle = this.backColor;
    context.beginPath();
    context.fillRect(this.backX, 0, this.backWidth, this.height);
    context.closePath();
    context.strokeStyle = this.handleBorderColor;
    context.fillStyle = this.handleColor;
    context.beginPath();
    context.rect(0, this.handleY, this.width, this.handleHeight);
    context.closePath();
    context.fill();
    context.stroke();
    context.restore();
  };

  Slider.prototype.updateValue = function () {
    var old_value = this.value,
        handleRange = this.height    this.handleHeight,
        valueRange = this.max    this.min;

    this.value = (handleRange - this.handleY) / handleRange * valueRange + this.min;

    if (typeof this.onchange === 'function' && this.value !== old_value) {
      this.onchange();
    }
  };

  Slider.prototype.updatePosition = function () {
    var handleRange = this.height    this.handleHeight,
        valueRange = this.max    this.min;

    this.handleY = handleRange - ((this.value - this.min) / valueRange) * handleRange;
  };

  Slider.prototype.captureMouse = function (element) {
    var self = this,
        mouse = utils.captureMouse(element),
        bounds = {};

    setHandleBounds();

    element.addEventListener('mousedown', function () {
```

```
      if (utils.containsPoint(bounds, mouse.x, mouse.y)) {
        element.addEventListener('mouseup', onMouseUp, false);
        element.addEventListener('mousemove', onMouseMove, false);
      }
    }, false);

    function onMouseUp () {
      element.removeEventListener('mousemove', onMouseMove, false);
      element.removeEventListener('mouseup', onMouseUp, false);
      setHandleBounds();
    }

    function onMouseMove () {
      var pos_y = mouse.y   self.y;
      self.handleY = Math.min(self.height   self.handleHeight, Math.max(pos_y, 0));
      self.updateValue();
    }

    function setHandleBounds () {
      bounds.x = self.x;
      bounds.y = self.y + self.handleY;
      bounds.width = self.width;
      bounds.height = self.handleHeight;
    }
};
```

For this slider (which you can see in Figure 13-2), you can pass in the **minimum**, **maximum**, and **value** arguments when you instantiate it. In the following example, we set the **minimum** to –90, the **maximum** to 90, and the **value** to 0. For the slider to "see" the mouse, we need to register the canvas element with it using **slider.captureMouse(canvas)**. This is similar to the way we use the **utils.captureMouse(canvas)** function in previous examples. It adds a couple of mouse event listeners to the canvas element and checks to see whether the position of the mouse cursor falls within the bounds of the slider. In this example, you can see the slider in action by using it to rotate a segment (**02-single-segment.html**):

```
<!doctype html>
<html>
 <head>
  <meta charset="utf-8">
  <title>Single Segment</title>
  <link rel="stylesheet" href="style.css">
 </head>
 <body>
  <canvas id="canvas" width="400" height="400"></canvas>
  <script src="utils.js"></script>
  <script src="segment.js"></script>
  <script src="slider.js"></script>
  <script>
  window.onload = function () {
    var canvas = document.getElementById('canvas'),
        context = canvas.getContext('2d'),
        segment = new Segment(100, 20),
```

```
      slider = new Slider(-90, 90, 0);

  segment.x = 100;
  segment.y = 100;

  slider.x = 300;
  slider.y = 20;
  slider.captureMouse(canvas);
  slider.onchange = drawFrame;

  function drawFrame () {
    context.clearRect(0, 0, canvas.width, canvas.height);

    segment.rotation = slider.value * Math.PI / 180;
    segment.draw(context);
    slider.draw(context);
  }

  drawFrame(); //call once for initial display
};
</script>
</body>
</html>
```

In this example, whenever the slider is moved, it calls the function that's assigned as its **slider.onchange** method—here, **drawFrame**—which sets the rotation of **segment** to the slider's value. Try that out, and you should see something like Figure 13-2. If it all works, you completed the first phase of forward kinematics.

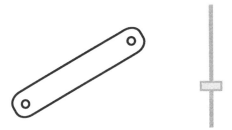

Figure 13-2. It moves!

Moving Two Segments

Now that we've set up a single segment to rotate with a slider, we can move on to something a little more exciting … two segments! Rename the the original slider and segment to **slider0** and **segment0**, respectively. Create another instance of **Segment**, name it **segment1**, and also create another slider instance and call it **slider1**. The new slider will control the rotation of the new segment, which is positioned at the point returned by the **getPin()** method of **segment0**. Here's the code for example **03-two-segments.html**:

```
<!doctype html>
<html>
```

```
<head>
 <meta charset="utf-8">
 <title>Two Segments</title>
 <link rel="stylesheet" href="style.css">
</head>
<body>
 <canvas id="canvas" width="400" height="400"></canvas>
 <script src="utils.js"></script>
 <script src="segment.js"></script>
 <script src="slider.js"></script>
 <script>
 window.onload = function () {
   var canvas = document.getElementById('canvas'),
       context = canvas.getContext('2d'),
       segment0 = new Segment(100, 20),
       segment1 = new Segment(100, 20),
       slider0 = new Slider(-90, 90, 0),
       slider1 = new Slider(-90, 90, 0);

   segment0.x = 100;
   segment0.y = 100;

   slider0.x = 320;
   slider0.y = 20;
   slider0.captureMouse(canvas);
   slider0.onchange = drawFrame;

   slider1.x = 340;
   slider1.y = 20;
   slider1.captureMouse(canvas);
   slider1.onchange = drawFrame;

   function drawFrame () {
     context.clearRect(0, 0, canvas.width, canvas.height);

     segment0.rotation = slider0.value * Math.PI / 180;
     segment1.rotation = slider1.value * Math.PI / 180;
     segment1.x = segment0.getPin().x;
     segment1.y = segment0.getPin().y;

     segment0.draw(context);
     segment1.draw(context);
     slider0.draw(context);
     slider1.draw(context);
   }

   drawFrame(); //call once for initial display
 };
 </script>
</body>
</html>
```

299

Take a look at the new code in the **drawFrame** function; you see that it now contains code to position **segment1** based on the return value of **segment0.getPin()**. The **drawFrame** function is first called after the objects are initialized, to make sure they are positioned properly at the start.

You set up **slider1** to call the **drawFrame** function in the same way as **slider0**, by assigning the function to its **onchange** property. And, obviously, you have **segment1**'s rotation now based on **slider1**.

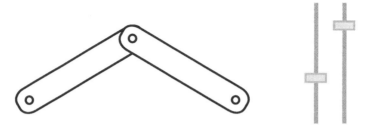

Figure 13-3. Forward kinematics with two segments

If you test this file in your browser, you see that as you rotate **segment0** around, **segment1** remains attached to the end of it, as shown in Figure 13-3. But there is no actual attachment between the two segments—it's all done with math. You can also rotate **segment1** independently with its slider. For some fun, change the height and width of the segments and see that it all still works perfectly. One thing that looks a bit strange is that although **segment1** *moves* with **segment0**, it doesn't *rotate* with it. It's like there's some gyro-stabilizer inside of it, holding its orientation steady. Because this is not how our arms move naturally, it doesn't look right. What really should happen is that **segment1**'s rotation should be **segment0**'s rotation plus the value of **slider1**. The document **04-two-segments-2.html** handles this with the following code:

```
function drawFrame () {
  context.clearRect(0, 0, canvas.width, canvas.height);

  segment0.rotation = slider0.value * Math.PI / 180;
  segment1.rotation = segment0.rotation + (slider1.value * Math.PI / 180);
  segment1.x = segment0.getPin().x;
  segment1.y = segment0.getPin().y;

  segment0.draw(context);
  segment1.draw(context);
  slider0.draw(context);
  slider1.draw(context);
}
```

Now, that looks more like a real arm. Of course, if you're thinking about a human arm, you might not like the way the elbow can bend in both directions. To look more normal, change the range of **slider1** so **minimum** is something like −160 and **maximum** is 0, as in the following code.

```
var slider1 = new Slider(-160, 0, 0);
```

This might be a good time to reflect on the term *forward kinematics* again. The base of this system is the pivot point of **segment0**. The free end is the other end of **segment1**, where you might imagine a hand. The rotation and position of the base determine the position of **segment1**. And **segment1**'s rotation and position determine the position of the free end. The free end has no say in where it is, should be, or would like to be—it just goes along for the ride. Thus, control moves forward from the base to the free end.

Automating the Process

All these sliders for rotation give you a lot of control, but what you've created is something like a piece of construction machinery with hydraulic levers to move around the parts. If you want to make something really walk, step back and give it some self-control.

You need a way for each segment to smoothly swing back and forth, and then somehow synchronize them all. That sounds like a job for a sine wave.

In example **05-walking-1.html**, we replaced the sliders with a trigonometry function. It takes the sine of the **cycle** variable (which is initialized to 0) and multiplies it by 90, resulting in a value from 90 to –90. The **cycle** variable is constantly increased, so you get an oscillation. For now, we used the resulting **angle** variable to control both segments. The **drawFrame** function has been converted to an animation loop that controls the action, so the motion is continuous. The output looks like the previous example, except this time the motion is automated.

```
<!doctype html>
<html>
 <head>
  <meta charset="utf-8">
  <title>Walking 1</title>
  <link rel="stylesheet" href="style.css">
 </head>
 <body>
  <canvas id="canvas" width="400" height="400"></canvas>
  <script src="utils.js"></script>
  <script src="segment.js"></script>
  <script>
  window.onload = function () {
    var canvas = document.getElementById('canvas'),
        context = canvas.getContext('2d'),
        segment0 = new Segment(100, 20),
        segment1 = new Segment(100, 20),
        cycle = 0;

    segment0.x = 200;
    segment0.y = 200;

    segment1.x = segment0.getPin().x;
    segment1.y = segment0.getPin().y;

    (function drawFrame () {
      window.requestAnimationFrame(drawFrame, canvas);
      context.clearRect(0, 0, canvas.width, canvas.height);

      cycle += 0.02;
```

```
        var angle = (Math.sin(cycle) * 90) * Math.PI / 180;

        segment0.rotation = angle;
        segment1.rotation = segment0.rotation + angle;
        segment1.x = segment0.getPin().x;
        segment1.y = segment0.getPin().y;

        segment0.draw(context);
        segment1.draw(context);
    }());
};
</script>
</body>
</html>
```

Building a Natural Walk Cycle

Now you have something moving around looking vaguely arm-like, but let's turn it into a leg. Start with the following changes:

- Make the system point down by adding 90 to **segment0**'s rotation and reducing its range of motion from 90 degrees in both directions to 45 degrees.

- Use a separate angle for each segment, so you have **angle0** and **angle1**.

- Reduce **angle1**'s range to 45, and then add 45 to it. This makes its final range 0 to 90, so that it bends in only one direction, like a real knee. If that isn't totally clear, try it with and without the added 45 to see what it's doing, and try some other numbers until you get a feel for how it all fits together.

You end up with the following code from **06-walking-2.html**. Only the **drawFrame** method is shown, because nothing else has changed:

```
(function drawFrame () {
  window.requestAnimationFrame(drawFrame, canvas);
  context.clearRect(0, 0, canvas.width, canvas.height);

  cycle += 0.02;
  var angle0 = (Math.sin(cycle) * 45 + 90) * Math.PI / 180,
      angle1 = (Math.sin(cycle) * 45 + 45) * Math.PI / 180;

  segment0.rotation = angle0;
  segment1.rotation = segment0.rotation + angle1;
  segment1.x = segment0.getPin().x;
  segment1.y = segment0.getPin().y;

  segment0.draw(context);
  segment1.draw(context);
}());
```

Well, you're getting there, as shown in Figure 13-4. This is starting to look like a leg, or at least starting to move like one.

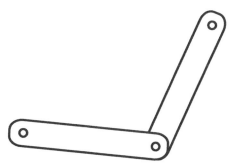

Figure 13-4. The beginnings of a walk cycle

But it doesn't really look like it's walking. Maybe it's a half-hearted attempt to kick a ball, but it's not walking. What's happening now is that both segments are moving in the same direction at the same time. They are in sync, which, if you were to analyze an actual walk cycle, is not how it works.

The segments are in sync because they are both using the **cycle** variable to calculate their angle. To throw them out of sync, you can resort to using **cycle0** and **cycle1** variables, but you don't need to go that far with it. Instead, you can offset **cycle** a bit when using it to find **angle1**, like so:

```
var angle1 = Math.sin(cycle + offset) * 45 + 45;
```

You need to define **offset** earlier in the code, but how much should **offset** be? Experiment until you find something that looks good, but here's a hint: It should be a number between **Math.PI** and **-Math.PI** (or 3.14 and -3.14). Anything more or less than that is going to double back on itself. For instance, we use -**Math.PI/2**, which puts it a quarter of a cycle behind **angle0**. Of course, -**Math.PI/2** is about -1.57, so you might want to try other numbers around that value, like −1.7 or -1.3, and see whether that looks better or worse. A little later, we throw in a slider to do it all dynamically. The file with this offset included is in **07-walking-3.html**.

We should probably add another leg while we're at it. Start by throwing in two more segments, named **segment2** and **segment3**. **segment2** should be in the same position as **segment0**, because it will also be the top level, or base, of the whole leg, and **segment3** should be positioned using **segment2**'s **getPin()** method.

Rather than duplicate all the code that makes **segment0** and **segment1** walk, it has been abstracted into its own method, called **walk**:

```
function walk (segA, segB, cyc) {
  var angle0 = (Math.sin(cyc) * 45 + 90) * Math.PI / 180,
      angle1 = (Math.sin(cyc + offset) * 45 + 45) * Math.PI / 180;

  segA.rotation = angle0;
  segB.rotation = segA.rotation + angle1;
  segB.x = segA.getPin().x;
  segB.y = segA.getPin().y;
}
```

This function has three parameters: two segments (**segA** and **segB**) and **cyc**, which stands for **cycle**. The rest of the code is what you've been using. Now, to make **segment0** and **segment1** walk, just call it like this:

```
walk(segment0, segment1, cycle);
```

And now you're ready to make **segment2** and **segment3** walk as well. This is what your **drawFrame** function ends up as:

```
(function drawFrame () {
  window.requestAnimationFrame(drawFrame, canvas);
  context.clearRect(0, 0, canvas.width, canvas.height);

  cycle += 0.02;
  walk(segment0, segment1, cycle);
  walk(segment2, segment3, cycle);

  segment0.draw(context);
  segment1.draw(context);
  segment2.draw(context);
  segment3.draw(context);
}());
```

But if you try that, you're not going to see the second leg. The problem is that both legs are moving exactly in sync, so they appear as one. Once again, you need to desynchronize. Last time, you offset the bottom segment's position on the cycle from the top segment's position. This time, you offset the second leg from the first. Again, this comes down to changing the value it's using for **cycle**. And once again, rather than keeping track of two different variables, just add something to or subtract something from **cycle** before you send it into the **walk** method. So, the **drawFrame** function becomes the following:

```
(function drawFrame () {
  window.requestAnimationFrame(drawFrame, canvas);
  context.clearRect(0, 0, canvas.width, canvas.height);

  cycle += 0.02;
  walk(segment0, segment1, cycle);
  walk(segment2, segment3, cycle + Math.PI);

  segment0.draw(context);
  segment1.draw(context);
  segment2.draw(context);
  segment3.draw(context);
}());
```

We use **Math.PI** to put the second leg 180 degrees out of sync with the first, so the first leg moves forward while the second is moving back, and vice versa. You can try it out with some different values, say **Math.PI/2**, and see that it looks a lot more like a gallop than a walk or run—which you might need to use someday!

The file is available as **08-walking-4.html** and looks like Figure 13-5. The base segments (the "thighs") have been made a bit larger than the lower segments (the "calves"). And because of the dynamic way everything is set up, it all works no matter what the sizes are. In the next version, you make more things dynamic with sliders. You should play around with some of these variables now manually, by changing the values in the code and seeing how the values affect things.

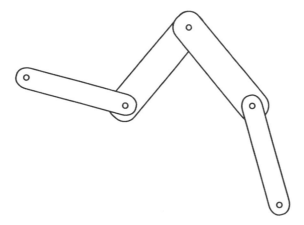

Figure 13-5. Behold! It walks!

Making It Dynamic

Next, let's work with this walk cycle and see just how much you can change it by altering the various values that go into it. The **09-walking-5.html** example brings back the **Slider** class so you can start changing some of these variables instantly.

In this example, we create and position five of these sliders across the top of the animation, as shown in Figure 13-6.

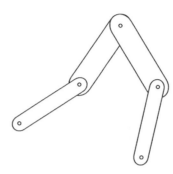

Figure 13-6. Adding the sliders to control the walk

Table 13-1 shows the slider names (from left to right), what they do, and the settings to use for them. These are just ranges and values that seem to work well, but feel free to experiment with other values.

Table 13-1. The Sliders for Controlling the Walk Cycle

Instance	Description	Settings
speedSlider	Controls the speed at which the system moves.	minimum: 0 maximum: 0.2 value: 0.08
thighRangeSlider	Controls how far back and forth the top-level segments (thighs) can move.	minimum: 0 maximum: 90 value: 45
thighBaseSlider	Controls the base angle of the top-level segments. So far, this has been 90, meaning that the legs point straight down and move back and forth from there. But you can get some interesting effects by changing this value.	minimum: 0 maximum: 180 value: 90
calfRangeSlider	Controls how much range of motion the lower segments (calves) have.	minimum: 0 maximum: 90 value: 45
calfOffsetSlider	Controls the offset value (you've been using -Math.PI/2).	minimum: −3.14 maximum: 3.14 value: −1.57

Now, change the code so that it uses the values provided by the sliders, rather than hard-coded values.

```
<!doctype html>
<html>
 <head>
  <meta charset="utf-8">
  <title>Walking 5</title>
  <link rel="stylesheet" href="style.css">
 </head>
 <body>
  <canvas id="canvas" width="400" height="400"></canvas>
  <script src="utils.js"></script>
  <script src="segment.js"></script>
  <script src="slider.js"></script>
  <script>
  window.onload = function () {
    var canvas = document.getElementById('canvas'),
        context = canvas.getContext('2d'),
        segment0 = new Segment(100, 30),
        segment1 = new Segment(100, 20),
        segment2 = new Segment(100, 30),
        segment3 = new Segment(100, 20),
        speedSlider = new Slider(0, 0.2, 0.08),
        thighRangeSlider = new Slider(0, 90, 45),
        thighBaseSlider = new Slider(0, 180, 90),
        calfRangeSlider = new Slider(0, 90, 45),
        calfOffsetSlider = new Slider(-3.14, 3.14, -1.57),
        cycle = 0;

    segment0.x = 200;
    segment0.y = 200;

    segment1.x = segment0.getPin().x;
    segment1.y = segment0.getPin().y;

    segment2.x = 200;
    segment2.y = 200;

    segment3.x = segment2.getPin().x;
    segment3.y = segment2.getPin().y;

    speedSlider.x = 10;
    speedSlider.y = 10;
    speedSlider.captureMouse(canvas);

    thighRangeSlider.x = 30;
    thighRangeSlider.y = 10;
    thighRangeSlider.captureMouse(canvas);

    thighBaseSlider.x = 50;
    thighBaseSlider.y = 10;
    thighBaseSlider.captureMouse(canvas);

    calfRangeSlider.x = 70;
```

```
        calfRangeSlider.y = 10;
        calfRangeSlider.captureMouse(canvas);

        calfOffsetSlider.x = 90;
        calfOffsetSlider.y = 10;
        calfOffsetSlider.captureMouse(canvas);

    function walk (segA, segB, cyc) {
        var angle0 = (Math.sin(cyc) * thighRangeSlider.value + thighBaseSlider.value) * Math.PI
/ 180,
            angle1 = (Math.sin(cyc + calfOffsetSlider.value) * calfRangeSlider.value +
calfRangeSlider.value) * Math.PI / 180;

        segA.rotation = angle0;
        segB.rotation = segA.rotation + angle1;
        segB.x = segA.getPin().x;
        segB.y = segA.getPin().y;
    }

    (function drawFrame () {
        window.requestAnimationFrame(drawFrame, canvas);
        context.clearRect(0, 0, canvas.width, canvas.height);

        cycle += speedSlider.value;
        walk(segment0, segment1, cycle);
        walk(segment2, segment3, cycle + Math.PI);

        segment0.draw(context);
        segment1.draw(context);
        segment2.draw(context);
        segment3.draw(context);
        speedSlider.draw(context);
        thighRangeSlider.draw(context);
        thighBaseSlider.draw(context);
        calfRangeSlider.draw(context);
        calfOffsetSlider.draw(context);
    }());
  };
  </script>
 </body>
</html>
```

This code is exactly as it was before, but now it uses the slider values rather than hard-coded values. You can have a lot of fun with this exercise, exploring different variations of the walk cycle.

Making It Really Walk

You have a couple of legs moving around in a manner that looks realistic, but they are just floating in space. Earlier in the book, you got something moving with velocity and acceleration, and then had it interact with the environment. It's time to do the same thing here.

This portion of the chapter gets pretty complex, so we go through the code one concept at a time. The final document, with all of these concepts incorporated, is **10-real-walk.html**.

Giving It Some Space

Because this thing is actually going to be walking around the screen, let's make all the parts a bit smaller so that there is room for it to move around. Take the original four segments and make them half of what they were:

```
var segment0 = new Segment(50, 15),
    segment1 = new Segment(50, 10),
    segment2 = new Segment(50, 15),
    segment3 = new Segment(50, 10);
```

Next, because it will move around and react with boundaries, define variables for **vx** and **vy**:

```
var vx = 0,
    vy = 0;
```

At this point, if you run the file, you'd have a miniature, working version of the previous example.

Adding Gravity

Now you need to create some gravity; otherwise—even if you add in the boundary detection—the legs are just going to float in space. The gravity variable is controlled by another slider, so, create a new slider object, name it **gravitySlider**, and set its **minimum** to 0, **maximum** to 1, and **value** to 0.2. Here's the relevant of code that initializes that last slider:

```
var gravitySlider = new Slider(0, 1, 0.2);

gravitySlider.x = 110;
gravitySlider.y = 10;
gravitySlider.captureMouse(canvas);
```

You also need to do the velocity calculations, along with the gravity acceleration. Rather than jamming all this into the **drawFrame** function, make a call to another function named **setVelocity**:

```
(function drawFrame () {
  window.requestAnimationFrame(drawFrame, canvas);
  context.clearRect(0, 0, canvas.width, canvas.height);

  cycle += speedSlider.value;
  setVelocity();
  walk(segment0, segment1, cycle);
  walk(segment2, segment3, cycle + Math.PI);

  segment0.draw(context);
  segment1.draw(context);
  segment2.draw(context);
  segment3.draw(context);
  speedSlider.draw(context);
```

```
    thighRangeSlider.draw(context);
    thighBaseSlider.draw(context);
    calfRangeSlider.draw(context);
    calfOffsetSlider.draw(context);
    gravitySlider.draw(context);
}());
```

And in that function, add gravity to **vy**, and then add **vx** and **vy** to the position of **segment0** and **segment2**. Remember that you don't need to worry about **segment1** and **segment3**, because their positions are calculated in relationship to the higher-level segments.

```
function setVelocity () {
    vy += gravitySlider.value;
    segment0.x += vx;
    segment0.y += vy;
    segment2.x += vx;
    segment2.y += vy;
}
```

You can test this version if you want, but it won't be very exciting. There's no x velocity happening yet, and gravity pulls the legs right through the floor. So, you need to check the floor to see whether the legs have hit it, and that means it's time for collision detection.

Handling the Collision

To start, make **drawFrame** call another function: **checkFloor**. This happens after the calls to **walk**, so it operates on the latest positions. We check only **segment1** and **segment3** the lower-level segments—to see whether they hit the floor. So, we pass them both to **checkFloor**.

```
(function drawFrame () {
    window.requestAnimationFrame(drawFrame, canvas);
    context.clearRect(0, 0, canvas.width, canvas.height);

    cycle += speedSlider.value;
    setVelocity();
    walk(segment0, segment1, cycle);
    walk(segment2, segment3, cycle + Math.PI);
    checkFloor(segment1);
    checkFloor(segment3);

    segment0.draw(context);
    segment1.draw(context);
    segment2.draw(context);
    segment3.draw(context);
    speedSlider.draw(context);
    thighRangeSlider.draw(context);
    thighBaseSlider.draw(context);
    calfRangeSlider.draw(context);
    calfOffsetSlider.draw(context);
    gravitySlider.draw(context);
}());
```

Now comes the first interesting part: the collision detection. You want to know whether the bottom of the segment in question has gone below the bottom boundary. In this example, that's specified by `canvas.height`.

Probably the easiest way to do this is by performing a rough calculation of our segment bottom by getting the y position of its pin, and adding on the extra space of the segment end. Then check whether it is greater than the height of the canvas. It's not the most precise measurement, but it serves the purposes of this example, so that's how you start the **checkFloor** function:

```
function checkFloor (seg) {
  var yMax = seg.getPin().y + (seg.height / 2);

  if (yMax > canvas.height) {
    //do reaction...
  }
}
```

If you've determined that **yMax** is greater than the `canvas.height` (or, if the leg has hit the floor), what do you do? Just as in other boundary collisions, you first want to move the object so it's touching the boundary. If **yMax** is the lowest edge of the segment and `canvas.height` is the floor, you need to move the segment back up exactly the distance between them. In other words, say `canvas.height` is 400 and **yMax** is 420. You need to change the segment's y position by –20, but you don't want to move *only* the segment. You want to move *all* the segments by that amount, because they are all part of the same body and must move as one. So, you get something like this:

```
function checkFloor (seg) {
  var yMax = seg.getPin().y + (seg.height / 2);

  if (yMax > canvas.height) {
    var dy = yMax   canvas.height;
    segment0.y -= dy;
    segment1.y -= dy;
    segment2.y -= dy;
    segment3.y -= dy;
  }
}
```

This iteration of the example is worth playing with some more. Adjust the slider values to see the different walk cycles in action. You get more of a feel for them with the legs interacting with the environment. Of course, it's still not really walking yet—that's up next.

Handling the Reaction

The legs are successfully colliding with the floor, but other than repositioning themselves, there's no real reaction. The whole reason you walk is to get some horizontal motion going—x velocity, in this case. Furthermore, your walk cycle should give you a bit of y velocity as well, at least enough to briefly counteract gravity. You see this more in a fast run, where you might get slightly airborne during a cycle.

One way of looking at this is that your foot is moving down. When it hits the floor, it can't move down any more, so that vertical momentum goes back up to your body, moving it up. The stronger your foot is moving down, the more lift you get. Likewise, if your foot moves backward when it hits, the horizontal momentum goes back to your body, moving it forward. The faster your foot moves back, the more horizontal thrust you get.

If you can keep track of the foot's x and y velocity, then when you get a collision, you can subtract that x and y velocity from the **vx** and **vy** values. But, you don't have any feet yet. You can add some and calculate their positions, or instead, use the position of virtual feet, which is the value returned by **getPin()** on the lower segments.

If you keep track of where the pin is before the segment moves and where it is after the segment moves, you can subtract the two and get the foot's velocity on both x and y. You can do that in the walk function and store the values in the **vx** and **vy** properties of the segment (now you see where those come in).

```
function walk (segA, segB, cyc) {
  var angle0 = (Math.sin(cyc) * thighRangeSlider.value + thighBaseSlider.value) * Math.PI / 180,
      angle1 = (Math.sin(cyc + calfOffsetSlider.value) * calfRangeSlider.value +
calfRangeSlider.value) * Math.PI / 180,
      foot = segB.getPin();

  segA.rotation = angle0;
  segB.rotation = segA.rotation + angle1;
  segB.x = segA.getPin().x;
  segB.y = segA.getPin().y;
  segB.vx = segB.getPin().x    foot.x;
  segB.vy = segB.getPin().y    foot.y;
}
```

Each bottom segment has a **vx** and **vy** property, which represents not the velocity of the segment itself, but the velocity of the bottom pivot point, or virtual foot.

So, what do you do with this velocity? You wait until you have a collision with the floor, and then you subtract it from the overall velocity. In other words, if the foot moves down at 3 pixels per frame (a **vy** of 3) when it hits, subtract 3 from the overall **vy**. You do the same with the **vx**. In code, it's really simple:

```
function checkFloor (seg) {
  var yMax = seg.getPin().y + (seg.height / 2);

  if (yMax > canvas.height) {
    var dy = yMax    canvas.height;
    segment0.y -= dy;
    segment1.y -= dy;
    segment2.y -= dy;
    segment3.y -= dy;
    vx -= seg.vx;
    vy -= seg.vy;
  }
}
```

This is an extremely simplified, and possibly a completely inaccurate, representation of how the forces involved in walking actually work. If you test it, there is a pair of legs walking across the screen!

Screen Wrapping, Revisited

Now the legs walk off screen, never to return—but a little screen wrapping fixes that. When the legs go off to the right, you move them back to the left. It's a little more complex than before, because now you move four pieces around in unison, instead of a single object. But then again, remember that you need to check only one of the two top segments, because they are always in the same position, and the positions of the lower segments are determined by the upper ones. Add a call to a function named `checkWalls` after the floor checks in `drawFrame`:

```
(function drawFrame () {
  window.requestAnimationFrame(drawFrame, canvas);
  context.clearRect(0, 0, canvas.width, canvas.height);

  cycle += speedSlider.value;
  setVelocity();
  walk(segment0, segment1, cycle);
  walk(segment2, segment3, cycle + Math.PI);
  checkFloor(segment1);
  checkFloor(segment3);
  checkWalls();

  segment0.draw(context);
  segment1.draw(context);
  segment2.draw(context);
  segment3.draw(context);
  speedSlider.draw(context);
  thighRangeSlider.draw(context);
  thighBaseSlider.draw(context);
  calfRangeSlider.draw(context);
  calfOffsetSlider.draw(context);
  gravitySlider.draw(context);
}());
```

Let's leave a general margin of 100 pixels, so that either leg can move 100 pixels off the right of the canvas element before wrapping. If it goes past that, reposition everything way over to the left, which is the width of the canvas plus 200, for the 100-pixel margin on each side. Start your `if` statement in the `checkWalls` function like so:

```
function checkWalls () {
  var w = canvas.width + 200;

  if (segment0.x > canvas.width + 100) {
    segment0.x -= w;
    segment1.x -= w;
    segment2.x -= w;
    segment3.x -= w;
  }
}
```

Then do the same thing for the left edge, because some walk cycles can make the legs go backward. Here's the complete `checkWalls` function:

```
function checkWalls () {
  var w = canvas.width + 200;

  if (segment0.x > canvas.width + 100) {
    segment0.x -= w;
    segment1.x -= w;
    segment2.x -= w;
    segment3.x -= w;
  } else if (segment0.x < -100) {
    segment0.x += w;
    segment1.x += w;
    segment2.x += w;
    segment3.x += w;
  }
}
```

And there you have it. If you thought this section was a bit confusing, here's the entire code listing (and can be found in document **10-real-walk.html**):

```
<!doctype html>
<html>
 <head>
  <meta charset="utf-8">
  <title>Real Walk</title>
  <link rel="stylesheet" href="style.css">
 </head>
 <body>
  <canvas id="canvas" width="400" height="400"></canvas>
  <script src="utils.js"></script>
  <script src="segment.js"></script>
  <script src="slider.js"></script>
  <script>
  window.onload = function () {
    var canvas = document.getElementById('canvas'),
        context = canvas.getContext('2d'),
        segment0 = new Segment(50, 15),
        segment1 = new Segment(50, 10),
        segment2 = new Segment(50, 15),
        segment3 = new Segment(50, 10),
        speedSlider = new Slider(0, 0.2, 0.08),
        thighRangeSlider = new Slider(0, 90, 45),
        thighBaseSlider = new Slider(0, 180, 90),
        calfRangeSlider = new Slider(0, 90, 45),
        calfOffsetSlider = new Slider(-3.14, 3.14, -1.57),
        gravitySlider = new Slider(0, 1, 0.2),
        cycle = 0,
        vx = 0,
        vy = 0;

    segment0.x = 200;
    segment0.y = 200;

    segment1.x = segment0.getPin().x;
    segment1.y = segment0.getPin().y;
```

```
        segment2.x = 200;
        segment2.y = 200;

        segment3.x = segment2.getPin().x;
        segment3.y = segment2.getPin().y;

        speedSlider.x = 10;
        speedSlider.y = 10;
        speedSlider.captureMouse(canvas);

        thighRangeSlider.x = 30;
        thighRangeSlider.y = 10;
        thighRangeSlider.captureMouse(canvas);

        thighBaseSlider.x = 50;
        thighBaseSlider.y = 10;
        thighBaseSlider.captureMouse(canvas);

        calfRangeSlider.x = 70;
        calfRangeSlider.y = 10;
        calfRangeSlider.captureMouse(canvas);

        calfOffsetSlider.x = 90;
        calfOffsetSlider.y = 10;
        calfOffsetSlider.captureMouse(canvas);

        gravitySlider.x = 110;
        gravitySlider.y = 10;
        gravitySlider.captureMouse(canvas);

        function setVelocity () {
          vy += gravitySlider.value;
          segment0.x += vx;
          segment0.y += vy;
          segment2.x += vx;
          segment2.y += vy;
        }

        function walk (segA, segB, cyc) {
          var angle0 = (Math.sin(cyc) * thighRangeSlider.value + thighBaseSlider.value) * Math.PI
 / 180,
              angle1 = (Math.sin(cyc + calfOffsetSlider.value) * calfRangeSlider.value +
 calfRangeSlider.value) * Math.PI / 180,
              foot = segB.getPin();

          segA.rotation = angle0;
          segB.rotation = segA.rotation + angle1;
          segB.x = segA.getPin().x;
          segB.y = segA.getPin().y;
          segB.vx = segB.getPin().x    foot.x;
          segB.vy = segB.getPin().y    foot.y;
        }
```

```
    function checkFloor (seg) {
      var yMax = seg.getPin().y + (seg.height / 2);

      if (yMax > canvas.height) {
        var dy = yMax   canvas.height;
        segment0.y -= dy;
        segment1.y -= dy;
        segment2.y -= dy;
        segment3.y -= dy;
        vx -= seg.vx;
        vy -= seg.vy;
      }
    }

    function checkWalls () {
      var w = canvas.width + 200;

      if (segment0.x > canvas.width + 100) {
        segment0.x -= w;
        segment1.x -= w;
        segment2.x -= w;
        segment3.x -= w;
      } else if (segment0.x < -100) {
        segment0.x += w;
        segment1.x += w;
        segment2.x += w;
        segment3.x += w;
      }
    }

    (function drawFrame () {
      window.requestAnimationFrame(drawFrame, canvas);
      context.clearRect(0, 0, canvas.width, canvas.height);

      cycle += speedSlider.value;
      setVelocity();
      walk(segment0, segment1, cycle);
      walk(segment2, segment3, cycle + Math.PI);
      checkFloor(segment1);
      checkFloor(segment3);
      checkWalls();

      segment0.draw(context);
      segment1.draw(context);
      segment2.draw(context);
      segment3.draw(context);
      speedSlider.draw(context);
      thighRangeSlider.draw(context);
      thighBaseSlider.draw(context);
      calfRangeSlider.draw(context);
      calfOffsetSlider.draw(context);
      gravitySlider.draw(context);
    }());
  };
```

```
    </script>
  </body>
</html>
```

Summary

You've done some pretty powerful stuff in this chapter, conquering the basics of forward kinematics. The methods presented here are probably not the only solutions to the subject, they're tailored toward a particular application of the technology: making something walk. Feel free to leave things out, change things, or add whatever you want to this system. Experiment and see what you can come up with.

Next up, you look at the other side of the coin: inverse kinematics.

Chapter 14

Inverse Kinematics: Dragging and Reaching

What we'll cover in this chapter:

- Reaching and dragging single segments

- Dragging multiple segments

- Reaching with multiple segments

- Using the standard inverse kinematics method

In Chapter 13, we covered the basics of kinematics and the difference between inverse and forward kinematics. The last chapter was about forward kinematics, and now you're ready for its close relative, inverse kinematics: the movements for dragging and reaching.

As with the forward kinematics examples, the code in this chapter build systems from individual segments. You begin with single segments, and then move on to multiple segments. First, you'll see the simplest method for calculating the various angles and positions. This just approximates measurements using the basic trigonometry you've already seen in action. Then, we briefly cover another method using the law of cosines, which can be more accurate at the cost of being more complex—that familiar trade-off.

Reaching and Dragging Single Segments

When the free end of the system reaches for a target, the other end of the system, the base, might be unmovable. So the free end might never be able to get all the way to the target if it is out of range. An example of this is when you grab hold of something. Your fingers move toward the object, your wrist pivots to put your fingers as close as possible, and your elbow, shoulder, and the rest of your body move in whatever way they can, to give you as much reach as possible. Sometimes, the combination of all these positions put your fingers in contact with the object, and other times, you won't be able to reach it. If the object moves from side to side, all your limbs constantly reposition themselves to keep your fingers reaching as close as they can to the object. Inverse kinematics shows you how to position all the pieces to give the best reach.

The other type of inverse kinematics is when something is dragged. In this case, the free end is moved by some external force. Wherever it is, the rest of the parts of the system follow along behind it, positioning themselves in whatever way is physically possible. For this, imagine another person lying on the floor, that you grab by the hand and drag around. The force you apply to their hand causes the wrist, elbow, shoulder, and rest of their body to pivot and move in whatever way they can as they are dragged along. In this case, inverse kinematics shows you how the pieces fall into the correct positions as they are dragged.

To give you an idea of the difference between these two methods—drag and reach—let's run through an example of each one with a single segment. You need the **Segment** class we used in the Chapter 13, so make sure you include that script in your document.

Reaching with a Single Segment

For reaching, all the segment is able to do is turn toward the target. The target, in these examples, is the mouse cursor. To turn the segment toward the target, you need the distance between the two on the x and y axes. You then can use **Math.atan2** to get the angle between them in radians, which we use to rotate the segment. Here's the code (which you also find in **01-one-segment.html**):

```
<!doctype html>
<html>
 <head>
  <meta charset="utf-8">
  <title>One Segment</title>
  <link rel="stylesheet" href="style.css">
 </head>
 <body>
  <canvas id="canvas" width="400" height="400"></canvas>
  <script src="utils.js"></script>
  <script src="segment.js"></script>
  <script>
  window.onload = function () {
    var canvas = document.getElementById('canvas'),
        context = canvas.getContext('2d'),
        mouse = utils.captureMouse(canvas),
        segment0 = new Segment(100, 20);

    segment0.x = canvas.width / 2;
    segment0.y = canvas.height / 2;

    (function drawFrame () {
      window.requestAnimationFrame(drawFrame, canvas);
      context.clearRect(0, 0, canvas.width, canvas.height);

      var dx = mouse.x - segment0.x,
          dy = mouse.y - segment0.y;
```

```
        segment0.rotation = Math.atan2(dy, dx);

        segment0.draw(context);
    }());
};
</script>
</body>
</html>
```

Figure 14-1 shows the result. Test this and watch how the segment follows the mouse around. Even if the segment is too far away, you can see how it seems to be reaching for the mouse.

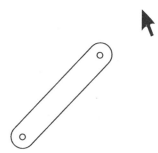

Figure 14-1. A single segment reaching toward the mouse

Dragging with a Single Segment

Now, let's try dragging. The first part of the dragging method is the same as the reaching method: You rotate the object toward the mouse. But then you go a step further and move the segment to a position that places the second pivot point exactly where the mouse is. To do that, you need to know the distance between the two pins on each axis. You can get this from the difference (on each axis) between the segment's `getPin()` point and its actual x, y location—we call these **w** and **h**. Then subtract **w** and **h** from the current mouse position, and you know where to put the segment. Here's the `drawFrame` function from `02-one-segment-drag.html`, which is the only part that has changed from the previous example:

```
(function drawFrame () {
  window.requestAnimationFrame(drawFrame, canvas);
  context.clearRect(0, 0, canvas.width, canvas.height);

  var dx = mouse.x - segment0.x,
      dy = mouse.y - segment0.y;

  segment0.rotation = Math.atan2(dy, dx);

  var w = segment0.getPin().x - segment0.x,
      h = segment0.getPin().y - segment0.y;

  segment0.x = mouse.x - w;
  segment0.y = mouse.y - h;
```

```
    segment0.draw(context);
}());
```

The segment is now permanently attached to the mouse and rotates to drag along behind it. You can even push the segment around in the opposite direction.

Dragging Multiple Segments

Dragging a system with inverse kinematics is a bit simpler than reaching, so we cover that first. We begin moving a couple of segments.

Dragging Two Segments

Starting with the previous example, create another segment, **segment1**, at the top of the script. Because **segment0** is already dragging to the mouse position, you have **segment1** drag on **segment0**. To start with, you can use some of the same code as before—just change a few references. The new additions to the **drawFrame** function are shown in bold:

```
(function drawFrame () {
    window.requestAnimationFrame(drawFrame, canvas);
    context.clearRect(0, 0, canvas.width, canvas.height);

    var dx = mouse.x - segment0.x,
        dy = mouse.y - segment0.y;

    segment0.rotation = Math.atan2(dy, dx);

    var w = segment0.getPin().x - segment0.x,
        h = segment0.getPin().y - segment0.y:

    segment0.x = mouse.x - h;
    segment0.y = mouse.y - w;

    dx = segment0.x - segment1.x;
    dy = segment0.y - segment1.y;

    segment1.rotation = Math.atan2(dy, dx);

    w = segment1.getPin().x - segment1.x;
    h = segment1.getPin().y - segment1.y;
    segment1.x = segment0.x - w;
    segment1.y = segment0.y - h;

    segment0.draw(context);
    segment1.draw(context);
}());
```

In the new section of code, you figure out the distance from **segment1** to **segment0**, and use that for the angle, rotation, and position of **segment1**—reusing the variables from the previous calculation. You can test this example and see how it's a pretty realistic two-segment system.

In the next example, we remove some of the duplicated code by creating a new function named **drag**. The parameters for this are the segment to drag and the x, y point to drag to. Then you move **segment0** to point **mouse.x**, **mouse.y** and **segment1** to point **segment0.x**, **segment0.y**. Here's the complete code listing for document **03-two-segment-drag.html**:

```html
<!doctype html>
<html>
 <head>
  <meta charset="utf-8">
  <title>Two Segment Drag</title>
  <link rel="stylesheet" href="style.css">
 </head>
 <body>
  <canvas id="canvas" width="400" height="400"></canvas>
  <script src="utils.js"></script>
  <script src="segment.js"></script>
  <script>
  window.onload = function () {
    var canvas = document.getElementById('canvas'),
        context = canvas.getContext('2d'),
        mouse = utils.captureMouse(canvas),
        segment0 = new Segment(100, 20),
        segment1 = new Segment(100, 20);

    function drag (segment, xpos, ypos) {
      var dx = xpos - segment.x,
          dy = ypos - segment.y;

      segment.rotation = Math.atan2(dy, dx);

      var w = segment.getPin().x - segment.x,
          h = segment.getPin().y - segment.y;

      segment.x = xpos - w;
      segment.y = ypos - h;
    }

    (function drawFrame () {
      window.requestAnimationFrame(drawFrame, canvas);
      context.clearRect(0, 0, canvas.width, canvas.height);

      drag(segment0, mouse.x, mouse.y);
      drag(segment1, segment0.x, segment0.y);

      segment0.draw(context);
      segment1.draw(context);
    }());
  };
  </script>
 </body>
</html>
```

Dragging More Segments

Now you can add as many segments as you want. In the next example, add five segments, named
segment0 through segment4, and store them in an array. Each segment is passed as an argument to the
drag function. Here's the code (document 04-multi-segment-drag.html):

```
<!doctype html>
<html>
 <head>
  <meta charset="utf-8">
  <title>Multi Segment Drag</title>
  <link rel="stylesheet" href="style.css">
 </head>
 <body>
  <canvas id="canvas" width="400" height="400"></canvas>
  <script src="utils.js"></script>
  <script src="segment.js"></script>
  <script>
  window.onload = function () {
    var canvas = document.getElementById('canvas'),
        context = canvas.getContext('2d'),
        mouse = utils.captureMouse(canvas),
        segments = [],
        numSegments = 5;

    while (numSegments--) {
      segments.push(new Segment(50, 10));
    }

    function drag (segment, xpos, ypos) {
      var dx = xpos - segment.x,
          dy = ypos - segment.y;

      segment.rotation = Math.atan2(dy, dx);

      var w = segment.getPin().x - segment.x,
          h = segment.getPin().y - segment.y;

      segment.x = xpos - w;
      segment.y = ypos - h;
    }

    function move (segment, i) {
      if (i !== 0) {
        drag(segment, segments[i-1].x, segments[i-1].y);
      }
    }

    function draw (segment, i) {
      segment.draw(context);
    }

    (function drawFrame () {
```

```
    window.requestAnimationFrame(drawFrame, canvas);
    context.clearRect(0, 0, canvas.width, canvas.height);

    drag(segments[0], mouse.x, mouse.y);
    segments.forEach(move);

    segments.forEach(draw);
  }());
};
</script>
</body>
</html>
```

In the **drawFrame** animation loop, the first segment is positioned at the mouse cursor. Then, each segment is passed to the **move** function as an argument, and positioned behind the segment before it (using the **drag** function). The first segment is ignored in the **move** function because it has already been positioned. Figure 14-2 shows the result.

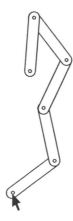

Figure 14-2. Multiple-segment dragging

Well, there you have the basics of inverse kinematics. You can add as many segments as you want by changing the **numSegments** variable. In Figure 14-3, you can see 50 segments, demonstrating just how robust this system is.

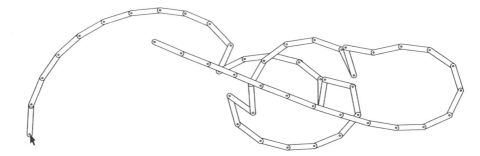

Figure 14-3. Dragging 50 segments

Reaching with Multiple Segments

The following excercises build off the first example in this chapter, **01-one-segment.html**, and add to that. That animation contained a segment rotating to a target, which was the mouse position.

Reaching for the Mouse

To reach with multiple segments, first determine the position of the segment for it to touch the target, which is the same calculation you use to position the segment when you drag. In this case, you don't move the segment; you just find the position. You use the position as the target of the next segment up the line and have the segment rotate to that position. When you reach the base of the system, you then work back through the line, positioning each piece on the end of its parent. Figure 14-4 illustrates how this works.

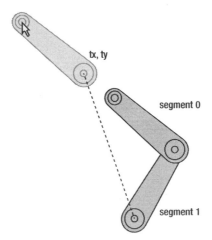

Figure 14-4. segment0 is moved to the mouse cursor. In turn, segment1 follows segment0, positioning itself toward point tx, ty.

For our example, we first need to add another segment to work with. At the top of the script, create an additional segment and position it in the center of the canvas element. Since this segment will now act as the base, remove the initial positioning for **segment0** as well:

```
var segment1 = new Segment(100, 20);

segment1.x = canvas.width / 2;
segment1.y = canvas.height / 2;
```

The next step is to find the point where **segment0** will hit the target. Once again, this is the same point you moved the segment to in the dragging examples, but don't move it, just store the position. So, you get this:

```
(function drawFrame () {
  window.requestAnimationFrame(drawFrame, canvas);
  context.clearRect(0, 0, canvas.width, canvas.height);

  var dx = mouse.x - segment0.x,
      dy = mouse.y - segment0.y;

  segment0.rotation = Math.atan2(dy, dx);

  var w = segment0.getPin().x - segment0.x,
      h = segment0.getPin().y - segment0.y,
      tx = mouse.x - w,
      ty = mouse.y - h;

  segment0.draw(context);
  segment1.draw(context);
}());
```

We called the point **tx**, **ty** because it will be the target for **segment1** to rotate to.

Next, you add the rotation code for **segment1** to rotate to its target. This code is the same as the calculation for **segment0**, but it uses a different segment and different target:

```
(function drawFrame () {
  window.requestAnimationFrame(drawFrame, canvas);
  context.clearRect(0, 0, canvas.width, canvas.height);

  var dx = mouse.x - segment0.x,
      dy = mouse.y - segment0.y;

  segment0.rotation = Math.atan2(dy, dx);

  var w = segment0.getPin().x - segment0.x,
      h = segment0.getPin().y - segment0.y,
      tx = mouse.x - w,
      ty = mouse.y - h;

  dx = tx - segment1.x;
  dy = ty - segment1.y;

  segment1.rotation = Math.atan2(dy, dx);
```

```
  segment0.draw(context);
  segment1.draw(context);
}());
```

Finally, reposition **segment0** so it sits on the end of **segment1**, because **segment1** is now rotated to a different position:

```
(function drawFrame () {
  window.requestAnimationFrame(drawFrame, canvas);
  context.clearRect(0, 0, canvas.width, canvas.height);

  var dx = mouse.x - segment0.x,
      dy = mouse.y - segment0.y;

  segment0.rotation = Math.atan2(dy, dx);

  var w = segment0.getPin().x - segment0.x,
      h = segment0.getPin().y - segment0.y,
      tx = mouse.x - w,
      ty = mouse.y - h;

  dx = tx - segment1.x;
  dy = ty - segment1.y;

  segment1.rotation = Math.atan2(dy, dx);

  segment0.x = segment1.getPin().x;
  segment0.y = segment1.getPin().y;

  segment0.draw(context);
  segment1.draw(context);
}());
```

When you test this example, you see that the segments work as a unit to reach for the mouse. Now, let's clean up the code so you can add more segments to it easily. Move all of the rotation code into its own function, named **reach**:

```
function reach (segment, xpos, ypos) {
  var dx = xpos - segment.x,
      dy = ypos - segment.y;

  segment.rotation = Math.atan2(dy, dx);

  var w = segment.getPin().x - segment.x,
      h = segment.getPin().y - segment.y;

  return {
    x: xpos - w,
    y: ypos - h
  };
}
```

This function sets the rotation of the **segment** parameter, and then uses it to return an object with **x** and **y** properties based on our previous calculations for **tx** and **ty**. This allows you to call the **reach** function to rotate a segment, and returns a target you can pass to the next call. So, the **drawFrame** function becomes the following:

```
(function drawFrame () {
  window.requestAnimationFrame(drawFrame, canvas);
  context.clearRect(0, 0, canvas.width, canvas.height);

  var target = reach(segment0, mouse.x, mouse.y);
  reach(segment1, target.x, target.y);

  segment0.draw(context);
  segment1.draw(context);
}());
```

Here, **segment0** reaches toward the mouse, and **segment1** reaches toward **segment0**. We then move the positioning code into its own function:

```
function position (segmentA, segmentB) {
  segmentA.x = segmentB.getPin().x;
  segmentA.y = segmentB.getPin().y;
}
```

Then you can position **segment0** on the end of **segment1** by calling:

```
position(segment0, segment1);
```

Here's the final code for **05-two-segment-reach.html**:

```
<!doctype html>
<html>
 <head>
  <meta charset="utf-8">
  <title>Two Segment Reach</title>
  <link rel="stylesheet" href="style.css">
 </head>
 <body>
  <canvas id="canvas" width="400" height="400"></canvas>
  <script src="utils.js"></script>
  <script src="segment.js"></script>
  <script>
  window.onload = function () {
    var canvas = document.getElementById('canvas'),
        context = canvas.getContext('2d'),
        mouse = utils.captureMouse(canvas),
        segment0 = new Segment(100, 20),
        segment1 = new Segment(100, 20);

    segment1.x = canvas.width / 2;
    segment1.y = canvas.height / 2;

    function reach (segment, xpos, ypos) {
```

```
      var dx = xpos - segment.x,
          dy = ypos - segment.y;

      segment.rotation = Math.atan2(dy, dx);

      var w = segment.getPin().x - segment.x,
          h = segment.getPin().y - segment.y;

      return {
        x: xpos - w,
        y: ypos - h
      };
    }

    function position (segmentA, segmentB) {
      segmentA.x = segmentB.getPin().x;
      segmentA.y = segmentB.getPin().y;
    }

    (function drawFrame () {
      window.requestAnimationFrame(drawFrame, canvas);
      context.clearRect(0, 0, canvas.width, canvas.height);

      var target = reach(segment0, mouse.x, mouse.y);
      reach(segment1, target.x, target.y);
      position(segment0, segment1);

      segment0.draw(context);
      segment1.draw(context);
    }());
  };
  </script>
 </body>
</html>
```

Building off this example, it's easy to create an array to hold as many segments as you like. The next exercise does just that, **06-multi-segment-reach.html**:

```
<!doctype html>
<html>
 <head>
  <meta charset="utf-8">
  <title>Multi Segment Reach</title>
  <link rel="stylesheet" href="style.css">
 </head>
 <body>
  <canvas id="canvas" width="400" height="400"></canvas>
  <script src="utils.js"></script>
  <script src="segment.js"></script>
  <script>
  window.onload = function () {
    var canvas = document.getElementById('canvas'),
        context = canvas.getContext('2d'),
        mouse = utils.captureMouse(canvas),
```

```
      segments = [],
      numSegments = 5,
      target; //referenced by drawFrame and move

  while (numSegments--) {
    segments.push(new Segment(50, 10));
  }

  //center the last one
  segments[segments.length - 1].x = canvas.width / 2;
  segments[segments.length - 1].y = canvas.height / 2;

  function reach (segment, xpos, ypos) {
    var dx = xpos - segment.x,
        dy = ypos - segment.y;

    segment.rotation = Math.atan2(dy, dx);

    var w = segment.getPin().x - segment.x,
        h = segment.getPin().y - segment.y;

    return {
      x: xpos - w,
      y: ypos - h
    };
  }

  function position (segmentA, segmentB) {
    segmentA.x = segmentB.getPin().x;
    segmentA.y = segmentB.getPin().y;
  }

  function move (segment, i) {
    if (i !== 0) {
      target = reach(segment, target.x, target.y);
      position(segments[i - 1], segment);
    }
  }

  function draw (segment) {
    segment.draw(context);
  }

  (function drawFrame () {
    window.requestAnimationFrame(drawFrame, canvas);
    context.clearRect(0, 0, canvas.width, canvas.height);

    target = reach(segments[0], mouse.x, mouse.y);
    segments.forEach(move);

    segments.forEach(draw);
  }());
};
```

```
  </script>
 </body>
</html>
```

You can see the results of this example in Figure 14-5. Of couse, the segment chain doesn't have to chase the mouse all day. Let's see what happens when we give it a toy to play with.

Figure 14-5. Multiple-segment reaching

Reaching for an Object

Again, we build off the previous example. This time we need the **Ball** class, so include that file in your document. Then create some new variables at the top of the script for the ball to use as it moves around:

```
var ball = new Ball(20),
    gravity = 0.5,
    bounce = -0.9;

ball.vx = 10; //start the ball with velocity on the x axis
```

We're also going to shrink the segments down a little bit, to give them more room to play. You can adjust these values to see what looks best in your animation:

```
while (numSegments--) {
  segments.push(new Segment(20, 10));
}
```

Create another function, **moveBall**, that allows us to separate the ball-moving code so it doesn't clutter up the program:

```
function moveBall () {
  ball.vy += gravity;
  ball.x += ball.vx;
  ball.y += ball.vy;

  if (ball.x + ball.radius > canvas.width) {
    ball.x = canvas.width - ball.radius;
    ball.vx *= bounce;
  } else if (ball.x - ball.radius < 0) {
```

```
    ball.x = ball.radius;
    ball.vx *= bounce;
  }
  if (ball.y + ball.radius > canvas.height) {
    ball.y = canvas.height - ball.radius;
    ball.vy *= bounce;
  } else if (ball.y - ball.radius < 0) {
    ball.y = ball.radius;
    ball.vy *= bounce;
  }
}
```

Finally, in the **drawFrame** animation loop, call the **moveBall** function, and have the first segment reach for the ball instead of the mouse:

```
(function drawFrame () {
  window.requestAnimationFrame(drawFrame, canvas);
  context.clearRect(0, 0, canvas.width, canvas.height);

  moveBall();
  target = reach(segments[0], ball.x, ball.y);
  segments.forEach(move);

  segments.forEach(draw);
  ball.draw(context);
}());
```

When you run this example you should see something like Figure 14-6. The ball now bounces around, and the arm follows it. Pretty amazing, right?

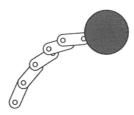

Figure 14-6. It likes to play ball.

Right now, the arm touches the ball, but the ball completely ignores the arm. Let's have them interact.

Adding Some Interaction

How the ball and the arm interact depends on what you want them to do. But, no matter what you do, the first thing you need is some collision detection. Then, you can have the reaction if there is a collision. Again, put all the code into its own function and call it from the **drawFrame** animation loop:

```
(function drawFrame () {
  window.requestAnimationFrame(drawFrame, canvas);
  context.clearRect(0, 0, canvas.width, canvas.height);
```

```
  moveBall();
  target = reach(segments[0], ball.x, ball.y);
  segments.forEach(move);
  checkHit();

  segments.forEach(draw);
  ball.draw(context);
}());
```

The collision detection is executed after the motion code, so everything is in its final position. Here's the start of the **checkHit** function:

```
function checkHit () {
  var segment = segments[0],
      dx = segment.getPin().x - ball.x,
      dy = segment.getPin().y - ball.y,
      dist = Math.sqrt(dx * dx + dy * dy);

  if (dist < ball.radius) {
    //reaction goes here
  }
}
```

The first thing you do is determine the distance from the end pin of the first arm to the ball, and use distance-based collision detection to see whether it hits the ball.

Now you need to do something when you detect a hit. For this example, the arm throws the ball up in the air (negative y velocity) and moves it randomly on the x axis (random x velocity), like so:

```
function checkHit () {
  var segment = segments[0],
      dx = segment.getPin().x - ball.x,
      dy = segment.getPin().y - ball.y,
      dist = Math.sqrt(dx * dx + dy * dy);

  if (dist < ball.radius) {
    ball.vx += Math.random() * 2 - 1;
    ball.vy -= 1;
  }
}
```

This works out pretty well, and the final code can be found in **07-play-ball.html**. If the arm happens to lose its ball, don't be sad, you can always refresh your browser to keep playing. But this example is just that, an example. You might want to use this technique to have the arm catch the ball and throw it toward a target, or play catch with another arm. Try different reactions, because you certainly know enough now to do some interesting things.

Using the Standard Inverse Kinematics Method

The method we describe for inverse kinematics is relatively easy to understand and program, doesn't require a lot of system resources to process, and most importantly, works. But there is a more standard, mathematical, solution to this problem using the law of cosines. We take a look at the standard way of doing inverse kinematics, so then you have a couple different methods at your disposal and can choose whichever one you like.

Introducing the Law of Cosines

This way of calculating inverse kinematics uses something called the *law of cosines*. Recall that in Chapter 3, all the examples used right triangles, which are triangles with one right angle (90 degrees). The rules for such triangles are fairly simple: Sine equals opposite over hypotenuse, cosine equals adjacent over hypotenuse, etc. We use these rules quite extensively throughout the book.

But what if you have a triangle that doesn't have a 90-degree angle? Well, that's where the law of cosines fits in, it can help us figure out the various angles and lengths of this kind of triangle. It is a little more complex, but if you have enough information about the triangle, you can use this formula to figure out the rest. So what does this have to do with inverse kinematics? Take a look at the diagram in Figure 14-7.

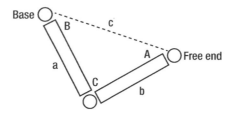

Figure 14-7. Two segments form a triangle with sides a, b, c, and angles A, B, C.

Here, you have two segments. The one on the left (side *a*) is the base, which is fixed, so you know that location. You want to put the free end at the position shown. Thus, you've formed a triangle.

What do we know about this triangle? You can easily find the distance between the two ends—the length of side *c*. And you know the length of each segment—sides *a* and *b*. So, you know all three lengths.

What do you need to know about this triangle? You just need the two angles of the two segments—angles *B* and *C*. This is where the law of cosines can help you:

$$c^2 = a^2 + b^2 - 2 \times a \times b \times \cos C$$

Now, you need to know angle *C*, so you can isolate that on one side. We won't go through each step, but, with a little algebra, you should wind up with this:

$$C = \text{acos} \left((a^2 + b^2 - c^2) / (2 \times a \times b) \right)$$

The `acos` there is arccosine, or inverse cosine. The cosine of an angle gives you a ratio, and the arccosine of that ratio gives you back the angle. The JavaScript function for this is `Math.acos`. Because you know sides *a*, *b*, and *c*, you can now find angle *C*. Similarly, you need to know angle *B*, and the law of cosines says this:

$$b^2 = a^2 + c^2 - 2 \times a \times c \times \cos B$$

Which, when isolating angle *B*, boils down to this:

$$B = \text{acos}((a^2 + c^2 - b^2) / (2 \times a \times c))$$

Converting these equations to JavaScript gives you this:

```
var B = Math.acos((a * a + c * c - b * b) / (2 * a * c)),
    C = Math.acos((a * a + b * b - c * c) / (2 * a * b));
```

Now you have *almost* everything you need to position things. Almost, because the angles *B* and *C* aren't really the angles of rotation you use for the segments. Look at the next diagram in Figure 14-8.

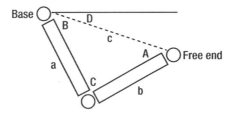

Figure 14-8. Figuring the rotation of side a

Although you know angle *B*, you still need to determine how much to actually rotate side *a* (**segment1**). This is how far from zero, or horizontal, it's going to be, and is represented by angles *D* plus *B*. To get angle *D*, call **Math.atan2** using the difference between the free end and base position. For the rotation of side *b* (**segment0**), you know angle *C*, but that is only in relation to side *a* So you take the rotation of side *a*, plus 180, plus angle *C*, (as shown in Figure 14-9), and this is your angle *E*.

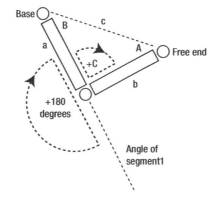

Figure 14-9. Figuring out angle E and the rotation of side b

Yes, this way requires a lot more math. But let's see how this looks in code, which should hopefully make the calculations a little clearer.

Programming the Law of Cosines

First, here's the complete code listing for next example (**08-cosines-1.html**), then we'll step throught it:

```html
<!doctype html>
<html>
 <head>
  <meta charset="utf-8">
  <title>Cosines 1</title>
  <link rel="stylesheet" href="style.css">
 </head>
 <body>
  <canvas id="canvas" width="400" height="400"></canvas>
  <script src="utils.js"></script>
  <script src="segment.js"></script>
  <script>
  window.onload = function () {
    var canvas = document.getElementById('canvas'),
        context = canvas.getContext('2d'),
        mouse = utils.captureMouse(canvas),
        segment0 = new Segment(100, 20),
        segment1 = new Segment(100, 20);

    segment1.x = canvas.width / 2;
    segment1.y = canvas.height / 2;

    (function drawFrame () {
      window.requestAnimationFrame(drawFrame, canvas);
      context.clearRect(0, 0, canvas.width, canvas.height);

      var dx = mouse.x - segment1.x,
          dy = mouse.y - segment1.y,
          dist = Math.sqrt(dx * dx + dy * dy),
          a = 100,
          b = 100,
          c = Math.min(dist, a + b),
          B = Math.acos((b * b - a * a - c * c) / (-2 * a * c)),
          C = Math.acos((c * c - a * a - b * b) / (-2 * a * b)),
          D = Math.atan2(dy, dx),
          E = D + B + Math.PI + C;

      segment1.rotation = (D + B);

      var target = segment1.getPin();
      segment0.x = target.x;
      segment0.y = target.y;
      segment0.rotation = E;

      segment0.draw(context);
      segment1.draw(context);
    }());
  };
  </script>
 </body>
</html>
```

Here's the procedure for this excercise:

- Get the distance from **segment1** to the mouse.

- Get the lengths of the three sides. Sides **a** and **b** are easy. They're equal to 100, because that's how long we made the segments. Side **c** is equal to **dist** or **a** + **b**, whichever is smaller. This is because one side of a triangle can't be longer than the other two sides added together.

- Figure out angles **B** and **C** using the law of cosines formula, and angle **D** using **Math.atan2**. angle **E**, as mentioned, is **D** + **B** + 180 + **C**. But in code, you substitute **Math.PI** radians for 180 degrees.

- Just as the diagram in Figure 14-8 shows, use the angle **D** + **B** as **segment1**'s rotation. Use the same angle to find the end point of **segment1** and position **segment0** on it.

- Finally, **segment0**'s rotation is angle **E**.

So that's inverse kinematics using the law of cosines. You might notice that the joint always bends the same way. This might be good if you're building something like an elbow or a knee that can bend only one way, but what if you want to bend it the other way?

When you figure out the angles analytically like this, there are two solutions to the problem: It can bend this way, or it can bend that way. You coded it to bend one way by *adding D* and *B*, and then *adding C*. If you subtracted them all, you get the same effect, but the segment bends in the other direction. Here's the modified **drawFrame** function to see how this looks (document **09-cosines-2.html**):

```
(function drawFrame () {
  window.requestAnimationFrame(drawFrame, canvas);
  context.clearRect(0, 0, canvas.width, canvas.height);

  var dx = mouse.x - segment1.x,
      dy = mouse.y - segment1.y,
      dist = Math.sqrt(dx * dx + dy * dy),
      a = 100,
      b = 100,
      c = Math.min(dist, a + b),
      B = Math.acos((b * b - a * a - c * c) / (-2 * a * c)),
      C = Math.acos((c * c - a * a - b * b) / (-2 * a * b)),
      D = Math.atan2(dy, dx),
      E = D - B + Math.PI - C;

  segment1.rotation = (D - B);

  var target = segment1.getPin();
  segment0.x = target.x;
  segment0.y = target.y;
  segment0.rotation = E;

  segment0.draw(context);
  segment1.draw(context);
}());
```

If you want it to bend either way, you need to figure out some kind of conditional logic to say: "If it's in this position, bend this way; otherwise, bend that way." But these examples should give you plenty to get started.

Important Formulas in This Chapter

For the standard form of inverse kinematics, you use the law of cosines formula.

Law of Cosines

$$a^2 = b^2 + c^2 - 2 \times b \times c \times \cos A$$
$$b^2 = a^2 + c^2 - 2 \times a \times c \times \cos B$$
$$c^2 = a^2 + b^2 - 2 \times a \times b \times \cos C$$

Law of Cosines in JavaScript

```
var A = Math.acos((b * b + c * c - a * a) / (2 * b * c)),
    B = Math.acos((a * a + c * c - b * b) / (2 * a * c)),
    C = Math.acos((a * a + b * b - c * c) / (2 * a * b));
```

Summary

Inverse kinematics is a vast subject—far more than can ever be covered in a single chapter. Even so, this chapter described some pretty interesting and useful things. You saw how to set up an inverse kinematics system and two ways of looking at it: dragging and reaching. Hopefully you've seen that there's some fun stuff you can build with it, and it doesn't have to be that complex. There's much more that can be done with inverse kinematics, and you should be ready to go discover it and put it to use.

In the next chapter, you enter a whole new dimension, which enables you to add some depth to your animations.

Part IV

3D Animation

Chapter 15

3D Basics

What we'll cover in this chapter:

- The third dimension and perspective
- Velocity and acceleration
- Bouncing
- Gravity
- Wrapping
- Easing and springing
- Coordinate rotation
- Collision detection

Up to now, everything in this book has been in just two (and sometimes only one) dimensions, and you've created some pretty interesting animations. Now, let's take it to the next level.

Creating graphics in 3D is exciting because the extra dimension seems to make things really come to life. We move through the basics of programming 3D fairly quickly, and after that, we'll see how the motion effects discussed in the previous chapters can be done with a third dimension. Specifically, this chapter covers velocity, acceleration, friction, gravity, bouncing, wrapping, easing, springing, coordinate rotation, and collision detection.

For now, you are primarily concerned with taking an object and moving it around in 3D space, using perspective to calculate its size and position on the screen. The object we draw is flat, of course. It won't have a back, side, top, or bottom that you can see. Over the next couple of chapters, you do some modeling of points, lines, shapes, and solids in 3D.

It's worth mentioning there is currently, at the time of writing, a 3D specification in development for the canvas element, called WebGL. However, it is not considered part of the HTML5 specification, and is not supported across all the major web browsers at this time (and it is not known if it ever will be). WebGL is, by design, a low-level means to execute code on the computer's graphics card. Although WebGL is a powerful way to run hardware-accelerated graphics in the browser, it's rather advanced and uses JavaScript more as a way to tie together other programs, called *shaders*, which are written in a separate shader language and are compiled when the browser loads the document. But WebGL could provide the foundation for the next generation of web-based graphics, on which other, easier to use, libraries and 3D-engines are built. There are still a number of issues facing its broad adoption by all browsers, but it does offer a glimpse into the future of graphics and games on the web.

The third dimension and perspective

The main concept behind 3D is the existence of another dimension beyond the x and y axes. This is the dimension of depth, and it is usually labeled z.

The canvas element does not have a built-in z dimension, but it isn't too difficult to create one with JavaScript. And it's actually less complex than a lot of the stuff you did in the previous chapters!

The z axis

To begin with, you must decide which direction the z-axis will go: in or out. If you recall back to the description of the canvas coordinate system in Chapter 3, it is in some ways opposite to most other commonly used coordinate systems. The y axis goes down instead of up, and angles are measured clockwise instead of counterclockwise.

If an object's z position increases, is it going away from you or toward you on the z-axis? Neither way is necessarily more *correct* than the other. In fact, this subject has been addressed enough times that there are even names to describe the two methods: left-hand system and right-hand system.

Take either hand, and point the fingers in the direction of the positive x-axis and curl them toward the positive y-axis. The direction your thumb points, either toward you or away from you, is the direction that the positive z-axis points for that coordinate system. So, if you take your right-hand, point it away from you following the positive x-axis, and then curl the fingers to the ground, toward the positive y-axis, your thumb will point in front of you—the positive z-axis for the right-handed coordinate system. So in code, this means the z-axis increases as it goes away from the viewer, and decreases as it goes toward the viewer, as shown in Figure 15-1.

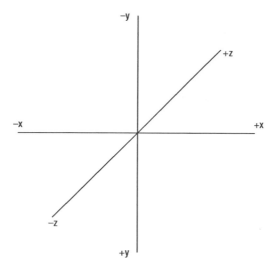

Figure 15-1. Right-hand coordinate system

If you try it with your left hand, you get the opposite result—your thumb is pointing behind you. Figure 15-2 shows the left-hand coordinate system.

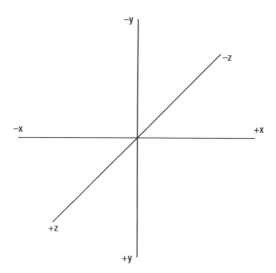

Figure 15-2. Left-hand coordinate system

We use the right-hand coordinate system (refer to Figure 15-1) for the examples here, so as an object's z position increases, it moves further in front of us. But that is just the preference of this book, there's no reason that you couldn't make a left-hand system.

The next step in creating a third (z) dimension is to figure out how to simulate perspective.

Perspective

Perspective is how we determine whether something is closer to us or farther away, or—to put it another way—how we make something look like it is closer or farther. There are a number of techniques for presenting perspective, but we concentrate on two here:

- Things get smaller as they get farther away.

- Things converge on a vanishing point as they get farther away.

You've probably seen examples of train tracks coming to a point on the horizon to illustrate the vanishing point. So, when you move something on the z axis, you need to do two things:

- Scale it up or down.

- Move it closer to or farther away from the vanishing point.

When working with only two dimensions, you can get away with using the screen x and y coordinates for your object's x and y position—you just do a one-to-one mapping. But this won't work in 3D, because two objects can have the same x and y position, and yet, due to their depth, have a different position on the screen. Each object you move in 3D should have its own x, y, and z coordinates that have nothing to do with the screen position, these coordinates describe the object's position in virtual space. The perspective calculation tells you where to put the object on the screen.

The perspective formula

The idea is that as something moves farther away (z increases), its scale approaches 0 and its x, y position converges on the 0, 0 of the vanishing point. Because the ratio of distance to scale is the same as the ratio of distance to convergence, you need to figure out what that ratio is for a given distance and use it in both places. The diagram in Figure 15-3 helps to explain this concept.

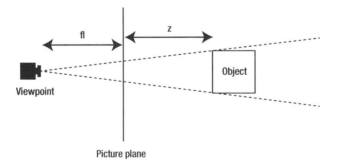

Figure 15-3. Perspective seen from the side

Here, you have an object off in the distance, a viewpoint we look from (the camera), and a picture plane, which we look through to see the scene. You have the distance of the object to the picture plane, which is the z value, and, you have the distance from the viewpoint to the picture plane. This last one is similar to the focal length of a camera lens, so we use the variable fl to represent it. A long focal length can be compared to a telephoto lens on a camera, with a narrow view that compresses the distance between objects. A short focal length is like a wide-angle lens, where you see a lot of the scene, but with a lot of distortion. A medium focal length approximates what the human eye sees, and uses a value for `fl` that's between 200 and 300. Here's the perspective formula:

```
scale = fl / (fl + z)
```

This usually yields a number between 0.0 and 1.0, which is your ratio for scaling and converging on the vanishing point. However, as z approaches `-fl`, `(fl + z)` approaches 0 and `scale` approaches infinity. This is the coding equivalent to being poked in the eye.

What do you do with this scale value? Well, you can adjust the scale of the canvas context before drawing the object. For example, in the `Ball` class we've used throughout the book, there are `scaleX` and `scaleY` properties that are referenced in its `draw` method, like so:

```
context.scale(this.scaleX, this.scaleY);
```

Once the scale as been determined, you multiply the object's x and y position by this factor to find its screen x and y position.

Let's look at an example where we use 250 as the focal length. If z is zero—in other words, the object is exactly on the picture plane—then the scale will be 250 / (250 + 0). This comes out to exactly 1.0. That's your `scaleX` and `scaleY` (remember that for scale, 1.0 means 100%). Multiplying 1.0 by the object's x and y positions gives the same numbers back as a result, so the object's screen position is exactly equal to its x and y.

Now move it out so that z is 250. That makes the scale equal to 250 / (250 + 250), or 0.5 for `scaleX` and `scaleY`. It also moves the object's screen position. If the object were at 200, 300 on the x and y axis, its screen position would now be 100, 150—it has moved halfway to the vanishing point. (Actually, the screen position would be in relation to the vanishing point, which you see shortly.)

Move z out to 9750. This makes the scale equal to 250/10000, or 0.025 for `scaleX` and `scaleY`. The object becomes just a speck that is close to the vanishing point.

Now we see how to write all of this in code.

Programming perspective

We use the `Ball` class again for these examples, and for interaction, let's get fancy and use the mouse *and* keyboard. The mouse controls the ball's x and y position, and the up and down keys on the keyboard move the ball forward and back on the z-axis. The variables `xpos`, `ypos`, and `zpos` are used to represent the 3D position. Here's the code for example `01-perspective-1.html`:

```html
<!doctype html>
<html>
 <head>
  <meta charset="utf-8">
  <title>Perspective 1</title>
  <link rel="stylesheet" href="style.css">
 </head>
 <body>
  <canvas id="canvas" width="400" height="400"></canvas>
```

```
<script src="utils.js"></script>
<script src="ball.js"></script>
<script>
window.onload = function () {
  var canvas = document.getElementById('canvas'),
      context = canvas.getContext('2d'),
      mouse = utils.captureMouse(canvas),
      ball = new Ball(),
      xpos = 0,
      ypos = 0,
      zpos = 0,
      fl = 250,
      vpX = canvas.width / 2,
      vpY = canvas.height / 2;

  window.addEventListener('keydown', function (event) {
    if (event.keyCode === 38) {          //up
      zpos += 5;
    } else if (event.keyCode === 40) {   //down
      zpos -= 5;
    }
  }, false);

  (function drawFrame () {
    window.requestAnimationFrame(drawFrame, canvas);
    context.clearRect(0, 0, canvas.width, canvas.height);

    var scale = fl / (fl + zpos);
    xpos = mouse.x - vpX;
    ypos = mouse.y - vpY;
    ball.scaleX = ball.scaleY = scale;
    ball.x = vpX + xpos * scale;
    ball.y = vpY + ypos * scale;

    ball.draw(context);
  }());
};
</script>
</body>
</html>
```

First, you create variables for xpos, ypos, and zpos, as well as fl. Then you create a vanishing point, vpX, vpY. Remember, as objects move off in the distance, they converge on 0, 0. If you don't offset this somehow, everything converges at the top-left corner of the screen, which is not what you want. You use vpX, vpY to make the center of the canvas element the vanishing point.

Next, add a listener for the keydown event that changes the zpos variable. If the up key is pressed, zpos increases, and pressing the down key decreases it. This makes the ball move farther from, or closer to, the viewer.

In the drawFrame animation loop, set xpos and ypos to the mouse position, as offset by the vanishing point. In other words, if the mouse is 200 pixels right of center, xpos is 200. If it's 200 pixels left of center, xpos is –200.

Calculate `scale` using the perspective formula we just covered, and size and position the ball accordingly. The x and y positions of the ball on the canvas element are calculated from the vanishing point, adding on the `xpos` and `ypos` times the `scale`. Thus, as scale becomes small, the ball converges on the vanishing point.

When this example is run in your browser, at first it looks like you're simply dragging the ball with the mouse. This is because `zpos` is zero, making `scale` 1.0. So, no noticeable perspective is applied. As you press the up cursor key, the ball appears to slide into the distance, as shown in Figure 15-4. Now as you move the mouse around, the ball moves with it, but much less, giving you a parallax effect. If you want to set up a scene to use parallax, hard-code the z value for each layer, rather than calculating it dynamically.

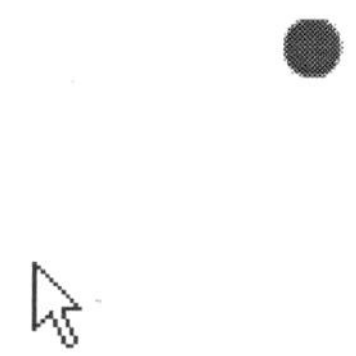

Figure 15-4. Perspective in action

You might notice that if you keep pressing the down key, the ball gets very large. This is expected—if you hold a pebble close to your eye, it looks like a boulder. However, if you continue to press the down key, you see that the ball grows to an infinite size and then shrinks down again. (It's actually upside down and reversed, but it's difficult to tell that from a circle.) This is the ball going *behind* the viewpoint.

Mathematically, what happens is that when `zpos` is equal to `-fl`, the formula `scale = fl / (fl + zpos)` becomes `scale = fl / 0`. In many languages, dividing by zero gives you an error. In JavaScript, it gives you `Infinity`. As you decrease `zpos` even more, you divide `fl` by a negative number. `scale` becomes negative, which when applied to the canvas context, has the effect of flipping the image coordinate system, so your ball looks upside down and backward.

A simple way to handle this is to make the ball invisible if it goes past a certain point. If `zpos` is less than or equal to `-fl`, you have a problem, so you can test for that condition and handle it. Here's the updated `drawFrame` function in document `02-perspective-2.html` (the rest of the script is the same as the previous example):

```
(function drawFrame () {
  window.requestAnimationFrame(drawFrame, canvas);
  context.clearRect(0, 0, canvas.width, canvas.height);

  if (zpos > -fl) {
    var scale = fl / (fl + zpos);
    xpos = mouse.x - vpX;
    ypos = mouse.y - vpY;
    ball.scaleX = ball.scaleY = scale;
    ball.x = vpX + xpos * scale;
    ball.y = vpY + ypos * scale;
    ball.visible = true;
```

```
  } else {
    ball.visible = false;
  }

  if (ball.visible) {
    ball.draw(context);
  }
}());
```

If the ball is not in front of us, there's no need to scale and position it. And if the ball isn't visible, there is no need to draw it to the canvas.

Well, there you have it, the bare-bones basics of 3D. Not so painful, is it? Make sure you play around with this example and get a good feel for it. In particular, change the value of fl and see how it affects how the scene is rendered. This is the equivalent of changing the lens on a camera.

The rest of the chapter is devoted to programming the various motion effects covered in previous chapters, but now in 3D.

Velocity and acceleration

Accomplishing velocity and acceleration in 3D is surprisingly easy. For 2D, you have **vx** and **vy** variables to represent velocity on two axes. Now you just need to add the **vz** variable for the third dimension. Similarly, if you have something such as **ax** and **ay** for acceleration, you add **az**.

You can modify the last exercise to make it work sort of like the earlier spaceship examples, but in 3D. It's all keyboard-controlled now, with the cursor keys providing the thrust on the x and y axes, and the Shift and Control keys used for z thrust. Here's the code for document 03-velocity-3d.html:

```
<!doctype html>
<html>
 <head>
  <meta charset="utf-8">
  <title>Velocity 3D</title>
  <link rel="stylesheet" href="style.css">
 </head>
 <body>
  <canvas id="canvas" width="400" height="400"></canvas>
  <script src="utils.js"></script>
  <script src="ball.js"></script>
  <script>
  window.onload = function () {
    var canvas = document.getElementById('canvas'),
        context = canvas.getContext('2d'),
        ball = new Ball(),
        xpos = 0,
        ypos = 0,
        zpos = 0,
        vx = 0,
        vy = 0,
        vz = 0,
```

```
      friction = 0.98,
      fl = 250,
      vpX = canvas.width / 2,
      vpY = canvas.height / 2;

  window.addEventListener('keydown', function (event) {
    switch (event.keyCode) {
    case 38:          //up
      vy -= 1;
      break;
    case 40:          //down
      vy += 1;
      break;
    case 37:          //left
      vx -= 1;
      break;
    case 39:          //right
      vx += 1;
      break;
    case 16:          //shift
      vz += 1;
      break;
    case 17:          //control
      vz -= 1;
      break;
    }
  }, false);

  (function drawFrame () {
    window.requestAnimationFrame(drawFrame, canvas);
    context.clearRect(0, 0, canvas.width, canvas.height);

    xpos += vx;
    ypos += vy;
    zpos += vz;
    vx *= friction;
    vy *= friction;
    vz *= friction;

    if (zpos > -fl) {
      var scale = fl / (fl + zpos);
      ball.scaleX = ball.scaleY = scale;
      ball.x = vpX + xpos * scale;
      ball.y = vpY + ypos * scale;
      ball.visible = true;
    } else {
      ball.visible = false;
    }

    if (ball.visible) {
      ball.draw(context);
    }
  }());
```

```
  };
  </script>
 </body>
</html>
```

All we did here is add variables for velocity on each axis and some friction. When one of the six keys is pressed, it adds or subtracts from the appropriate velocity (remember that acceleration changes velocity). Then it adds the velocity to the position on each axis and computes friction.

Now you have a 3D object moving with acceleration, velocity, and friction. And done quite easily.

Bouncing

For the purposes of this section, we bounce a ball off a flat surface—in other words, one that aligns perfectly with the x, y, or z axis. This is analogous to bouncing off the sides of our canvas element you did in 2D.

Single object bouncing

When bouncing in 3D, again you detect when the object has gone past a boundary, adjust it to touch that boundary, and then reverse its velocity on the appropriate axis. One of the differences with 3D is in how you decide where the boundaries are. In 2D, you generally use the canvas element or some other visible rectangular area. In 3D, things aren't quite so simple because there is no real concept of a visible edge—unless you draw one. You will draw in 3D in the next chapter, so for now, bounce your objects off arbitrarily placed, invisible walls.

The boundaries are set up as before, but now you position them in 3D space, which means that they can be negative as well as positive. And a boundary can be set up on the z-axis. For the next example, our boundaries look like this:

```
var top = -100,
    bottom = 100,
    left = -100,
    right = 100,
    front = -100,
    back = 100;
```

After determining the object's new position, check it against all six boundaries. Remember that you take half of the object's width into account when checking for the collision, and that you already stored that value in a property of the Ball class called radius. Here's the full code listing for 3D bouncing (document 04-bounce-3d.html):

```
<!doctype html>
<html>
 <head>
  <meta charset="utf-8">
  <title>Bounce 3d</title>
  <link rel="stylesheet" href="style.css">
 </head>
 <body>
```

```
<canvas id="canvas" width="400" height="400"></canvas>
<script src="utils.js"></script>
<script src="ball.js"></script>
<script>
window.onload = function () {
  var canvas = document.getElementById('canvas'),
      context = canvas.getContext('2d'),
      ball = new Ball(),
      xpos = 0,
      ypos = 0,
      zpos = 0,
      vx = Math.random() * 10   5,
      vy = Math.random() * 10   5,
      vz = Math.random() * 10   5,
      fl = 250,
      vpX = canvas.width / 2,
      vpY = canvas.height / 2,
      top = -100,
      bottom = 100,
      left = -100,
      right = 100,
      front = -100,
      back = 100;

  (function drawFrame () {
    window.requestAnimationFrame(drawFrame, canvas);
    context.clearRect(0, 0, canvas.width, canvas.height);

    xpos += vx;
    ypos += vy;
    zpos += vz;

    //check boundaries
    if (xpos + ball.radius > right) {
      xpos = right   ball.radius;
      vx *= -1;
    } else if (xpos - ball.radius < left) {
      xpos = left + ball.radius;
      vx *= -1;
    }
    if (ypos + ball.radius > bottom) {
      ypos = bottom   ball.radius;
      vy *= -1;
    } else if (ypos - ball.radius < top) {
      ypos = top + ball.radius;
      vy *= -1;
    }
    if (zpos + ball.radius > back) {
      zpos = back   ball.radius;
      vz *= -1;
    } else if (zpos - ball.radius < front) {
      zpos = front + ball.radius;
      vz *= -1;
```

```
    }
    if (zpos > -fl) {
      var scale = fl / (fl + zpos);
      ball.scaleX = ball.scaleY = scale;
      ball.x = vpX + xpos * scale;
      ball.y = vpY + ypos * scale;
      ball.visible = true;
    } else {
      ball.visible = false;
    }

    if (ball.visible) {
      ball.draw(context);
    }
  }());
};
</script>
</body>
</html>
```

All of the key-handling code has been removed from the previous example, and the ball has been given a random velocity on each axis. Now you can see the ball is definitely bouncing around, but you can't really tell what it is bouncing against—remember that these are arbitrarily placed invisible boundaries.

Multiple object bouncing

One thing you can do to visualize the walls a little better is to fill up the space with more objects. To do this, we need multiple instances of the Ball class. But then each instance needs its own xpos, ypos, zpos, and velocities on each axis as well. It can get messy keeping track of all of that in the main code, so we'll create a new class, Ball3d, to keep track of the values for us. Save the following script to the file ball3d.js and we'll import it into the next examples:

```
function Ball3d (radius, color) {
  if (radius === undefined) { radius = 40; }
  if (color === undefined) { color = "#ff0000"; }
  this.x = 0;
  this.y = 0;
  this.xpos = 0;
  this.ypos = 0;
  this.zpos = 0;
  this.vx = 0;
  this.vy = 0;
  this.vz = 0;
  this.radius = radius;
  this.mass = 1;
  this.rotation = 0;
  this.scaleX = 1;
  this.scaleY = 1;
  this.color = utils.parseColor(color);
  this.lineWidth = 1;
  this.visible = true;
```

```
}

Ball3d.prototype.draw = function (context) {
  context.save();
  context.translate(this.x, this.y);
  context.rotate(this.rotation);
  context.scale(this.scaleX, this.scaleY);
  context.lineWidth = this.lineWidth;
  context.fillStyle = this.color;
  context.beginPath();
  context.arc(0, 0, this.radius, 0, (Math.PI * 2), true);
  context.closePath();
  context.fill();
  if (this.lineWidth > 0) {
    context.stroke();
  }
  context.restore();
};
```

As you can see, all this does is add properties for position and velocity on each axis to our ball. In `05-multi-bounce-3d.html`, we created 50 instances of this new class. Each one now has its own values for `xpos`, `ypos`, and `zpos`, and `vx`, `vy`, `vz`. The `drawFrame` animation loop now iterates twice over each `Ball3d` object, passing it to the `move` and `draw` functions. This code does the same thing to each ball that the previous example did to just one. Here's the example `05-multi-bounce-3d.html`:

```
<!doctype html>
<html>
 <head>
  <meta charset="utf-8">
  <title>Multi Bounce 3d</title>
  <link rel="stylesheet" href="style.css">
 </head>
 <body>
  <canvas id="canvas" width="400" height="400"></canvas>
  <script src="utils.js"></script>
  <script src="ball3d.js"></script>
  <script>
  window.onload = function () {
    var canvas = document.getElementById('canvas'),
        context = canvas.getContext('2d'),
        balls = [],
        numBalls = 50,
        fl = 250,
        vpX = canvas.width / 2,
        vpY = canvas.height / 2,
        top = -100,
        bottom = 100,
        left = -100,
        right = 100,
        front = -100,
        back = 100;

    for (var ball, i = 0; i < numBalls; i++) {
```

```
      ball = new Ball3d(15);
      ball.vx = Math.random() * 10   5;
      ball.vy = Math.random() * 10   5;
      ball.vz = Math.random() * 10   5;
      balls.push(ball);
  }

  function move (ball) {
    ball.xpos += ball.vx;
    ball.ypos += ball.vy;
    ball.zpos += ball.vz;

    //check boundaries
    if (ball.xpos + ball.radius > right) {
      ball.xpos = right   ball.radius;
      ball.vx *= -1;
    } else if (ball.xpos - ball.radius < left) {
      ball.xpos = left + ball.radius;
      ball.vx *= -1;
    }
    if (ball.ypos + ball.radius > bottom) {
      ball.ypos = bottom   ball.radius;
      ball.vy *= -1;
    } else if (ball.ypos - ball.radius < top) {
      ball.ypos = top + ball.radius;
      ball.vy *= -1;
    }
    if (ball.zpos + ball.radius > back) {
      ball.zpos = back   ball.radius;
      ball.vz *= -1;
    } else if (ball.zpos - ball.radius < front) {
      ball.zpos = front + ball.radius;
      ball.vz *= -1;
    }

    if (ball.zpos > -fl) {
      var scale = fl / (fl + ball.zpos);
      ball.scaleX = ball.scaleY = scale;
      ball.x = vpX + ball.xpos * scale;
      ball.y = vpY + ball.ypos * scale;
      ball.visible = true;
    } else {
      ball.visible = false;
    }
  }

  function draw (ball) {
    if (ball.visible) {
      ball.draw(context);
    }
  }

  (function drawFrame () {
```

```
        window.requestAnimationFrame(drawFrame, canvas);
        context.clearRect(0, 0, canvas.width, canvas.height);

        balls.forEach(move);
        balls.forEach(draw);
    }());
};
</script>
</body>
</html>
```

When you run this script, you'll see the balls fill up the space between the six boundaries, as shown in Figure 15-5, and you can get an idea of the shape of this space.

Figure 15-5. Bouncing 3D balls

Z-sorting

Now, this addition of multiple objects brings up an issue lacking in the code you have so far—something called *z-sorting*. Z-sorting is how objects are sorted on the z-axis, or which one goes in front of another one. If you look closely at the ball outlines, you can see which ball is on top of which. This pretty much ruins the whole 3D effect, because smaller objects are now appearing in front of larger ones. But we can fix the order the balls are drawn to the canvas element by applying z-sorting.

Our code draws the balls in the order they are positioned in the balls array. In the prior example, that order is determined when the balls are first initialized and added to the array. So if we want to draw the balls according to their position on the z-index, we need to reorder them accordingly. To reorder an array in JavaScript, we need to define a function to sort it.

JavaScript arrays have a sort method that is defined as Array.sort([compareFunction]). The method has an optional function parameter that defines the sort order by comparing each element. If this argument omitted, the array is sorted alphabetically by the element names.

The `compareFunction` parameter is a function that in turn takes two arguments, and these are the array elements that are compared as it iterates over the entire collection. How the array is ordered is determined by the numeric return value of the `compareFunction` when passed successive elements using the following rules:

Let n = `compareFunction(a, b)`,

- If n is less than 0, sort element a to a lower index than element b.

- If n returns 0, leave element a and element b unchanged.

- If n is greater than 0, sort element b to a lower index than element a.

For example, to sort an array of numbers in ascending order:

```
var arr = [3, 5, 1, 4, 2];
arr.sort(function (a, b) { return (a - b); });

console.log(arr); //prints [1, 2, 3, 4, 5]
```

In terms of 3D depth ordering, index 0 is the bottom, and any objects with a higher number appear in front of objects with a lower number. You want to sort the array of objects from the highest depth (farthest away) to lowest (closest). The following code defines our sort function, and then orders the `balls` array:

```
function zSort (a, b) {
  return (b.zpos - a.zpos);
}

balls.sort(zSort);
```

This sorts the array based on the `zpos` property of each object, in reverse numerical order—in other words, from high to low. The result is that the ball that is farthest away (highest `zpos` value) is first in the array and therefore drawn first to the canvas element. The closest ball is the last element in the array and drawn on top of every other ball.

Once you add this function to previous example, you need to call it *before* you draw the balls:

```
(function drawFrame () {
  window.requestAnimationFrame(drawFrame, canvas);
  context.clearRect(0, 0, canvas.width, canvas.height);

  balls.forEach(move);
  balls.sort(zSort);
  balls.forEach(draw);
}());
```

The rest of the code remains the same as the previous exercise. The full listing can be found in document `06-z-sort.html`.

Gravity

In this section, we look at simple gravity as seen from the earth's surface, and as described in Chapter 5. In this case, gravity works pretty much the same in 3D as it does in 2D. Choose a number for the force gravity that is exerting on the object, and add that number to the object's y velocity on each animation frame.

Gravity in 3D may be simple, but something simple can create a great looking effect. In this example, we combine gravity with bouncing to give the appearance of dumping a bucket of tiny rubber bouncy balls onto the floor.

You need an object to represent a single rubber bouncy ball, so we again use the Ball3d class, but with a smaller radius. Make each ball a random color, and it also helps to change the background color to black. Here's the code for exercise, 07-bouncy-balls.html:

```
<!doctype html>
<html>
 <head>
  <meta charset="utf-8">
  <title>Fireworks</title>
  <link rel="stylesheet" href="style.css">
  <style>
  #canvas {
    background-color: #000000;
  }
  </style>
 </head>
<body>
 <canvas id="canvas" width="400" height="400"></canvas>
 <script src="utils.js"></script>
 <script src="ball3d.js"></script>
 <script>
 window.onload = function () {
   var canvas = document.getElementById('canvas'),
       context = canvas.getContext('2d'),
       balls = [],
       numBalls = 100,
       fl = 250,
       vpX = canvas.width / 2,
       vpY = canvas.height / 2,
       gravity = 0.2,
       floor = 200,
       bounce = -0.6;

   for (var ball, i = 0; i < numBalls; i++) {
     ball = new Ball3d(3, Math.random() * 0xffffff);
     ball.ypos = -100;
     ball.vx = Math.random() * 6 - 3;
     ball.vy = Math.random() * 6 - 3;
     ball.vz = Math.random() * 6 - 3;
     balls.push(ball);
   }
```

```
function move (ball) {
  ball.vy += gravity;
  ball.xpos += ball.vx;
  ball.ypos += ball.vy;
  ball.zpos += ball.vz;

  if (ball.ypos > floor) {
    ball.ypos = floor;
    ball.vy *= bounce;
  }

  if (ball.zpos > -fl) {
    var scale = fl / (fl + ball.zpos);
    ball.scaleX = ball.scaleY = scale;
    ball.x = vpX + ball.xpos * scale;
    ball.y = vpY + ball.ypos * scale;
    ball.visible = true;
  } else {
    ball.visible = false;
  }
}

function zSort (a, b) {
  return (b.zpos - a.zpos);
}

function draw (ball) {
  if (ball.visible) {
    ball.draw(context);
  }
}

(function drawFrame () {
  window.requestAnimationFrame(drawFrame, canvas);
  context.clearRect(0, 0, canvas.width, canvas.height);

  balls.forEach(move);
  balls.sort(zSort);
  balls.forEach(draw);
}());
};
</script>
</body>
</html>
```

Here, we add a few properties: gravity, bounce, and floor. The first two you should know by now, and the floor property is just that—the bottom-most y value that the balls can hit before they bounce.

Other than the one line that adds gravity to each ball's **vy** property, and the bouncing when each one hits the floor, there's not a lot going on here that we haven't covered, but things are starting to look pretty nice.

The result looks something like Figure 15-6.

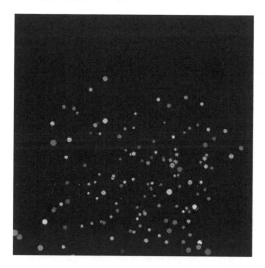

Figure 15-6. A bunch of rubber bouncy balls! (Trust me, it looks much better in motion.)

Wrapping

Recall in Chapter 6, we discussed three possible reactions when an object hits a boundary. We just covered bouncing, and there was also wrapping and regeneration. For 3D, wrapping can be useful, but primarily on the z axis.

In 2D wrapping, you check whether the object went off the screen on the x or y axis. This works pretty well, because when the object goes beyond one of those boundaries, you can't see it anymore, so you can easily reposition it without jarring the viewer's attention. You don't have that luxury in 3D.

In 3D wrapping, there are only two points where it's safe to remove and reposition an object. One is when the object has gone behind the viewpoint. The previous examples test for this and make the object invisible in such a case. The other is when the object is so far in the distance and shrunk to such a small size that it's practically invisible. This means that you can safely wrap on the z axis. When something goes behind you, you toss it way out in front of you, and let it come at you again. Or, if something has gone so far out that you can barely see it, remove it and replace it behind you. If you want, you can try wrapping on the x or y axis as well, but in most cases, you're going to wind up with an unnatural popping in and out of existence effect.

It's worth mentioning, if an object has moved too far out of sight on the x or y axis, you can always reposition it along the z-axis. This is not really screen wrapping, but can be an effective way to reuse objects.

But z-axis wrapping can be useful, especially in 3D racing type games, and we'll create a basic setup here. The idea is to place various 3D objects in front of the viewpoint, then, you move those objects toward the viewpoint. In other words, you give them some negative z velocity. Depending on how you set it up, this can either look like a lot of objects coming toward you, or it can trick the eye to look like you're moving toward the objects. Once an object has gone behind the viewpoint, replace it way out in the distance. That way there is a never-ending supply of objects to move past.

The objects we use in the next example are simple, stylized trees with randomized branch positions. This is the `Tree` class, which has the 3D position properties and draws a somewhat random stick figure tree. This code will be file `tree.js`:

```
function Tree () {
  this.x = 0;
  this.y = 0;
  this.xpos = 0;
  this.ypos = 0;
  this.zpos = 0;
  this.scaleX = 1;
  this.scaleY = 1;
  this.color = "#ffffff";
  this.alpha = 1;
  this.lineWidth = 1;
  this.branch = [];

  //generate some random branch positions
  this.branch[0] = -140 - Math.random() * 20;
  this.branch[1] = -30 - Math.random() * 30;
  this.branch[2] = Math.random() * 80 - 40;
  this.branch[3] = -100 - Math.random() * 40;
  this.branch[4] = -60 - Math.random() * 40;
  this.branch[5] = Math.random() * 60 - 30;
  this.branch[6] = -110 - Math.random() * 20;
}

Tree.prototype.draw = function (context) {
  context.save();
  context.translate(this.x, this.y);
  context.scale(this.scaleX, this.scaleY);
  context.lineWidth = this.lineWidth;
  context.strokeStyle = utils.colorToRGB(this.color, this.alpha);
  context.beginPath();
  context.moveTo(0, 0);
  context.lineTo(0, this.branch[0]);
  context.moveTo(0, this.branch[1]);
  context.lineTo(this.branch[2], this.branch[3]);
  context.moveTo(0, this.branch[4]);
  context.lineTo(this.branch[5], this.branch[6]);
  context.stroke();
  context.restore();
};
```

Again, for this example, we use a white on a black background color. The script creates several trees, and they are spread out randomly on the x-axis, 1,000 pixels in either direction. They are also spread out on the z-axis, from 0 to 10,000. They all have the same y position though, based on the `floor` property, which gives the impression of a ground plane.

The following code is for excercise `08-trees-1.html`, and you can see what it looks like in Figure 15-7.

```
<!doctype html>
<html>
 <head>
  <meta charset="utf-8">
  <title>Trees 1</title>
  <link rel="stylesheet" href="style.css">
  <style>
  #canvas {
    background-color: #000000;
  }
  </style>
 </head>
 <body>
  <canvas id="canvas" width="400" height="400"></canvas>
  <script src="utils.js"></script>
  <script src="tree.js"></script>
  <script>
  window.onload = function () {
    var canvas = document.getElementById('canvas'),
        context = canvas.getContext('2d'),
        trees = [],
        numTrees = 100,
        fl = 250,
        vpX = canvas.width / 2,
        vpY = canvas.height / 2,
        floor = 200,
        vz = 0,
        friction = 0.98;

    for (var tree, i = 0; i < numTrees; i++) {
      tree = new Tree();
      tree.xpos = Math.random() * 2000 - 1000;
      tree.ypos = floor;
      tree.zpos = Math.random() * 10000;
      trees.push(tree);
    }

    window.addEventListener('keydown', function (event) {
      if (event.keyCode === 38) {          //up
        vz -= 1;
      } else if (event.keyCode === 40) {   //down
        vz += 1;
      }
    }, false);

    function move (tree) {
      tree.zpos += vz;
      if (tree.zpos < -fl) {
        tree.zpos += 10000;
      }
      if (tree.zpos > 10000 - fl) {
        tree.zpos -= 10000;
      }
```

363

```
      var scale = fl / (fl + tree.zpos);
      tree.scaleX = tree.scaleY = scale;
      tree.x = vpX + tree.xpos * scale;
      tree.y = vpY + tree.ypos * scale;
      tree.alpha = scale;
    }

    function zSort (a, b) {
      return (b.zpos - a.zpos);
    }

    function draw (tree) {
      tree.draw(context);
    }

    (function drawFrame () {
      window.requestAnimationFrame(drawFrame, canvas);
      context.clearRect(0, 0, canvas.width, canvas.height);

      trees.forEach(move);
      vz *= friction;
      trees.sort(zSort);
      trees.forEach(draw);
    }());
  };
  </script>
 </body>
</html>
```

There is only a single variable for z velocity, because the trees won't move on the x or y axis, and all move in unison on the z-axis. We attached a **keydown** event listener to the document, which increments or decrements **vz** accordingly. Applying a little friction in the **drawFrame** function keeps the speed from increasing infinitely, and slows you down if no key is pressed.

The code then loops through each tree, updating its z position with the current z velocity. Then it checks whether a tree has gone behind you. If so, rather than making it invisible, it moves the tree 10,000 pixels into the z axis. Likewise, if it has gone past 10,000 - fl, it moves the tree back 10,000.

You then do the standard perspective actions. Here, we also add another little extra to enhance the illusion of depth:

```
tree.alpha = scale;
```

This sets the transparency of the tree in relation to its depth on the z-axis. The farther away it goes, the more it fades out. This is atmospheric perspective, simulating the effect of the atmosphere between the viewer and the object. This is particularly effective when you have objects moving way out in the distance, as in this example. The effect is applied to the canvas context within the tree's **draw** method:

```
context.strokeStyle = utils.colorToRGB(this.color, this.alpha);
```

This specific calculation for transparency gives the effect of a dark, spooky night. You might want to try something like the following:

```
tree.alpha = scale * 0.7 + 0.3;
```

This gives the trees an opacity of at least 30%—not quite so foggy. There are no right or wrong values for most of this, just different values that create different effects.

We left the z-sorting method in there, though, in this particular case, it doesn't make much of a visual difference because the trees are just simple lines of the same color. If you draw more complex, overlapping objects, it is pretty important.

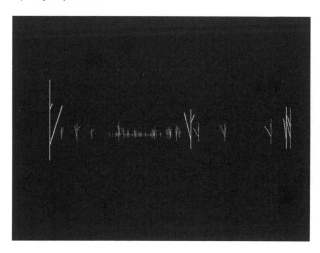

Figure 15-7. Watch out for the trees!

Let's add a few enhancements beyond the scope of screen wrapping, just to give you an idea of where this can go. Here is the result (which can also be found in `09-trees-2.html`):

```
<!doctype html>
<html>
 <head>
  <meta charset="utf-8">
  <title>Trees 2</title>
  <link rel="stylesheet" href="style.css">
  <style>
  #canvas {
    background-color: #000000;
  }
  </style>
 </head>
 <body>
  <canvas id="canvas" width="400" height="400"></canvas>
  <script src="utils.js"></script>
  <script src="tree.js"></script>
  <script>
  window.onload = function () {
    var canvas = document.getElementById('canvas'),
        context = canvas.getContext('2d'),
```

```
            trees = [],
            numTrees = 100,
            fl = 250,
            vpX = canvas.width / 2,
            vpY = canvas.height / 2,
            floor = 50,
            ax = 0,
            ay = 0,
            az = 0,
            vx = 0,
            vy = 0,
            vz = 0,
            gravity = 0.3,
            friction = 0.95;

        for (var tree, i = 0; i < numTrees; i++) {
          tree = new Tree();
          tree.xpos = Math.random() * 2000 - 1000;
          tree.ypos = floor;
          tree.zpos = Math.random() * 10000;
          trees.push(tree);
        }

        window.addEventListener('keydown', function (event) {
          switch (event.keyCode) {
          case 38:         //up
            az = -1;
            break;
          case 40:         //down
            az = 1;
            break;
          case 37:         //left
            ax = 1;
            break;
          case 39:         //right
            ax = -1;
            break;
          case 32:         //space
            ay = 1;
            break;
          }
        }, false);

        window.addEventListener('keyup', function (event) {
          switch (event.keyCode) {
          case 38:         //up
          case 40:         //down
            az = 0;
            break;
          case 37:         //left
          case 39:         //right
            ax = 0;
            break;
```

```
      case 32:          //space
        ay = 0;
        break;
      }
    }, false);

    function move (tree) {
      tree.xpos += vx;
      tree.ypos += vy;
      tree.zpos += vz;
      if (tree.ypos < floor) {
        tree.ypos = floor;
      }
      if (tree.zpos < -fl) {
        tree.zpos += 10000;
      }
      if (tree.zpos > 10000 - fl) {
        tree.zpos -= 10000;
      }
      var scale = fl / (fl + tree.zpos);
      tree.scaleX = tree.scaleY = scale;
      tree.x = vpX + tree.xpos * scale;
      tree.y = vpY + tree.ypos * scale;
      tree.alpha = scale;
    }

    function zSort (a, b) {
      return (b.zpos - a.zpos);
    }

    function draw (tree) {
      tree.draw(context);
    }

    (function drawFrame () {
      window.requestAnimationFrame(drawFrame, canvas);
      context.clearRect(0, 0, canvas.width, canvas.height);

      vx += ax;
      vy += ay;
      vz += az;
      vy -= gravity;
      trees.forEach(move);
      vx *= friction;
      vy *= friction;
      vz *= friction;
      trees.sort(zSort);
      trees.forEach(draw);
    }());
  };
  </script>
  </body>
</html>
```

Here, we add velocity for the x and y axis, as well as some gravity. We also do some fancy footwork to detect multiple key presses by attaching a **keydown** and **keyup** event listener. When the key is pressed, we set the acceleration on the appropriate axis to 1 or –1;then when that key is released, we set the acceleration back to 0. The acceleration for each axis gets added to the velocity on that axis in the **drawFrame** animation loop. The left and right cursor keys were obvious choices for the x velocity, and we use the spacebar for y. One interesting point is that we are *subtracting* gravity from **vy**. This is because we want it to seem like the *viewer* is the one who is falling down to where the trees are, as shown in Figure 15-8. Really, the trees are "falling up" to where the viewpoint is, but it winds up looking the same. The y position of the trees is limited to 50, which makes it look like you landed on the ground.

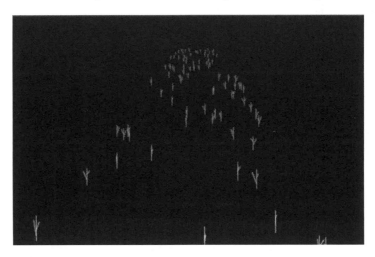

Figure 15-8. Look, I'm flying!

There is nothing to limit movement on the x-axis, which means you can go off to the side of the forest if you want. As an additional exercise, it wouldn't be too hard for you to set up some side boundaries.

Easing and springing

Easing and springing are also not much more complex in 3D than they are in 2D (the subject of Chapter 8). Just add another variable or two for the z-axis, and you're all set.

Easing

There's not a lot to cover on easing. In 2D, you have **tx** and **ty** as a target point. You just add **tz** for the z-axis. On each animation frame, you measure the distance from the object to the target on each axis, and move it a fraction of the way there.

Let's look at a simple example that eases an instance of **Ball3d** to a random target in 3D space. When the ball arrives at the coordinate, it picks another target and moves there. Here's the code (document **10-easing-3d.html**):

```html
<!doctype html>
<html>
 <head>
  <meta charset="utf-8">
  <title>Easing 3d</title>
  <link rel="stylesheet" href="style.css">
 </head>
 <body>
  <canvas id="canvas" width="400" height="400"></canvas>
  <script src="utils.js"></script>
  <script src="ball3d.js"></script>
  <script>
  window.onload = function () {
    var canvas = document.getElementById('canvas'),
        context = canvas.getContext('2d'),
        ball = new Ball3d(),
        tx = Math.random() * 500 - 250,
        ty = Math.random() * 500 - 250,
        tz = Math.random() * 500,
        easing = 0.1,
        fl = 250,
        vpX = canvas.width / 2,
        vpY = canvas.height / 2;

    (function drawFrame () {
      window.requestAnimationFrame(drawFrame, canvas);
      context.clearRect(0, 0, canvas.width, canvas.height);

      var dx = tx - ball.xpos,
          dy = ty - ball.ypos,
          dz = tz - ball.zpos,
          dist = Math.sqrt(dx * dx + dy * dy + dz * dz);

      ball.xpos += dx * easing;
      ball.ypos += dy * easing;
      ball.zpos += dz * easing;

      if (dist < 1) {
        tx = Math.random() * 500 - 250;
        ty = Math.random() * 500 - 250;
        tz = Math.random() * 500;
      }

      if (ball.zpos > -fl) {
        var scale = fl / (fl + ball.zpos);
        ball.scaleX = ball.scaleY = scale;
        ball.x = vpX + ball.xpos * scale;
        ball.y = vpY + ball.ypos * scale;
        ball.visible = true;
      } else {
        ball.visible = false;
      }
```

```
      if (ball.visible) {
        ball.draw(context);
      }
    }());
  };
  </script>
 </body>
</html>
```

The most interesting part of this code is calculating the 3D distance:

```
var dist = Math.sqrt(dx * dx + dy * dy + dz * dz);
```

If you remember, in 2D, you measure the distance between two points by the following equation:

```
var dist = Math.sqrt(dx * dx + dy * dy);
```

To move into 3D distances, just add the square of the distance on the third axis. It's pretty simple.

Springing

Springing, a close cousin to easing, requires a similar adjustment for 3D. You use the distance to the target to change the velocity, rather than the position. In this example, 11-spring-3d.html, clicking the mouse creates a new random target for the ball to spring to:

```
<!doctype html>
<html>
 <head>
  <meta charset="utf-8">
  <title>Spring 3d</title>
  <link rel="stylesheet" href="style.css">
 </head>
 <body>
  <canvas id="canvas" width="400" height="400"></canvas>
  <script src="utils.js"></script>
  <script src="ball3d.js"></script>
  <script>
  window.onload = function () {
    var canvas = document.getElementById('canvas'),
        context = canvas.getContext('2d'),
        ball = new Ball3d(),
        tx = Math.random() * 500 - 250,
        ty = Math.random() * 500 - 250,
        tz = Math.random() * 500,
        spring = 0.1,
        friction = 0.94,
        fl = 250,
        vpX = canvas.width / 2,
        vpY = canvas.height / 2;

    window.addEventListener('mousedown', function () {
      tx = Math.random() * 500 - 250;
      ty = Math.random() * 500 - 250;
```

```
      tz = Math.random() * 500;
    }, false);

    (function drawFrame () {
      window.requestAnimationFrame(drawFrame, canvas);
      context.clearRect(0, 0, canvas.width, canvas.height);

      var dx = tx - ball.xpos,
          dy = ty - ball.ypos,
          dz = tz - ball.zpos;

      ball.vx += dx * spring;
      ball.vy += dy * spring;
      ball.vz += dz * spring;
      ball.xpos += ball.vx;
      ball.ypos += ball.vy;
      ball.zpos += ball.vz;
      ball.vx *= friction;
      ball.vy *= friction;
      ball.vz *= friction;

      if (ball.zpos > -fl) {
        var scale = fl / (fl + ball.zpos);
        ball.scaleX = ball.scaleY = scale;
        ball.x = vpX + ball.xpos * scale;
        ball.y = vpY + ball.ypos * scale;
        ball.visible = true;
      } else {
        ball.visible = false;
      }

      if (ball.visible) {
        ball.draw(context);
      }
    }());
  };
  </script>
 </body>
</html>
```

This code uses the basic spring formula from Chapter 8, but with a third axis.

Coordinate rotation

Next up is coordinate rotation in 3D. This gets a bit more complex than 2D, which you saw in Chapters 10 and 11. Not only can you choose between three different axes to rotate on, you can even rotate on more than one of them at once.

In 2D coordinate rotation, the points rotate around the z-axis, as shown in Figure 15-9. Think of a spinning windmill with an axle through the center. The axle is the z-axis. Only the x and y coordinates change.

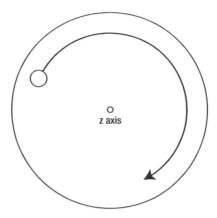

Figure 15-9. Rotation on the z axis

In 3D, you can also rotate on the x or y axis. An x-axis rotation looks like a car tire rolling toward you, as shown in Figure 15-10, with the axle as the x-axis. Points rotate around that and change their y and z positions.

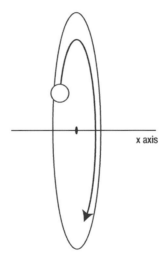

Figure 15-10. Rotation on the x axis

For y-axis rotation, imagine a record player, something like Figure 15-11. The spindle is the y-axis, and the points move on the x and z axes.

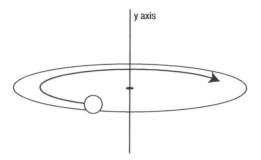

Figure 15-11. Rotation on the y axis

Thus, for 3D, when you rotate an object on one axis, its position changes on the other two axes.

In Chapter 10, we calculated 2D coordinate rotation using the formula:

```
x1 = x * cos(angle) - y * sin(angle)
y1 = y * cos(angle) + x * sin(angle)
```

In 3D, you do basically the same thing, but you need to specify which angle you're talking about: x, y, or z. Thus, you get the following three formulas:

```
x1 = x * cos(angleZ) - y * sin(angleZ)
y1 = y * cos(angleZ) + x * sin(angleZ)

x1 = x * cos(angleY) - z * sin(angleY)
z1 = z * cos(angleY) + x * sin(angleY)

y1 = y * cos(angleX) - z * sin(angleX)
z1 = z * cos(angleX) + y * sin(angleX)
```

We'll perform a y-axis rotation in the next example, `12-rotate-y.html`. It creates 50 instances of `Ball3d` and randomly positions them. Then, it gets a y angle based on the mouse's x position. The farther right the mouse goes, the higher the number for the angle. This makes the objects seem to follow the mouse in their rotation.

```
<!doctype html>
<html>
 <head>
  <meta charset="utf-8">
  <title>Rotate Y</title>
  <link rel="stylesheet" href="style.css">
 </head>
 <body>
  <canvas id="canvas" width="400" height="400"></canvas>
  <script src="utils.js"></script>
  <script src="ball3d.js"></script>
  <script>
  window.onload = function () {
    var canvas = document.getElementById('canvas'),
        context = canvas.getContext('2d'),
```

```
      mouse = utils.captureMouse(canvas),
      balls = [],
      numBalls = 50,
      fl = 250,
      vpX = canvas.width / 2,
      vpY = canvas.height / 2,
      angleY; //referenced in drawFrame and move

  for (var ball, i = 0; i < numBalls; i++) {
    ball = new Ball3d(15);
    ball.xpos = Math.random() * 200 - 100;
    ball.ypos = Math.random() * 200 - 100;
    ball.zpos = Math.random() * 200 - 100;
    balls.push(ball);
  }

  function rotateY (ball, angle) {
    var cos = Math.cos(angle),
        sin = Math.sin(angle),
        x1 = ball.xpos * cos - ball.zpos * sin,
        z1 = ball.zpos * cos + ball.xpos * sin;

    ball.xpos = x1;
    ball.zpos = z1;

    if (ball.zpos > -fl) {
      var scale = fl / (fl + ball.zpos);
      ball.scaleX = ball.scaleY = scale;
      ball.x = vpX + ball.xpos * scale;
      ball.y = vpY + ball.ypos * scale;
      ball.visible = true;
    } else {
      ball.visible = false;
    }
  }

  function move (ball) {
    rotateY(ball, angleY);
  }

  function zSort (a, b) {
    return (b.zpos - a.zpos);
  }

  function draw (ball) {
    if (ball.visible) {
      ball.draw(context);
    }
  }

  (function drawFrame () {
    window.requestAnimationFrame(drawFrame, canvas);
    context.clearRect(0, 0, canvas.width, canvas.height);
```

```
    angleY = (mouse.x - vpX) * 0.001;

    balls.forEach(move);
    balls.sort(zSort);
    balls.forEach(draw);
  }());
};
</script>
</body>
</html>
```

The important parts are in bold. You get an angle, and pass it and each ball to the `rotateY` function. Inside this function, you get the sine and cosine of the angle, calculate the rotation, and assign `x1` and `z1` back to the ball's **xpos** and **zpos** properties. After that, it's just standard perspective and z-sorting. Figure 15-12 shows the result.

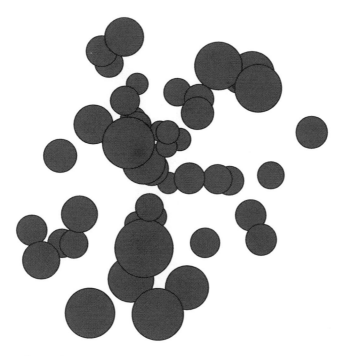

Figure 15-12. Rotation on the y-axis

After you try that, you can switch the example over to an x-axis rotation. Add a new **angleX** variable to the top of the script, and update the `drawFrame` and **move** functions:

```
function move (ball) {
  rotateX(ball, angleX);
}

(function drawFrame () {
```

```
  window.requestAnimationFrame(drawFrame, canvas);
  context.clearRect(0, 0, canvas.width, canvas.height);

  angleX = (mouse.y - vpY) * 0.001;

  balls.forEach(move);
  balls.sort(zSort);
  balls.forEach(draw);
}());
```

Then, you just need to create the `rotateX` function to perform the rotation:

```
function rotateX (ball, angle) {
  var cos = Math.cos(angle),
      sin = Math.sin(angle),
      y1 = ball.ypos * cos - ball.zpos * sin,
      z1 = ball.zpos * cos + ball.ypos * sin;

  ball.ypos = y1;
  ball.zpos = z1;

  if (ball.zpos > -fl) {
    var scale = fl / (fl + ball.zpos);
    ball.scaleX = ball.scaleY = scale;
    ball.x = vpX + ball.xpos * scale;
    ball.y = vpY + ball.ypos * scale;
    ball.visible = true;
  } else {
    ball.visible = false;
  }
}
```

The angle is based on the mouse's y position. You take the cosine and sine of the angle, and use them to get `y1` and `z1`, which are passed to the ball's `ypos` and `zpos` properties.

For the next example, let's combine the two rotations. Here's the code for `13-rotate-xy.html`:

```
<!doctype html>
<html>
 <head>
  <meta charset="utf-8">
  <title>Rotate XY</title>
  <link rel="stylesheet" href="style.css">
 </head>
 <body>
  <canvas id="canvas" width="400" height="400"></canvas>
  <script src="utils.js"></script>
  <script src="ball3d.js"></script>
  <script>
  window.onload = function () {
    var canvas = document.getElementById('canvas'),
        context = canvas.getContext('2d'),
        mouse = utils.captureMouse(canvas),
        balls = [],
```

```
    numBalls = 50,
    fl = 250,
    vpX = canvas.width / 2,
    vpY = canvas.height / 2,
    angleX, angleY; //referenced in drawFrame and move

for (var ball, i = 0; i < numBalls; i++) {
  ball = new Ball3d(15);
  ball.xpos = Math.random() * 200 - 100;
  ball.ypos = Math.random() * 200 - 100;
  ball.zpos = Math.random() * 200 - 100;
  balls.push(ball);
}

function rotateX (ball, angle) {
  var cos = Math.cos(angle),
      sin = Math.sin(angle),
      y1 = ball.ypos * cos - ball.zpos * sin,
      z1 = ball.zpos * cos + ball.ypos * sin;

  ball.ypos = y1;
  ball.zpos = z1;
}

function rotateY (ball, angle) {
  var cos = Math.cos(angle),
      sin = Math.sin(angle),
      x1 = ball.xpos * cos - ball.zpos * sin,
      z1 = ball.zpos * cos + ball.xpos * sin;

  ball.xpos = x1;
  ball.zpos = z1;
}

function setPerspective (ball) {
  if (ball.zpos > -fl) {
    var scale = fl / (fl + ball.zpos);
    ball.scaleX = ball.scaleY = scale;
    ball.x = vpX + ball.xpos * scale;
    ball.y = vpY + ball.ypos * scale;
    ball.visible = true;
  } else {
    ball.visible = false;
  }
}

function move (ball) {
  rotateX(ball, angleX);
  rotateY(ball, angleY);
  setPerspective(ball);
}

function zSort (a, b) {
```

```
    return (b.zpos - a.zpos);
  }

  function draw (ball) {
    if (ball.visible) {
      ball.draw(context);
    }
  }

  (function drawFrame () {
    window.requestAnimationFrame(drawFrame, canvas);
    context.clearRect(0, 0, canvas.width, canvas.height);

    angleX = (mouse.y - vpY) * 0.001;
    angleY = (mouse.x - vpX) * 0.001;

    balls.forEach(move);
    balls.sort(zSort);
    balls.forEach(draw);
  }());
};
</script>
</body>
</html>
```

Here, you find both **angleY** and **angleX**, and call both **rotateX** and **rotateY** functions for each ball. The perspective code has been moved out of the **rotate** functions and into its own function, **setPerspective**, since it doesn't need to be called twice. You can easily add a **rotateZ** function based on what you learned and the preceding formulas.

Collision detection

The last thing to cover in this introduction to 3D is collision detection. The only feasible way of calculating collision detection in 3D with the canvas and JavaScript is distance-based. This is not too much different from collision detection in 2D: You find the distance between two objects (using the 3D distance formula), and if that is less than the sum of their radii, you have a hit.

For a 3D collision detection example, we alter one of the earlier 3D bouncing examples, giving it fewer objects and more space. First, we perform the normal 3D motion and perspective, and then do a double iteration to compare the locations of all the balls and check for a collision. If any are less distance apart than twice their radius, it's a hit, and we change the color of both balls to blue. Here's the code for exercise **14-collision-3d.html**:

```
<!doctype html>
<html>
 <head>
  <meta charset="utf-8">
  <title>Collision 3d</title>
  <link rel="stylesheet" href="style.css">
 </head>
 <body>
```

```
<canvas id="canvas" width="400" height="400"></canvas>
<script src="utils.js"></script>
<script src="ball3d.js"></script>
<script>
window.onload = function () {
  var canvas = document.getElementById('canvas'),
      context = canvas.getContext('2d'),
      balls = [],
      numBalls = 20,
      fl = 250,
      vpX = canvas.width / 2,
      vpY = canvas.height / 2,
      top = -200,
      bottom = 200,
      left = -200,
      right = 200,
      front = -200
      back = 200;

  for (var ball, i = 0; i < numBalls; i++) {
    ball = new Ball3d(15);
    ball.xpos = Math.random() * 400 - 200;
    ball.ypos = Math.random() * 400 - 200;
    ball.zpos = Math.random() * 400 - 200;
    ball.vx = Math.random() * 5 - 1;
    ball.vy = Math.random() * 5 - 1;
    ball.vz = Math.random() * 5 - 1;
    balls.push(ball);
  }

  function move (ball) {
    ball.xpos += ball.vx;
    ball.ypos += ball.vy;
    ball.zpos += ball.vz;

    //check boundaries
    if (ball.xpos + ball.radius > right) {
      ball.xpos = right - ball.radius;
      ball.vx *= -1;
    } else if (ball.xpos - ball.radius < left) {
      ball.xpos = left + ball.radius;
      ball.vx *= -1;
    }
    if (ball.ypos + ball.radius > bottom) {
      ball.ypos = bottom - ball.radius;
      ball.vy *= -1;
    } else if (ball.ypos - ball.radius < top) {
      ball.ypos = top + ball.radius;
      ball.vy *= -1;
    }
    if (ball.zpos + ball.radius > back) {
      ball.zpos = back - ball.radius;
      ball.vz *= -1;
    } else if (ball.zpos - ball.radius < front) {
```

```
      ball.zpos = front + ball.radius;
      ball.vz *= -1;
    }

    if (ball.zpos > -fl) {
      var scale = fl / (fl + ball.zpos);
      ball.scaleX = ball.scaleY = scale;
      ball.x = vpX + ball.xpos * scale;
      ball.y = vpY + ball.ypos * scale;
      ball.visible = true;
    } else {
      ball.visible = false;
    }
  }

  function checkCollision (ballA, i) {
    for (var ballB, dx, dy, dz, dist, j = i + 1; j < numBalls; j++) {
      ballB = balls[j];
      dx = ballA.xpos    ballB.xpos;
      dy = ballA.ypos    ballB.ypos;
      dz = ballA.zpos    ballB.zpos;
      dist = Math.sqrt(dx * dx + dy * dy + dz * dz);

      if (dist < ballA.radius + ballB.radius) {
        ballA.color = "#0000ff";
        ballB.color = "#0000ff";
      }
    }
  }

  function zSort (a, b) {
    return (b.zpos - a.zpos);
  }

  function draw (ball) {
    if (ball.visible) {
      ball.draw(context);
    }
  }

  (function drawFrame () {
    window.requestAnimationFrame(drawFrame, canvas);
    context.clearRect(0, 0, canvas.width, canvas.height);

    balls.forEach(move);
    balls.forEach(checkCollision);
    balls.sort(zSort);
    balls.forEach(draw);
  }());
};
</script>
</body>
</html>
```

The important parts of this code are in bold. The balls start out all red, and as they collide, they change color. Before long, all are blue.

Important formulas in this chapter

The important formulas in this chapter are those for 3D perspective, coordinate rotation, and distance.

Basic perspective

```
scale = fl / (fl + zpos);
object.scaleX = object.scaleY = scale;
object.alpha = scale; // optional
object.x = vanishingPointX + xpos * scale;
object.y = vanishingPointY + ypos * scale;
```

Z-sorting

```
//assumes an array of 3D objects with a zpos property
function zSort (a, b) {
  return (b.zpos - a.zpos);
}

objects.sort(zSort);
```

Coordinate rotation

```
x1 = xpos * cos(angleZ) - ypos * sin(angleZ);
y1 = ypos * cos(angleZ) + xpos * sin(angleZ);

x1 = xpos * cos(angleY) - zpos * sin(angleY);
z1 = zpos * cos(angleY) + xpos * sin(angleY);

y1 = ypos * cos(angleX) - zpos * sin(angleX);
z1 = zpos * cos(angleX) + ypos * sin(angleX);
```

3D distance

```
dist = Math.sqrt(dx * dx + dy * dy + dz * dz);
```

Summary

You now have the basics of 3D under your belt, and you've seen most of the basic motion code adapted for 3D. It's surprising how much of it is the same as the 2D animation code, but with an additional z variable. It turns out that much of these examples were rather simple.

You use a lot of what you learned here in the next chapter, where you actually begin to sculpt 3D forms with points and lines.

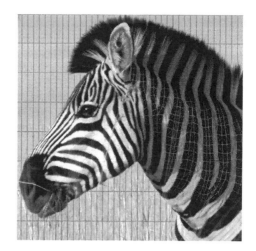

Chapter 16

3D Lines and Fills

What we'll cover in this chapter:

- Creating points and lines

- Making shapes

- Creating 3D fills

- Modeling 3D solids

- Moving 3D solids

The last chapter introduced 3D, but the objects were only positioned in 3D space by calculating their size and screen position—the objects themselves were actually 2D. If you were to move your viewpoint position in this space, the object would always seem to turn and face you. However, that object is not turning. It only appears to turn because, as a 2D object, it's the only view you have of it.

In this chapter, we construct 3D models that are rendered using the canvas drawing API. In particular, we look at how to create and use 3D points, lines, fills, and solids. By the end of this chapter, you'll be able to create a variety of shapes, move them, and rotate them, all in 3D.

Creating points and lines

Since a point, by definition, is invisible because it has no dimension, it doesn't make sense to create points in 3D without making lines in 3D to connect them. But to start with, you continue to use an instance of the **Ball3d** class—with a small radius—as a point so you can see where it is. From there, you draw lines to connect the balls. You already did similar things, but now the points have perspective applied to them, to put them in a 3D space.

In the first example, we make the points black and with a diameter of 10 pixels. We create a few of these points, rotate them based on the mouse position, and then draw lines between them. The code is almost identical to the example `13-rotate-xy.html` from the previous chapter. The difference is that we add some drawing code to the **move** function, and remove the **sortZ** function—because the depth of the points does not matter when drawing a wire-frame model. Here's the code for document `01-lines-3d-1.html`, and is shown in Figure 16-1:

```
<!doctype html>
<html>
 <head>
  <meta charset="utf-8">
  <title>Lines 3d 1</title>
  <link rel="stylesheet" href="style.css">
 </head>
 <body>
  <canvas id="canvas" width="400" height="400"></canvas>
  <script src="utils.js"></script>
  <script src="ball3d.js"></script>
  <script>
  window.onload = function () {
    var canvas = document.getElementById('canvas'),
        context = canvas.getContext('2d'),
        mouse = utils.captureMouse(canvas),
        balls = [],
        numBalls = 15,
        fl = 250,
        vpX = canvas.width / 2,
        vpY = canvas.height / 2,
        angleX, angleY; //referenced in drawFrame and move

    for (var ball, i = 0; i < numBalls; i++) {
      ball = new Ball3d(5, "#000000");
      ball.xpos = Math.random() * 200    100;
      ball.ypos = Math.random() * 200    100;
      ball.zpos = Math.random() * 200    100;
      balls.push(ball);
    }

    function rotateX (ball, angle) {
      var cos = Math.cos(angle),
          sin = Math.sin(angle),
          y1 = ball.ypos * cos - ball.zpos * sin,
          z1 = ball.zpos * cos + ball.ypos * sin;

      ball.ypos = y1;
      ball.zpos = z1;
    }

    function rotateY (ball, angle) {
      var cos = Math.cos(angle),
          sin = Math.sin(angle),
          x1 = ball.xpos * cos - ball.zpos * sin,
```

```
        z1 = ball.zpos * cos + ball.xpos * sin;

      ball.xpos = x1;
      ball.zpos = z1;
    }

    function setPerspective (ball) {
      if (ball.zpos > -fl) {
        var scale = fl / (fl + ball.zpos);
        ball.scaleX = ball.scaleY = scale;
        ball.x = vpX + ball.xpos * scale;
        ball.y = vpY + ball.ypos * scale;
        ball.visible = true;
      } else {
        ball.visible = false;
      }
    }

    function move (ball, i) {
      rotateX(ball, angleX);
      rotateY(ball, angleY);
      setPerspective(ball);

      //don't draw line to first ball
      if (i !== 0) {
        context.lineTo(balls[i].x, balls[i].y);
      }
    }

    function draw (ball) {
      if (ball.visible) {
        ball.draw(context);
      }
    }

    (function drawFrame () {
      window.requestAnimationFrame(drawFrame, canvas);
      context.clearRect(0, 0, canvas.width, canvas.height);

      angleX = (mouse.y - vpY) * 0.001;
      angleY = (mouse.x - vpX) * 0.001;

      context.beginPath();
      //line starts at first ball
      context.moveTo(balls[0].x, balls[0].y);
      balls.forEach(move);
      context.stroke();
      balls.forEach(draw);
    }());
  };
  </script>
 </body>
</html>
```

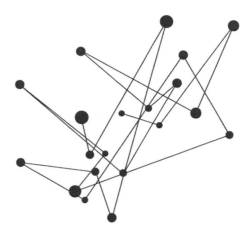

Figure 16-1. 3D points and lines

When you really model 3D solids, you want to remove all the black dots. The simple solution is to set the radius of each **Ball3d** instance to 0, like so:

```
var ball = new Ball3d(0);
```

You can see the results of this in Figure 16-2.

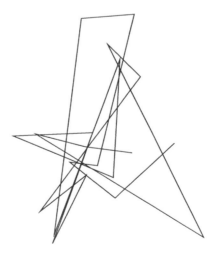

Figure 16-2. 3D lines with invisible points

But if you look at the **Ball3d** class definition, you see that parts of the code are now superfluous. The properties **scaleX**, **scaleY**, and **visible** are irrelevant for an invisible point, because there's nothing there to see or scale. In fact, the entire class is primarily a convenient place to store drawing commands. Because a 3D point needs to keep track of only a few properties, we can create another, simpler, class to contain the values we need. Additionally, the perspective and coordinate rotation functions have been moved into this new class, so we can keep our main document clean. Here's the **Point3d** class we use throughout this chapter and the next (file **point3d.js**):

```javascript
function Point3d (x, y, z) {
  this.x = (x === undefined) ? 0 : x;
  this.y = (y === undefined) ? 0 : y;
  this.z = (z === undefined) ? 0 : z;
  this.fl = 250; //focal length
  this.vpX = 0;  //vanishing point
  this.vpY = 0;
  this.cX = 0;   //center
  this.cY = 0;
  this.cZ = 0;
}

Point3d.prototype.setVanishingPoint = function (vpX, vpY) {
  this.vpX = vpX;
  this.vpY = vpY;
};

Point3d.prototype.setCenter = function (cX, cY, cZ) {
  this.cX = cX;
  this.cY = cY;
  this.cZ = cZ;
};

Point3d.prototype.rotateX = function (angleX) {
  var cosX = Math.cos(angleX),
      sinX = Math.sin(angleX),
      y1 = this.y * cosX - this.z * sinX,
      z1 = this.z * cosX + this.y * sinX;

  this.y = y1;
  this.z = z1;
};

Point3d.prototype.rotateY = function (angleY) {
  var cosY = Math.cos(angleY),
      sinY = Math.sin(angleY),
      x1 = this.x * cosY - this.z * sinY,
      z1 = this.z * cosY + this.x * sinY;

  this.x = x1;
  this.z = z1;
};

Point3d.prototype.rotateZ = function (angleZ) {
  var cosZ = Math.cos(angleZ),
      sinZ = Math.sin(angleZ),
      x1 = this.x * cosZ - this.y * sinZ,
      y1 = this.y * cosZ + this.x * sinZ;

  this.x = x1;
```

```
  this.y = y1;
};

Point3d.prototype.getScreenX = function () {
  var scale = this.fl / (this.fl + this.z + this.cZ);
  return this.vpX + (this.cX + this.x) * scale;
};

Point3d.prototype.getScreenY = function () {
  var scale = this.fl / (this.fl + this.z + this.cZ);
  return this.vpY + (this.cY + this.y) * scale;
};
```

To create a 3D point, you initialize the **Point3d** class by specifying its x, y, and z positions in 3D space. The class also contains properties for its focal length, its vanishing point, and its center. You can rotate the point around its center on any axis using the three rotate methods. The class also has methods to perform all the perspective calculations for you. When you position and rotate the point, call **getScreenX** and **getScreenY** to return the coordinate of the point on the canvas element with all the perspective calculations applied. Ready-built classes like this have been kept to a minimum in this book, but this one helps you understand the examples much easier over the next couple of chapters. Refactor the prior rotating lines example using the new **Point3d** class and it becomes simple, as seen in **02-lines-3d-2.html**:

```
<!doctype html>
<html>
 <head>
  <meta charset="utf-8">
  <title>Lines 3d 2</title>
  <link rel="stylesheet" href="style.css">
 </head>
 <body>
  <canvas id="canvas" width="400" height="400"></canvas>
  <script src="utils.js"></script>
  <script src="point3d.js"></script>
  <script>
  window.onload = function () {
    var canvas = document.getElementById('canvas'),
        context = canvas.getContext('2d'),
        mouse = utils.captureMouse(canvas),
        points = [],
        numPoints = 50,
        fl = 250,
        vpX = canvas.width / 2,
        vpY = canvas.height / 2,
        angleX, angleY; //referenced in drawFrame and move

    for (var point, i = 0; i < numPoints; i++) {
      point = new Point3d(Math.random() * 200    100,
                          Math.random() * 200    100,
                          Math.random() * 200    100);
      point.setVanishingPoint(vpX, vpY);
      points.push(point);
```

```
    }

    function move (point) {
      point.rotateX(angleX);
      point.rotateY(angleY);
    }

    function draw (point, i) {
      //ignore first point
      if (i !== 0) {
        context.lineTo(point.getScreenX(), point.getScreenY());
      }
    }

    (function drawFrame () {
      window.requestAnimationFrame(drawFrame, canvas);
      context.clearRect(0, 0, canvas.width, canvas.height);

      angleX = (mouse.y - vpY) * 0.001;
      angleY = (mouse.x - vpX) * 0.001;

      points.forEach(move);

      context.beginPath();
      //line starts at first point
      context.moveTo(points[0].getScreenX(), points[0].getScreenY());
      points.forEach(draw);
      context.stroke();
    }());
  };
  </script>
 </body>
</html>
```

The main changes are in bold and you should be able to follow them pretty easily. Just remember to include the correct path to new **point3d.js** file in your document.

Making shapes

Random lines look nice for demonstrations, but we can impose a bit of order on that mess. All you need to do is get rid of the initial loop that created random x, y, and z values for the points and replace them with specific, predetermined values. For example, let's make a square. Figure 16-3 shows the square you draw and the 3D locations of its four corners.

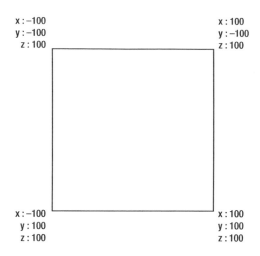

Figure 16-3. Coordinates of a square in 3D space

The z values are all the same because a square lies on a plane. The easiest way to keep the square on the plane is to give all of its points the same measurement on one axis (here we chose the z-axis) and define the square on the other two (x and y axes).

Here's the code that replaces the loop that created random points:

```
points[0] = new Point3d(-100, -100, 100);
points[1] = new Point3d( 100, -100, 100);
points[2] = new Point3d( 100,  100, 100);
points[3] = new Point3d(-100,  100, 100);
```

You then have to manually set the vanishing point for each point, which can be done by iterating over the **points** array:

```
points.forEach(function (point) {
  point.setVanishingPoint(vpX, vpY);
});
```

The rest of the code should work fine, but make one more addition: a line to connect the last point with the first, to close the shape. That's done with a call to **context.closePath** in the animation loop after the other lines have been drawn. Here's the full code as found in **03-square-3d.html** (Figure 16-4 shows the result):

```
<!doctype html>
<html>
 <head>
  <meta charset="utf-8">
  <title>Square 3d</title>
  <link rel="stylesheet" href="style.css">
 </head>
 <body>
  <canvas id="canvas" width="400" height="400"></canvas>
```

```
<script src="utils.js"></script>
<script src="point3d.js"></script>
<script>
window.onload = function () {
  var canvas = document.getElementById('canvas'),
      context = canvas.getContext('2d'),
      mouse = utils.captureMouse(canvas),
      points = [],
      fl = 250,
      vpX = canvas.width / 2,
      vpY = canvas.height / 2,
      angleX, angleY; //referenced in drawFrame and move

  //create 4 points
  points[0] = new Point3d(-100, -100, 100);
  points[1] = new Point3d( 100, -100, 100);
  points[2] = new Point3d( 100,  100, 100);
  points[3] = new Point3d(-100,  100, 100);

  points.forEach(function (point) {
    point.setVanishingPoint(vpX, vpY);
  });

  function move (point) {
    point.rotateX(angleX);
    point.rotateY(angleY);
  }

  function draw (point, i) {
    if (i !== 0) {
      context.lineTo(point.getScreenX(), point.getScreenY());
    }
  }

  (function drawFrame () {
    window.requestAnimationFrame(drawFrame, canvas);
    context.clearRect(0, 0, canvas.width, canvas.height);

    angleX = (mouse.y - vpY) * 0.0005;
    angleY = (mouse.x - vpX) * 0.0005;

    points.forEach(move);

    context.beginPath();
    context.moveTo(points[0].getScreenX(), points[0].getScreenY());
    points.forEach(draw);
    context.closePath();
    context.stroke();
  }());
};
</script>
</body>
</html>
```

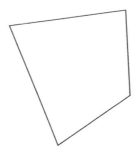

Figure 16-4. 3D spinning square

Look at that, a spinning square! You should be able to create just about any flat shape now. You might find it easier to create shapes by first plotting the points out on a grid before you translate the positions to code (as shown in Figure 16-5).

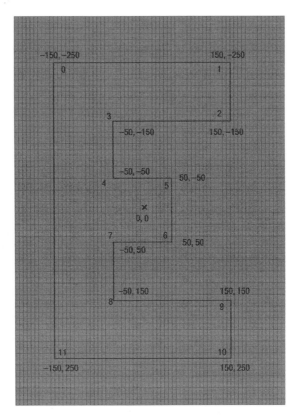

Figure 16-5. Using a grid to plot out the points for the letter E

Using this sketch as a reference, create the points like so:

```
points[0]  = new Point3d(-150, -250, 100);
points[1]  = new Point3d( 150, -250, 100);
points[2]  = new Point3d( 150, -150, 100);
points[3]  = new Point3d( -50, -150, 100);
points[4]  = new Point3d( -50,  -50, 100);
points[5]  = new Point3d(  50,  -50, 100);
points[6]  = new Point3d(  50,   50, 100);
points[7]  = new Point3d( -50,   50, 100);
points[8]  = new Point3d( -50,  150, 100);
points[9]  = new Point3d( 150,  150, 100);
points[10] = new Point3d( 150,  250, 100);
points[11] = new Point3d(-150,  250, 100);
```

Now you have a spinning letter E as seen in **04-spinning-e.html** and in Figure 16-6.

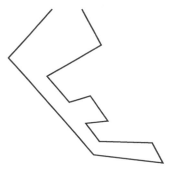

Figure 16-6. 3D spinning letter E

When you start playing around with different shapes, you may notice that if some of the points get too close, they do that inversion bug you saw in the first 3D examples in the last chapter. Your first thought might be to increase the z value of all the points, but that would make the effect worse. For example, say we made z 500. As it rotated, z moves from 500 to –500, putting some of the points even farther behind the viewpoint and making a real mess of things. Instead, use the **setCenter** method to push the whole set of points out on the z axis, like so:

```
points.forEach(function (point) {
  point.setVanishingPoint(vpX, vpY);
  point.setCenter(0, 0, 200);
});
```

If you look back at the **Point3d** class, you see this equation being used to calculate the **scale**:

```
var scale = this.fl / (this.fl + this.z + this.cZ);
```

So when we set the center of the point, it pushes the entire system, including the rotation of the system, out 200 pixels. The value for z remains the same, but because perspective is calculated on higher values, everything is in front of the viewer. Use other values and see how it works. A little later, we play with moving the shape around on the other axes.

Creating 3D fills

As you might imagine, a large part of the work for fills has already been done. You already created the points for a shape and connected them from one end to the other with a line. All you need to do is set the `context.fillStyle` and add `context.fill` to the drawing code. The code in the **05-filled-e.html** file does just that (see Figure 16-7 for the results). Here's the relevant section of **drawFrame** code with the changes in bold:

```
(function drawFrame () {
  window.requestAnimationFrame(drawFrame, canvas);
  context.clearRect(0, 0, canvas.width, canvas.height);

  angleX = (mouse.y - vpY) * 0.0005;
  angleY = (mouse.x - vpX) * 0.0005;

  points.forEach(move);

  context.fillStyle = "#ff0000";
  context.beginPath();
  context.moveTo(points[0].getScreenX(), points[0].getScreenY());
  points.forEach(draw);
  context.closePath();
  context.stroke();
  context.fill();
}());
```

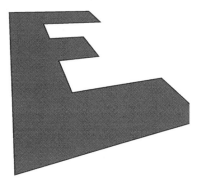

Figure 16-7. First 3D fills

It's a good idea to understand how traditional 3D programs model shapes and solids. In the previous examples, both the square and the letter E are *polygons*. A polygon is a closed shape made of at least three vertices. Thus, a triangle is the simplest polygon. In many 3D modeling and rendering programs—even those that use patches, meshes, NURBS, and complex polygons—all 3D forms are finally reduced to a set of triangles just prior to being rendered.

Using triangles

There are a number of advantages to using triangles. With a triangle, no matter where you place its three vertices, you can be sure that all the points of the polygon are always on the same plane, with the face of the triangle pointing in a single direction. This direction, or *surface normal*, is perpendicular to the face of the triangle and is shown in Figure 16-8. If you move the vertices using another type of polygon, it's possible that the points could wind up on multiple planes and distort the shape. Using the previous example, take some of the points that make up the letter E, and randomly change their z position. Although you might get some interesting results, they can also quickly become unexpected and unpredictable.

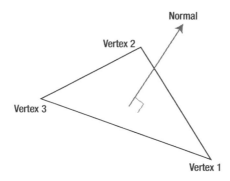

Figure 16-8. The surface normal of a 3D triangle

Another advantage for triangles, is that any complex polygon can be drawn by only using triangles. Consider Figure 16-9, for example.

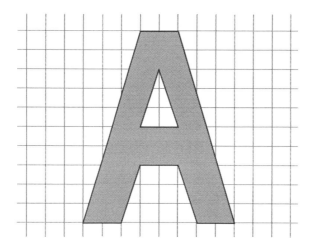

Figure 16-9. More complex 3D shape

This type of closed shape would be difficult to create using a single polygon. You'd find yourself in a situation where every polygon you create would have a different number of points and require special handling to move the pen around. On the other hand, by combining triangles, you can model every shape in a consistent, and efficient, manner—no special handling required. In Figure 16-10 you see how the same closed shape can be broken down into smalled polygons by using triangles..

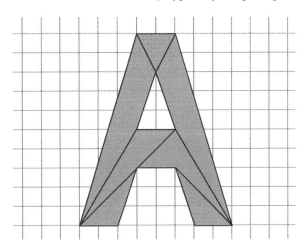

Figure 16-10. The same shape as in Figure 16-9, rendered with triangles

You can then set up a function that takes three points and renders a single triangle. From there, you just need a list of points and then a list of triangles. One loop goes through the list of points, positions them, and applies perspective. Another loop goes through the triangle list and renders each one.

Using triangles enables further optimizations when setting up the geometry as well. Triangle fans and triangle strips are common ways that 3D geometry is stored, because they allow for efficient traversal of all the vertices, while eliminating redundant points. Yet another benefit to using triangles is that we can use trigonometry to manipulate them using well-known calculations, as covered throughout this book.

This isn't to say that you must use a triangle-only approach. You can make a function that dynamically renders a polygon of any number of sides. But to keep things simple and flexible here, let's go with the triangles.

We can try it out using the letter A example. First, you need to define all of your points and triangles. As shown in Figure 16-11, we laid out the shape and numbered all of its points and each of its triangles.

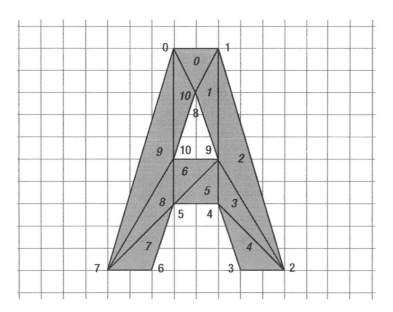

Figure 16-11. The points and polygons that make up this shape

When you graph all the points, you get the following values:

```
points[0]  = new Point3d( -50, -250, 100);
points[1]  = new Point3d(  50, -250, 100);
points[2]  = new Point3d( 200,  250, 100);
points[3]  = new Point3d( 100,  250, 100);
points[4]  = new Point3d(  50,  100, 100);
points[5]  = new Point3d( -50,  100, 100);
points[6]  = new Point3d(-100,  250, 100);
points[7]  = new Point3d(-200,  250, 100);
points[8]  = new Point3d(   0, -150, 100);
points[9]  = new Point3d(  50,    0, 100);
points[10] = new Point3d( -50,    0, 100);
```

Next, you define the triangles. Each triangle is simply a list of three points, and we'll call them **a**, **b**, and **c**. Make a Triangle class to keep track of the points for each triangle and give it a **draw** method so it knows how to render itself to the canvas element. It's listed here, and you see how to use it in a moment (file **triangle.js**):

```
function Triangle (a, b, c, color) {
  this.pointA = a;
  this.pointB = b;
  this.pointC = c;
  this.color = (color === undefined) ? "#ff0000" : utils.parseColor(color);
  this.lineWidth = 1;
  this.alpha = 1;
}
```

```
Triangle.prototype.draw = function (context) {
  context.save();
  context.lineWidth = this.lineWidth;
  context.fillStyle = context.strokeStyle = utils.colorToRGB(this.color, this.alpha);
  context.beginPath();
  context.moveTo(this.pointA.getScreenX(), this.pointA.getScreenY());
  context.lineTo(this.pointB.getScreenX(), this.pointB.getScreenY());
  context.lineTo(this.pointC.getScreenX(), this.pointC.getScreenY());
  context.closePath();
  context.fill();
  if (this.lineWidth > 0) {
    context.stroke();
  }
  context.restore();
};
```

We need another array to hold the list of triangles. So at the top of the script, define the array:

```
var triangles = [];
```

Then, after defining all the points, you create the triangles using three points and a color:

```
triangles[0]  = new Triangle(points[0], points[1],  points[8],  "#ffcccc");
triangles[1]  = new Triangle(points[1], points[9],  points[8],  "#ffcccc");
triangles[2]  = new Triangle(points[1], points[2],  points[9],  "#ffcccc");
triangles[3]  = new Triangle(points[2], points[4],  points[9],  "#ffcccc");
triangles[4]  = new Triangle(points[2], points[3],  points[4],  "#ffcccc");
triangles[5]  = new Triangle(points[4], points[5],  points[9],  "#ffcccc");
triangles[6]  = new Triangle(points[9], points[5],  points[10], "#ffcccc");
triangles[7]  = new Triangle(points[5], points[6],  points[7],  "#ffcccc");
triangles[8]  = new Triangle(points[5], points[7],  points[10], "#ffcccc");
triangles[9]  = new Triangle(points[0], points[10], points[7],  "#ffcccc");
triangles[10] = new Triangle(points[0], points[8],  points[10], "#ffcccc");
```

We order the points of each triangle to go in a clockwise direction. That isn't important at this stage, but it becomes important in the next chapter, so it's a good habit to get into.

> *If you think that plotting all these points and triangles by hand is tedious, that's because it is tedious. And it's going to get worse when you model solid forms. That's why most 3D programs have visual modeling front ends to them, which give you tools to create forms and extract all the points and polygons for you. Although creating a 3D modeling program is beyond the scope of this book, a good strategy might be to parse an open 3D model format, like COLLADA, and store the vertex positions in a format like JSON. You can then load this file into your document and construct the model.*

Now, your rendering loop looks like the following (don't worry, you'll see the complete file in a bit):

```
function draw (triangle) {
  triangle.draw(context);
}

(function drawFrame () {
  window.requestAnimationFrame(drawFrame, canvas);
  context.clearRect(0, 0, canvas.width, canvas.height);

  angleX = (mouse.y - vpY) * 0.0005;
  angleY = (mouse.x - vpX) * 0.0005;

  points.forEach(move);
  triangles.forEach(draw);
}());
```

Here, all the triangles are iterated over and passed to the **draw** function, which in turn calls the **draw** method of each triangle. That's all there is to it! The triangle begins a fill based on its defined color, moves to the position of the first point, draws its shape, and ends the fill. You can see the results of this example in Figure 16-12.

Figure 16-12. The A shape

And, here's the entire code listing for document **06-triangles.html**:

```
<!doctype html>
<html>
 <head>
  <meta charset="utf-8">
  <title>Triangles</title>
  <link rel="stylesheet" href="style.css">
 </head>
 <body>
  <canvas id="canvas" width="400" height="400"></canvas>
  <script src="utils.js"></script>
  <script src="point3d.js"></script>
  <script src="triangle.js"></script>
  <script>
  window.onload = function () {
    var canvas = document.getElementById('canvas'),
        context = canvas.getContext('2d'),
        mouse = utils.captureMouse(canvas),
        points = [],
        triangles = [],
```

```
      fl = 250,
      vpX = canvas.width / 2,
      vpY = canvas.height / 2,
      angleX, angleY; //referenced in drawFrame and move

//the letter 'A', using 11 points
points[0]  = new Point3d( -50, -250, 100);
points[1]  = new Point3d(  50, -250, 100);
points[2]  = new Point3d( 200,  250, 100);
points[3]  = new Point3d( 100,  250, 100);
points[4]  = new Point3d(  50,  100, 100);
points[5]  = new Point3d( -50,  100, 100);
points[6]  = new Point3d(-100,  250, 100);
points[7]  = new Point3d(-200,  250, 100);
points[8]  = new Point3d(   0, -150, 100);
points[9]  = new Point3d(  50,    0, 100);
points[10] = new Point3d( -50,    0, 100);

points.forEach(function (point) {
  point.setVanishingPoint(vpX, vpY);
  point.setCenter(0, 0, 200);
});

//create 11 triangle objects from our points
triangles[0]  = new Triangle(points[0], points[1],  points[8],  "#ffcccc");
triangles[1]  = new Triangle(points[1], points[9],  points[8],  "#ffcccc");
triangles[2]  = new Triangle(points[1], points[2],  points[9],  "#ffcccc");
triangles[3]  = new Triangle(points[2], points[4],  points[9],  "#ffcccc");
triangles[4]  = new Triangle(points[2], points[3],  points[4],  "#ffcccc");
triangles[5]  = new Triangle(points[4], points[5],  points[9],  "#ffcccc");
triangles[6]  = new Triangle(points[9], points[5],  points[10], "#ffcccc");
triangles[7]  = new Triangle(points[5], points[6],  points[7],  "#ffcccc");
triangles[8]  = new Triangle(points[5], points[7],  points[10], "#ffcccc");
triangles[9]  = new Triangle(points[0], points[10], points[7],  "#ffcccc");
triangles[10] = new Triangle(points[0], points[8],  points[10], "#ffcccc");

function move (point) {
  point.rotateX(angleX);
  point.rotateY(angleY);
}

function draw (triangle) {
  triangle.draw(context);
}

(function drawFrame () {
  window.requestAnimationFrame(drawFrame, canvas);
  context.clearRect(0, 0, canvas.width, canvas.height);

  angleX = (mouse.y - vpY) * 0.0005;
  angleY = (mouse.x - vpX) * 0.0005;

  points.forEach(move);
  triangles.forEach(draw);
```

```
    }());
  };
  </script>
  </body>
</html>
```

Modeling 3D solids

In the computing world, the first example in any book or tutorial is almost always "Hello, World!", a program that in one way or another prints the words to the screen. When drawing your first 3D solid, the equivalent seems to be a spinning cube, so let's start with that.

Modeling a spinning cube

To model a cube, you need eight points to define its eight corners. These are shown in Figure 16-13.

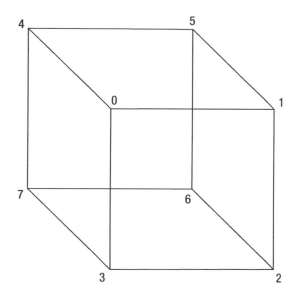

Figure 16-13. The points of a 3D cube

The position of the points are defined like this for our code:

```
//front four corners
points[0] = new Point3d(-100, -100, -100);
points[1] = new Point3d( 100, -100, -100);
points[2] = new Point3d( 100,  100, -100);
points[3] = new Point3d(-100,  100, -100);

//back four corners
points[4] = new Point3d(-100, -100, 100);
points[5] = new Point3d( 100, -100, 100);
```

```
points[6] = new Point3d( 100,  100, 100);
points[7] = new Point3d(-100,  100, 100);
```

Then, you need to define the triangles. Each face of the cube consists of two triangles, so there are 12 triangles altogether—two each for the six faces. Again, we list the points for each triangle in a clockwise direction, as seen from the outer face of the triangle. It gets a little tricky, but rotate the cube in your mind so that the triangle you're defining is facing you, and then list the points in clockwise order from that viewpoint. For example, the front face is easy, and Figure 16-14 shows the two triangles. While continuing to rotate the cube in your mind, you can see the top face in Figure 16-15, and Figure 16-16 shows the back.

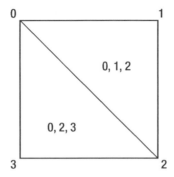

Figure 16-14. The front face of the cube

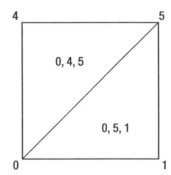

Figure 16-15. The top face of the cube

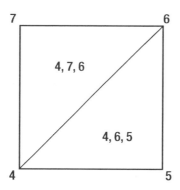

Figure 16-16. The back face of the cube

Moving to each cube face, you come up with the following triangle definitions:

```
//front
triangles[0]  = new Triangle(points[0], points[1], points[2], "#6666cc");
triangles[1]  = new Triangle(points[0], points[2], points[3], "#6666cc");

//top
triangles[2]  = new Triangle(points[0], points[5], points[1], "#66cc66");
triangles[3]  = new Triangle(points[0], points[4], points[5], "#66cc66");

//back
triangles[4]  = new Triangle(points[4], points[6], points[5], "#cc6666");
triangles[5]  = new Triangle(points[4], points[7], points[6], "#cc6666");

//bottom
triangles[6]  = new Triangle(points[3], points[2], points[6], "#cc66cc");
triangles[7]  = new Triangle(points[3], points[6], points[7], "#cc66cc");

//right
triangles[8]  = new Triangle(points[1], points[5], points[6], "#66cccc");
triangles[9]  = new Triangle(points[1], points[6], points[2], "#66cccc");

//left
triangles[10] = new Triangle(points[4], points[0], points[3], "#cccc66");
triangles[11] = new Triangle(points[4], points[3], points[7], "#cccc66");
```

Each face has a different color, because the two triangles that make up the face are the same color. Again, this clockwise orientation doesn't matter right now, but in the next chapter, you use this for *backface culling*. This term refers to a way of determining which surfaces are facing you and which are facing away. You see why this is important in a moment.

The **07-cube.html** example is the same as **06-triangles.html**, with these new point and triangle definitions at the top of the script.

Run this in your browser, and … it's all messed up! You can see some of the back faces, some of the time. Other faces seem invisible all the time. What's going on? Well, the faces on the back of the cube (the back faces) are always being drawn. And the triangles are being drawn in the same order, based on their

403

position in the **triangles** array. So the faces at the bottom of the list always draw over the faces at the top of the list, and you get bizarre, unpredictable results like this. You need to *cull* (get rid of) those back faces, because you don't need to render them.

Backface culling is covered in detail in the next chapter, and you also learn how to apply some basic lighting on each surface, based on its angle. But as a temporary fix for the rest of this chapter, in the definition of the **Triangle** class, set the value of the **alpha** property to 0.5:

```
function Triangle (a, b, c, color) {
  this.pointA = a;
  this.pointB = b;
  this.pointC = c;
  this.color = (color === undefined) ? "#ff0000" : utils.parseColor(color);
  this.lineWidth = 1;
  this.alpha = 0.5;
}
```

Now you can see through any side of the cube, and makes the whole solid look like it's made from colored glass. Again, this is a temporary workaround until we get to backface culling.

Figure 16-17 shows the finished 3D cube.

Figure 16-17. The resulting 3D cube

Modeling other shapes

Now that you've mastered the spinning cube, you can model all kinds of shapes. Just draw them out on a grid, mark up the points and triangles, and put them into the arrays. It often helps to draw several views of the object, rotated so you can see each face and what points make up the triangles. This section offers a few to get you started.

Pyramid

Here's the code for a 3D pyramid (which you can also find in **08-pyramid.html**), starting with the points:

```
points[0] = new Point3d(   0, -100,    0);
points[1] = new Point3d( 100,  100, -100);
points[2] = new Point3d(-100,  100, -100);
points[3] = new Point3d(-100,  100,  100);
points[4] = new Point3d( 100,  100,  100);
```

And here's the code for the triangles:

```
triangles[0] = new Triangle(points[0], points[1], points[2], "#6666cc");
triangles[1] = new Triangle(points[0], points[2], points[3], "#66cc66");
triangles[2] = new Triangle(points[0], points[3], points[4], "#cc6666");
triangles[3] = new Triangle(points[0], points[4], points[1], "#66cccc");
triangles[4] = new Triangle(points[1], points[3], points[2], "#cc66cc");
triangles[5] = new Triangle(points[1], points[4], points[3], "#cc66cc");
```

Figure 16-18 shows the result.

Figure 16-18. A 3D pyramid

Extruded letter A

In **09-extruded-a.html**, we extrude—pull the shape out to give it depth—the earlier letter A example. This means copying the first 11 points, moving one set on the z-axis to −50 and the other set to +50, creating triangles for the second set (making sure they are still going clockwise as seen from the back), and finally making triangles to join the two sides. It's tedious, but looks nice when it's done (you can see the result in Figure 16-19).

```
//first set
points[0]  = new Point3d( -50, -250, -50);
points[1]  = new Point3d(  50, -250, -50);
points[2]  = new Point3d( 200,  250, -50);
points[3]  = new Point3d( 100,  250, -50);
points[4]  = new Point3d(  50,  100, -50);
points[5]  = new Point3d( -50,  100, -50);
points[6]  = new Point3d(-100,  250, -50);
points[7]  = new Point3d(-200,  250, -50);
points[8]  = new Point3d(   0, -150, -50);
points[9]  = new Point3d(  50,    0, -50);
points[10] = new Point3d( -50,    0, -50);

//second set
points[11] = new Point3d( -50, -250,  50);
points[12] = new Point3d(  50, -250,  50);
points[13] = new Point3d( 200,  250,  50);
points[14] = new Point3d( 100,  250,  50);
points[15] = new Point3d(  50,  100,  50);
points[16] = new Point3d( -50,  100,  50);
```

```
points[17] = new Point3d(-100,  250,  50);
points[18] = new Point3d(-200,  250,  50);
points[19] = new Point3d(   0, -150,  50);
points[20] = new Point3d(  50,    0,  50);
points[21] = new Point3d( -50,    0,  50);

triangles[0]  = new Triangle(points[0],  points[1],  points[8],  "#6666cc");
triangles[1]  = new Triangle(points[1],  points[9],  points[8],  "#6666cc");
triangles[2]  = new Triangle(points[1],  points[2],  points[9],  "#6666cc");
triangles[3]  = new Triangle(points[2],  points[4],  points[9],  "#6666cc");
triangles[4]  = new Triangle(points[2],  points[3],  points[4],  "#6666cc");
triangles[5]  = new Triangle(points[4],  points[5],  points[9],  "#6666cc");
triangles[6]  = new Triangle(points[9],  points[5],  points[10], "#6666cc");
triangles[7]  = new Triangle(points[5],  points[6],  points[7],  "#6666cc")
triangles[8]  = new Triangle(points[5],  points[7],  points[10], "#6666cc");
triangles[9]  = new Triangle(points[0],  points[10], points[7],  "#6666cc");
triangles[10] = new Triangle(points[0],  points[8],  points[10], "#6666cc");
triangles[11] = new Triangle(points[11], points[19], points[12], "#cc6666");
triangles[12] = new Triangle(points[12], points[19], points[20], "#cc6666");
triangles[13] = new Triangle(points[12], points[20], points[13], "#cc6666");
triangles[14] = new Triangle(points[13], points[20], points[15], "#cc6666");
triangles[15] = new Triangle(points[13], points[15], points[14], "#cc6666");
triangles[16] = new Triangle(points[15], points[20], points[16], "#cc6666");
triangles[17] = new Triangle(points[20], points[21], points[16], "#cc6666");
triangles[18] = new Triangle(points[16], points[18], points[17], "#cc6666");
triangles[19] = new Triangle(points[16], points[21], points[18], "#cc6666");
triangles[20] = new Triangle(points[11], points[18], points[21], "#cc6666");
triangles[21] = new Triangle(points[11], points[21], points[19], "#cc6666");
triangles[22] = new Triangle(points[0],  points[11], points[1],  "#cccc66");
triangles[23] = new Triangle(points[11], points[12], points[1],  "#cccc66");
triangles[24] = new Triangle(points[1],  points[12], points[2],  "#cccc66");
triangles[25] = new Triangle(points[12], points[13], points[2],  "#cccc66");
triangles[26] = new Triangle(points[3],  points[2],  points[14], "#cccc66");
triangles[27] = new Triangle(points[2],  points[13], points[14], "#cccc66");
triangles[28] = new Triangle(points[4],  points[3],  points[15], "#cccc66");
triangles[29] = new Triangle(points[3],  points[14], points[15], "#cccc66");
triangles[30] = new Triangle(points[5],  points[4],  points[16], "#cccc66");
triangles[31] = new Triangle(points[4],  points[15], points[16], "#cccc66");
triangles[32] = new Triangle(points[6],  points[5],  points[17], "#cccc66");
triangles[33] = new Triangle(points[5],  points[16], points[17], "#cccc66");
triangles[34] = new Triangle(points[7],  points[6],  points[18], "#cccc66");
triangles[35] = new Triangle(points[6],  points[17], points[18], "#cccc66");
triangles[36] = new Triangle(points[0],  points[7],  points[11], "#cccc66");
triangles[37] = new Triangle(points[7],  points[18], points[11], "#cccc66");
triangles[38] = new Triangle(points[8],  points[9],  points[19], "#cccc66");
triangles[39] = new Triangle(points[9],  points[20], points[19], "#cccc66");
triangles[40] = new Triangle(points[9],  points[10], points[20], "#cccc66");
triangles[41] = new Triangle(points[10], points[21], points[20], "#cccc66");
triangles[42] = new Triangle(points[10], points[8],  points[21], "#cccc66");
triangles[43] = new Triangle(points[8],  points[19], points[21], "#cccc66");
```

Figure 16-19. An extruded letter A

As you can see, triangles build up quickly when you create 3D models. The original, flat, A had 11 triangles. Extruding it somehow quadrupled that! This code still runs pretty smoothly, but you aren't going to get any massive 3D worlds with thousands of polygons by drawing them out on the canvas element this way. Still, you can do some pretty cool things. And with web browsers improving in performance with each release, and new technologies like WebGL on the horizon, who knows what the future holds?

Cylinder

Here's one more shape example, and this time we'll create points and triangles with some math. The only thing we change in this example, **10-cylinder.html**, is at the top of the script. Instead of defining points and triangles by hand, we create an algorithm to do it for us and make a cylinder. Here's that portion of the code:

```
var points = [],
    numFaces = 20;

for (var angle, xpos, ypos, i = 0, idx = 0; i < numFaces; i++) {
  angle = Math.PI * 2 / numFaces * i;
  xpos = Math.cos(angle) * 200;
  ypos = Math.sin(angle) * 200;
  points[idx]   = new Point3d(xpos, ypos, -100);
  points[idx+1] = new Point3d(xpos, ypos,  100);
  idx += 2;
}

points.forEach(function (point) {
  point.setVanishingPoint(vpX, vpY);
  point.setCenter(0, 0, 200);
});

for (i = 0, idx = 0; i < numFaces - 1; i++) {
  triangles[idx] = new Triangle(points[idx], points[idx+3], points[idx+1], "#6666cc");
  triangles[idx+1] = new Triangle(points[idx], points[idx+2], points[idx+3], "#6666cc");
  idx += 2;
}
```

```
triangles[idx] = new Triangle(points[idx], points[1], points[idx+1], "#6666cc");
triangles[idx+1] = new Triangle(points[idx], points[0], points[1], "#6666cc");
```

This probably isn't the most straightforward code, so let's step through it with some explanation and maybe a diagram or two.

You loop around in a full circle and create points at certain intervals. For each iteration you calculate an angle, which is the full circle, divided by the number of faces, times the particular segment you're working on.

With that angle (and some trigonometry you should be well used to by now), determine the x, y position for the point on the circle. You then make two points, one with a z of -100 and one with a z of +100. When this loop is done, you have two circles of points, one close to you and one a bit farther away. Now you need to connect them with triangles.

Again, you iterate over each face, this time creating two triangles. Seen from the side, the first face looks like Figure 16-20.

This makes the two triangles:

```
0, 3, 1
0, 2, 3
```

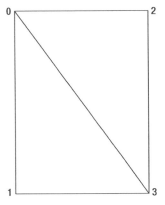

Figure 16-20. The first face of the cylinder

Because the index (**idx**) variable is initialized to 0, you can also define these like so:

```
idx, idx + 3, idx + 1
idx, idx + 2, idx + 3
```

This is exactly how you define the two triangles. You then increase **idx** by 2 to handle the next face with points 2, 3, 4, and 5.

You continue iterating up to the second-to-last face, and then connect the last one back to the first two points, 0 and 1, as shown in Figure 16-21.

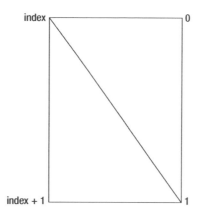

Figure 16-21. The last face of the cylinder

These wind up as follows:

```
idx, 1, idx + 1
idx, 0, 1
```

The result is shown in Figure 16-22. If you want to make the construction of this shape a little clearer, increase the `lineWidth` property of each `Triangle` object.

Figure 16-22. The resulting 3D cylinder

Moving 3D solids

Moving a 3D solid is easy now that you have the `Point3d` class, just change its center with the `setCenter` method. You've already moved a shape on the z-axis, and it's the same for positioning on the x and y axis. But let's take a quick look at what happens when you change those values. It's all in the `getScreenX` and `getScreenY` methods of the `Point3d` class:

```
Point3d.prototype.getScreenX = function () {
  var scale = this.fl / (this.fl + this.z + this.cZ);
```

```
    return this.vpX + (this.cX + this.x) * scale;
};

Point3d.prototype.getScreenY = function () {
  var scale = this.fl / (this.fl + this.z + this.cZ);
  return this.vpY + (this.cY + this.y) * scale;
};
```

The center z value (`this.cZ`) is added to the z position (`this.z`) when the scale is calculated, effectively pushing the point out into the distance without altering the z position itself.

The same thing happens with **this.cX** and **this.cY**. They are added to the x and y positions, and then the scale is applied. This pushes the point off in one of those directions, without permanently altering its position. Because we are not changing any of these values, the point—and thus the larger shape that it is part of—continues to rotate around its own center, rather than orbiting around the center of the 3D coordinate space for our scene.

Let's see this in action. Go back to the **07-cube.html** example, and add two variables at the top of the script:

```
var offsetX = 0,
    offsetY = 0;
```

Now add a **keydown** event handler to change the offset using the arrow keys:

```
window.addEventListener('keydown', function (event) {
  if (event.keyCode === 37) {          //left
    offsetX = -5;
  } else if (event.keyCode === 39) {   //right
    offsetX = 5;
  } else if (event.keyCode === 38) {   //up
    offsetY = -5;
  } else if (event.keyCode === 40) {   //down
    offsetY = 5;
  }

  points.forEach(function (point) {
    point.x += offsetX;
    point.y += offsetY;
  });
}, false);
```

This loops through each point and adds or subtracts 5 from its value (you can find the complete file in **11-move-cube-1.html**). Because the actual positions of all the points are changing, the model now orbits around the center of the 3D space. This might or might not be what you want it to do. If you want to move the whole model, and still have it rotate around its own center, you need to use the point's **setCenter** method. Change the event handler code we just added to the following:

```
window.addEventListener('keydown', function (event) {
  if (event.keyCode === 37) {          //left
    offsetX -= 5;
  } else if (event.keyCode === 39) {   //right
    offsetX += 5;
```

```
  } else if (event.keyCode === 38) {  //up
    offsetY -= 5;
  } else if (event.keyCode === 40) {  //down
    offsetY += 5;
  }

  points.forEach(function (point) {
    point.setCenter(offsetX, offsetY, 200);
  });
}, false);
```

This example can be found in document 12-move-cube-2.html. Now the entire cube moves as a whole and continues to rotate around its center, but it does not orbit around the center of the scene's 3D coordinate space.

Summary

With what you learned in this chapter, you should be on your way to modeling your own 3D shapes on and manipulating them in 3D space.

This chapter concentrated on creating 3D geometry and how to draw the lines and color fills. In the next chapter, you explore how to create more solid-looking solids. All that material builds on the foundation of points, lines, and fills that you covered here. So, when you're ready, let's move on!

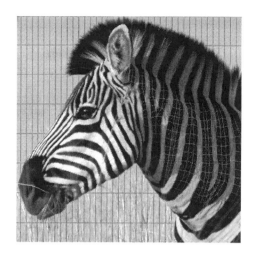

Chapter 17

Backface Culling and 3D Lighting

What we'll cover in this chapter:

- Backface culling
- Enhanced depth sorting
- 3D lighting

In the previous chapter, we looked at the basics of modeling 3D solids: how to create the points, lines, and polygons that make up a form, and how to give each polygon a color. But if you recall, that color was left at 50% transparency, so you could see right through it. Although we created some complex 3D shapes, the models still lack a lot in terms of realism.

In this chapter, we fix that by learning about backface culling (not drawing the polygons facing away from you), enhanced depth sorting (we covered this a bit in Chapter 15, but we take a new look at it in terms of polygons), and 3D lighting.

You should be amazed at the results on your 3D models once these three techniques are applied. After the first two, you will be able to create 3D solids that look solid. And with 3D lighting, they really come alive.

In the examples presented here, we build on the rotating, extruded, 3D letter A that was created in the previous chapter. This serves as a sufficiently complex model that makes it obvious if you do something wrong, and looks pretty good when you do everything right! The foundation of this chapter was provided by the techniques described by Todd Yard in Chapter 10 of *Macromedia Flash MX Studio* (friends of ED, 2002).

Backface culling

Backface culling was mentioned a couple of times in the previous chapter, and now you find out what it is all about and exactly how it works.

Remember that in the earlier models, you made all the color fills semitransparent. The reason for this was that you were always drawing every polygon, and you had no control over what order they were drawn in. So a polygon on the back of the model might get drawn on top of one on the front of the model, creating some odd looking results. Giving every face an alpha value of 50% made them all relatively equal and let us put off this discussion while you concentrated on your modeling techniques. Now, you are going to deal with it.

In principle, backface culling is simple. You draw the polygons that are facing you, and you don't draw the ones that are facing away from you. The tricky part is determining which are which.

You were constantly reminded to define the points of each polygon in a clockwise direction. Even though that is unnecessary for the examples so far, you now see why this is so important, and why it is good to get into the habit from the start.

It's an interesting observation that if the points of a polygon are arranged in a clockwise fashion when the triangle is facing you, they are counterclockwise when the polygon is facing away from you. You can see this demonstrated in Figure 17-1, which has a triangle facing you. (A note on terminology in this book: For the most part, "polygon" is used as a general term, and "triangle" for a specific triangular polygon under discussion.)

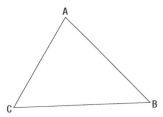

Figure 17-1. A triangle facing you has points in a clockwise direction.

In Figure 17-2, the triangle has been rotated so it is facing in the opposite direction.

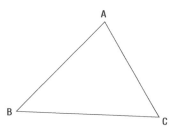

Figure 17-2. A triangle facing away from you has points in a counterclockwise direction.

Now you see that points go around in a counterclockwise direction.

But what does it mean when a polygon is "facing you"? It means that the *exterior* side of the polygon is facing you. Although it's not obvious when we look at a single triangle, remember that we're talking about solids in 3D space. In that case, each polygon has one exterior side and one interior side.

There are times when you want to draw the opposite side of the triangle. For example, if the viewport is located inside a cube and looking out, you want to see the interior sides—the walls, ceiling, and floor. But for the examples here, looking *at* a model, you want to view the exterior sides of the geometry that it's made of.

When determining if a polygon is clockwise or counterclockwise, we refer to the *screen* positions of the points—not the 3D x, y, and z positions, but the getScreenX(), getScreenY() position that is the location on the canvas determined by applying perspective.

You can reverse the setup and make a system where counterclockwise polygons face you, and clockwise ones faced away. Either way works as long as you are consistent.

So again, we return to the question: How do you determine whether three points are arranged in a clockwise or counterclockwise direction? It's such an easy thing for your eyes to pick out, but when it comes to writing it down in code, the problem suddenly seems like an abstract concept.

What you do is add a method to the Triangle class, called isBackface. This evaluates the three points that make up the triangle, and returns true if they are counterclockwise and false if they are clockwise. Here is the updated Triangle class with the new method (file triangle.js). Notice that alpha is set to 1, since we are drawing opaque shapes in this chapter:

```
function Triangle (a, b, c, color) {
  this.pointA = a;
  this.pointB = b;
  this.pointC = c;
  this.color = (color === undefined) ? "#ff0000" : utils.parseColor(color);
  this.lineWidth = 1;
  this.alpha = 1;
}

Triangle.prototype.draw = function (context) {
  if (this.isBackface()) {
    return;
  }

  context.save();
  context.lineWidth = this.lineWidth;
  context.fillStyle = context.strokeStyle = utils.colorToRGB(this.color, this.alpha);
  context.beginPath();
  context.moveTo(this.pointA.getScreenX(), this.pointA.getScreenY());
  context.lineTo(this.pointB.getScreenX(), this.pointB.getScreenY());
  context.lineTo(this.pointC.getScreenX(), this.pointC.getScreenY());
  context.closePath();
  context.fill();
  if (this.lineWidth > 0) {
    context.stroke();
```

```
  }
  context.restore();
};

Triangle.prototype.isBackface = function () {
  var cax = this.pointC.getScreenX() - this.pointA.getScreenX(),
      cay = this.pointC.getScreenY() - this.pointA.getScreenY(),
      bcx = this.pointB.getScreenX() - this.pointC.getScreenX(),
      bcy = this.pointB.getScreenY() - this.pointC.getScreenY();
  return (cax * bcy > cay * bcx);
};
```

For a quick explanation, the isBackface function calculates the lengths of two sides of the triangle, and with some multiplication and comparison involving the triangle's normal vector relative to the camera, is able to tell which direction they are going.

So, how do you use this method? Well, you don't really need to think about it; the function is called only from within the Triangle.draw method. If it returns true, it is a back-face triangle and should not be drawn, so the draw method stops there and returns. If isBackface returns false, the triangle is facing forward and is rendered as usual using the canvas drawing API.

Now, you can run 01-extruded-a.html, or any other 3D model you created, and you see that things look quite a bit different. As you rotate the shape around, you see that as soon as a particular face is facing the other way, it is no longer drawn. Things aren't perfect yet, because there are still parts that are farther away drawing on top of parts that are closer, but we're getting there. If the term "z-sorting," or "depth sorting," just came to mind, you're right on track—and that's what's coming up next.

Right now you should be looking at something similar to what appears in Figure 17-3.

Figure 17-3. Backface culling in action

Enhanced depth sorting

Depth sorting, or z-sorting, is something we discussed in Chapter 15, when you applied perspective to the shapes. In that case, you sorted the array of objects (which had 3D properties) by their zpos property.

But now, you are not dealing with multiple objects. Whenever a particular polygon is drawn, it is drawn on top of any that have been drawn earlier. Rather than swapping an object's depth, you need to determine the order that each polygon is drawn. Specifically, you want to draw the ones that are farthest away first; then you draw the rest, working your way forward, so that the closest polygons are drawn last, covering anything they might be in front of.

So how do you do that? Well, you have all the polygons in an array called triangles. When you draw the shape, you iterate through this array drawing each triangle from first element through the end. You must sort this array so that the triangle that is farthest away is in element zero, and the one closest to the viewer is in the last element of the array.

This is similar to what we did when sorting the array of objects, but here, the triangles are just a collection of three Point3d objects. They don't have a single property that describes the overall depth of the triangle. However, it is easy enough to create such a property. It turns out that the value that works best is the minimum z value of the three points within a triangle. In other words, if a triangle had three points with depths 200, 250, and 300, we should say this triangle is at a z position of 200.

We can use the Math.min function to determine the minimum z value of all three points. We do this within a new getDepth method that we add to our Triangle class. Here's that function to add to the file triangle.js:

```
Triangle.prototype.getDepth = function () {
  return Math.min(this.pointA.z, this.pointB.z, this.pointC.z);
};
```

Now you can sort the array of triangle objects and know which to draw first and which to draw last. Again, you want to sort it in descending order so that the one with the highest depth (farthest away) is first. You calculate this in the drawFrame animation loop, before you draw any of the triangles. Here's the updated section of our example in 02-extruded-a-depth.html:

```
function depth (a, b) {
  return (b.getDepth() - a.getDepth());
}

(function drawFrame () {
  window.requestAnimationFrame(drawFrame, canvas);
  context.clearRect(0, 0, canvas.width, canvas.height);

  angleX = (mouse.y - vpY) * 0.0005;
  angleY = (mouse.x - vpX) * 0.0005;

  points.forEach(move);
  triangles.sort(depth);
  triangles.forEach(draw);
}());
```

When you run this exercise in your browser, you should have a perfectly rendered solid, as shown in Figure 17-4. You've made real progress here, and the next step boosts this example over the top in terms of realism!

Figure 17-4. Sorting the depths puts it all right!

3D lighting

Although the previous example does a nice job with the render accuracy, it still lacks a bit of realism—it's a bit flat. You already know where we're heading with this, so let's add some 3D lighting.

Like backface culling, the specifics behind 3D lighting can get complex and math intensive. We don't want to get into a detailed discussion of all the finer points, but there's plenty of information on the web about the equations. What you have here are the basics, along with some functions you can use and adapt as needed.

First, you need a light source. The simplest light source has two properties: location and brightness. In more complex 3D systems, it might point in a certain direction, have a color of its own, have falloff rates, conical areas, and so on. But all that is beyond the scope of what you are doing here.

Let's start out by making a Light class to hold the two properties we just mentioned: location and brightness. Save this code as file light.js:

```
function Light (x, y, z, brightness) {
  this.x = (x === undefined) ? -100 : x;
  this.y = (y === undefined) ? -100 : y;
  this.z = (z === undefined) ? -100 : z;
  this.brightness = (brightness === undefined) ? 1 : brightness;
}

Light.prototype.setBrightness = function (b) {
  this.brightness = Math.min(Math.max(b, 0), 1);
};
```

Now, at the top of your script, you can create a new default light like so:

```
var light = new Light();
```

Or, you can create a light with a particular position and location like this:

```
var light = new Light(100, 200, 300, 0.5);
```

Two things are important here. The distance between the object and light position has no affect on how brightly the object is lit. The coordinates of the light are used only to calculate the angle that the light ray bounces off the object and into the viewpoint for us to see it. Because the strength of the light you are creating does not fall off with distance, changing the x, y, and z to -1,000,000 or down to -1 makes no difference to the object brightness. Only the brightness property changes that characteristic of the light. You can certainly add this functionality, altering the brightness value based on the distance from the light to the area it is hitting, but that exercise is left to you.

Also, brightness must be a number from 0.0 to 1.0. If you go outside of that range, you can wind up with some odd results from the forthcoming calculations. This is something you can play around with, but for more realistic lighting effects, you want to stay within this range. For this reason, the brightness property is adjusted using the method setBrightness. This enables us to validate the number that is passed in, to make sure it falls within the specified range; this is known as *clamping* the light.

Now, the light source changes the brightness of the color of a triangle, based on the angle of the light that is falling on that polygon. If the polygon is facing directly at the light, it displays the full value of its color. As it turns away from the light, it gets darker and darker. Finally, when it is facing in the opposite direction of the light source, it is completely in shadow and colored black.

Because Triangle objects keep track of their own color and know how to draw themselves, each triangle also needs access to this light to perform calculations in its drawing function. So, in the Triangle constructor, give it a light property:

```
function Triangle (a, b, c, color) {
  this.pointA = a;
  this.pointB = b;
  this.pointC = c;
  this.color = (color === undefined) ? "#ff0000" : utils.parseColor(color);
  this.lineWidth = 1;
  this.alpha - 1;
  this.light = null;
}
```

Then in the main script, assign each triangle a reference to the light object that we created:

```
triangles.forEach(function (triangle) {
  triangle.light = light;
});
```

Now, each Triangle object requires a way to look at its base color and the angle and brightness of the light, and return an adjusted color. Here is that method:

```
Triangle.prototype.getAdjustedColor = function () {
  var color = utils.parseColor(this.color, true),
```

```
      red = color >> 16,
      green = color >> 8 & 0xff,
      blue = color & 0xff,
      lightFactor = this.getLightFactor();

  red *= lightFactor;
  green *= lightFactor;
  blue *= lightFactor;
  return utils.parseColor(red << 16 | green << 8 | blue);
};
```

This method first splits the triangle's base color into red, green, and blue components (see Chapter 4). The command `utils.parseColor(this.color, true)` converts the color from a string format to a number. There is a call to `getLightFactor`, which we'll look at next, but for now, it returns a number from 0.0 to 1.0. This is the amount to alter the color of that particular triangle, 1.0 being full brightness, and 0.0 being black.

Each of the component colors is then multiplied by that light factor, and they are joined back into a single color value—using `utils.parseColor` to convert it back to a string—and is returned as the adjusted color. This is the color of the triangle, based on its lighting.

Now, how do you come up with this `lightFactor` method? Let's look:

```
Triangle.prototype.getLightFactor = function () {
  var ab = {
    x: this.pointA.x - this.pointB.x,
    y: this.pointA.y - this.pointB.y,
    z: this.pointA.z - this.pointB.z
  };
  var bc = {
    x: this.pointB.x - this.pointC.x,
    y: this.pointB.y - this.pointC.y,
    z: this.pointB.z - this.pointC.z
  };
  var norm = {
    x:  (ab.y * bc.z) - (ab.z * bc.y),
    y:-((ab.x * bc.z) - (ab.z * bc.x)),
    z:  (ab.x * bc.y) - (ab.y * bc.x)
  };
  var dotProd = norm.x * this.light.x +
                norm.y * this.light.y +
                norm.z * this.light.z;
  var normMag = Math.sqrt(norm.x * norm.x +
                          norm.y * norm.y +
                          norm.z * norm.z);
  var lightMag = Math.sqrt(this.light.x * this.light.x +
                           this.light.y * this.light.y +
                           this.light.z * this.light.z);
  return (Math.acos(dotProd / (normMag * lightMag)) / Math.PI) * this.light.brightness;
};
```

Now that is quite a function to take in. To *fully* understand all that's going on here, you need a good grasp of advanced vector math, but we'll walk through the basics of it.

First, you need to find the normal of the triangle. This is a vector that is perpendicular to the surface of the triangle, depicted in Figure 17-5 and mentioned briefly in the last chapter. Imagine you had a triangular piece of wood and you put a nail through the back of it so it stuck out directly through the face. The nail represents the normal of that surface. If you study anything about 3D rendering and lighting, you see all kinds of references to surface normals.

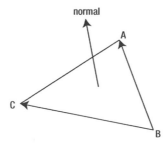

Figure 17-5. The normal is perpendicular to the surface of the triangle.

You can find the normal of a surface by taking two vectors that make up that surface plane and calculating their *cross product*. A cross product of two vectors is a new vector, which is perpendicular to those two. The two vectors you use are the lines between points A and B, and points B and C. Each vector is held in an object with x, y, and z properties.

```
var ab = {
  x: this.pointA.x - this.pointB.x,
  y: this.pointA.y - this.pointB.y,
  z: this.pointA.z - this.pointB.z
};

var bc = {
  x: this.pointB.x - this.pointC.x,
  y: this.pointB.y - this.pointC.y,
  z: this.pointB.z - this.pointC.z
};
```

Then you calculate the normal, which is another vector, and you call this object norm. The following code computes the cross product of the vectors ab and bc, using a standard formula from linear algebra:

```
var norm = {
  x:   (ab.y * bc.z) - (ab.z * bc.y),
  y: -((ab.x * bc.z) - (ab.z * bc.x)),
  z:   (ab.x * bc.y) - (ab.y * bc.x)
};
```

Now you need to know how closely that normal aligns with the angle of the light. Another bit of vector math is the *dot product,* which is the difference between two vectors. You have the vector of the normal, and the vector of the light. The following calculates that dot product:

```
var dotProd = norm.x * this.light.x +
```

```
          norm.y * this.light.y +
          norm.z * this.light.z;
```

As you can see, dot products are a bit simpler than cross products!

Next, you calculate the magnitude of the normal and the magnitude of the light, which you might recognize as the 3D version of the Pythagorean Theorem:

```
var normMag = Math.sqrt(norm.x * norm.x +
                        norm.y * norm.y +
                        norm.z * norm.z);
var lightMag = Math.sqrt(this.light.x * this.light.x +
                         this.light.y * this.light.y +
                         this.light.z * this.light.z);
```

This `lightMag` variable is calculated every time a triangle is rendered, which allows for a moving light source. If you know that the light source is going to be fixed, you can create this variable at the beginning of the code and calculate it one time as soon as the light is created or assigned to the triangle. Alternatively, you can add a `lightMag` property to the `Light` class. This can be calculated any time its x, y, or z properties changed.

Finally, you take all these pieces you just calculated, and put them into the magic formula:

```
return (Math.acos(dotProd / (normMag * lightMag)) / Math.PI) * this.light.brightness;
```

Basically, `dotProd` is one measurement and (`normMag * lightMag`) is another. Dividing these two gives you a ratio. Recall from our discussion in Chapter 3 that the cosine of an angle gives you a ratio, and the arccosine of a ratio gives you an angle. So using `Math.acos` here on this ratio of measurements gives you an angle. This is essentially the angle at which the light is striking the surface of the polygon. It is in the range of 0 to `Math.PI` radians (0 to 180 degrees), meaning it's either hitting head on or completely from behind.

Dividing this angle by `Math.PI` gives you a percentage, and multiplying that by the percentage of brightness gives you your final light factor, which you use to alter the base color.

All this was just to get a new color for the surface! Implementing it in your existing code is pretty easy—you add it to the `draw` method of the `Triangle` class. Instead of using the base color, use the adjusted color, like so:

```
context.fillStyle = context.strokeStyle = this.getAdjustedColor();
```

To wrap things up, here is the complete and final code for `triangle.js` and the document `03-extruded-a-light.html`.

First, here's the `Triangle` class:

```
function Triangle (a, b, c, color) {
  this.pointA = a;
  this.pointB = b;
  this.pointC = c;
  this.color = (color === undefined) ? "#ff0000" : utils.parseColor(color);
  this.lineWidth = 1;
  this.alpha = 1;
```

```
  this.light = null;
}

Triangle.prototype.draw = function (context) {
  if (this.isBackface()) {
    return;
  }

  context.save();
  context.lineWidth = this.lineWidth;
  context.fillStyle = context.strokeStyle = this.getAdjustedColor();
  context.beginPath();
  context.moveTo(this.pointA.getScreenX(), this.pointA.getScreenY());
  context.lineTo(this.pointB.getScreenX(), this.pointB.getScreenY());
  context.lineTo(this.pointC.getScreenX(), this.pointC.getScreenY());
  context.closePath();
  context.fill();
  if (this.lineWidth > 0) {
    context.stroke();
  }
  context.restore();
};

Triangle.prototype.isBackface = function () {
  var cax = this.pointC.getScreenX() - this.pointA.getScreenX(),
      cay = this.pointC.getScreenY() - this.pointA.getScreenY(),
      bcx = this.pointB.getScreenX() - this.pointC.getScreenX(),
      bcy = this.pointB.getScreenY() - this.pointC.getScreenY();
  return (cax * bcy > cay * bcx);
};

Triangle.prototype.getDepth = function () {
  return Math.min(this.pointA.z, this.pointB.z, this.pointC.z);
};

Triangle.prototype.getAdjustedColor = function () {
  var color = utils.parseColor(this.color, true),
      red = color >> 16,
      green = color >> 8 & 0xff,
      blue = color & 0xff,
      lightFactor = this.getLightFactor();
  red *= lightFactor;
  green *= lightFactor;
  blue *= lightFactor;
  return utils.parseColor(red << 16 | green << 8 | blue);
};

Triangle.prototype.getLightFactor = function () {
  var ab = {
    x: this.pointA.x - this.pointB.x,
    y: this.pointA.y - this.pointB.y,
    z: this.pointA.z - this.pointB.z
  };
```

423

```
  var bc = {
    x: this.pointB.x - this.pointC.x,
    y: this.pointB.y - this.pointC.y,
    z: this.pointB.z - this.pointC.z
  };
  var norm = {
    x:  (ab.y * bc.z) - (ab.z * bc.y),
    y:-((ab.x * bc.z) - (ab.z * bc.x)),
    z:  (ab.x * bc.y) - (ab.y * bc.x)
  };
  var dotProd = norm.x * this.light.x +
                norm.y * this.light.y +
                norm.z * this.light.z;
  var normMag = Math.sqrt(norm.x * norm.x +
                          norm.y * norm.y +
                          norm.z * norm.z);
  var lightMag = Math.sqrt(this.light.x * this.light.x +
                           this.light.y * this.light.y +
                           this.light.z * this.light.z);
  return (Math.acos(dotProd / (normMag * lightMag)) / Math.PI) *
  this.light.brightness;
};
```

And here's the code for example 03-extruded-a-light.html:

```
<!doctype html>
<html>
 <head>
  <meta charset="utf-8">
  <title>Extruded A Light</title>
  <link rel="stylesheet" href="style.css">
 </head>
 <body>
  <canvas id="canvas" width="400" height="400"></canvas>
  <script src="utils.js"></script>
  <script src="point3d.js"></script>
  <script src="triangle.js"></script>
  <script src="light.js"></script>
  <script>
  window.onload = function () {
    var canvas = document.getElementById('canvas'),
        context = canvas.getContext('2d'),
        mouse = utils.captureMouse(canvas),
        light = new Light(),
        points = [],
        triangles = [],
        fl = 250,
        vpX = canvas.width / 2,
        vpY = canvas.height / 2,
        angleX, angleY; //referenced in drawFrame and move

    //first set
    points[0]  = new Point3d( -50, -250, -50);
    points[1]  = new Point3d(  50, -250, -50);
```

```
points[2]  = new Point3d( 200,  250, -50);
points[3]  = new Point3d( 100,  250, -50);
points[4]  = new Point3d(  50,  100, -50);
points[5]  = new Point3d( -50,  100, -50);
points[6]  = new Point3d(-100,  250, -50);
points[7]  = new Point3d(-200,  250, -50);
points[8]  = new Point3d(   0, -150, -50);
points[9]  = new Point3d(  50,    0, -50);
points[10] = new Point3d( -50,    0, -50);

//second set
points[11] = new Point3d( -50, -250,  50);
points[12] = new Point3d(  50, -250,  50);
points[13] = new Point3d( 200,  250,  50);
points[14] = new Point3d( 100,  250,  50);
points[15] = new Point3d(  50,  100,  50);
points[16] = new Point3d( -50,  100,  50);
points[17] = new Point3d(-100,  250,  50);
points[18] = new Point3d(-200,  250,  50);
points[19] = new Point3d(   0, -150,  50);
points[20] = new Point3d(  50,    0,  50);
points[21] = new Point3d( -50,    0,  50);

points.forEach(function (point) {
  point.setVanishingPoint(vpX, vpY);
  point.setCenter(0, 0, 200);
});

triangles[0]  = new Triangle(points[0],  points[1],  points[8],  "#cccccc");
triangles[1]  = new Triangle(points[1],  points[9],  points[8],  "#cccccc");
triangles[2]  = new Triangle(points[1],  points[2],  points[9],  "#cccccc");
triangles[3]  = new Triangle(points[2],  points[4],  points[9],  "#cccccc");
triangles[4]  = new Triangle(points[2],  points[3],  points[4],  "#cccccc");
triangles[5]  = new Triangle(points[4],  points[5],  points[9],  "#cccccc");
triangles[6]  = new Triangle(points[9],  points[5],  points[10], "#cccccc");
triangles[7]  = new Triangle(points[5],  points[6],  points[7],  "#cccccc");
triangles[8]  = new Triangle(points[5],  points[7],  points[10], "#cccccc");
triangles[9]  = new Triangle(points[0],  points[10], points[7],  "#cccccc");
triangles[10] = new Triangle(points[0],  points[8],  points[10], "#cccccc");
triangles[11] = new Triangle(points[11], points[19], points[12], "#cccccc");
triangles[12] = new Triangle(points[12], points[19], points[20], "#cccccc");
triangles[13] = new Triangle(points[12], points[20], points[13], "#cccccc");
triangles[14] = new Triangle(points[13], points[20], points[15], "#cccccc");
triangles[15] = new Triangle(points[13], points[15], points[14], "#cccccc");
triangles[16] = new Triangle(points[15], points[20], points[16], "#cccccc");
triangles[17] = new Triangle(points[20], points[21], points[16], "#cccccc");
triangles[18] = new Triangle(points[16], points[18], points[17], "#cccccc");
triangles[19] = new Triangle(points[16], points[21], points[18], "#cccccc");
triangles[20] = new Triangle(points[11], points[18], points[21], "#cccccc");
triangles[21] = new Triangle(points[11], points[21], points[19], "#cccccc");
triangles[22] = new Triangle(points[0],  points[11], points[1],  "#cccccc");
triangles[23] = new Triangle(points[11], points[12], points[1],  "#cccccc");
triangles[24] = new Triangle(points[1],  points[12], points[2],  "#cccccc");
triangles[25] = new Triangle(points[12], points[13], points[2],  "#cccccc");
```

```
triangles[26] = new Triangle(points[3],  points[2],  points[14], "#cccccc");
triangles[27] = new Triangle(points[2],  points[13], points[14], "#cccccc");
triangles[28] = new Triangle(points[4],  points[3],  points[15], "#cccccc");
triangles[29] = new Triangle(points[3],  points[14], points[15], "#cccccc");
triangles[30] = new Triangle(points[5],  points[4],  points[16], "#cccccc");
triangles[31] = new Triangle(points[4],  points[15], points[16], "#cccccc");
triangles[32] = new Triangle(points[6],  points[5],  points[17], "#cccccc");
triangles[33] = new Triangle(points[5],  points[16], points[17], "#cccccc");
triangles[34] = new Triangle(points[7],  points[6],  points[18], "#cccccc");
triangles[35] = new Triangle(points[6],  points[17], points[18], "#cccccc");
triangles[36] = new Triangle(points[0],  points[7],  points[11], "#cccccc");
triangles[37] = new Triangle(points[7],  points[18], points[11], "#cccccc");
triangles[38] = new Triangle(points[8],  points[9],  points[19], "#cccccc");
triangles[39] = new Triangle(points[9],  points[20], points[19], "#cccccc");
triangles[40] = new Triangle(points[9],  points[10], points[20], "#cccccc");
triangles[41] = new Triangle(points[10], points[21], points[20], "#cccccc");
triangles[42] = new Triangle(points[10], points[8],  points[21], "#cccccc");
triangles[43] = new Triangle(points[8],  points[19], points[21], "#cccccc");

triangles.forEach(function (triangle) {
  triangle.light = light;
});

function move (point) {
  point.rotateX(angleX);
  point.rotateY(angleY);
}

function depth (a, b) {
  return (b.getDepth() - a.getDepth());
}

function draw (triangle) {
  triangle.draw(context);
}

(function drawFrame () {
  window.requestAnimationFrame(drawFrame, canvas);
  context.clearRect(0, 0, canvas.width, canvas.height);

  angleX = (mouse.y - vpY) * 0.0005;
  angleY = (mouse.x - vpX) * 0.0005;

  points.forEach(move);
  triangles.sort(depth);
  triangles.forEach(draw);
}());
};
</script>
</body>
</html>
```

As you can see, there are only minor changes to the main document, because most of the work happens in Triangle class. However, all the triangles are now the same color, which shows off the lighting effect much better (see Figure 17-6).

Figure 17-6. 3D solid with backface culling, depth sorting, and 3D lighting

Summary

That was a lot to cover in just a few pages! But the results are incredible and you now have the tools to make some stunning 3D animations. There are a lot of variations you can throw in here; for instance, in the last example, the light is stationary and the object moves. Try moving the light around instead. (It's just a matter of altering its x, y, and/or z positions.)

That about wraps up our main discussion of 3D. In the next chapter, you look at matrix math, which is often used as an alternative to some of the scaling and rotation methods you used so far, and thus is something you often see in 3D programming.

Part V

Additional Techniques

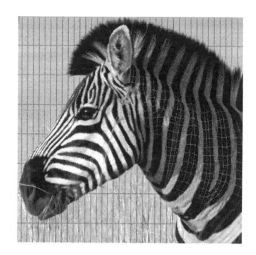

Chapter 18

Matrix Math

What we'll cover in this chapter:

- Matrix basics
- Matrix operations
- Canvas transforms

Although this chapter does not introduce any new types of motion or methods of rendering graphics, it does introduce *matrices,* which provide an alternative way of applying visual transformations, something we've done throughout the book.

Matrices are used quite often in 3D systems for rotating, scaling, and translating (moving) 3D points. They are also used quite a bit in various 2D graphics transformations. In this chapter, you see how to create a system of matrices to manipulate objects and look at several methods built into the canvas that are used to work with matrices.

Matrix basics

A matrix, by simplest definition, is a grid of numbers. It can have one or more horizontal rows and one or more vertical columns. Figure 18-1 shows some matrices.

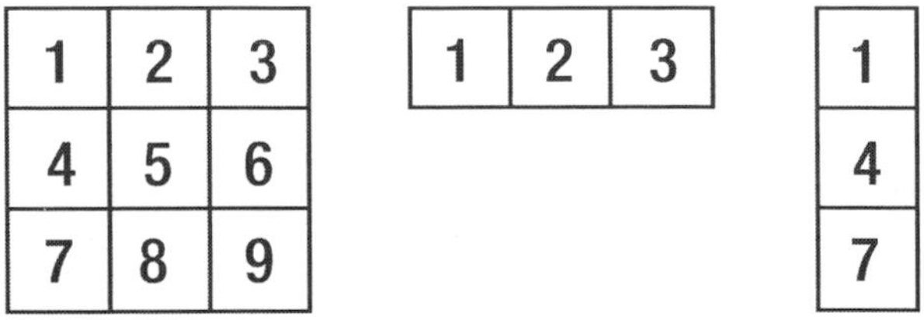

1	2	3
4	5	6
7	8	9

1	2	3

1
4
7

Figure 18-1. A 3 × 3 matrix, a 1 × 3 matrix, and a 3 × 1 matrix; each uses the rows by columns notation.

Any particular matrix is usually represented by a variable, such as M. To refer to a specific cell in a matrix, you use the variable name with the row and column number in subscript. For example, if the 3 × 3 matrix in Figure 18-1 is denoted as M, then using the rows by colums notation, $M_{2,3}$ is equal to 6, as it refers to the second row, third column. Matrix indices start at 1, which is different than the notation for JavaScript arrays, which start at 0.

The cells of a matrix can contain not only numbers, but also formulas and variables. If you've ever used a spreadsheet, it is basically one big matrix. You can have one cell hold the sum of a column, and another cell multiply that sum by some number that's held in another cell, and so on. So, you see that matrices can be rather useful.

Matrix operations

A spreadsheet is kind of a free-form matrix, but the matrices we use are a lot more structured and have all kinds of rules for what we can do with them and how to do those things.

There are usually two ways to teach matrix math. The first approach describes how to do the operations in detail, using matrices full of seemingly random numbers. You learn the rules, but you have no idea why you are doing certain things or what the result means. It's like playing a game where you arrange the numbers in a pretty pattern.

The second approach is to describe the contents of the matrices in detail and skim over the operation. Using vague instructions such as "and then you just multiply these two matrices together and get this …", leaving the reader with no idea how this multiplication is done.

In this chapter, we walk the line between these two methods. We start by looking at matrices that contain meaningful values, and then we see how to manipulate them.

Matrix addition

One of the more common uses of matrices is manipulating 3D points, which contain a value for its x, y, and z positions. We can easily view this as a 1 × 3 matrix, like so:

x y z

To move this point in space—also called *translating* the point—you need to know how far to move it on each axis. You can put this in a *translation matrix*, which is another 1 × 3 matrix that looks something like this:

dx dy dz

Here, dx, dy, and dz are the distances to move on each axis. Now you need to apply the transformation matrix to the point matrix; this is done with matrix addition. You just add each corresponding cell together to make a new matrix containing the sum of each cell. To add two matrices, they need to be the same size. So for translation, you do this:

x y z + dx dy dz = (x + dx) (y + dy) (z + dz)

The resulting matrix can be called x1, y1, z1, and it contains the new position of the point after it has been translated. So, if you had a point at 100, 50, 75 on x, y, z, and then wanted to move it -10, 20, -35, here's how that would look:

100 50 75 + -10 20 -35 = (100 - 10) (50 + 20) (75 - 35)

Thus, when you perform the addition, you get 90, 70, 40 as the point's new position. You probably already noticed the correlation to velocity, where the velocity on each axis is added to the position on that axis. It's the same here, but we're just looking at it a bit differently.

If you had a larger matrix, you would still use the same process, matching up the cells. We won't be dealing with matrix addition for anything larger than 1 × 3 matrices here, but here's an abstract example:

```
a b c     j k l     (a + j) (b + k) (c + l)
d e f  +  m n o  =  (d + m) (e + n) (f + o)
g h i     p q r     (g + p) (h + q) (i + r)
```

That's all you need to know about matrix addition. After we cover matrix multiplication, you see how to put together some actual functions to use in a matrix-based 3D engine.

Matrix multiplication

A more common way of calculating 3D transformations is using *matrix multiplication,* which is usually used for scaling and rotating. We won't actually use 3D scaling in this book, as the examples cover using either points, which can't be scaled, or a drawn shape, which does not have any 3D "thickness" and is therefore scaled only in two dimensions. Of course, you can build a more complex engine that can scale an entire 3D solid, but you'd then need to write additional functions that would alter the 3D points of the solid to the new size. That's beyond the scope of what we're doing here, but because scaling is a simple and clear demonstration of matrix multiplication, we'll run through an example.

Scaling with a matrix

First, you need to know an object's existing width, height, and depth—in other words, its measurement of size on each of the three axes. This creates a 1 × 3 matrix:

w h d

Here, w, h, and d stand for width, height, and depth. Next, you need a scaling matrix like the following:

```
sx  0   0
 0  sy  0
 0   0  sz
```

In this matrix, sx, sy, and sz are the percentages to scale on that particular axis. These would be in terms of a fraction or decimal, so that 1.0 is 100%, 2.0 is 200%, 0.5 is 50%, etc. You'll see why the matrix is laid out this way in a minute.

One thing you need to know about matrix multiplication is that in order to multiply two matrices, the first matrix must have the same number of *columns* as the second one has *rows*. The first one can have any number of rows, and the second can have any number of columns, as long as these criteria have been met. In this case, you are fine, as the first matrix has three columns (w, h, d), and the scaling matrix has three rows.

So, how do you multiply these things? Let's just go ahead and do it and see if you can see the pattern:

```
          sx  0  0
w h d  *   0 sy  0
           0  0 sz
```

This produces the following matrix as a result:

(w * sx + h * 0 + d * 0) (w * 0 + h * sy + d * 0) (w * 0 + h * 0 + d * sz)

When you get rid of all the zeros, it ends up as this:

(w * sx) (h * sy) (d * sz)

This is logical, as you are multiplying the width (x-axis measurement) by the x scaling factor, the height by the y scaling factor, and the depth by the z scaling factor. But, what exactly did we do there? All those zeros kind of clutter things up, so let's abstract it a bit to make the pattern clearer.

```
         a b c
u v w  * d e f
         g h i
```

Now you can see the pattern emerge in this result:

(u * a + v * d + w * g) (u * b + v * e + w * h) (u * c + v * f + w * i)

You can see that you move across the first row of the first matrix (u, v, w) and multiply by each first element in each row of the second (a, d, g). Adding those together gives you the first element for the first row of the resulting matrix. Doing the same with the second column of the second matrix (b, e, h) gives you the second column result.

If you have more than one row in the first matrix, you repeat the actions with that second row, which gives you the second row of the result:

```
u v w    a b c
x y z  * d e f
         g h i
```

This returns a 2 × 3 matrix:

(u * a + v * d + w * g) (u * b + v * e + w * h) (u * c + v * f + w * i)
(x * a + y * d + z * g) (x * b + y * e + z * h) (x * c + y * f + z * i)

The size of the resulting matrix is the number of rows in the first matrix by the number of columns in the second matrix.

Now let's see some matrix multiplication for something that you can actually use: coordinate rotation. Hopefully this scaling example will make it more clear what we're doing.

Coordinate rotation with a matrix

First, we'll use the 3D point matrix:

```
x y z
```

This holds the coordinates of the point you want to rotate. Now you need a rotation matrix, which, as you know, can rotate on any one of three axes. You'll create each of these types of rotation as separate matrices. Let's start with an x-axis rotation matrix:

```
1   0    0
0   cos  sin
0  -sin  cos
```

This matrix contains some sines and cosines, but sines and cosines of what? Well, it's the sine or cosine of whatever angle you're rotating by. If you're rotating that point by 45 degrees, it would be the sine and cosine of 45 degrees. (Of course in code, you'd use radians.)

Now, let's perform matrix multiplication with this and a 3D point matrix and see the results.

```
          1   0    0
x y z  *  0   cos  sin
          0  -sin  cos
```

For that, you get:

```
(x * 1 + y * 0 + z * 0) (x * 0 + y * cos   z * sin) (x * 0 + y * sin + z * cos)
```

Cleaning that up gives you:

```
(x) (y * cos   z * sin) (z * cos + y * sin)
```

We can write this in JavaScript as:

```
x = x;
y = y * Math.cos(rotation)   z * Math.sin(rotation);
z = z * Math.cos(rotation) + y * Math.sin(rotation);
```

If you look back to the section about 3D coordinate rotation in Chapter 15, you can see this is exactly how to accomplish x-axis rotation. This isn't a big surprise, as matrix math is just a different way of organizing various formulas and equations.

From here, you can easily create a matrix for y-axis rotation:

```
 cos  0   sin
   0  1   0
-sin  0   cos
```

Finally, here is one for rotation on the z-axis:

```
 cos  sin   0
-sin  cos   0
   0    0   1
```

It's good practice to go ahead and multiply each of these by an x, y, z matrix and verify that you get the same formulas you used for coordinate rotation on those two axes in Chapter 15.

Coding with matrices

Now you know enough of the basics to start programming with matrices. We're going to reuse and alter the 13-rotate-xy.html example from Chapter 15, so open that up. That exercise had a rotateX and rotateY function to perform the 3D coordinate rotation. We will change these so they work with matrices.

Start with the rotateX function. The updated code takes the ball's x, y, z coordinates, puts them in a 1 × 3 matrix, and then creates an x rotation matrix based on the given angle. These matrices are in the form of arrays. It then multiplies these two matrices together using the matrixMultiply function, which you also need to create. The result of the multiplication is another array, so you have to assign those values back to the ball's x, y, and z coordinates. Here's the new version of the rotateX function:

```
function rotateX (ball, angle) {
  var position = [ball.xpos, ball.ypos, ball.zpos],
      sin = Math.sin(angle),
      cos = Math.cos(angle),
      xRotMatrix = [];

  xRotMatrix[0] = [1,    0,    0];
  xRotMatrix[1] = [0,  cos,  sin];
  xRotMatrix[2] = [0, -sin,  cos];

  var result = matrixMultiply(position, xRotMatrix);
  ball.xpos = result[0];
  ball.ypos = result[1];
  ball.zpos = result[2];
}
```

And here is the function used for matrix multiplication:

```
function matrixMultiply (matrixA, matrixB) {
  var result = [];
  result[0] = matrixA[0] * matrixB[0][0] +
              matrixA[1] * matrixB[1][0] +
              matrixA[2] * matrixB[2][0];
  result[1] = matrixA[0] * matrixB[0][1] +
              matrixA[1] * matrixB[1][1] +
              matrixA[2] * matrixB[2][1];
  result[2] = matrixA[0] * matrixB[0][2] +
              matrixA[1] * matrixB[1][2] +
              matrixA[2] * matrixB[2][2];
  return result;
}
```

This function is hard-coded to multiply a 1 × 3 matrix by a 3 × 3 matrix, because that's what we need it to do. You can make a more dynamic function that can handle any sized matrices using iteration techniques, but let's keep things simple here.

Finally, create the `rotateY` function, which, if you understand the `rotateX` function, should look similar. You just create a y rotation matrix instead of an x rotation matrix.

```
function rotateY (ball, angle) {
  var position = [ball.xpos, ball.ypos, ball.zpos],
      sin = Math.sin(angle),
      cos = Math.cos(angle),
      yRotMatrix = [];

  yRotMatrix[0] = [ cos, 0, sin];
  yRotMatrix[1] = [   0, 1,   0];
  yRotMatrix[2] = [-sin, 0, cos];

  var result = matrixMultiply(position, yRotMatrix);
  ball.xpos = result[0];
  ball.ypos = result[1];
  ball.zpos = result[2];
}
```

Save the updated example as `01-rotate-xy.html` and run it in your browser. Compare the output of this to the version from Chapter 15 and they should look exactly the same. If you want, you can also create a `rotateZ` function, but because we don't actually need that for this example, that's left as an exercise for you to do on your own.

Even if you don't use matrices for 3D, you'll still find them useful for other purposes. We cover these next. Their use here provides a nice introduction because you can see how they relate to formulas you already know. Also, because matrices are used extensively in other graphics environments, if your programming life takes you elsewhere, you'll be ready!

Canvas transforms

One poweful feature of matricies is that they can be used to manipulate the canvas display. By applying a transformation, we can rotate, scale, and translate how the shapes are drawn, altering their form, size, and position. The canvas context uses a 3 × 3 transformation matrix set up like so:

```
a c dx
b d dy
u v w
```

This setup is known as an *affine transformation*, which means we are representing a 2-vector (x, y) as a 3-vector (x, y, 1). Because we won't use u, v, w, the extra space is filled in with 0, except for the lower-right corner that is set to 1. These remain unchanged, so you don't have to worry about them.

You can set the transformation of the canvas context by calling:

```
context.setTransform(a, b, c, d, dx, dy);
```

To multiply the current canvas context transformation with a matrix, call:

```
context.transform(a, b, c, d, dx, dy);
```

If the matrix elements are all stored in an array, it can be handy to apply the entire array as arguments:

```
context.transform.apply(context, [a, b, c, d, dx, dy]);
```

If there haven't been any transformations, then it's assumed we're using an *identity matrix* or a null transform. This matrix is described as:

```
1 0 0
0 1 0
0 0 1
```

Multiplying this matrix does nothing to the transformation. So, if you ever want to reset the canvas context, set its transformation to an identity matrix, like so:

```
context.setTransform(1, 0, 0, 1, 0, 0);
```

But back to the components of a matrix, what do all these letters mean? Well, dx and dy control the position of the canvas context by translating it on the x and y axis—remember coordinate 0, 0 is at the top-left corner. The a, b, c, and d positions in the matrix are a little trickier because they are so dependent on each other. If you set b and c to 0, you can use a and d to scale the object on the x and y axis. If you set a and d to 1, you can use b and c to skew the object on the y and x axis. And, you can use a, b, c, and d together in a way that you'll find familiar when laid out like this:

```
cos -sin  dx
sin  cos  dy
 u    v   w
```

This contains a rotation matrix. Naturally, cos and sin refer to the cosine and sine of an angle (in radians) that you wish to rotate the canvas context by. Let's try that one out in the next example, 02-matrix-rotate.html, which draws a red box in the animation loop:

```
<!doctype html>
<html>
 <head>
  <meta charset="utf-8">
  <title>Matrix Rotate</title>
  <link rel="stylesheet" href="style.css">
 </head>
 <body>
  <canvas id="canvas" width="400" height="400"></canvas>
  <script src="utils.js"></script>
  <script>
  window.onload = function () {
    var canvas = document.getElementById('canvas'),
        context = canvas.getContext('2d'),
        angle = 0;

    (function drawFrame () {
      window.requestAnimationFrame(drawFrame, canvas);
```

```
      context.clearRect(0, 0, canvas.width, canvas.height);

      angle += 0.03;

      var cos = Math.cos(angle),
          sin = Math.sin(angle),
          dx = canvas.width / 2,
          dy = canvas.height / 2;

      context.save();
      context.fillStyle = "#ff0000";
      context.transform(cos, sin, -sin, cos, dx, dy);
      context.fillRect(-50, -50, 100, 100);
      context.restore();
    }());
  };
  </script>
 </body>
</html>
```

Here you have an `angle` variable that increases on each frame. We find the sine and cosine of that angle and feed them to the `context.transform` method, in the way specified for rotation. We also apply a translation based on the canvas width and height, centering the rectangle. Test this and you have a spinning box.

In the `drawFrame` function, we wrapped the rectangle drawing code within calls to `context.save` and `context.restore`. These methods are used to save and retrieve the canvas drawing state, which is basically a snapshot of all the styles and transformations that have been applied. By using these, we can traverse through multiple matrix transformations by pushing and popping to the stack. You can nest multiple save and restores; just be mindful of which transformation you're working on. If you ever need to reset the canvas context, just set an identity matrix.

To demonstrate something a little more practical, we look at skewing. Skewing means stretching something out on one axis so that one part goes one way and the other part goes the other way. Think of italic letters and the way they slope; this is like a skew. The top part of the letters goes to the right and the bottom part to the left. This is something that can be tricky to implement using formulas, but is easy when applying a transformation matrix. As mentioned previously, you set a and d of the matrix to 1, and the b value is the amount to skew on the y-axis, and c controls the skew on the x-axis. Let's try an x skew first. In `03-skew-x.html`, we used almost the exact same setup as the last example, but since we're using the mouse position, make sure you include our helpful utility function at the top of the script:

```
var mouse = utils.captureMouse(canvas);
```

Now change how the matrix is applied in the `drawFrame` function:

```
(function drawFrame () {
  window.requestAnimationFrame(drawFrame, canvas);
  context.clearRect(0, 0, canvas.width, canvas.height);

  var skewX = (mouse.x - canvas.width / 2) * 0.01,
      dx = canvas.width / 2,
      dy = canvas.height / 2;
```

```
    context.save();
    context.fillStyle = "#ff0000";
    context.transform(1, 0, skewX, 1, dx, dy);
    context.fillRect(-50, -50, 100, 100);
    context.restore();
}());
```

The skewX variable is relative to the mouse's x position, and offset from the center of the canvas. The value is multiplied by 0.01 to keep the skew in a manageable range; it is then fed to context.transform. When you test this example, you can see the entire shape is skewed, as shown in Figure 18-2.

Figure 18-2. Rectangle skewed on the x-axis

In the example 04-skew-xy.html, we did the same thing on the y-axis:

```
(function drawFrame () {
    window.requestAnimationFrame(drawFrame, canvas);
    context.clearRect(0, 0, canvas.width, canvas.height);

    var skewX = (mouse.x - canvas.width / 2) * 0.01,
        skewY = (mouse.y - canvas.height / 2) * 0.01,
        dx = canvas.width / 2,
        dy = canvas.height / 2;

    context.save();
    context.fillStyle = "#ff0000";
    context.transform(1, skewY, skewX, 1, dx, dy);
    context.fillRect(-50, -50, 100, 100);
    context.restore();
}());
```

Figure 18-3 shows you how skewing a shape on two axes looks.

Figure 18-3. Rectangle skewed on both axes

It's amazing to be able to do this kind of effect so easily. Skewing is used often for pseudo-3D, and as you move your mouse around in the previous example, you can see how it appears to have some perspective—as if the shape leaned over and spun around. It's not particularly accurate 3D, but it can be used for some convincing effects.

Summary

Matrices are powerful tools and are used in many different applications of computer graphics. They are used extensively for computer vision filters, image manipulation (such as edge detection), sharpening, and blur transformations. As you continue into more advanced computer graphics programming, you'll no doubt see matrices used extensively.

We covered the basics of what matrices are, how to use and combine them, and we created some cool effects with them in this chapter. Now that you have the concepts in your head, you're ready to take advantage of the power that matrices can offer, and hopefully won't run away when you encounter them elsewhere.

Coming up in the final chapter, we tie up a few loose ends and look at some other tips and tricks. Topics such as random motion, random distribution, and integrating sound; these are techniques that can make your animations really interesting.

Chapter 19

Tips and Tricks

What we'll cover in this chapter:

- Brownian (random) motion

- Random distribution

- Interval- and timer-based animation

- Collisions between same-mass objects

- Integrating sound

Well, you made it to the last chapter. This chapter has been set aside for all the little things that didn't really fit in anywhere else. Because these various topics are just random bits and pieces (albeit useful bits), each section is a stand-alone unit.

Brownian (random) motion

One day, a botanist named Robert Brown looked at some grains of pollen in a drop of water and found that they randomly moved around. Even though there was no current or motion in the water, those little grains never settled down. He found the same thing happened with dust particles, so he concluded that the pollen swam on its own. Even though he didn't know why they behaved like this and there wasn't a scientific explanation for several decades, the phenomenon is named after him—just for noticing it!

Brownian motion is explained by the fact that there are zillions of water molecules in a drop of water and are in constant motion, even if the water appears to be still. Some of these molecules collide with the pollen or dust particle, and in doing so, transfer some of their momentum to it. Because even a speck of dust is a million times heavier than a single water molecule, each collision doesn't do much. But when you have so many millions of collisions per second, it starts to add up.

Some of the molecules might hit on one side, and some on the other. Overall, they are going to generally average out. But over time, you see fluctuations. Where more molecules hit, say, on the left side, is enough to start the particle moving a bit to the right. Then more might hit on the bottom, and the particle moves upward. Again, these eventually average out, so it doesn't usually result in much momentum in any one direction. You get this random floating-around motion.

We can easily simulate effect in an animation. On each frame, you calculate random numbers to add to the x and y velocity of a moving object. The random numbers should be calculated to be either positive or negative, and usually quite small, say in a range from -0.1 to +0.1. You can do that like so:

```
vx += Math.random() * 0.2 - 0.1;
vy += Math.random() * 0.2 - 0.1;
```

Multiplying the random decimal by 0.2 gives you a number from 0.0 to 0.2, and subtracting 0.1 makes it -0.1 to 0.1. It's important to add some friction into this, otherwise the velocities will build up, and things zip around unnaturally. In the example `01-brownian-1.html`, we create 50 particles and have them floating around with Brownian motion. The particles are instances of our familiar `Ball` class, made small and colored black. Here is the code:

```
<!doctype html>
<html>
  <head>
    <meta charset="utf-8">
    <title>Brownian 1</title>
    <link rel="stylesheet" href="style.css">
  </head>
  <body>
    <canvas id="canvas" width="400" height="400"></canvas>
    <script src="utils.js"></script>
    <script src="ball.js"></script>
    <script>
    window.onload = function () {
      var canvas = document.getElementById('canvas'),
          context = canvas.getContext('2d'),
          dots = [],
          numDots = 50,
          friction = 0.95;

      for (var dot, i = 0; i < numDots; i++) {
        dot = new Ball(1, "#000000");
        dot.x = Math.random() * canvas.width;
        dot.y = Math.random() * canvas.height;
        dot.vx = 0;
        dot.vy = 0;
        dots.push(dot);
      }

      function draw (dot) {
        dot.vx += Math.random() * 0.2 - 0.1;
```

```
      dot.vy += Math.random() * 0.2 - 0.1;
      dot.x += dot.vx;
      dot.y += dot.vy;
      dot.vx *= friction;
      dot.vy *= friction;

      if (dot.x > canvas.width) {
        dot.x = 0;
      } else if (dot.x < 0) {
        dot.x = canvas.width;
      }
      if (dot.y > canvas.height) {
        dot.y = 0;
      } else if (dot.y < 0) {
        dot.y = canvas.height;
      }

      dot.draw(context);
    }

    (function drawFrame () {
      window.requestAnimationFrame(drawFrame, canvas);
      context.clearRect(0, 0, canvas.width, canvas.height);

      dots.forEach(draw);
    }());
  };
  </script>
 </body>
</html>
```

Most of this setup is old news to you, so we put the relevant parts in bold. Figure 19-1 shows how running this code appears on screen.

Figure 19-1. Brownian motion without the motion

In the next example, `02-brownian-2.html`, we make some adjustments to the previous exercise so we can see the path each dot takes. At the top of the script, reduce the number of dots to 20, and add two variables, `decay` and `decayColor`, that we use as the new canvas clearing color:

```
var numDots = 20,
    decay = 0.01,
    decayColor = utils.colorToRGB("#ffffff", decay);
```

Because the clearing color contains transparency, we use our utility function `utils.colorToRGB` to return the CSS-style RGBA string: `'rgba(255,255,255,0.01)'`.

Then remove our normal canvas clearing call to `context.clearRect` and replace it with a fill rectangle using our color. Now the animation loop no longer erases the dot's trail on each frame, it just gradually makes the image lighter and lighter.

```
(function drawFrame () {
  window.requestAnimationFrame(drawFrame, canvas);

  context.fillStyle = decayColor;
  context.fillRect(0, 0, canvas.width, canvas.height);

  dots.forEach(draw);
}());
```

Run this example in your browser and you can see the path that each dot takes, as shown in Figure 19-2. The active part of the trail is in black, whereas the remaining path decays to gray.

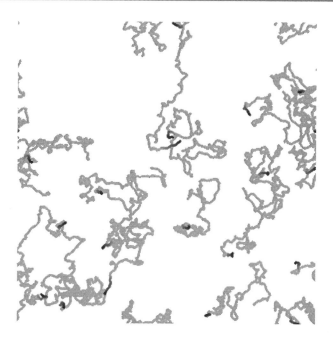

Figure 19-2. Brownian motion with trails

Brownian motion is useful any time you want something to move around as if it were floating with no particular direction in mind, with no forces really acting on it. You can also add it to an object that has some other motion applied to it, to give it a sense of randomness. An example is a fly or bee that's buzzing around. You might have it move along in some path, but adding in some random motion can make it look much more lifelike.

Random distribution

From time to time, you might want to create several objects and place them at random positions. You already did this many times throughout the book, but here we focus on a few different methods of doing this, and the different results that they give you.

Square distribution

If you want the objects to randomly cover the entire canvas element, that's simple. Choose a random number up to the canvas's width for x, and a random number up to the canvas's height for y. In fact, you did just that in the previous exercises:

```
dot.x = Math.random() * canvas.width;
dot.y = Math.random() * canvas.height;
```

But if you want to clump the dots in near the center of the canvas—say 100 pixels to either side, top, or bottom of the center—you can do something like the following, which is example 03-random-1.html:

```
<!doctype html>
<html>
 <head>
  <meta charset="utf-8">
  <title>Random 1</title>
  <link rel="stylesheet" href="style.css">
 </head>
 <body>
  <canvas id="canvas" width="400" height="400"></canvas>
  <script>
  window.onload = function () {
    var canvas = document.getElementById('canvas'),
        context = canvas.getContext('2d'),
        numDots = 50;

    while (numDots--) {
      var x = canvas.width / 2 + Math.random() * 200 - 100,
          y = canvas.height / 2 + Math.random() * 200 - 100;

      //draw circle...
      context.fillStyle = "#000000";
      context.beginPath();
      context.arc(x, y, 2, 0, (Math.PI * 2), true);
      context.closePath();
      context.fill();
    }
  };
  </script>
 </body>
</html>
```

This creates a random number from -100 to +100 and adds it to the center point of the canvas, so all of the dots are no farther than 100 pixels on either axis from the center. Figure 19-3 shows the result.

Figure 19-3. Randomly placed dots

Not too bad. But if you crowd them in a bit more by making more dots (300) and reducing the area to 100 by 100, you notice something odd starting to happen, which you can see in Figure 19-4. Here's the code for example 04-random-2.html:

```
<!doctype html>
<html>
 <head>
  <meta charset="utf-8">
  <title>Random 2</title>
  <link rel="stylesheet" href="style.css">
 </head>
 <body>
  <canvas id="canvas" width="400" height="400"></canvas>
  <script>
  window.onload = function () {
    var canvas = document.getElementById('canvas'),
        context = canvas.getContext('2d'),
        numDots = 300;

    while (numDots--) {
      var x = canvas.width / 2 + Math.random() * 100 - 50,
          y = canvas.height / 2 + Math.random() * 100 - 50;

      context.fillStyle = "#000000";
      context.beginPath();
      context.arc(x, y, 2, 0, (Math.PI * 2), true);
      context.closePath();
      context.fill();
    }
  };
  </script>
 </body>
</html>
```

Figure 19-4. This method starts to form a square. Not so random looking anymore.

As you see, the dots are starting to form a square. Maybe that's what you want, but if you try to make something like an explosion or star system, a square doesn't look too natural. So let's move on to the next technique.

Circular distribution

Although slightly more complex than a square distribution, circular distribution really isn't very difficult to do. First you need to know the radius of your circle. Let's keep it at 50, to match the last example. This is the maximum radius that a dot can be placed from the center. For each dot, you take a random number from zero to that number to use as the radius. Then you choose a random angle from 0 to PI * 2 radians (360 degrees), and use a little trigonometry to find an x and y position to place the dot. Here's the code for this example, 05-random-3.html:

```
<!doctype html>
<html>
 <head>
  <meta charset="utf-8">
  <title>Random 3</title>
  <link rel="stylesheet" href="style.css">
 </head>
 <body>
  <canvas id="canvas" width="400" height="400"></canvas>
  <script>
  window.onload = function () {
    var canvas = document.getElementById('canvas'),
        context = canvas.getContext('2d'),
        numDots = 300,
        maxRadius = 50;

    while (numDots--) {
      var radius = Math.random() * maxRadius,
          angle = Math.random() * (Math.PI * 2),
          x = canvas.width / 2 + Math.cos(angle) * radius,
          y = canvas.height / 2 + Math.sin(angle) * radius;
```

```
      context.fillStyle = "#000000";
      context.beginPath();
      context.arc(x, y, 2, 0, (Math.PI * 2), true);
      context.closePath();
      context.fill();
    }
  };
  </script>
 </body>
</html>
```

This gives you a picture like the one in Figure 19-5.

Figure 19-5. Circular random distribution

This is more natural looking for explosions; however, you might notice that the dots seem to be more clumped around the center of the circle. This is because an even distribution exists along the radius, meaning there are as many dots in the center as near the edge. But because the center has less area, they are more crowded.

We can make the dots appear more uniformly distributed throughout the circle, as you can see in example 06-random-4.html:

```
<!doctype html>
<html>
 <head>
  <meta charset="utf-8">
  <title>Random 4</title>
  <link rel="stylesheet" href="style.css">
 </head>
 <body>
  <canvas id="canvas" width="400" height="400"></canvas>
  <script>
  window.onload = function () {
    var canvas = document.getElementById('canvas'),
        context = canvas.getContext('2d'),
        numDots = 300,
        maxRadius = 50;

    while (numDots--) {
      var radius = Math.sqrt(Math.random()) * maxRadius,
```

```
        angle = Math.random() * (Math.PI * 2),
        x = canvas.width / 2 + Math.cos(angle) * radius,
        y = canvas.height / 2 + Math.sin(angle) * radius;

    context.fillStyle = "#000000";
    context.beginPath();
    context.arc(x, y, 2, 0, (Math.PI * 2), true);
    context.closePath();
    context.fill();
  }
};
</script>
</body>
</html>
```

By taking the square root of the random number—it has a bias toward 1 and away from 0—we can smooth out the distribution. You can see the result in Figure 19-6.

Figure 19-6. A smoother circular distribution

Biased distribution

You might want to give the random dots free range over the entire canvas, but have them tend to show up in the middle area. There would be some out on the edges, but the closer to the center you got, the more there are. This is somewhat like the first circular example, but applied to a rectangular area.

You do this by generating multiple random numbers for each position, and then averaging them to get the final value. For example, if the canvas element is 400 pixels wide, and you generate an x position for each object with just one random number, then each object has an equal chance of being anywhere in that range. But if you generate two random numbers from 0 to 400 and take the average, there's a bit higher chance that it will be somewhere in the middle rather than out toward the edges.

Let's look at that in a little more depth. There is some chance that both numbers might be in a high range, say from 300 to 400. There's about the same chance that both might be in a low range, from 0 to 100. But there's a higher chance that one will be high and one low, or one middle and one high or low, or even both in the middle. All of these possibilities average out to place most dots a bit closer to the middle.

To see it in code, as usual, we start on one dimension. Here's the example 07-random-5.html:

```
<!doctype html>
<html>
 <head>
  <meta charset="utf-8">
  <title>Random 5</title>
  <link rel="stylesheet" href="style.css">
 </head>
 <body>
  <canvas id="canvas" width="400" height="400"></canvas>
  <script>
  window.onload = function () {
    var canvas = document.getElementById('canvas'),
        context = canvas.getContext('2d'),
        numDots = 300;

    while (numDots--) {
      var x1 = Math.random() * canvas.width,
          x2 = Math.random() * canvas.width,
          x = (x1 + x2) / 2,
          y = canvas.height / 2 + Math.random() * 50 - 25;

      context.fillStyle = "#000000";
      context.beginPath();
      context.arc(x, y, 2, 0, (Math.PI * 2), true);
      context.closePath();
      context.fill();
    }
  };
  </script>
 </body>
</html>
```

Here you generate two random numbers, x1 and x2, and set the dot's x position to the average of them. The y position is simply randomly near the center. This example gives you something like what you see in Figure 19-7.

Figure 19-7. Biased distribution with one iteration

The effect isn't too pronounced here, but you can see that there is a bit more clumping in the center, and more space at the edges. Creating more random numbers and averaging them makes it more obvious. We can move this into a for loop to make it more versatile in the next example (08-random-6.html):

```
<!doctype html>
<html>
 <head>
  <meta charset="utf-8">
  <title>Random 6</title>
  <link rel="stylesheet" href="style.css">
```

```
    </head>
    <body>
     <canvas id="canvas" width="400" height="400"></canvas>
     <script>
     window.onload = function () {
       var canvas = document.getElementById('canvas'),
           context = canvas.getContext('2d'),
           numDots = 300,
           iterations = 6;

         while (numDots--) {
           for (var i = 0, xpos = 0; i < iterations; i++) {
             xpos += Math.random() * canvas.width;
           }

           var x = xpos / iterations,
               y = canvas.height / 2 + Math.random() * 50 - 25;

           context.fillStyle = "#000000";
           context.beginPath();
           context.arc(x, y, 2, 0, (Math.PI * 2), true);
           context.closePath();
           context.fill();
         }
     };
     </script>
    </body>
</html>
```

Here the `iterations` variable controls how many numbers you will average. You start with the variable xpos equal to zero, and add each random number to it. Finally, you divide that total by the number of iterations for the final value. Figure 19-8 shows the results.

Figure 19-8. Biased distribution with six iterations

It is now easy to do the same thing for the y-axis, and example `09-random-7.html` does just that:

```
<!doctype html>
<html>
 <head>
  <meta charset="utf-8">
  <title>Random 7</title>
  <link rel="stylesheet" href="style.css">
 </head>
 <body>
  <canvas id="canvas" width="400" height="400"></canvas>
```

```
<script>
window.onload = function () {
  var canvas = document.getElementById('canvas'),
      context = canvas.getContext('2d'),
      numDots = 300,
      iterations = 6;

  while (numDots--) {
    for (var i = 0, xpos = 0; i < iterations; i++) {
      xpos += Math.random() * canvas.width;
    }

    for (var j = 0, ypos = 0; j < iterations; j++) {
      ypos += Math.random() * canvas.height;
    }

    var x = xpos / iterations,
        y = ypos / iterations;

    context.fillStyle = "#000000";
    context.beginPath();
    context.arc(x, y, 2, 0, (Math.PI * 2), true);
    context.closePath();
    context.fill();
  }
};
</script>
</body>
</html>
```

This gives you a distribution like the one in Figure 19-9.

Figure 19-9. Two-dimensional biased distribution

This is the most random, explosive, star system-like distribution of them all, but it is also the most computationally intensive to generate.

Collision-based distribution

There are times when you might want objects distributed randomly within a particular shape or shapes. Perhaps the easiest way to accomplish this is to generate a random position on the screen, and use some collision testing to determine whether this point falls within a certain area of the screen. If the point is outside the shape, then discard it and generate a new random screen position, which we again test. Keep doing this process until you find a point that falls within the specified area.

In the next example, we distribute the dots randomly within two circles, which we reference using our `Ball` class. We use the distance-based collision detection formula from Chapter 9 to determine whether the dot falls within either of the two balls. And if it doesn't, keep trying until we find one. This example can be found in `10-random-8.html`:

```
<!doctype html>
<html>
 <head>
  <meta charset="utf-8">
  <title>Collision-Based Distribution</title>
  <link rel="stylesheet" href="style.css">
 </head>
 <body>
  <canvas id="canvas" width="400" height="400"></canvas>
  <script src="utils.js"></script>
  <script src="ball.js"></script>
  <script>
  window.onload = function () {
    var canvas = document.getElementById('canvas'),
        context = canvas.getContext('2d'),
        numDots = 300,
        ball0 = new Ball(),
        ball1 = new Ball(80);

    ball0.x = 100;
    ball0.y = canvas.height / 2;
    ball1.x = 300;
    ball1.y = canvas.height / 2;

    function detectCollision(x, y, ball) {
      var dx = x - ball.x,
          dy = y - ball.y,
          dist = Math.sqrt(dx * dx + dy * dy);
      return (dist < ball.radius);
    }

    while (numDots--) {
      //initialize variables
      var x = 0,
          y = 0;

      //if x, y not in ballA AND not in ballB, set new random position
      while (!detectCollision(x, y, ball0) && !detectCollision(x, y, ball1)) {
        //get random position on canvas
```

```
      x = Math.random() * canvas.width;
      y = Math.random() * canvas.height;
    }

    context.fillStyle = "#000000";
    context.beginPath();
    //x, y, radius, start_angle, end_angle, anti-clockwise
    context.arc(x, y, 2, 0, (Math.PI * 2), true);
    context.closePath();
    context.fill();
    }
  };
  </script>
 </body>
</html>
```

The distribution for this example can be seen in Figure 19-10.

Figure 19-10. Random distribution within two circles using distance-based collision detection

Here, we test whether a point falls with a circle, but the concept is the same no matter the shape (taking into account the limitations of collision detection described in Chapter 9). You generate the random position first, and then test whether it falls within a predefined area using the appropriate collision detection technique. The trade-off to this method is that you are potentially generating many more positions than you actually need. This technique is not something you want to run every animation frame, but it can be useful at the start of your program (for example, in a game, when you set up random starting positions for enemies).

Timer- and time-based animation

In the book examples so far, the animation is set up by placing the motion code within the `drawFrame` function and using `window.requestAnimationFrame` to build a loop. This is the preferred method for canvas-based animations, because web browsers can optimize this function for animation without degrading performance in the rest of the browser. We discussed this in detail in Chapter 2.

But in the days before all the multimedia support found in today's browsers, JavaScript timers were the only way to set up animations. This method uses intervals to control the animation playback rate, which we look at next.

After that, we discuss time-based animation, a technique that can be used with either frames or timers.

Timer-based animation

The JavaScript functions used for timer-based animations are `window.setTimeout` and `window.setInterval`. Each takes the same two arguments: a function to execute, and a number specifying the amount of milliseconds to wait before running that function.

```
function printMessage () {
  console.log("Hello, Timer!");
}
```

```
window.setTimeout(printMessage, 2000);
```

Here, the `printMessage` function is passed to the `window.setTimeout` and set to run in 2000 milliseconds. Once you execute this code, wait 2 seconds (1000 milliseconds is 1 second) and the message prints to the debugging console.

`window.setInterval` also executes a function, but instead of calling it once, it keeps running it again and again at the specified interval (unless you tell it to stop).

Setting up a timer-based canvas animation isn't much different than the other examples in this book that use `window.requestAnimationFrame`. You set up an interval for the frame rate and the timer runs the animation loop. Here's a simple example (document `11-timer.html`):

```
<!doctype html>
<html>
 <head>
  <meta charset="utf-8">
  <title>Timer</title>
  <link rel="stylesheet" href="style.css">
 </head>
 <body>
  <canvas id="canvas" width="400" height="400"></canvas>
  <script src="utils.js"></script>
  <script src="ball.js"></script>
  <script>
  window.onload = function () {
    var canvas = document.getElementById('canvas'),
        context = canvas.getContext('2d'),
        ball = new Ball(),
        fps = 30;

    ball.y = canvas.height / 2;
    ball.vx = 5;

    function drawFrame () {
      context.clearRect(0, 0, canvas.width, canvas.height);

      ball.x += ball.vx;
      ball.draw(context);
    }
```

```
    window.setInterval(drawFrame, 1000/fps);
  };
  </script>
 </body>
</html>
```

In this example, the animation loop is set to run at 30 frames per second using a timer. But since there is no way to accurately determine how fast the code will execute on the end user's machine, a timer-based animation winds up being no more accurate than a frame-based animation. You might not see a difference in a simple example like this one, but in a more processor intensive program, you will see a difference across computers.

If you really need accuracy, time-based animation is the way to go.

Time-based animation

Time-based animation is the method to use if the speed of objects in your animation needs to be consistent, which might be the case in some types of games. Neither frame- nor timer-based animation can be counted on for a specific rate of playback. A complex animation on an older, slower computer might run at a much lower speed than it was designed for. As you see shortly, when you use a time-based animation, you get speed you can count on, no matter the frame rate of the animation.

The first thing you need to do is change the way you think about velocity. Up to now, when you saw something like vx = 5, the units you used were *pixels per frame.* In other words, the object moved 5 pixels on the x-axis each time a new frame was encountered. In a timer-based animation, it is 5 pixels per timer interval.

For a time-based animation, you use real measurements of time, such as seconds. Because you deal with a whole second, rather than a small fraction of one, the value needs to be much higher. If something moves at 10 pixels per frame at 30 frames per second, that is roughly 300 pixels per second. For the next example, we take the 05-bouncing-2.html exercise from Chapter 6 and make a few changes, which are shown in bold (and can also be found in 12-time-based-1.html):

```
<!doctype html>
<html>
 <head>
  <meta charset="utf-8">
  <title>Time based 1</title>
  <link rel="stylesheet" href="style.css">
 </head>
 <body>
  <canvas id="canvas" width="400" height="400"></canvas>
  <script src="utils.js"></script>
  <script src="ball.js"></script>
  <script>
  window.onload = function () {

    var canvas = document.getElementById('canvas'),
```

```
    context = canvas.getContext('2d'),

    ball = new Ball(),

    start_time = new Date().getTime(),

    time = getTimer(),

    vx = 300,

    vy = -300,

    bounce = -0.7;


ball.x = canvas.width * Math.random();

ball.y = canvas.height / 2;


function getTimer () {

  return (new Date().getTime() - start_time); //milliseconds

}


(function drawFrame () {

  window.requestAnimationFrame(drawFrame, canvas);

  context.clearRect(0, 0, canvas.width, canvas.height);


  var elapsed = getTimer() - time,

      left = 0,

      right = canvas.width,

      top = 0,

      bottom = canvas.height;


  time = getTimer();
```

```
    ball.x += vx * elapsed / 1000;

    ball.y += vy * elapsed / 1000;

    if (ball.x + ball.radius > right) {

      ball.x = right - ball.radius;

      vx *= bounce;

    } else if (ball.x - ball.radius < left) {

      ball.x = left + ball.radius;

      vx *= bounce;

    }

    if (ball.y + ball.radius > bottom) {

      ball.y = bottom - ball.radius;

      vy *= bounce;

    } else if (ball.y - ball.radius < top) {

      ball.y = top + ball.radius;

      vy *= bounce;

    }

    ball.draw(context);

  }());

};
</script>
</body>
</html>
```

The velocities are bumped up, as described previously, and are left as hard-coded values, rather than randomly determined. There is a variable called time, that's set to the result of the function getTimer. The getTimer function is simple; it returns the number of milliseconds the animation runs—and that's all it does, it's just a counter.

If you call getTimer once and store its value, and then call it again later and subtract the two values, you know exactly—down to the millisecond—how much time elapsed between the two.

So this is the strategy we use: Call getTimer at the beginning of each frame and see how many milliseconds have elapsed since the last frame. If you divide that by 1,000, you have what fraction of a second elapsed. Because your vx and vy are now in terms of pixels per second, you can multiply them by this fraction and know how much to move the object. Also, don't forget to reset the value of the time so you can measure the next frame.

Test the example, and you see that the ball moves at about the same speed as the original. But the really amazing thing is that no matter what frame rate the animation is played at, it still moves at the same speed! Of course, higher rates make for a much smoother animation, and the lower ones are quite jumpy, but the velocity itself should be consistent.

This method can also be used in a timer-based animation. It's not listed here, but take a look at document 13-time-based-2.html and see that the regular animation loop has been replaced with window.setInterval, while continuing to apply velocity using getTimer. You can also adjust the fps variable and see how the animation looks at different frame rates.

You can use this technique with any example in the book that contains velocity. In doing so, you also need to apply a similar technique to any acceleration or repeated forces, such as gravity, because these are also time based. Values for acceleration have to be much larger when converted to this type of animation, because acceleration is defined as distance per time interval per time interval. For example, gravity is approximately 32 feet per second per second.

Where gravity might be something like 0.1 in our a frame-based animations, it has to be more like 300 here. Then you apply it like so:

```
vy += gravity * elapsed / 1000;
```

Go ahead and try gravity applied like this to the previous example, with a value of 300. You should find that it looks about equal to the same frame-based animation with a gravity of 0.1. You can find this code in the exercise 14-time-based-3.html.

Collisions between same-mass objects

Remember Chapter 11 and the conservation of momentum? That was some serious code. It happens you can make it a little bit simpler when two objects of the same mass collide. Along the line of collision, objects simply swap their velocities. Although you still use coordinate rotation to determine that line of collision, as well as the object's velocities on it, this wipes out the complex conservation of momentum stuff. To see how it works, let's go back to the example 06-multi-billiard-2.html in Chapter 11, and use that as the base for the next example, 15-same-mass.html. It's a big file, so all of the code from the original won't be listed here, but look at the for loop that create all the balls near the top of the script:

```
for (var radius, ball, i = 0; i < numBalls; i++) {
    radius = Math.random() * 20 + 15;
    ball = new Ball(radius, Math.random() * 0xffffff);
    ball.mass = radius;
    ball.x = Math.random() * canvas.width;
    ball.y = Math.random() * canvas.height;
    ball.vx = Math.random() * 10 - 5;
    ball.vy = Math.random() * 10 - 5;
    balls.push(ball);
}
```

For the new example, we remove the line in bold and create a new variable at the top of the script:

```
var radius = 20;
```

This makes all the balls the same size and mass.

Next, locate the checkCollision function and find this section:

```
//rotate ball0's velocity
vel0 = rotate(ball0.vx, ball0.vy, sin, cos, true),

//rotate ball1's velocity
vel1 = rotate(ball1.vx, ball1.vy, sin, cos, true),

//collision reaction
vxTotal = vel0.x - vel1.x;
vel0.x = ((ball0.mass - ball1.mass) * vel0.x + 2 * ball1.mass * vel1.x) /
         (ball0.mass + ball1.mass);
vel1.x = vxTotal + vel0.x;
```

This is the part that finds the velocities along the line of collision, and, along with their masses, figures out the result of the collision. The part labeled "collision reaction" is the code that factors in the conservation of momentum, and this is the section you can get rid of. You can replace that portion with code that simply swaps vel0 and vel1. This makes the whole section shown look like this:

```
//rotate ball0's velocity
vel0 = rotate(ball0.vx, ball0.vy, sin, cos, true),

//rotate ball1's velocity
vel1 = rotate(ball1.vx, ball1.vy, sin, cos, true);

//collision reaction, swap the two velocities
var temp = vel0;
vel0 = vel1;
vel1 = temp;
```

Here you eliminate a good bit of math, and if you test the file before and after, you should see the same thing.

Integrating sound

Something that has been conspicuously absent from this book has been the use of sound. Although sound is not directly a part of animation, well-done sound effects can go a long way to making an animation more immersive and realistic.

One of the most anticipated features of HTML5 is its support for the audio element, enabling native sound playback in the browser. The good news is that most browsers supporting HTML5 have some kind of support for audio. The bad news is, at least at the time of writing, the level of implementation varies across browsers. Because of licensing issues with audio formats, it is often unclear what browser plays which file type. Although this can be a frustrating environment to develop for, it is not an insurmountable one, if you take certain precautions. It's important to provide your audio samples in a range of formats so browsers can pick the one they support.

In this example, We again go back to the `05-bouncing-2.html` file from Chapter 6, with the ball that bounces off walls. Each time the ball hits a wall, it should make a sound.

The first thing you need is a sound to play. You can download one from the Internet, use one of your own, or use the audio clips that are provided with the rest of the example code. Place them in the same directory as your document.

Now you need to include the following audio tag in the body of your HTML document:

```
<audio id="sound">
  <source src="boing.ogg"/>
  <source src="boing.mp3"/>
  <p>This browser does not support the <code>audio</code> element.</p>
</audio>
```

Here we create an `audio` element and provide it with a pair of formats to pick from: Ogg Vorbis and MP3. Between these two, you should have all the major browsers covered. We also provide a fallback message to display in case the browser does not support the HTML5 `audio` element. This message is ignored if it does.

We can access the `audio` element from JavaScript using the DOM interface and assign it to a variable:

```
var sound = document.getElementById('sound');
```

The sound should be ready, and all you have to do is call its `play` method:

```
sound.play();
```

In the next example, we use JavaScript to check if the browser supports the audio element before we start the animation loop. If it's not supported, we display a blank canvas and throw an error message to the browser's debugging console. To test for audio support, you can check whether the audio object that returns from the DOM contains the `canPlayType` method:

```
if (typeof sound !== 'object' || !sound.canPlayType) {
  throw new Error("The audio element is not supported in this browser.");
}
```

Here's the code for the example, `16-sound-events.html`:

```
<!doctype html>
<html>
 <head>
  <meta charset="utf-8">
  <title>Sound Events</title>
  <link rel="stylesheet" href="style.css">
 </head>
 <body>
  <canvas id="canvas" width="400" height="400"></canvas>
  <audio id="sound">
    <source src="boing.ogg" />
```

```
  <source src="boing.mp3" />
  <p>This browser does not support the <code>audio</code> element.</p>
</audio>
<script src="utils.js"></script>
<script src="ball.js"></script>
<script>
window.onload = function () {
  var canvas = document.getElementById('canvas'),
      context = canvas.getContext('2d'),
      sound = document.getElementById('sound'),
      ball = new Ball(),
      vx = Math.random() * 10 - 5,
      vy = Math.random() * 10 - 5,
      bounce = -0.7;

  //the animation only runs with audio
  if (typeof sound !== 'object' || !sound.canPlayType) {
    throw new Error("This browser does not support the audio element.");
  }

  (function drawFrame () {
    window.requestAnimationFrame(drawFrame, canvas);
    context.clearRect(0, 0, canvas.width, canvas.height);

    var left = 0,
        right = canvas.width,
        top = 0,
        bottom = canvas.height;

    ball.x += vx;
    ball.y += vy;

    if (ball.x + ball.radius > right) {
      sound.play();
      ball.x = right - ball.radius;
      vx *= bounce;
    } else if (ball.x - ball.radius < left) {
      sound.play();
      ball.x = left + ball.radius;
      vx *= bounce;
    }
    if (ball.y + ball.radius > bottom) {
      sound.play();
      ball.y = bottom - ball.radius;
      vy *= bounce;
    } else if (ball.y - ball.radius < top) {
      sound.play();
      ball.y = top + ball.radius;
      vy *= bounce;
    }

    ball.draw(context);
  }());
};
```

```
    </script>
   </body>
  </html>
```

Test the animation and see ... make that, hear, the difference that sound makes. Of course, finding the *right* sounds to use in the right circumstances, and not overdoing it, is an art in itself.

Because of the inconsistencies in the way browsers have implemented the `audio` element, several JavaScript libraries have sprung up to smooth things out for the developer. If you come across problems with a particular browser, don't be afraid to look around for some projects that address this cross-platform need. Some of these libraries might even fallback to using Flash when all else fails, but at least you know the user will hear the sound.

Summary

Congratulations on finishing the book! It is no small accomplishment, and the techniques you learned here can be applied to many different types of graphics programming environments. But of course, perhaps the most exciting is the potential for web-based animations and games.

There's a bunch of examples provided in this book for you to reference, play around with, and break. That really is the best way to learn and move forward, tear the programs apart until you understand how each little piece affects the rest. Of course, reading how things work is important, but you must code, experiment, and put these ideas to use. And besides, that's the most fun part anyway. There's always more to learn, so don't get hung up about not knowing this type of math, or that new programming style; just hack it out, debug it, and get it to work. From there you can build on your successes and failures, and keep creating even better things.

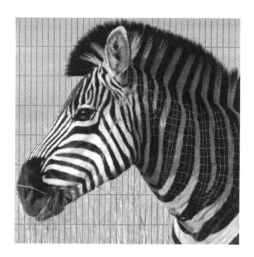

Appendix

Useful Formulas

Throughout the book, there are various formulas related to the different motions and effects you've created. These have been distilled down to the most useful and most commonly used formulas, equations, and code snippets, and are listed at the end of each chapter. These have been collected here to serve as a one-shot reference for those things you'll probably use the most.

Chapter 3

Calculate basic trigonometric functions

```
sine of angle = opposite / hypotenuse
cosine of angle = adjacent / hypotenuse
tangent of angle = opposite / adjacent
```

Convert radians to degrees and degrees to radians

```
radians = degrees * Math.PI / 180
degrees = radians * 180 / Math.PI
```

Rotate to the mouse (or any point)

```
//substitute mouse.x, mouse.y with the x, y point to rotate to
dx = mouseX - object.x;
dy = mouseY - object.y;
object.rotation = Math.atan2(dy, dx) * 180 / Math.PI; //radians to degrees
```

Create waves

```
(function drawFrame () {
  window.requestAnimationFrame(drawFrame, canvas);

  //assign value to x, y or other property of object
  value = center + Math.sin(angle) * range;
  angle += speed;
}());
```

Create circles

```
(function drawFrame () {
  window.requestAnimationFrame(drawFrame, canvas);

  //assign position to x, y of object, use as drawing coordinates
  xposition = centerX + Math.cos(angle) * radius;
  yposition = centerY + Math.sin(angle) * radius;
  angle += speed;
}());
```

Create ovals

```
(function drawFrame () {
  window.requestAnimationFrame(drawFrame, canvas);

  //assign position to x, y of object, use as drawing coordinates
  xposition = centerX + Math.cos(angle) * radiusX;
  yposition = centerY + Math.sin(angle) * radiusY;
  angle += speed;
}());
```

Get the distance between two points

```
//points are x1, y1 and x2, y2
//can be object positions, mouse coordinates, etc.
dx = x2 - x1;
dy = y2 - y1;
dist = Math.sqrt(dx * dx + dy * dy);
```

Chapter 4

Convert hex to decimal

```
console.log(hexValue);
```

Convert decimal to hex

```
console.log(decimalValue.toString(16));
```

Combine component colors

```
color = red << 16 | green << 8 | blue;
```

Extract component colors

```
red = color24 >> 16 & 0xFF;
green = color24 >> 8 & 0xFF;
blue = color24 & 0xFF;
```

Draw a curve through a point

```
//xt, yt is the point you want to draw through
//x0, y0 and x2, y2 are the end points of the curve
x1 = xt * 2 - (x0 + x2) / 2;
y1 = yt * 2 - (y0 + y2) / 2;

context.moveTo(x0, y0);
context.quadraticCurveTo(x1, y1, x2, y2);
```

Chapter 5

Convert angular velocity to x, y velocity

```
vx = speed * Math.cos(angle);
vy = speed * Math.sin(angle);
```

Convert angular acceleration (any force acting on an object) to x, y acceleration

```
ax = force * Math.cos(angle);
ay = force * Math.sin(angle);
```

Add acceleration to velocity

```
vx += ax;
vy += ay;
```

Add velocity to position

```
object.x += vx;
object.y += vy;
```

Chapter 6

Remove an out-of-bounds object

```
if (object.x - object.width / 2 > right ||
    object.x + object.width / 2 < left ||
    object.y - object.height / 2 > bottom ||
    object.y + object.height / 2 < top) {
  //code to remove object
}
```

Regenerate an out-of-bounds object

```
if (object.x - object.width / 2 > right ||
    object.x + object.width / 2 < left ||
    object.y - object.height / 2 > bottom ||
    object.y + object.height / 2 < top) {
  //reset object position and velocity
}
```

Screen wrapping for an out-of-bounds object

```
if (object.x - object.width / 2 > right) {
  object.x = left - object.width / 2;
} else if (object.x + object.width / 2 < left) {
  object.x = right + object.width / 2;
}
if (object.y - object.height / 2 > bottom) {
  object.y = top - object.height / 2;
} else if (object.y + object.height / 2 < top) {
  object.y = bottom + object.height / 2;
}
```

Apply friction (the correct way)

```
speed = Math.sqrt(vx * vx + vy * vy);
angle = Math.atan2(vy, vx);

if (speed > friction) {
  speed -= friction;
} else {
  speed = 0;
}

vx = Math.cos(angle) * speed;
vy = Math.sin(angle) * speed;
```

Apply friction (the easy way)

```
vx *= friction;
vy *= friction;
```

Chapter 8

Simple easing, long form

```
var dx = targetX - object.x,
    dy = targetY - object.y;

vx = dx * easing;
vy = dy * easing;
object.x += vx;
object.y += vy;
```

Simple easing, abbreviated form

```
vx = (targetX - object.x) * easing;
vy = (targetY - object.y) * easing;
object.x += vx;
object.y += vy;
```

Simple easing, short form

```
object.x += (targetX - object.x) * easing;
object.y += (targetY - object.y) * easing;
```

Simple spring, long form

```
var ax = (targetX - object.x) * spring,
    ay = (targetY - object.y) * spring;

vx += ax;
vy += ay;
vx *= friction;
vy *= friction;
object.x += vx;
object.y += vy;
```

Simple spring, abbreviated form

```
vx += (targetX - object.x) * spring;
vy += (targetY - object.y) * spring;
vx *= friction;
vy *= friction;
object.x += vx;
object.y += vy;
```

Simple spring, short form

```
vx += (targetX - object.x) * spring;
vy += (targetY - object.y) * spring;
object.x += (vx *= friction);
object.y += (vy *= friction);
```

Offset spring

```
var dx = object.x - fixedX,
    dy = object.y - fixedY,
    angle = Math.atan2(dy, dx),
    targetX = fixedX + Math.cos(angle) * springLength,
    targetY = fixedY + Math.sin(angle) * springLength;

//spring to targetX, targetY as above
```

Chapter 9

Distance-based collision detection

```
//starting with objectA and objectB
//if using an object without a radius property,
//you can use width or height divided by 2
var dx = objectB.x - objectA.x,
    dy = objectB.y - objectA.y,
    dist = Math.sqrt(dx * dx + dy * dy);

if (dist < objectA.radius + objectB.radius) {
  //handle collision
}
```

Multiple-object collision detection

```
objects.forEach(function (objectA, i) {
  for (var j = i + 1; j < objects.length; j++) {
    //evaluate reference using j. For example:
    var objectB = objects[j];
    //perform collision detection between objectA and objectB
  }
});
```

Chapter 10

Coordinate rotation

```
x1 = x * Math.cos(rotation) - y * Math.sin(rotation);
y1 = y * Math.cos(rotation) + x * Math.sin(rotation);
```

Reverse coordinate rotation

```
x1 = x * Math.cos(rotation) + y * Math.sin(rotation);
y1 = y * Math.cos(rotation) - x * Math.sin(rotation);
```

Chapter 11

Conservation of momentum, in straight mathematical terms

$$voFinal = \frac{(mO - m1) \times vO + 2 \times m1 \times v1}{mO + m1}$$

$$v1Final = \frac{(m1 - mO) \times v1 + 2 \times mO \times vO}{mO + m1}$$

Conservation of momentum in JavaScript, with a shortcut

```
var vxTotal = vx0 - vx1;
vx0 = ((ball0.mass - ball1.mass) * vx0 + 2 * ball1.mass * vx1) / (ball0.mass + ball1.mass);
vx1 = vxTotal + vx0;
```

Chapter 12

Basic gravity

$$force = G \times m_1 \times m_2 / distance^2$$

JavaScript-friendly gravity implementation

```
function gravitate (partA, partB) {
  var dx = partB.x - partA.x,
      dy = partB.y - partA.y,
      distSQ = dx * dx + dy * dy,
      dist = Math.sqrt(distSQ),
      force = partA.mass * partB.mass / distSQ,
      ax = force * dx / dist,
      ay = force * dy / dist;

  partA.vx += ax / partA.mass;
  partA.vy += ay / partA.mass;
  partB.vx -= ax / partB.mass;
  partB.vy -= ay / partB.mass;
}
```

Chapter 14

Law of cosines

$a^2 = b^2 + c^2 - 2 \times b \times c \times \cos A$
$b^2 = a^2 + c^2 - 2 \times a \times c \times \cos B$
$c^2 = a^2 + b^2 - 2 \times a \times b \times \cos C$

Law of cosines in JavaScript

```
var A = Math.acos((b * b + c * c - a * a) / (2 * b * c)),
    B = Math.acos((a * a + c * c - b * b) / (2 * a * c)),
    C = Math.acos((a * a + b * b - c * c) / (2 * a * b));
```

Chapter 15

Basic perspective

```
scale = fl / (fl + zpos);
object.scaleX = object.scaleY = scale;
object.alpha = scale;    //optional
object.x = vanishingPointX + xpos * scale;
object.y = vanishingPointY + ypos * scale;
```

Z-sorting

```
//assumes an array of 3D objects with a zpos property
function zSort (a, b) {
  return (b.zpos - a.zpos);
}

objects.sort(zSort);
```

Coordinate rotation

```
x1 = xpos * cos(angleZ) - ypos * sin(angleZ);
y1 = ypos * cos(angleZ) + xpos * sin(angleZ);

x1 = xpos * cos(angleY) - zpos * sin(angleY);
z1 = zpos * cos(angleY) + xpos * sin(angleY);

y1 = ypos * cos(angleX) - zpos * sin(angleX);
z1 = zpos * cos(angleX) + ypos * sin(angleX);
```

3D distance

```
dist = Math.sqrt(dx * dx + dy * dy + dz * dz);
```

Index

Z

Made in the USA
Lexington, KY
13 August 2012